Learning C# 2005

Other Microsoft .NET resources from O'Reilly

Related titles

Programming C#

C# Cookbook™

Visual C# 2005: A
  Developer's Notebook™

**.NET Books
Resource Center**

dotnet.oreilly.com is a complete catalog of O'Reilly's books on
.NET and related technologies, including sample chapters and
code examples.

ONDotnet.com provides independent coverage of fundamental,
interoperable, and emerging Microsoft .NET programming and
web services technologies.

Conferences

O'Reilly brings diverse innovators together to nurture the ideas
that spark revolutionary industries. We specialize in documenting the latest tools and systems, translating the innovator's
knowledge into useful skills for those in the trenches. Visit *con-
ferences.oreilly.com* for our upcoming events.

Safari Bookshelf (*safari.oreilly.com*) is the premier online reference library for programmers and IT professionals. Conduct
searches across more than 1,000 books. Subscribers can zero in
on answers to time-critical questions in a matter of seconds.
Read the books on your Bookshelf from cover to cover or simply flip to the page you need. Try it today for free.

SECOND EDITION

Learning C# 2005

Jesse Liberty and Brian MacDonald

Beijing · Cambridge · Farnham · Köln · Paris · Sebastopol · Taipei · Tokyo

Learning C# 2005, Second Edition
by Jesse Liberty and Brian MacDonald

Copyright © 2006, 2002 O'Reilly Media, Inc. All rights reserved.
Printed in the United States of America.

Published by O'Reilly Media, Inc., 1005 Gravenstein Highway North, Sebastopol, CA 95472.

O'Reilly books may be purchased for educational, business, or sales promotional use. Online editions
are also available for most titles (*safari.oreilly.com*). For more information, contact our
corporate/institutional sales department: (800) 998-9938 or *corporate@oreilly.com*.

Editor: John Osborn	**Cover Designer:** Hanna Dyer
Production Editor: Matt Hutchinson	**Interior Designer:** David Futato
Production Services: Octal Publishing, Inc.	**Illustrators:** Robert Romano, Jessamyn Read, and Lesley Borash

Printing History:

September 2002: First Edition.

February 2006: Second Edition.

Nutshell Handbook, the Nutshell Handbook logo, and the O'Reilly logo are registered trademarks of
O'Reilly Media, Inc. *Learning C# 2005*, the image of a goldfish, and related trade dress are trademarks
of O'Reilly Media, Inc.

Microsoft, MSDN, the .NET logo, Visual Basic, Visual C++, Visual Studio, and Windows are registered
trademarks of Microsoft Corporation.

Many of the designations used by manufacturers and sellers to distinguish their products are claimed as
trademarks. Where those designations appear in this book, and O'Reilly Media, Inc. was aware of a
trademark claim, the designations have been printed in caps or initial caps.

While every precaution has been taken in the preparation of this book, the publisher and authors
assume no responsibility for errors or omissions, or for damages resulting from the use of the
information contained herein.

 This book uses RepKover™, a durable and flexible lay-flat binding.

ISBN-10: 0-596-10209-7
ISBN-13: 978-0-596-10209-8
[M] [9/07]

*This book is dedicated to the
National Eating Disorder Association
and to Something-Fishy.org—and to all those
who struggle to overcome these most dangerous
and misunderstood afflictions.*

Table of Contents

Preface

In the summer of 2000, Microsoft released C# 1.0, which together with the .NET Framework, represented a major change in the way Windows applications and web applications were to be built.

In November 2005, Microsoft released C# 2.0, also known as C# 2005, and an upgraded platform, class library, and set of tools, including Visual Studio 2005. Throughout this book, we'll refer to C# 2.0 as C# 2005. Although not quite as revolutionary a step as the launch of .NET itself, 2.0 represents a significant maturation of the .NET platform and of the C# language, along with greatly enhanced tools to significantly increase programmer productivity.

About This Book

Learning C# 2005, Second Edition is a primer on the C# 2005 language specifically, and object-oriented software development in general. This book focuses on the fundamentals of the C# programming language, both syntactical and semantic. After mastering these concepts, you should be ready to move on to a more advanced programming guide that will help you create large-scale web and Windows applications.

Who This Book Is For

Learning C# 2005 was written for programmers with little or no object-oriented programming experience, as well as for novice programmers. Those coming from another language may have a slight advantage, but I've tried to provide an on-ramp for beginners as well, by defining all terms, demonstrating the relationships among the various constructs, and reviewing key concepts along the way.

How the Book Is Organized

Chapter 1, *C# and .NET Programming*
Introduces you to the C# language and the .NET platform.

Chapter 2, *Visual Studio 2005*
Provides a guided tour of Visual Studio 2005—the tool you will use to build all the applications in the book, and perhaps all the applications you'll build from now on.

Chapter 3, *C# Language Fundamentals*
Introduces the basic syntax and structure of the C# language, including the intrinsic types, variables, statements, and expressions.

Chapter 4, *Operators*
Describes some of the symbols that cause C# to take an action, such as assigning a value to a variable and arithmetically operating on values (adding, subtracting, and so forth).

Chapter 5, *Branching*
Shows how to create programs that branch based on conditions that may change while the program is running.

Chapter 6, *Object-Oriented Programming*
Explains the principles behind object-oriented programming, including encapsulation, specialization, and polymorphism.

Chapter 7, *Classes and Objects*
Introduces the key concepts of programmer-defined types (classes) and instances of those types (objects). Classes and objects are the building blocks of object-oriented programming.

Chapter 8, *Inside Methods*
Delves into the specific programming instructions you'll write to define the behavior of objects.

Chapter 9, *Basic Debugging*
Introduces the debugger integrated into the Visual Studio 2005 Integrated Development Environment.

Chapter 10, *Arrays*
Introduces the array, an indexed collection of objects that are all the same type.

Chapter 11, *Inheritance and Polymorphism*
Explores two of the key concepts behind object-oriented programming, inheritance and polymorphism, and demonstrates how you might implement them in your code.

Chapter 12, *Operator Overloading*
Explains how to add standard operators to the types you define.

Chapter 13, *Interfaces*

Explains how you can define a set of behaviors (an interface) that any number of classes might implement.

Chapter 14, *Generics and Collections*

Explains generics and shows how generics are used to create type-safe and efficient collections. Chapter 14 then introduces the standard .NET Framework generic collections: List, Stack, Queue, and Dictionary.

Chapter 15, *Strings*

Discusses the manipulation of strings of characters, the C# string class, and regular expression syntax.

Chapter 16, *Throwing and Catching Exceptions*

Explains how to handle errors and abnormal conditions that may arise in relation to your programs through the use of exceptions.

Chapter 17, *Delegates and Events*

Discusses how to write code to respond to programming occurrences like mouse clicks, keystrokes, and other events, through the use of delegates and the event keyword.

Chapter 18, *Creating Windows Applications*

Shows you how to bring all these skills to bear to create a Windows application.

Chapter 19, *Programming ASP.NET Applications*

Applies the same skills to building a web application.

Appendix, *Answers to Quizzes and Exercises*

Answers to all the chapter quizzes and exercises, with complete code examples.

Conventions Used in This Book

The following font conventions are used in this book:

Italic

Used for pathnames, filenames, program names, Internet addresses (such as domain names and URLs), and new terms where they are defined

`Constant Width`

Used for command lines and options that should be typed verbatim, C# keywords, and code examples

`Constant Width Italic`

Used for replaceable items, such as variables or optional elements, within syntax lines or code

`Constant Width Bold`

Used for emphasis within program code

Pay special attention to notes set apart from the text with the following icons:

This is a tip. It contains useful supplementary information about the topic at hand.

This is a warning. It helps you solve and avoid annoying problems.

Using Code Examples

This book is here to help you get your job done. In general, you may use the code in this book in your programs and documentation. You do not need to contact us for permission unless you're reproducing a significant portion of the code. For example, writing a program that uses several chunks of code from this book does not require permission. Selling or distributing a CD-ROM of examples from O'Reilly books *does* require permission. Answering a question by citing this book and quoting example code does not require permission. Incorporating a significant amount of example code from this book into your product's documentation *does* require permission.

We appreciate, but do not require, attribution. An attribution usually includes the title, author, publisher, and ISBN. For example: "*Learning C# 2005*, Second Edition, by Jesse Liberty and Brian MacDonald. Copyright 2006 O'Reilly Media, Inc., 0-596-10209-7."

If you feel your use of code examples falls outside fair use or the permission given above, feel free to contact us at *permissions@oreilly.com*.

Support

I provide ongoing support for my books through my web site (click on "books"):

> *http://www.LibertyAssociates.com*

On this web site, you'll also find the source code for all the examples in *Learning C# 2005,* Second Edition, as well as access to a free online support discussion forum. You'll also find an errata, FAQ, and other useful resources.

We'd Like to Hear from You

We have tested and verified the information in this book to the best of our ability, but you may find that features have changed (or even that we have made mistakes!).

Please let us know about any errors you find, as well as your suggestions for future editions, by writing to:

O'Reilly Media, Inc.
1005 Gravenstein Highway North
Sebastopol, CA 95472
(800) 998-9938 (in the U.S. or Canada)
(707) 829-0515 (international/local)
(707) 829-0104 (fax)

We have a web page for this book where we list examples and any plans for future editions. You can access this information at:

http://www.oreilly.com/catalog/learncsharp2

You can also send messages electronically. To be put on the mailing list or request a catalog, send email to:

info@oreilly.com

To comment on the book, send email to:

bookquestions@oreilly.com

For more information about this book and others, as well as additional technical articles and discussion on the C# and the .NET Framework, see the O'Reilly web site:

http://www.oreilly.com

and the O'Reilly .NET DevCenter:

http://www.oreillynet.com/dotnet

ONDotnet.com provides independent coverage of fundamental, interoperable, and emerging Microsoft .NET programming and web services technologies.

Safari® Enabled

 When you see a Safari® Enabled icon on the cover of your favorite technology book, that means the book is available online through the O'Reilly Network Safari Bookshelf.

Safari offers a solution that's better than e-books. It's a virtual library that lets you easily search thousands of top tech books, cut and paste code samples, download chapters, and find quick answers when you need the most accurate, current information. Try it for free at *http://safari.oreilly.com*.

Acknowledgments

Jesse Liberty

John Osborn signed me to O'Reilly, for which I will forever be in his debt. William Hamilton and Nicholas Paldino helped make this book better than what I'd written. Rob Romano created a number of the illustrations and improved the others. Tim O'Reilly provided support and resources.

Special thanks are due to my co-author, Brian MacDonald, who made this book far superior to what I'd originally written.

Brian MacDonald

First and foremost, thanks to Jesse for giving me the opportunity to participate in this book. Many thanks also to John Osborn, for getting me involved with O'Reilly in the first place. Finally, thanks to my wife, Carole, who provided both moral support and technical assistance.

CHAPTER 1

C# and .NET Programming

Learning C# 2005 introduces C# 2005 and the .NET 2.0 development platform. This book is targeted at new programmers and those migrating from VB6 or from non-object-oriented languages. Along the way, you will learn a great deal about writing high-quality, industrial-strength programs for .NET.

> Programmers migrating from Java or C++ may find the material in *Programming C#* by Jesse Liberty (O'Reilly, 2005) a more appropriate fit for their skills.

This brief introduction will show you how C# fits into the .NET picture, what you can do with the language, and what benefits this language has over its predecessors.

> Unless otherwise specified, when we refer to C#, we mean *C# 2005*; when we refer to .NET, we mean the *.NET 2005* (.NET 2.0) *Framework*; and when we refer to Visual Studio, we mean *Visual Studio 2005*.
>
> Finally, when we refer to using Visual Studio 2005, you may well be using Visual C# 2005 Express instead.

In the following pages, you will also learn some of the concepts integral to object-oriented programming, which has revolutionized how web and Windows applications are developed. Object-oriented programming is closely tied to the semantics of the C# language; that is, the meaning behind the code you write. Obviously, you need to have a basic understanding of the syntax of the C# language, but you also need to understand what you are actually trying to accomplish. This book will explain it all, in the context of creating applications to run either on the Web or on a Windows desktop.

C# 2005 and .NET 2.0

In the past, you might have learned a language like C or Java without much concern about the platform on which you would be programming. These cross-platform languages were as comfortable on a Unix box as they were on a PC running Windows.

C#, however, was created specifically for .NET. Although .NET may become cross-platform some day soon—there already exists a working open-source Unix version—for now, the overwhelming majority of .NET programs will be written to run on a machine running one of the Windows operating systems.

The .NET Platform

When Microsoft announced C# 1.0 in July 2000, its unveiling was part of a much larger event: the announcement of the .NET platform. The .NET platform is a development framework that provides a new way to create Windows applications. However, .NET goes beyond traditional Windows programming to facilitate creating web applications quickly and easily.

Microsoft reportedly devoted 80% of its research and development budget to .NET and its associated technologies. The results of this commitment were very impressive. In 2005, Microsoft rolled out Version 2 of the language, the platform, and the tools. Their goal was to radically reduce the amount of boilerplate code you have to write, and to make the creation of web and desktop applications easier by "encapsulating" much of the "plumbing" of a typical application in objects.

That means that rather than writing a lot of the code to connect to databases, the Internet, or your filesystem, .NET provides fully tested controls that you can drag onto your form, and they will do all the heavy lifting for you.

The scope of .NET is huge. The platform consists of three separate product groups:

- A set of languages, including C# and Visual Basic 2005; a set of development tools, including Visual Studio 2005; and powerful tools for building applications, including the *Common Language Runtime* (CLR), a platform for compiling, debugging, and executing .NET applications.
- A set of .NET Enterprise Servers, including SQL Server 2005, Exchange, Biz-Talk, and so on, that provide specialized functionality for relational data storage, email, B2B (business-to-business) commerce, etc.
- New .NET-enabled non-PC devices, from cell phones to game boxes.

The .NET 2.0 Framework

Central to the .NET platform is a development environment known as the *.NET Framework*. The Framework specifies how .NET programming constructs such as intrinsic types, classes, and interfaces are implemented. You will learn about these constructs in the chapters ahead.

The .NET Framework sits on top of any flavor of the Windows operating system. The most important components of the Framework are the Common Language Runtime (CLR), described in the preceding section, and the *Framework Class Library* (FCL), which provides an enormous number of predefined types or classes for you to use in your programs. You will learn how to define your own classes in Chapter 7.

 Detailed coverage of all the FCL classes is beyond the scope of this book. For more information, see *C# in a Nutshell* (O'Reilly) and the MSDN Library (*http://msdn.microsoft.com/library*).

The C# Language

The C# language is disarmingly simple, but C# is highly expressive when it comes to implementing modern programming concepts. C# includes all the support for structured, component-based, object-oriented programming that one expects of a modern language built on the shoulders of C++ and Java.

A small team led by two distinguished Microsoft engineers, Anders Hejlsberg and Scott Wiltamuth, developed the original C# language. Hejlsberg is also known for creating Turbo Pascal, a popular language for PC programming, and for leading the team that designed Borland Delphi, one of the first successful Integrated Development Environments for client/server programming.

The goal of C# is to provide a simple, safe, object-oriented, Internet-centric, high-performance language for .NET development. C# is simple because there are relatively few *keywords*. This makes it easy to learn and easy to adapt to your specific needs.

 Keywords are special words reserved by the language that have a specific meaning within all C# programs. Keywords include if, while, and for. You'll learn about these keywords in the coming chapters.

C# is considered safe because the language is *type-safe*, an important mechanism to help you find bugs early in the development process. This makes for code that is easier to maintain and programs that are more reliable. C# 2005 was enhanced in many ways, one of which was to add support for *generics* (see Chapter 14), which makes collections type-safe as well, thus greatly improving the reliability of advanced applications.

C# was designed, from the very start, to support object-oriented programming. This book will explain not only how to write object-oriented programs, but also why object-oriented programming has become so popular. The short answer is this: programs are becoming increasingly complex, and object-oriented programming techniques help you manage that complexity.

C# was designed for .NET, and .NET was designed for developing web and web-aware programs. The Internet is a primary resource in most .NET applications.

The Structure of C# Applications

At the most fundamental level, a C# application consists of *source code*. Source code is human-readable text written in a text editor. A text editor is like a word processor, but it puts no special characters into the file to support formatting, only the text. A classic text editor is Notepad.

Example 1-1 shows an example of a very simple source code file.

Example 1-1. A source code file

```
namespace NotePad
{
  class HelloWorld
  {
    // every console app starts with Main
    static void Main( )
    {
      System.Console.WriteLine("Hello world!");
    }
  }
}
```

This program is explained in detail below. For now, observe that the program is readable; it is in normal text. The words may be strange and the layout unusual, but there are no special characters—just the normal text produced by your keyboard.

Once you write your program in an editor, you must compile it. For that, you need a compiler (explained shortly). Once compiled, your program must be run and tested.

Although you *can* perform all of these tasks using Notepad (or another text editor) and various command-line tools, your programming life will be much easier if you use the Integrated Development Environment (IDE) called Visual Studio 2005. Visual Studio 2005 was designed with .NET development in mind, and greatly simplifies the writing of C# program code. This book assumes you are using Visual C# 2005 Express or Visual Studio 2005, both of which provide the Visual Studio 2005 development environment.

The overwhelming majority of C# programmers will be building Windows and web applications for the .NET platform using the Visual Studio 2005, and all the examples for this book have been tested in that environment.

A free version of this popular product, called Visual C# 2005 Express Edition, is available for download at *http://msdn.microsoft.com/vstudio/express/visualcsharp/*.

There are excellent open source C# compilers available, such as those from the Mono project (*http://www.mono-project.com*) and SharpDevelop (*http://www.icsharpcode.net/OpenSource/SD/*). Everything in this book should work with those compilers, but we have not tested with them and can not guarantee 100% compatibility.

The Development Environment

The Visual Studio 2005 Integrated Development Environment (*IDE*) provides enormous advantages to the C# programmer. This book tacitly assumes that you'll use Visual Studio 2005 for your work. However, the discussion focuses more on the language and the platform than on the tools.

Nonetheless, Chapter 2 provides an introduction to the IDE in some detail. Chapter 9 returns to the IDE to examine the debugger, which will help you find and correct problems in your code.

You can use the C# language to develop four types of applications:

- Console applications, which display no graphics
- Windows applications, which use the standard Windows interface
- Web applications, which can be accessed with a browser
- Web services, which can be accessed using standard Internet protocols and which provide services such as current stock quotes, ISBN to title conversions, etc., that can be used by other applications

This book will focus primarily on the basics of the C# language, using simple console applications for most of the examples, to illustrate language fundamentals. The last two chapters will show you how to use C# within the context of building Windows and web applications, respectively.

The .NET platform is web-centric. The C# language was developed to allow .NET programmers to create very large, powerful, high-quality web applications quickly and easily. The .NET technology for creating web applications and web services is called *ASP.NET*.

Typically, you'll create an ASP.NET application when you want your program to be available to end users on any platform (e.g., Windows, Mac, Unix). By serving your application over the Web, end users can access your program with any browser.

When you want the richness and power of a native application running directly on the Windows platform, you will create a desktop Windows application. The .NET tools for building Windows applications are called Windows Forms.

However, if you don't need a Graphical User Interface (GUI) and just want to write a simple application that writes to a console window (i.e., what we used to call a DOS box), you might consider creating a console application. This book makes extensive use of console applications to illustrate the basics of the C# language.

Console applications

A console application runs in a console window, as shown in Figure 1-1. A console window (or DOS box) provides simple text-based output. Console applications are very helpful when learning a language because they strip away the distraction of the Graphical User Interface. Rather than spending your time creating complex windowing applications, you can focus on the details of the language constructs, such as how you create classes and methods, how you branch based on runtime conditions, and how you loop. All these topics will be covered in detail in later chapters.

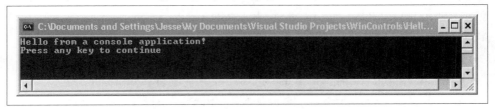

Figure 1-1. A console application

Windows applications

A Windows application runs on a PC's desktop. You are already familiar with Windows applications such as Microsoft Word or Excel. Windows applications are much more complex than console applications and can take advantage of the full suite of menus, controls, and other widgets you've come to expect in a modern desktop application. Figure 1-2 shows the output of a simple Windows application.

ASP.NET applications

An ASP.NET application runs on a web server and delivers its functionality through a browser, typically over the Web. ASP.NET technology facilitates developing web applications quickly and easily. Figure 1-3 shows a message from a simple ASP.NET application.

Figure 1-2. A Windows application

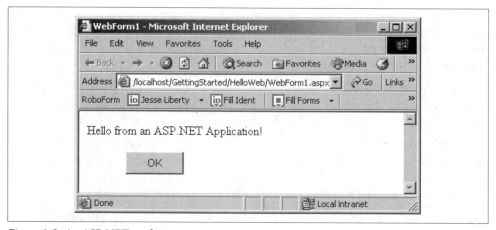

Figure 1-3. An ASP.NET application

Although most commercial applications will be either Windows or ASP.NET programs, console applications have a tremendous advantage in a C# primer. Windows and ASP.NET applications bring a lot more overhead; there is great complexity in managing the window and all the events associated with the window. (Events are covered in Chapter 17.) Console applications keep things simple—allowing you to focus on the features of the language.

This book does not go into all the myriad details of building robust Windows and ASP.NET applications. For complete coverage of these topics, please see *Programming ASP.NET* and *Programming .NET Windows Applications*, both by Jesse Liberty and Dan Hurwitz (O'Reilly).

What's in a Program?

A program consists of English-language instructions called *source code*. The *syntax* for these instructions is strictly defined by the language.

In C#, source code consists of a series of statements. A *statement* is an instruction to the complier. Each instruction must be formed correctly, and one task you'll face when learning C# will be to learn the correct syntax of the language. For example, in C#, every statement ends with a semicolon.

Each instruction has a *semantic* meaning that expresses what you are trying to accomplish. Although you must follow the rules of C# syntax, the semantics of the language are far more important in developing effective object-oriented programs. This book will provide insight into both the syntax and the semantics of good C# programs.

Your First Program: Hello World

In this first example, you will create a very simple application that does nothing more than display the words "Hello World" to your monitor. This console application is the traditional first program for learning any new language; it demonstrates some of the basic elements of a C# program.

Once you write your "Hello World" program and compile it, this chapter will provide a line-by-line analysis of the source code. This analysis gives something of a preview of the language; Chapter 3 describes the fundamentals much more fully.

As explained earlier, you can create C# programs with any text editor. You can, for example, create each of the three programs shown previously (in Figures 1-1, 1-2, and 1-3) with Notepad. To demonstrate that this is possible, you'll write your very first C# program using Notepad.

Begin by opening Notepad and typing in the program exactly as shown in Example 1-2.

Example 1-2. Hello World in Notepad

```
namespace NotePad
{
    class HelloWorld
    {
        // every console app starts with Main
        static void Main()
        {
            System.Console.WriteLine("Hello world!");
        }
    }
}
```

That is the entire program. Save it to your disk as a file called *helloworld.cs*.

We'll examine this program in some detail in just a moment. First, however, it must be compiled.

The Compiler

Once you save your program to disk, you must compile the code to create your application. Compiling your source code means running a compiler and identifying the source code file. You run the compiler by opening a command prompt (DOS box) and entering the program name *csc*. Then you "pass in" your source code file by entering the filename on the command line, as in the following:

```
csc HelloWorld.cs
```

The job of the compiler is to turn your source code into a working program. It turns out to be just slightly more complicated than that because .NET uses an intermediate language called Microsoft Intermediate Language (MSIL, sometimes abbreviated as IL).

The compiler reads your source code and produces IL. When you run the program, the .NET Just In Time (JIT) compiler reads your IL code and produces an executable application in memory.

 The IL code is actually stored in a *.exe* file, but this file does not contain executable code. It contains the information needed by the JIT to execute the code when you run it.

Microsoft provides a command window with the correct environment variables set. Open the command window by selecting the following menu items in this order (your installation may vary slightly): Start → Programs → Microsoft Visual Studio 2005 → Visual Studio Tools → Visual Studio 2005 Command Prompt.

Navigate to the directory in which you created your code file and enter the following command:

```
csc helloworld.cs
```

The Microsoft C# compiler compiles your code; when you display the directory, you'll find the compiler has produced an executable file called *helloworld.exe*. Type *helloworld* at the command prompt, and your program executes, as shown in Figure 1-4.

Presto! You are a C# programmer. That's it, close the book, you've done it. Okay, don't close the book—there are details to examine, but take a moment to congratulate yourself. Have a cookie.

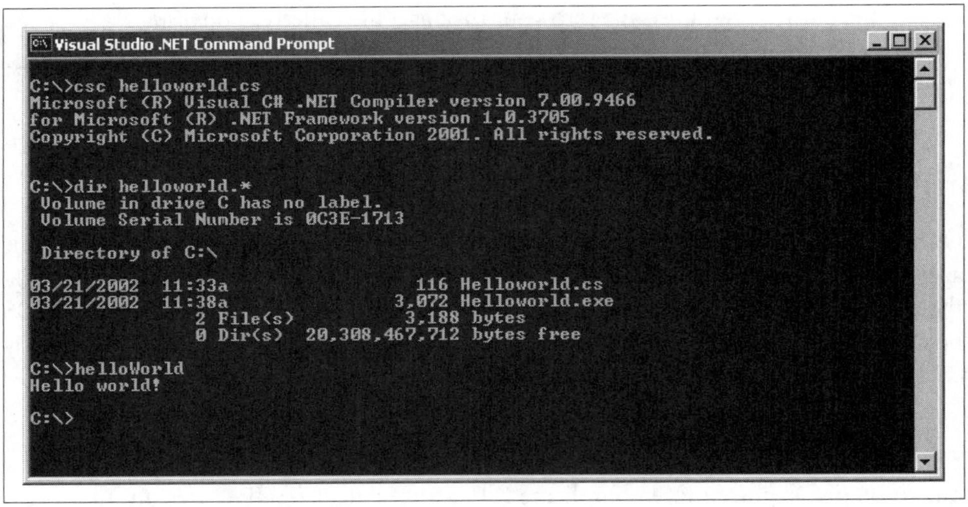

```
Visual Studio .NET Command Prompt                              _ | □ | X

C:\>csc helloworld.cs
Microsoft (R) Visual C# .NET Compiler version 7.00.9466
for Microsoft (R) .NET Framework version 1.0.3705
Copyright (C) Microsoft Corporation 2001. All rights reserved.


C:\>dir helloworld.*
 Volume in drive C has no label.
 Volume Serial Number is 0C3E-1713

 Directory of C:\

03/21/2002  11:33a              116 Helloworld.cs
03/21/2002  11:38a            3,072 Helloworld.exe
               2 File(s)        3,188 bytes
               0 Dir(s)  20,308,467,712 bytes free

C:\>helloWorld
Hello world!

C:\>
```

Figure 1-4. Compiling and running Hello World

Granted, the program you created is one of the simplest C# programs imaginable, but it is a complete C# program, and it can be used to examine many of the elements common to C# programs.

Examining Your First Program

The single greatest challenge when learning to program is that you must learn everything before you can learn anything. Even this simple "Hello World" program uses many features of the language that will be discussed in coming chapters, including classes, namespaces, statements, static methods, objects, strings, blocks, and libraries.

It is as if you were learning to drive a car. You must learn to steer, accelerate, brake, and understand the flow of traffic. Right now, we're going to get you out on the highway and just let you steer for a while. Over time, you'll learn how to speed up and slow down. Along the way, you'll learn to set the radio and adjust the heat so that you'll be more comfortable. In no time you'll be driving, and then won't your parents begin to worry.

Hang on tight; we're going to zip through this quickly and come back to the details in subsequent chapters.

The first line in the program defines a *namespace*:

```
namespace NotePad
```

You will create many names when programming in C#. Every object and every type of object must be named. It is possible for the names you assign to conflict with the names assigned by Microsoft or other vendors. A namespace is a way of saying "These names are mine."

In this program, you've created a namespace called NotePad. The items defined in your namespace must be enclosed in braces ({}). Thus, the second line of the Hello World program is an open brace to mark the beginning of the NotePad namespace. The open brace is matched by a closing brace at the end of the program.

Within the braces of the namespace, you write other programming constructs. For instance, you might define a class. *Classes* define a category, or *type*, of object. A class is a new, user-defined type. The .NET Framework provides thousands of classes, and you can define new ones of your own as well. Classes are used to define the attributes and behavior of Windows controls (buttons, listboxes, etc.), as well as constructs that mimic the important attributes or behavior of things in the world, such as employees, students, telephones, and so on.

Classes are the core of C# and object-oriented programming. You'll learn about classes in detail in Chapters 6 and 7.

Every class named within the namespace braces is implicitly prefixed with the name NotePad. The dot operator (.) separates the namespace from the name of the class within the namespace. Thus, if you were to create a class MyClass within the namespace NotePad, the real name of that class would be NotePad.MyClass. You can read this as either "NotePad dot MyClass" or "NotePad MyClass." Actually, you use the dot operator quite a lot; you'll see various other uses as we proceed.

The third line in our Hello World program creates a class named, aptly, HelloWorld. Like a namespace, a class is defined within braces. The following code represents the opening of the HelloWorld class definition:

```
class HelloWorld
{
```

A *method* is a relatively small block of code that performs an action. The Main( ) method is the "entry point" for every C# console application; it is where your program begins. The next few lines in Hello World mark the beginning of the Main( ) method:

```
static void Main( )
{
```

Methods are covered in detail in Chapter 8, but are mentioned in virtually every chapter in this book.

A *comment* (here in bold) appears just before the start of the Main( ) method:

```
// every console app starts with Main
static void Main( )
{
```

A comment is just a note to yourself. You insert comments to make the code more readable to yourself and other programmers. You'll be surprised how helpful those comments are six months later when you have no idea what a line of code you wrote actually does.

You can place comments anywhere in your program that you think the explanation will be helpful; they have no effect on the running program.

C# recognizes three styles of comments. The comment in Hello World begins with two slashes (//). The slashes indicate that everything to the right on the same line is a comment.

The second style is to begin your comment with a forward slash followed by an asterisk (/*) and to end your comment with the opposite pattern (*/). These pairs of characters are called the opening C-style comment and the closing C-style comment, respectively.

These comment symbols were inherited from the C language—thus the names used to identify them. They are also used in C++ and Java.

Everything between these comment symbols is a comment. C-style comments can span more than one line, as in the following:

```
/* This begins a comment
This line is still within the comment
Here comes the end of the comment */
```

The third and final style of comments uses three forward slashes (///). This is an XML-style comment and is used for advanced documentation techniques. XML comments are beyond the scope of this book.

You will note that I use few comments in the examples in this book. Even so, I tend to use more comments in a book than I do in professional code. It's not that I don't believe in fully documenting code; it's just that I may disagree with others about what "fully documented" means. My personal set of guidelines is this:

- Prefer self-documenting code to comments (see *http://en.wikipedia. org/wiki/Self-documenting*).
- Use comments when you need to explain *why* you did it, not *what* you did.
- Comments that say what the code is doing are a sign that the code may not be written well—it should be *obvious* what the code is doing, and if not, the code will be hard to maintain.
- Remember that comments rust. The code changes, and inevitably the comments are not fully updated.
- Comments that mislead are far worse than no comments at all.

Notice that the Main( ) method is defined with the keywords static and void.

```
static void Main( )
```

The static keyword indicates that you can access this method without having an object of your class available. While a class defines a type, each instance of that type is an *object* (much as Car defines a type of vehicle, and your aging rust-bucket is an individual instance of Car). Thus, while `Button` defines a type of control for a Windows program, any individual program will have many `Button` objects, each with its own label (e.g., OK, Cancel, Retry).

Normally, methods can be called only if you have an object, but static methods are special and are called without an object. (The use of static methods, other than `Main( )`, is fairly advanced and won't be covered until Chapter 7.)

The second keyword in the statement defining the `Main( )` method is `void`:

```
static void Main( )
```

Typically, one method calls another. The called method will do work, and it can return a value to the calling method. (You'll see how methods call one another and return values in Chapter 8.) If a method does not return a value, it is declared void. The keyword void is a signal to the compiler that your method will not return a value to the calling method.

The operating system calls `Main( )` when the program is invoked. It is possible for `Main( )` to return a value (typically an error code) that might be used by the operating system. In this case, you've declared that `Main( )` will not return a value.

Every method name is followed by parentheses:

```
static void Main( )
```

It is possible to pass values into a method so that the method can manipulate or use those values. These values are called *parameters* or *arguments*. (Method parameters are covered in Chapter 8.) In this case, `Main( )` has no parameters.

All methods are enclosed within braces. Within the braces for `Main( )` is a single line of code:

```
System.Console.WriteLine("Hello world!");
```

The `Console` is an object that represents your screen. The `Console` class is defined within the `System` namespace, and so its full identification is `System.Console`.

The `Console` class has a static method, `WriteLine( )`, which you access not with an instance of `Console`, but through the `Console` class itself. Because you access the method with the dot operator, you write `System.Console.WriteLine`.

The `WriteLine( )` method declares a single parameter: the string you want to display. When you pass a string in to the method, the string is an *argument*. The argument ("Hello world") corresponds to the parameter the method expects, and the string is displayed. The complete call to the method is:

```
System.Console.WriteLine("Hello world!");
```

If you will use many objects from the System namespace, you can save typing by telling the compiler that many of the objects you'll refer to are in that namespace. You do so by adding a using directive to the beginning of your program:

```
using System;
```

Once you add this line, you can use the Console class name without explicitly identifying that it is in the System namespace. If you add the using declaration, you can rewrite the contents of Main( ) as follows:

```
Console.WriteLine("Hello world!");
```

The final series of lines close the various nested opening braces. The first closes the brace for Main( ), the second closes the brace for the class, and the third closes the brace for the namespace. Each open brace must be matched by a closing brace.

The class is defined within the namespace declaration, and thus you do not close the namespace until you've closed the class. Similarly, the method Main( ) is declared within the class, so you do not close the class until you've closed the method.

Whew! That was a lot to take in all at once! Don't panic; all the concepts introduced here are explained in detail in coming chapters. Oh, and that's the last time you'll use Notepad to write a program (if you know what is good for you!). From now on, we'll use Visual Studio 2005 (or Visual C# 2005 Express).

Summary

- C# was initially created specifically for use with the .NET platform but has been submitted to and been accepted by ECMA as a standardized programming language.
- C# is designed to be simple, type-safe, object-oriented, high-performance, and Internet-centric.
- C# applications consist of human-readable source code, written in a text editor. The source code is compiled into Microsoft Intermediate Language (MSIL) which, at run time, is compiled into machine code.
- You can use C# to develop console applications, Windows applications, web applications, and web services.
- Classes are the core building blocks of C# and object-oriented programming because they allow you to create new types that model types in the "problem domain"—that is, that model things in the area you are concerned with.
- A method is a named block of code that performs an action and that may *return* a value.
- A comment is a note for the programmer and does not affect the running of the application.

Quiz

Question 1-1. What is the CLR?

Question 1-2. What are the four types of applications you can build in .NET?

Question 1-3. What is the .NET Framework?

Question 1-4. What is the FCL?

Question 1-5. What does it mean to say that C# is a "safe" language?

Question 1-6. What is a keyword?

Question 1-7. What is a namespace?

Question 1-8. What does the compiler do?

Question 1-9. What is MSIL?

Question 1-10. What is the JIT?

Exercise

Exercise 1-1. Write an application that emits the words "What a great book" to the console window.

Hint: Open Visual Studio, create a console application, and, if you get stuck, consider copying or modifying the code shown in the chapter. Remember, these exercises are for your own edification, no one is grading them, and making mistakes is an opportunity to explore and learn more—this is true in just about everything except nuclear physics (Written on the back of a tee shirt: "I am a nuclear technician. If I am running, try to keep up").

So, *Don't Panic*!

CHAPTER 2

Visual Studio 2005

In Chapter 1, you learned that you *can* create your C# applications using Notepad. In this chapter, you'll learn why you never *will*. Microsoft developed Visual Studio 2005 to facilitate the creation of Windows and web applications. You will find that this Integrated Development Environment (IDE) is a *very* powerful tool that will greatly simplify your work.

Visual Studio 2005 offers many advantages to the .NET developer, among them:

- A modern interface, using a tabbed document metaphor for code and layout screens, and dockable toolbars and information windows.

- Convenient access to multiple design and code windows (this will make more sense when you are creating web applications, as shown in Chapter 19).

- WYSIWYG (What You See Is What You Get) visual design of Windows and Web Forms.

- Code completion, which allows you to enter code with fewer errors and less typing.

- IntelliSense, which displays tips for every method, providing the return type and the types of all the parameters.

- Dynamic, context-sensitive help, which allows you to view topics and samples relevant to the code you are writing at the moment. You can also search the complete SDK library from within the IDE.

- Immediate flagging of syntax errors, which allows you to fix problems as they are entered.

- A Start Page, which provides easy access to new and existing projects.

- The same code editor for all .NET languages, which shortens the learning curve. Each language can have specialized aspects, but all languages benefit from shared features, such as incremental search, code outlining, collapsing text, line numbering, and color-coded keywords.

- An HTML editor, which provides both Design and HTML views that update each other in real time.

- A Solution Explorer, which displays in outline form all the files comprising your solution.
- An integrated debugger, which allows you to step through code, observe program runtime behavior, and set breakpoints, even across multiple languages and multiple processes.
- Customization capability, which allows you to set user preferences for IDE appearance and behavior.
- Integrated support for source control software.
- A built-in task list.
- Ability to modify your controls' properties, either declaratively or through a properties window.
- Ability to integrate custom controls that you create or purchase from a third party.
- Rapid and easy deployment, including the ability to copy an entire web site development project from one machine to another.
- Ability to integrate third-party tools into Visual Studio.
- Ability to program extensions to Visual Studio.
- Ability to rename methods, properties, etc. and have them renamed automatically throughout the program.

In addition, Microsoft has added these new features to VS2005:

- Support for all three coding models: inline, code-behind, and mixed inline and code-behind.
- Access to web sites through the filesystem, FTP, IIS, or Front Page Server Extensions. (You no longer need to install IIS on the developer's machine, because a built-in web server is provided.)
- Full support for look-and-feel features, such as skins, themes, and master pages.
- A Server Explorer, which allows you to log on to servers that you have network access to, access the data and services on those servers, drag and drop data sources onto controls, and perform a variety of other chores.
- Ability to import and export user preferences.
- Integrated build and compile support.
- Ability to drag and drop controls onto your web page, either in design mode or in HTML mode.

Visual Studio 2005 is a highly useful tool that can save you hours of repetitive tasks. It is also a large and complex program, so it is impossible in this chapter to explore every nook and cranny. Instead, this chapter will lay the foundation for understanding and using Visual Studio 2005, and will point out some of the nastier traps you might run into along the way.

Before You Read Further

This chapter has a lot of information in it, and you won't need all of it all at once. In fact, much of the information will not even apply to console applications, but will be valuable when you are ready to create Windows or web applications.

Many readers like to skim this chapter the first time through, and then come back for the details later. But it is your book, you paid for it (you *did* pay for it, didn't you?), and so you are free to read the entire chapter, take notes as you go, skip it entirely, or otherwise use it to your best advantage.

Whether or not you read this chapter, I do strongly recommend you spend time (lots and lots of time) exploring Visual Studio in detail. You will forever be surprised at how much is in there and how much you can set it up to behave as you want; it is your principal development tool. Ignoring Visual Studio would be like a race car driver never looking under the hood. In time, you not only want to know how to change the oil, but you also want to understand how the valves work and why the linkage sticks.

Start Page

The Start Page is the first thing you see when you open Visual Studio 2005 (unless you configure it otherwise). From here, you can create new projects or open a project you worked on in a previous session. You can also find out what is new in .NET, access .NET newsgroups and web sites, search for help online, download useful code, or adjust Visual Studio 2005 to your personal requirements. Figure 2-1 shows a typical Start Page.

The Start Page includes a list of recent projects (clicking on one will open it), along with the ability to open any project on your computer or to create a new one. The Getting Started box provides links to features and helpful sites, and the large box on the right contains useful articles from MSDN online.

Projects and Solutions

A C# program is built from source files, which are text files containing the code you write. Source code files are named with the *.cs* extension. The *HelloWorld.cs* file you created in Chapter 1 is an example.

A typical Visual Studio 2005 application can have a number of other files (such as assembly information files, references, icons, data connections, and more). Visual Studio 2005 organizes these files into a container called a *project*.

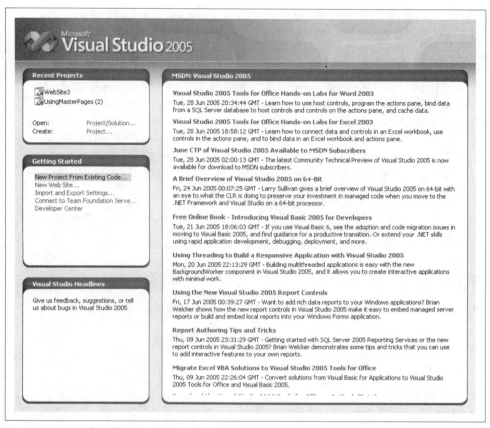

Figure 2-1. Visual Studio start page

Visual Studio 2005 provides two types of containers for your source code, folders, files, and related material: the project and the solution. A *project* is a set of files that work together to create an executable program (*.exe*) or a dynamic link library (*.dll*). Large, complex projects may contain multiple *.dll* files.

A *solution* is a set of related projects, although it may also have just one project. Each time you create a new project, Visual Studio 2005 either adds it to an existing solution or creates a new solution.

Solutions are defined within a file named for the solution, and have the extension *.sln*. The *.sln* file contains metadata, which is basically information about the data. The metadata describes the projects that compose the solution and information about building the solution.

Visual Studio 2005 also creates a file with the same base name as the *.sln* file, but with the filename extension *.sou* (such as *mySolution.sln* and *mySolution.sou*). The *.sou* file contains metadata used to customize the IDE.

There are a number of ways to open an existing solution. The simplest way is to select Open Project from the Start menu (which opens a project and its enclosing solution). Alternatively, you can open a solution in Visual Studio 2005 just by double-clicking the *.sln* file in Windows Explorer.

Typically, the build process results in the contents of a project being compiled into an executable (*.exe*) file or a dynamic link library (*.dll*) file. This book focuses on creating executable files.

> The metadata describing the project is contained in a separate file named after the project with the extension *.csproj*. The project file contains version information, build settings, and references to other source files to include as part of the project.
>
> Note that the metadata for the program you are creating is a different thing entirely, and is contained within the executable (*.exe*) or the DLL. What we are discussing here is metadata used by Visual Studio.

Web Sites

You can create many types of projects in Visual Studio 2005, including:

- Console Application
- Windows Application
- Windows Service
- Windows Control Libray
- Web Control Library
- Class Library
- Pocket PC templates
- SmartPhone templates
- Windows CE templates
- Crystal Reports Windows Application
- SQL Server Project
- Word and Excel Document and Template
- Screen Saver

Web applications are notable in their absence from the list of projects you can create. Web applications do not use projects, just solutions.

A typical .NET web application is comprised of many items: content files (such as *.aspx* files), source files (such as *.cs* files), assemblies (such as *.exe* and *.dll* files) and assembly information files, data sources (such as *.mdb* files), references, and icons, as well as miscellaneous other files and folders. Visual Studio 2005 organizes these items into a folder that represents the web site. The web site folder is housed in a solution. When you create a new web site, Visual Studio 2005 automatically creates the solution.

Templates

When you create a new project, you get the New Project dialog box, shown in Figure 2-2.

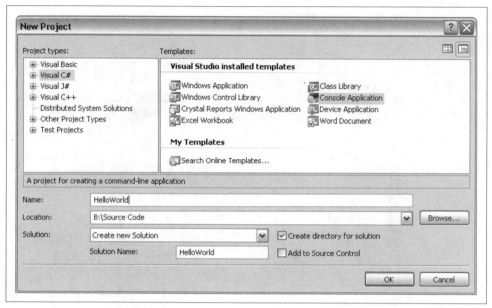

Figure 2-2. New Project dialog

In the New Project dialog, you select the project type (in the left-hand pane) and the template (in the right). There are a variety of templates for each project type. A *template* is a file that Visual Studio 2005 uses to set up the initial state of your project.

For the examples in this book, you'll always choose Visual C# for the project type, and in most cases, you'll choose Console Application as the template. Specify the name of the directory in which your project will be stored in the Location Box and name your project in the Name box.

> Project names can contain any standard characters, except leading or trailing spaces, Windows or DOS keywords, and any of the following special characters: # % & * | \ : " < > ? /.

Inside the Integrated Development Environment

The Visual Studio 2005 Integrated Development Environment (IDE) is centered around an editor. An editor is much like a word processor, except that it produces simple text (that is, text with no formatting, such as bold and italics). All source code files are simple text files.

The Visual Studio 2005 IDE also provides support for building Graphical User Interfaces (GUIs), which are integral to Windows and web projects. The following pages introduce some of the key features of the IDE.

The IDE is a Multiple Document Interface (MDI) application. There is a main window, and within the main window are a number of smaller windows. The central window is the text editing window. Figure 2-3 shows the basic layout.

Figure 2-3. The IDE

To the left of the editing window are a number of tabbed windows that contain tools used when creating Windows and web applications. To the right of the editing window are both stacked and tabbed windows. Shown on top is the Solution Explorer, which allows you to examine and manipulate the files in the solution. Below the Solution Explorer are two tabbed windows: Dynamic Help and Properties. The Properties window is used extensively when creating web and Windows desktop applications. Dynamic help will examine what you are doing and offer help on related topics.

At the bottom of the IDE are five tabbed windows: Error List, Task List, Output, Find Results, and Find Symbol Results.

All of these windows, plus the Toolbox, are resizable and dockable. They can be resized by placing the mouse cursor over the edge you want to move. The cursor will change to a double-arrow resizing cursor, at which point you can drag the window edge one way or the other.

Right-clicking on the title bar of a dockable window pops up a menu with five mutually exclusive check items:

Floating

The window will not dock when dragged against the edge of the Visual Studio 2005 window. The floating window can be placed anywhere on the desktop, even outside the Visual Studio 2005 window.

Dockable

The window can be dragged and docked along any side of the Visual Studio 2005 window, as you'll see later in the chapter.

Tabbed Document

The window occupies the work surface, with a set of tabs for navigation.

Auto Hide

The window will disappear, indicated only by a tab, when the cursor is not over the window. It will reappear when the cursor is over the tab. A pushpin in the upper-right corner of the window will be pointing down when Auto Hide is turned off and pointing sideways when it is turned on.

Hide

The window disappears. To see the window again (to unhide it), use the View main menu item.

If you click the title bar of a window and drag it, it floats free. You can now place it where you want. Visual Studio 2005 provides guides to help you with locating the window. To see this at work, grab the Solution Explorer and pull it free of its current position. As you move about, the IDE positioning indicators appear, as shown in Figure 2-4.

As you click on each positioning indicator, a shadow appears to show you where the window would go if you release the mouse. Notice in the center of the editing window that there is a cluster of five indicators. If you choose the center square, the window will be tabbed with the current window. To put the Solution Explorer back where it belongs, hover over the Dynamic Help window; a five-part indicator will appear, and you can select the upper indicator to place Solution Explorer above the tabbed set of Properties and Dynamic Help.

You can also double-click on either the title bar or the tab to dock and undock the window. Double-clicking on the title while docked undocks the entire group. Double-clicking on the tab just undocks the one window, leaving the rest of the group docked.

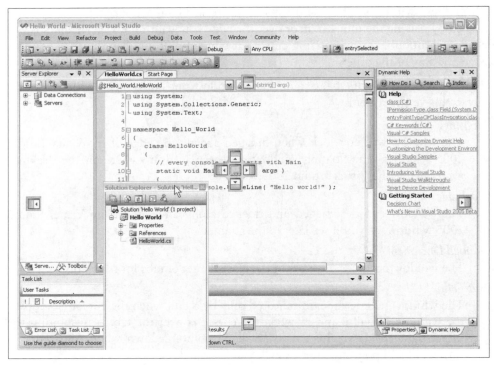

Figure 2-4. Positioning windows

Building and Running

You can run your application at any time by selecting either Start or Start Without Debugging from the Debug menu, or you can accomplish the same results by pressing either F5 or Ctrl-F5, respectively. You can also start the program by clicking the Start icon (▶) on the Standard toolbar.

For console applications, the advantage of running the program with Ctrl-F5 is that Visual Studio 2005 will open your application in a console window, display its results, and then add a line to press a key when you are ready, as shown in Figure 2-5. This keeps the window open until you've seen the results and pressed a key, at which point the window will close.

The program can be built (that is, the *.exe* and *.dll* files can be generated) by selecting a command under the Build menu. You have the option of building the entire solution or only the currently selected project.

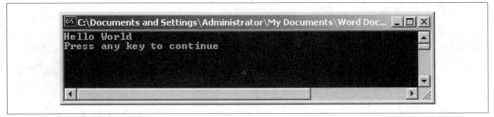

Figure 2-5. Running the application

Menus and Toolbars

The menus provide access to many of the commands and capabilities of Visual Studio 2005. The more commonly used menu commands are duplicated with toolbar buttons for ease of use.

The menus and toolbars are context-sensitive (the available selection is dependent on what part of the IDE is currently selected, and what activities are expected or allowed). For example, if the current active window is a code-editing window for a console window, the top-level menu commands are: File, Edit, View, Refactor, Project, Build, Debug, Data, Tools, Test, Window, Community, and Help.

Many of the menu items have keyboard shortcuts, listed adjacent to the menu item itself. These are comprised of one or more keys (referred to as a *chord*), pressed simultaneously. Shortcut keys can be a huge productivity boost, because you can perform common tasks quickly, without removing your hands from the keyboard.

The following sections describe some of the more important menu items and their submenus, focusing on those aspects that are interesting and different from common Windows commands.

File Menu

The File menu provides access to a number of file-, project-, and solution-related commands. Many of these commands are content-sensitive.

As in most Windows applications, the New menu item creates new items to be worked on by the application.

Edit Menu

The Edit menu contains the text editing and searching commands that one would expect, but also includes commands useful in editing code. The most useful are discussed next.

Cycle Clipboard Ring

The Clipboard Ring is like copy-and-paste on steroids. You can copy a number of different selections to the Windows clipboard, using the Edit → Cut (Ctrl-X) or Edit → Copy (Ctrl-C) commands. Then use Ctrl-Shift-V to cycle through all the selections, allowing you to paste the correct one when it comes around.

 Visual Studio Hot Keys can be changed systematically or individually; the ones referred to here and throughout this book are the "standard keys" used when programming in C#. Your mileage may vary.

This submenu item is context-sensitive and is visible only when editing a code window.

Find and Replace

Visual Studio 2005 includes a number of advanced Find and Replace options that you'll use frequently. The most common ones are discussed in this section.

Quick Find and Quick Replace. These are just slightly jazzed names for slightly jazzed versions of the typical Find and Replace. You can access Quick Find with Ctrl-F, and Quick Replace with Ctrl-H. Both commands call essentially the same dialog boxes, switchable by a tab at the top of the dialog box, as shown in Figure 2-6.

Figure 2-6. Find and Replace

The search string defaults to the text currently selected in the code window, or, if nothing is selected, to the text immediately after the current cursor location.

The Look in: drop-down offers the choice of the Current Document, All Open Documents, the Current Project, and the current method.

Search options can be expanded or collapsed by clicking on the plus/minus button next to Find Options. By default, Search hidden text is checked, which allows the search to include code sections currently collapsed in the code window. The Use checkbox allows the use of either regular expressions or wildcards.

 Regular expressions are a language unto themselves, expressly designed for incredibly powerful and sophisticated searches. A full explanation of regular expressions is beyond the scope of this book. For a complete discussion of regular expressions, see the SDK documentation or *Mastering Regular Expressions*, Second Edition, by Jeffrey E. F. Friedl (O'Reilly, 2002).

If the Use checkbox is checked, then the Expression Builder button to the right of the Find what textbox becomes enabled, providing a very handy way to insert valid regular expression or wildcard characters.

Once a search string has been entered in the Find what: text box, the Find Next button becomes enabled. In Quick Find mode, there is also a Bookmark All button, which finds all occurrences of the search string and places a bookmark (described below) next to the code.

In Quick Replace mode, there is also a Replace with text box, and buttons for replacing either a single occurrence or all occurrences of the search string.

Find in Files. Find in Files (Ctrl-Shift-F) is a very powerful search utility that finds text strings anywhere in a directory or in subdirectories (subfolders). It presents the dialog box shown in Figure 2-7. Checkboxes present several self-explanatory options, including the ability to search using either wildcards or regular expressions.

Find Symbol. Clicking the Find Symbol command (Alt-F12) will bring up the Find Symbol dialog box, which allows you to search for symbols (such as namespaces, classes, and interfaces) and their members (such as properties, methods, events, and variables). It also allows you to search in external components for which the source code is not available.

The search results will be displayed in a window labeled Find Symbol Results. From there, you can move to each location in the code by double-clicking on each result.

Go To...

This command brings up the Go To Line dialog box, which allows you to enter a line number and immediately go to that line. It is context-sensitive and is visible only when editing a text window.

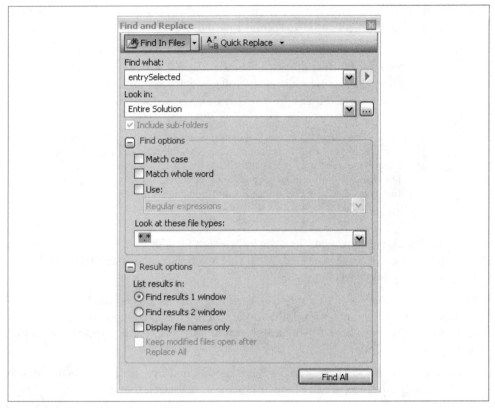

Figure 2-7. Find and Replace in Files

Find All References

This is somewhat similar to Find Symbol under Find and Replace, except that rather than searching for any symbol, it only allows searches for methods that are referenced elsewhere in the project.

Insert File As Text…

This command allows you to insert the contents of any file into your source code, as though you had typed it in. It is context-sensitive and is visible only when editing a text window.

A standard file-browsing dialog box is presented for searching for the file to be inserted. The default file extension will correspond to the project language, but you can search for any file with any extension.

Advanced

The Advanced command is context-sensitive and is visible only when editing a code window. It has many submenu items. These include commands for:

- Creating or removing tabs in a selection (converting spaces to tabs and vice versa)
- Forcing selected text to uppercase or lowercase
- Deleting horizontal whitespace
- Viewing whitespace (making tabs and space characters visible on the screen)
- Toggling word wrap
- Commenting and uncommenting blocks of text
- Increasing and decreasing line indenting
- Incremental searching (see the next section, "Incremental search")

Incremental search

Incremental search allows you to search an editing window by entering the search string character by character. As each character is entered, the cursor moves to the first occurrence of matching text.

To use incremental search in a window, select the command on the Advanced submenu, or press Ctrl-I. The cursor icon will change to a binocular with an arrow indicating the direction of search. Begin typing the text string to search for.

The case sensitivity of an incremental search will come from the previous Find, Replace, Find in Files, or Replace in Files search (described earlier).

The search will proceed downward and left to right from the current location. To search backward, use Ctrl-Shift-I.

The key combinations listed in Table 2-1 apply to incremental searching.

Table 2-1. Incremental searching

Key combination	Description
Esc	Stop the search.
Backspace	Remove a character from the search text.
Ctrl-Shift-I	Change the direction of the search.
Ctrl-I	Move to the next occurrence in the file for the current search text.

Bookmarks

Bookmarks are useful for marking spots in your code and easily navigating from marked spot to marked spot. There are several context-sensitive commands on the Bookmarks submenu (listed in Table 2-2). Note that, unless you add the item to the task list, bookmarks are lost when you close the file, although they are saved when you close the solution (so long as the file was still open).

Table 2-2. Bookmark commands

Command	Description
Toggle Bookmark	Place or remove a bookmark at the current line. When a bookmark is set, a blue rectangular icon will appear in the column along the left edge of the code window.
Enable/Disable	Enables or disables the checkboxes for all bookmarks in the Bookmarks window (does not remove bookmarks).
Previous Bookmark	Move to the previous bookmark.
Next Bookmark	Move to the next bookmark.
Clear	Remove bookmark.
Previous Bookmark in Folder	Move to the previous bookmark in the folder.
Next Bookmark in Folder	Move to the next bookmark in the folder.
Previous Bookmark in Document	Move to the previous bookmark in the current document.
Next Bookmark in Document	Move to the next bookmark in the current document.
Add Task List Shortcut	Add an entry to the Task List (described later in the "View Menu" section) for the current line. When a task list entry is set, a curved arrow icon appears in the column along the left edge of the code window.

This menu item only appears when a code window is the current window.

Outlining

Visual Studio 2005 allows you to *outline*, or collapse and expand, sections of your code to make it easier to view the overall structure. When a section is collapsed, it appears with a plus sign in a box along the left edge of the code window. Clicking on the plus sign expands the region.

You can nest the outlined regions, so that one section can contain one or more other collapsed sections. There are several commands to facilitate outlining (shown in Table 2-3).

Table 2-3. Outlining commands

Command	Description
Hide Selection	Collapses currently selected text.
Toggle Outlining Expansion	Reverses the current outlining state of the innermost section in which the cursor lies.
Toggle All Outlining	Sets all sections to the same outlining state. If some sections are expanded and some collapsed, then all become collapsed.
Stop Outlining	Expands all sections. Removes the outlining symbols from view.
Stop Hiding Current	Removes outlining information for currently selected section.
Collapse to Definitions	Automatically creates sections for each procedure in the code window and collapses them all.
Start Automatic Outlining	Restarts automatic outlining after it has been stopped.

The default behavior of outlining can be set using the Tools → Options menu item. Go to Text Editor, and then the specific language for which you want to set the options. The outlining options can be set for VB.NET under Basic → VB Specific, for Visual Basic 2005 under Visual Basic 2005 → Formatting, and for C++ under C/C++ → Formatting.

IntelliSense

Microsoft IntelliSense technology makes the lives of programmers much easier. It has real-time, context-sensitive help available, which appears right under your cursor. Code completion automatically completes your thoughts for you, drastically reducing your typing. Drop-down-lists provide all methods and properties possible in the current context, available at a keystroke or mouse click.

Unlike previous versions of Visual Studio, IntelliSense now works in all code windows, including not only the Visual Basic 2005 code-behind files, but also within both server- (i.e., script) and client-side (i.e., HTML) code in content files.

The default IntelliSense features can be configured by going to Tools → Options and then the language-specific pages under Text Editor.

Most of the IntelliSense features appear as you type inside a code window, or allow the mouse to hover over a portion of the code. In addition, the Edit → IntelliSense menu item offers numerous commands, the most important of which are shown in Table 2-4.

Table 2-4. IntelliSense commands

Command	Description
List Members	Displays a list of all possible members available for the current context. Keystrokes incrementally search the list. Press any key to insert the highlighted selection into your code; that key becomes the next character after the inserted name. Use the Tab key to select without entering any additional characters.
	This can also be accessed by right-clicking and selecting List Member from the context-sensitive menu.
Parameter Info	Displays a list of number, names, and types of parameters required for a method, sub, function, or attribute.
Quick Info	Displays the complete declaration for any identifier (such as a variable name or class name) in your code. This is also enabled by hovering the mouse cursor over any identifier.
Complete Word	Automatically completes the typing of any identifier once you type in enough characters to uniquely identify it. This only works if the identifier is being entered in a valid location in the code.
Insert Snippet	Displays a selection of code snippets to insert, such as the complete syntax for a `switch` case block or an `if` block.
Surround With	Displays a selection of code snippets to surround a block of code, such as a class declaration.

The member list presents itself when you type a dot operator following any class or member name.

Every member of the class is listed, and each member's type is indicated by an icon. There are icons for methods, fields, properties, events, and so forth. In addition, each icon may have a second icon overlaid to indicate the accessibility of the member: public, private, protected, and so on. If there is no accessibility icon, then the member is public.

 If the member list does not appear, make sure that you have added all the necessary using statements.

Two of the subcommands under the IntelliSense menu item, Insert Snippet and Surround With, tap into a great feature to reduce typing and minimize errors: *code snippets*. A code snippet is a chunk of code that replaces an alias. A short alias is replaced with a much longer code snippet. For example, the alias switch would be replaced with:

```
switch ( switch_on )
{
    default:
}
```

with the expression switch_on highlighted in yellow and the cursor in place, ready to type in your own expression. In fact, all the editable fields will be highlighted, and you can use the Tab key to navigate through them, or Shift-Tab to go backwards. Any changes made to the editable field are immediately propagated to all the instances of that field in the code snippet. Press Enter or Esc to end the field editing and return to normal editing.

To do a straight alias replacement, either select Insert Snippet from the menu, or more easily, press Ctrl-K, Ctrl-X. Alternatively, just type an alias in the code window and an IntelliSense menu will pop up with a list of aliases, with the current one highlighted.

Alternatively, a code snippet can surround highlighted lines of code, say with a for construct. To surround lines of code with a code snippet construct, highlight the code, then either select Surround With from the menu, or press Ctrl-K, Ctrl-S.

View Menu

The View menu is a context-sensitive menu that provides access to the myriad of windows available in the Visual Studio 2005 IDE. You will probably keep many of these windows open all the time; others you will use rarely, if at all.

The View menu is context-sensitive. For example, with an ASP.NET content file on the work surface, the first three menu items will be Code, Designer, and Markup, while the Code and Designer menu items will be omitted if looking at a code-behind file.

When the application is running, a number of other windows, primarily used for debugging, become visible or available. These windows are accessed via the Debug → Windows menu item, not from the View menu item.

Visual Studio 2005 can store several different window layouts. In particular, it remembers a completely different set of open windows during debug sessions than it does during normal editing. These layouts are stored per-user, not per-project or per-solution.

Class View

The Class View (Ctrl-Shift-C) shows all the classes in the solution in a hierarchical manner. A typical Class View, somewhat expanded, is shown in Figure 2-8.

As with the Solution Explorer, any item in the class view can be right-clicked, which exposes a pop-up menu with a number of context-sensitive menu items. This can provide a convenient way to sort the display of classes in a project or solution, or to add a method, property, or field to a class.

The button on the left above the class list allows for sorting the classes listed, either alphabetically, by type, by access, or grouped by type. Clicking on the button itself sorts by the current sort mode, while clicking on the down arrow next to it presents the other sort buttons and changes the sort mode.

The button on the right above the class list allows you to create virtual folders for organizing the classes listed. These folders are saved as part of the solution in the *.suo* file.

These folders are virtual (that is, they are illusory). They are only used for viewing the list. As such, they have no effect on the actual items. Items copied to the folder are not physically moved, and if the folders are deleted, the items in them are not lost. Note that if you rename or delete an object from the code that is in a folder, you may need to manually drag the item into the folder again to clear the error node.

Code Definition

The Code Definition window (Ctrl-W, D) is used in developing web pages.

Error List

The Error List window (Ctrl-W, Ctrl-E), which is available in all editor views, displays errors, warnings, and messages generated as you edit and compile your project. Syntax errors flagged by IntelliSense are displayed here, as well as deployment errors. Double-clicking on an error in this list will open the offending file and move the cursor to the error location.

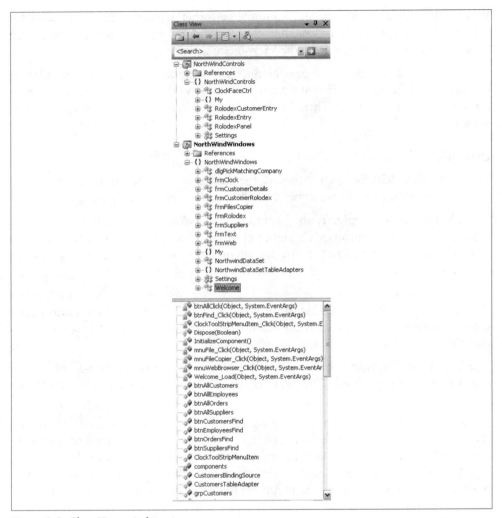

Figure 2-8. Class View window

Output

The Output window (Ctrl-Alt-O) displays status messages from the IDE, such as build progress. The Output window can be set to display by default when a build starts by going to Tools → Options → Projects and Solutions → General and checking "Show Output window when build starts."

This window is available in all editor views.

Properties

The Properties window (F4) displays all the properties for the currently selected item. Some of the properties (such as Font) may have subproperties, indicated by a plus sign next to their entries in the window. The property values on the right side of the window are editable.

One thing that can be confusing is that certain items have more than one set of properties. For example, a Form content file can show two different sets of properties, depending on whether you select the source file in the Solution Explorer or the form as shown in the Design view.

A typical Properties window is shown in Figure 2-9.

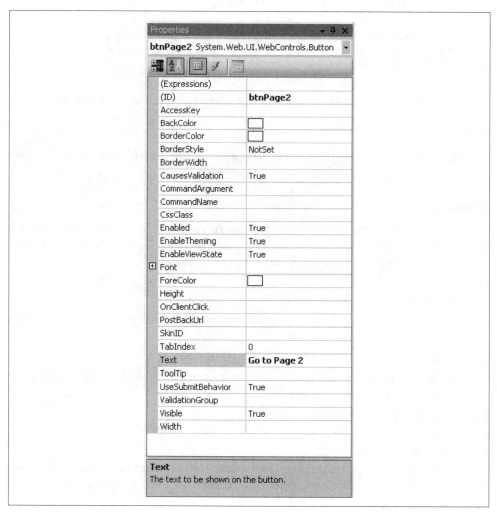

Figure 2-9. Properties window

The name and type of the current object is displayed in the field at the top of the window. In Figure 2-9, it is an object named btnPage2 of type Button, contained in the System.Web.UI.WebControls namespace.

Most properties can be edited in place in the Properties window. The Font property has subproperties that may be set directly in the window by clicking on the plus sign to expand its subproperties, and then editing the subproperties in place.

The Properties window has several buttons just below the name and type of the object. The first two buttons on the left toggle the list by category or alphabetically. The next two buttons from the left toggle between displaying properties for the selected item and displaying events for the selected item. The rightmost button displays property pages for the object, if there are any.

 Some objects have both a Properties window and property pages. The property pages display additional properties not shown in the Properties window.

The box below the list of properties displays a brief description of the selected property.

Task List

In large applications, keeping a to-do list can be quite helpful. Visual Studio 2005 provides this functionality with the Task List window.

Toolbox

The Toolbox command (Ctrl-Alt-X) displays the toolbox if it is not currently displayed. If it is currently displayed, nothing happens—it does not toggle the display. To hide the toolbox, click on the X in the toolbox title bar.

Other windows

There are several other windows that have been relegated to a submenu called Other Windows. These include:

Bookmark window (Ctrl-K, Ctrl-W)
: The Bookmark window displays bookmarks you create to allow you to return to a specific spot in your code quickly.

Command window (Ctrl-Alt-A)
: The Command window is used to enter commands directly.

Document Outline (Ctrl-Alt-T)
: The Document Outline displays the hierarchical structure of a web page or user control, including directives, script blocks, HTML elements, and server controls.

Macro Explorer (Alt-F8)
: Visual Studio 2005 offers the ability to automate repetitive chores with macros. A *macro* is a set of instructions written in VB.NET, either created manually or recorded by the IDE, saved in a file. The Macro Explorer is the one of the main

tools for viewing, managing, and executing macros. It provides access into the Macro IDE.

Object Browser (Ctrl-Alt-J)
The Object Browser is a tool for examining objects (such as namespaces, classes, and interfaces), and their members (such as methods, properties, variables, and events).

Resource View (Ctrl-Shift-E)
This window displays the resource files included in the project. Resources are nonexecutable data deployed with an application, such as icons and graphics, culture-specific text messages, and persistent data objects.

Server Explorer (Ctrl-Alt-S)
The Server Explorer allows you to access any server to which you have network access.

Refactor Menu

Refactoring is the process of taking code duplicated in various parts of your program and extracting them out to a callable method. This is an advanced procedure, so you won't see any refactoring in this book.

 For details on refactoring, we highly recommend the book *Refactoring: Improving the Design of Existing Code,* by Fowler, et al. (Addison Wesley, 1999).

The Refactor menu item is available when you're looking at a code window for a web page, user control, or language source code file. It is also available from context menus when right-clicking on an identifier in a Class View, Object Browser, or Solution Explorer window.

The refactoring menu items will modify your code—for example, extracting common code to a method and then calling that method in the place from which it was extracted.

Project Menu

The Project menu provides functionality related to project management. It is only visible when the solution is selected in the Solution Explorer. All of the functionality exposed by the Project menu is also available in the Solution Explorer, by right-clicking on the solution.

Build Menu

The Build menu offers menu items for building the current project (highlighted in Solution Explorer) or the solution. It also exposes the Configuration Manager for configuring the build process.

Debug Menu

The Debug menu allows you to start an application with or without debugging, set breakpoints in the code, and control the debugging session.

Data Menu

This context-sensitive menu is visible only when in design mode when creating, for example, web applications.

Format Menu

The Format menu is visible only in design mode when creating, for example, web applications; further, the commands under it are context-sensitive to the control(s) currently selected.

Tools Menu

The Tools menu presents commands accessing a wide range of functionality, ranging from connecting to databases to accessing external tools to setting IDE options. Some of the more useful commands are described in the following sections.

Connect To Device

The Connect To Device command brings up a dialog box that allows you to connect to either a physical mobile device or an emulator.

Connect To Database

The Connect To Database command default brings up the dialog box that allows you to select a server, log in to that server, and connect to the database on the server. Microsoft SQL Server is the default database (surprise!), but the Change button allows you to connect to any number of other databases, including any for which there are Oracle or ODBC providers.

Code Snippets Manager

The Code Snippets Manager command (Ctrl-K, Ctrl-B) brings up the Code Snippets Manager dialog box, which allows you to maintain the code snippets (described previously in the "IntelliSense" section). This dialog box allows you to add or remove code snippets for any of the supported languages. You can also import code snippets and search online for code snippets.

Choose Toolbox Items

This command brings up the Choose Toolbox dialog box, allowing you to add COM components and custom controls. The details of doing so are beyond the scope of this book, but are covered in full in *Programming ASP.NET* by Jesse Liberty and Dan Hurwitz (O'Reilly, 2005).

External Tools

Depending on the options selected at the time Visual Studio 2005 was installed on your machine, you may have one or more external tools available on the Tools menu. These might include tools such as Create GUID or Dotfuscator Community Edition. (Use of these tools is beyond the scope of this book.)

The Tools → External Tools... command allows you to add additional external tools to the Tools menu. When selected, you are presented with the External Tools dialog box. This dialog box has fields for the tool title, the command to execute the tool, any arguments and the initial directory, as well as several checkboxes for different behaviors.

Performance Tools

This menu item exposes a wizard for benchmarking and tuning performance, as well as a command for starting a new performance session.

Import and Export Settings

This command brings up the Import and Export Settings dialog box, which is a wizard for importing and exporting IDE environment settings. With this wizard, you can transfer your carefully wrought IDE settings from one machine to the next.

Options

The Options command also brings up the Options dialog box that allows you to set a wide range of options, ranging from the number of items to display in lists of recently used items to HTML Designer options.

Window Menu

The Window menu is a standard Windows application Window command. It displays a list of all the currently open windows, allowing you to bring any window to the foreground by clicking on it. Note that all the file windows currently displayed in the IDE also have tabs along the top edge of the work surface, below the toolbars (unless you have selected MDI mode in Tools → Options → Environment → General), and windows can be selected by clicking on a tab.

Help Menu

The Help menu provides access to a number of submenus.

If you are developing on a machine with enough horsepower, Dynamic Help is a wonderful thing. Otherwise, it can diminish the responsiveness of the IDE.

Summary

- Visual Studio 2005 is a powerful tool with many features, to make writing programs easier.
- The Start Page provides an overview of your programming environment, and a list of recent projects.
- A *solution* is a set of related projects, and a *project* is a set of related code files and associated resources such as images, and so on.
- Visual Studio 2005 has a number of templates that allow you to create particular types of projects, such as windows or web applications.
- Among other things, Visual Studio 2005 provides "what you see is what you get" (WSYWYG) support for building, testing, and debugging graphical user interfaces (GUI).
- Every window in Visual Studio 2005 can be resized and moved.
- To run your application, select Start or Start Without Debugging, or press F5 or Ctrl-F5.
- The Clipboard Ring can hold a number of different selections that you can cycle through.
- The Find and Replace feature lets you locate text strings in the current file or other files, using normal text or regular expressions.
- Bookmarks enable you to mark spots in your code so you can easily find them later.
- IntelliSense saves you keystrokes and can help you discover methods and required arguments by (for example) listing possible completions to what you're typing.
- The Properties window displays properties for the currently selected item.

Quiz

Question 2-1. What is the difference between a project and a solution?

Question 2-2. How do you move windows in the IDE?

Question 2-3. What does the pushpin do on a window?

Question 2-4. What is the difference between pressing F5 and Ctrl-F5 from within Visual Studio 2005?

Question 2-5. What is the Clipboard Ring?

Question 2-6. How do you retrieve items from the clipboard ring?

Question 2-7. What is "Find Symbol" for?

Question 2-8. What are bookmarks?

Question 2-9. What is IntelliSense?

Question 2-10. What is a code snippet?

Exercises

Exercise 2-1. Insert a bookmark before the `Console.Writeline()` statement in Hello World. Navigate away from it and then use the bookmarks menu item to return to it.

Exercise 2-2. Undock the Solution Explorer window from the right side of the IDE and move it to the left. Leave it there if you like, or move it back.

Exercise 2-3. Insert a code snippet for a for loop from the Edit → Intellisense menu into your Hello World program. (It won't do anything for now; you'll learn about for loops in Chapter 4.)

CHAPTER 3

C# Language Fundamentals

Chapter 1 demonstrates a very simple C# program that prints the text string "Hello world!" to the console screen and provides a line-by-line analysis of that program. However, even that very simple program was complex enough that some of the details had to be skipped over. In this chapter, I'll begin an in-depth exploration of the syntax and structure of the C# language. The *syntax* of a language is the order of the keywords, where you put semicolons and so forth. The *semantics* is what you are expressing in the code, and how your code fits together. Syntax is trivial and unimportant, but because compilers are absolute sticklers for correct syntax, novice programmers spend a lot of attention to syntax until they are comfortable. Fortunately, Visual Studio 2005 makes managing syntax much easier so that you can focus on semantics, which is far more important.

In this chapter, I'll introduce statements and expressions, the building blocks of any program. You'll learn about variables and constants, which let you store values for use in your program. I'll begin an explanation of types and we'll take a look at strings, which you saw briefly in the Hello World program.

Statements

In C#, a complete program instruction is called a *statement* and each statement ends with a semicolon (;). Programs consist of sequences of statements such as:

```
int myVariable;                        // a statement
myVariable = 23;                       // another statement
int anotherVariable = myVariable;      // yet another statement
```

The compiler starts at the beginning of a source code file and reads down, executing statement after statement in the order encountered. This would be entirely straightforward, and terribly limiting, were it not for branching. Branching allows you to change the order in which statements are evaluated. See Chapter 5 for more information about branching.

Types

C# is a *strongly typed* language. That means that every object you create or use in a C# program must have a specific *type* (e.g., you must declare the object to be an integer or a string or a Dog or a Button). Essentially, the type indicates how big the object is (in memory) and what it can do.

Types come in two flavors: those that are built into the language (intrinsic types) and those you create (classes and interfaces, discussed in Chapters 7 and 13). C# offers a number of intrinsic types, shown in Table 3-1.

Table 3-1. The intrinsic types

C# type	Size (in bytes)	.NET type	Description
byte	1	Byte	Unsigned (values 0–255).
char	2	Char	Unicode characters.
bool	1	Boolean	True or false.
sbyte	1	SByte	Signed (values –128 to 127).
short	2	Int16	Signed (short) (values –32,768 to 32,767).
ushort	2	UInt16	Unsigned (short) (values 0 to 65,535).
int	4	Int32	Signed integer values between –2,147,483,648 and 2,147,483,647.
uint	4	UInt32	Unsigned integer values between 0 and 4,294,967,295.
float	4	Single	Floating point number. Holds the values from approximately +/– $1.5 * 10^{-45}$ to approximately +/–$3.4 * 10^{38}$ with 7 significant figures.
double	8	Double	Double-precision floating point; holds the values from approximately +/-$5.0 * 10^{-324}$ to approximately +/–$1.8 * 10^{308}$ with 15–16 significant figures.
decimal	12	Decimal	Fixed-precision up to 28 digits and the position of the decimal point. This is typically used in financial calculations. Requires the suffix "m" or "M."
long	8	Int64	Signed integers ranging from -9,223,372,036,854,775,808 to 9,223,372,036,854,775,807.
ulong	8	UInt64	Unsigned integers ranging from 0 to approximately $1.85 * 10^{19}$.

Each type has a name (such as int) and a size (such as 4 bytes). The size tells you how many bytes each object of this type occupies in memory. (Programmers generally don't like to waste memory if they can avoid it, but with the cost of memory these days, you can afford to be mildly profligate if doing so simplifies your program.) The description field of Table 3-1 tells you the minimum and maximum values you can hold in objects of each type.

Each C# type corresponds to an underlying .NET type. Thus, what C# calls an int, .NET calls an Int32. This is interesting only if you care about sharing objects across languages.

Intrinsic types can't do much. You can use them to add two numbers together, and they can display their values as strings. User-defined types can do a lot more; their abilities are determined by the methods you create, as discussed in detail in Chapter 8.

Objects of an intrinsic type are called *variables*. Variables are discussed in detail later in this chapter.

Numeric Types

Most of the intrinsic types are used for working with numeric values (byte, sbyte, short, ushort, int, uint, float, double, decimal, long, and ulong).

The numeric types can be broken into two sets: unsigned and signed. An unsigned value (byte, ushort, uint, ulong) can hold only positive values. A signed value (sbyte, short, int, long) can hold positive or negative values, but the highest value is only half as large as the corresponding unsigned type. That is, a ushort can hold any value from 0 through 65,535, but a short can hold only –32,768 through 32,767. Notice that 32,767 is nearly half of 65,535 (it is off by one to allow for holding the value zero). The reason a ushort can hold up to 65,535 is that 65,536 is a round number in binary arithmetic (2^{16}) and one bit is devoted to 0.

Another way to categorize the types is into those used for integer values (whole numbers) and those used for floating-point values (fractional or rational numbers). The byte, sbyte, ushort, uint, ulong, short, int, and long types all hold whole number values.

The byte and sbyte types are not used very often and won't be described in this book.

The double and float types hold fractional values. For most uses, float will suffice, unless you need to hold a really big fractional number, in which case you might use a double. The decimal value type was added to the language to support scientific and financial applications.

Typically, you decide which size integer to use (short, int, or long) based on the magnitude of the value you want to store. For example, a ushort can only hold values from 0 through 65,535, while a uint can hold values from 0 through 4,294,967,295.

That said, in real life, most of the time you'll simply declare your numeric variables to be of type int, unless there is a good reason to do otherwise. (Most programmers choose signed types unless they have a good reason to use an unsigned value. This is, in part, just a matter of tradition.)

Suppose you need to keep track of inventory for a book warehouse. You expect to house up to 40,000 or even 50,000 copies of each book. A signed short can only hold up to 32,767 values. You might be tempted to use an unsigned short (which can hold up to 65,535 values), but it is easier and preferable to just use a signed int (with a maximum value of 2,147,483,647). That way, if you have a runaway best seller, your program won't break (if you anticipate selling more than 2 billion copies of your book, perhaps you'll want to use a long!).

 Throughout this book, we will use int wherever it works, even if short or byte might be workable alternatives. Memory is cheap, and programmer time expensive. There are circumstances where the difference in memory usage would be significant (for example, if you are going to hold a billion of them in memory), but we'll keep things simple by using the int type whenever possible.

float, double, and decimal offer varying degrees of size and precision. For most small fractional numbers, float is fine. Note that the compiler assumes that any number with a decimal point is a double unless you tell it otherwise. (The "Variables" section discusses how you tell it otherwise.)

Non-Numeric Types: char and bool

In addition to the numeric types, the C# language offers two other types: char and bool.

The char type is used from time to time when you need to hold a single character. The char type can represent a simple character (A), a Unicode character (\u0041), or an escape sequence ('\n'). You'll see escape sequences later in this book, and their use will be explained in context.

The one remaining important type is bool, which holds a Boolean value. A Boolean value is one that is either true or false. Boolean values are used frequently in C# programming, as you'll see throughout this book. Virtually every comparison (is myDog bigger than yourDog?) results in a Boolean value.

 The bool type was named after George Boole (1815–1864), an English mathematician who published *An Investigation into the Laws of Thought, on Which Are Founded the Mathematical Theories of Logic and Probabilities,* and thus created the science of Boolean algebra.

Types and Compiler Errors

The compiler will help you by complaining if you try to use a type improperly. The compiler complains in one of two ways: it issues a warning or it issues an error.

 You are well advised to treat warnings as errors. Stop what you are doing and figure out why there is a warning and fix the problem. Never ignore a compiler warning unless you are certain that you know exactly why the warning was issued and that you know something the compiler does not.

To have Visual Studio enforce this for you, follow these steps:

1. Right-click on the project.
2. Click on the Compile tab.
3. Make sure the "Treat all warnings as errors" checkbox is checked or set the Warnings that you want to treat as errors using the drop-down boxes.

Programmers talk about design-time, compile-time, and runtime. Design-time is when you are designing the program, compile-time is when you compile the program, and runtime is (surprise!) when you run the program.

The earlier in your development process that you unearth a bug, the better. It is easier to fix a bug in your logic at design-time than to fix the bug once it has been written into code. Likewise, it is better (and cheaper) to find bugs in your program at compile-time than at runtime. Not only is it better; it is more reliable. A compile-time bug will fail every time you run the compiler, but a runtime bug can hide. Runtime bugs slip under a crack in your logic and lurk there (sometimes for months), biding their time, waiting to come out when it will be most expensive (or most embarrassing) to you.

It will be a constant theme of this book that you *want* the compiler to find bugs. The compiler is your friend (though I admit, at times it feels like your Nemesis). The more bugs the compiler finds, the fewer bugs your users will find.

A strongly typed language like C# helps the compiler find bugs in your code. Here's how: suppose you tell the compiler that Milo is of type Dog. Sometime later you try to use Milo to display text (calling the ShowText method). Oops, Dogs don't display text. Your compiler will stop with an error:

```
Dog does not contain a definition for 'showText'
```

Very nice. Now you can go figure out if you used the wrong object or you called the wrong method.

Visual Studio .NET actually finds the error even before the compiler does. When you try to add a method, IntelliSense pops up a list of valid methods to help you, as shown in Figure 3-1.

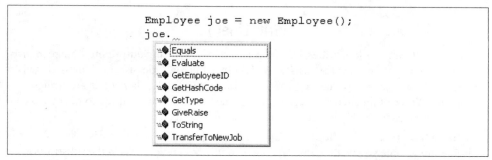

```
Employee joe = new Employee();
joe.
        Equals
        Evaluate
        GetEmployeeID
        GetHashCode
        GetType
        GiveRaise
        ToString
        TransferToNewJob
```

Figure 3-1. IntelliSense

When you try to add a method that does not exist, it won't be in the list. That is a pretty good clue that you are not using the object properly.

Variables

A variable is an instance of an intrinsic type (such as int) that can hold a value:

```
int myVariable = 15;
```

You *initialize* a variable by writing its type, its *identifier*, and then assigning a value to that variable.

An *identifier* is just an arbitrary name you assign to a variable, method, class, or other element. In this case, the variable's identifier is myVariable.

You can define variables without initializing them:

```
int myVariable;
```

You can then assign a value to myVariable later in your program:

```
int myVariable;
// some other code here
myVariable = 15; // assign 15 to myVariable
```

You can also change the value of a variable later in the program. That is why they're called variables; their values can vary.

```
int myVariable;
// some other code here
myVariable = 15; // assign 15 to myVariable
// some other code here
myVariable = 12; // now it is 12
```

Technically, a variable is a named storage location (that is, stored in memory) with a type. After the final line of code in the previous example, the value 12 is stored in the named location myVariable.

Example 3-1 illustrates the use of variables. To test this program, open Visual Studio .NET and create a console application. Type in the code as shown.

WriteLine( )

The .NET Framework provides a useful method for displaying output on the screen in console applications: System.Console.WriteLine( ). How you use this method will become clearer as you progress through the book, but the fundamentals are straightforward. You call the method, passing in a string that you want printed to the console (the screen), as in the Hello World application in Chapter 1.

You can also pass in substitution parameters. A *substitution parameter* is just a placeholder for a value you want to display. For example, you might pass in the substitution parameter {0}, and then when you run the program, you'll substitute the value held in the variable myInt, so that its value is displayed where the parameter {0} appears in the WriteLine( ) statement.

Here's how it works. You place a number between braces:

```
System.Console.WriteLine("After assignment, myInt: {0}", myInt);
```

Notice that you follow the quoted string with a comma and then a variable name. The value of the variable will be substituted into the parameter. Assuming myInt has the value 15, the statement shown previously causes the following to display:

```
After assignment, myInt: 15
```

If you have more than one parameter, the variable values will be substituted in order, as in the following:

```
System.Console.WriteLine("After assignment, myInt: {0} and
myOtherInt: {1}", myInt, myOtherInt);
```

Assuming myInt has the value 15, and myOtherInt has the value 20, this will cause the following to display:

```
After assignment, myInt: 15 and myOtherInt: 20.
```

You'll see a great deal more about WriteLine( ) in later chapters.

Example 3-1. Using variables

```
class Values
{
    static void Main( )
    {
        int myInt = 7;
        System.Console.WriteLine("Initialized, myInt: {0}",
        myInt);
        myInt = 5;
        System.Console.WriteLine("After assignment, myInt: {0}",
        myInt);
    }
}
```

Press F5 to build and run this application; the output looks like this:

```
Initialized, myInt: 7
After assignment, myInt: 5
```

Example 3-1 initializes the variable myInt to the value 7, displays that value, reassigns the variable with the value 5, and displays it again.

Definite Assignment

C# requires *definite assignment*; that is, variables must be initialized (or assigned to) before they are "used" (see "out Parameters and Definite Assignment" in Chapter 8). To test this rule, change the line that initializes myInt in Example 3-1 to:

```
int myInt;
```

Save the revised program shown in Example 3-2.

Example 3-2. Uninitialized variable

```
class Values
{
    static void Main( )
    {
        int myInt;
        System.Console.WriteLine
        ("Uninitialized, myInt: {0}",myInt);
        myInt = 5;
        System.Console.WriteLine("Assigned, myInt: {0}", myInt);
    }
}
```

When you try to compile Example 3-2, the C# compiler will display the following error message:

```
Use of unassigned local variable 'myInt'
```

It is not legal to use an uninitialized variable in C#; doing so violates the rule of definite assignment. In this case, "using" the variable myInt means passing it to WriteLine( ).

So does this mean you must initialize every variable? No, but if you don't initialize your variable, then you must assign a value to it before you attempt to use it. Example 3-3 illustrates a corrected program.

Example 3-3. Definite assignment

```
class Values
{
    static void Main( )
    {
        int myInt;
        //other code here...
        myInt = 7; // assign to it
```

Example 3-3. Definite assignment (continued)

```
        System.Console.WriteLine("Assigned, myInt: {0}", myInt);
        myInt = 5;
        System.Console.WriteLine("Reassigned, myInt: {0}", myInt);
    }
}
```

Constants

Variables are a powerful tool, but there are times when you want to manipulate a defined value, one whose value you want to ensure remains constant. A *constant* is like a variable in that it can store a value. However, unlike a variable, you cannot change the value of a constant while the program runs.

For example, you might need to work with the Fahrenheit freezing and boiling points of water in a program simulating a chemistry experiment. Your program will be clearer if you name the variables that store these values FreezingPoint and BoilingPoint, but you do not want to permit their values to be changed while the program is executing. The solution is to use a constant. Constants come in three flavors: *literals*, *symbolic constants*, and *enumerations*.

Literal Constants

A literal constant is just a value. For example, 32 is a literal constant. It does not have a name; it is just a literal value. And you can't make the value 32 represent any other value. The value of 32 is always 32. You can't assign a new value to 32, and you can't make 32 represent the value 99 no matter how hard you might try.

Symbolic Constants

Symbolic constants assign a name to a constant value. You declare a symbolic constant using the following syntax:

```
    const type identifier = value;
```

The const keyword is followed by a type, an identifier, the assignment operator (=), and the value with which you'll initialize the constant.

This is similar to declaring a variable, except that you start with the keyword const and symbolic constants *must* be initialized. Once initialized, a symbolic constant cannot be altered. For example, in the following declaration, 32 is a literal constant and FreezingPoint is a symbolic constant of type int:

```
    const int FreezingPoint = 32;
```

Example 3-4 illustrates the use of symbolic constants.

Example 3-4. Using symbolic constants

```
class Values
{
 static void Main( )
 {
 const int FreezingPoint = 32; // degrees Fahrenheit
 const int BoilingPoint = 212;

 System.Console.WriteLine("Freezing point of water: {0}",
 FreezingPoint );
 System.Console.WriteLine("Boiling point of water: {0}",
 BoilingPoint );
 //BoilingPoint = 21;

 }
}
```

Example 3-4 creates two symbolic integer constants: FreezingPoint and BoilingPoint. See the sidebar, "Naming Conventions," for a discussion of how to name symbolic constants.

Naming Conventions

Microsoft has promulgated white papers on how you should name the variables, constants, and other objects in your program. They define two types of naming conventions: Camel notation and Pascal notation.

In Camel notation, names begin with a lowercase letter. Multiword names (such as "my button") are written with no spaces and no underscore and with each word after the first capitalized. Thus, the correct name for "my button" is myButton.

Pascal notation is just like Camel notation except that the first letter is also uppercase (FreezingPoint).

Microsoft suggests that variables be written with Camel notation and constants with Pascal notation. In later chapters, you'll learn that member variables are named using Camel notation, while methods and classes are named using Pascal notation.

These constants serve the same purpose as using the literal values 32 and 212 for the freezing and boiling points of water, respectively, in expressions that require them. However, because the constants have names, they convey far more meaning. It might seem easier to just use the literal values 32 and 212 instead of going to the trouble of declaring the constants, but if you decide to switch this program to Celsius, you can reinitialize these constants at compile time to 0 and 100, respectively, and all the rest of the code should continue to work.

To prove to yourself that the constant cannot be reassigned, try un-commenting the last line of the preceding program by removing the two slash marks:

```
BoilingPoint = 21;
```

When you recompile, you receive this error:

```
The left-hand side of an assignment must be a variable, property or indexer
```

Enumerations

Enumerations provide a powerful alternative to literal or simple symbolic constants. An *enumeration* is a distinct value type, consisting of a set of named constants (called the enumerator list).

In Example 3-4, you created two related constants:

```
const int FreezingPoint = 32;
const int BoilingPoint = 212;
```

You might want to add a number of other useful constants to this list as well, such as:

```
const int LightJacketWeather = 60;
const int SwimmingWeather = 72;
const int WickedCold = 0;
```

Notice, however, that this process is somewhat cumbersome; also, this syntax shows no logical connection among these various constants. C# provides an alternate construct, the *enumeration*, which allows you to group logically related constants, as in the following:

```
enum Temperatures
{
    WickedCold = 0,
    FreezingPoint = 32,
    LightJacketWeather = 60,
    SwimmingWeather = 72,
    BoilingPoint = 212,
}
```

Many programmers like to leave a comma after the last entry in an enumeration as a convenience for adding more values later. Other programmers find this, at best, sloppy. The code will compile either way.

The complete syntax for specifying an enumeration uses the enum keyword, as follows:

```
[attributes] [modifiers] enum identifier
[:base-type] {enumerator-list};
```

In a specification statement like the preceding example, anything in square brackets is optional. Thus, you can declare an enum with no attributes, modifiers, or base-type.

The optional attributes and modifiers are considered later in this book. For now, let's focus on the rest of this declaration. An enumeration begins with the keyword enum, which is generally followed by an identifier; in this case, Temperatures:

```
enum Temperatures
```

The base-type is the underlying type for the enumeration. You might specify that you are declaring constant ints, constant longs, or something else. If you leave out this optional value (and often you will), it defaults to int, but you are free to use any of the integral types (ushort, long) except for char. For example, the following fragment declares an enumeration with unsigned integers (uint) as the base-type:

```
enum ServingSizes : uint
{
    Small = 1,
    Regular = 2,
    Large = 3
}
```

Notice that an enum declaration ends with the enumerator list, which contains the constant assignments for the enumeration, each separated by a comma. Example 3-5 rewrites Example 3-4 to use an enumeration.

Example 3-5. Using an enumeration

```
class Values
{
    // declare the enumeration
    enum Temperatures
    {
        WickedCold = 0,
        FreezingPoint = 32,
        LightJacketWeather = 60,
        SwimmingWeather = 72,
        BoilingPoint = 212,
    }

    static void Main( )
    {

        System.Console.WriteLine("Freezing point of water: {0}",
        (int) Temperatures.FreezingPoint );
        System.Console.WriteLine("Boiling point of water: {0}",
        (int) Temperatures.BoilingPoint );
    }
}
```

In Example 3-5, you declare an enumerated constant called Temperatures. When you want to use any of the values in an enumeration in a program, the values of the enumeration must be qualified by the enumeration name.

You cannot just refer to FreezingPoint; instead, you use the enumeration identifier (Temperature) followed by the dot operator and then the enumerated constant

(FreezingPoint). This is called *qualifying* the identifier FreezingPoint. Thus, to refer to the FreezingPoint, you use the full identifier Temperature.FreezingPoint.

You might want to display the value of an enumerated constant to the console, as in the following:

```
Console.WriteLine("The freezing point of water is {0}",
    (int) Temperature.FreezingPoint);
```

To make this work properly, you must cast the constant to its underlying type (int). When you *cast* a value, you tell the compiler "I know that this value is really of the indicated type." In this case, you are saying, "Treat this enumerated constant as an int. " Because the underlying type is int, this is safe to do. (See the sidebar, "Casting.")

Casting

Objects of one type can be converted into objects of another type. This is called *casting*. Casting can be either implicit or explicit.

An *implicit conversion* happens automatically; the compiler takes care of it for you. If you have a short, and you assign it to a variable of type int, the compiler automatically (and silently) casts it for you. You don't have to take any action. This is safe, because an int variable can hold any value that might have been in a short variable.

```
short myShort = 5;
// other code here...
int myint = myShort; // implicit conversion
```

You use *explicit conversions* when there is danger of losing data. For example, while the compiler will let you convert a short to an int implicitly (no chance you can lose data), it will not let you implicitly convert an int to a short (the short may not be able to hold all the information in the integer). To accomplish this, you must use an explicit conversion—a signal to the compiler that you want the conversion even though it is dangerous. You do so by placing the type you want to convert to in parentheses:

```
int myInt = 5;
// other code here...
short myShort = (short) myInt; // explicit conversion
```

Note the (int)—that is the explicit conversion.

The semantics of an explicit conversion are "Hey! Compiler! I know what I'm doing." This is sometimes called "hitting it with the big hammer" and can be very useful or very painful, depending on whether your thumb is in the way.

In Example 3-5, the values in the two enumerated constants FreezingPoint and BoilingPoint are both cast to type integer; then that integer value is passed to WriteLine( ) and displayed.

Each constant in an enumeration corresponds to a numerical value. In Example 3-5, each enumerated value is an integer. If you don't specifically set it otherwise, the enumeration begins at 0 and each subsequent value counts up from the previous. Thus, if you create the following enumeration:

```
enum SomeValues
{
    First,
    Second,
    Third = 20,
    Fourth
}
```

the value of First will be 0, Second will be 1, Third will be 20, and Fourth will be 21.

Strings

It is nearly impossible to write a C# program without creating strings. A string object holds a series of characters.

You declare a string variable using the string keyword much as you would create an instance of any type:

```
string myString;
```

You specify a *string literal* by enclosing it in double quotes:

```
"Hello World"
```

It is common to initialize a string variable that contains a string literal:

```
string myString = "Hello World";
```

Strings will be covered in much greater detail in Chapter 15.

Expressions

Statements that evaluate to a value are called *expressions*. You may be surprised how many statements do evaluate to a value. For example, an assignment such as:

```
myVariable = 57;
```

is an expression; it evaluates to the value assigned—in this case, 57.

 Note that the preceding statement assigns the value 57 to the variable myVariable. The assignment operator (=) does not test equality; rather, it causes whatever is on the right side (57) to be assigned to whatever is on the left side (myVariable). Chapter 4 discusses some of the more useful C# operators (including assignment and equality).

Because myVariable = 57 is an expression that evaluates to 57, it can be used as part of another assignment, such as:

```
mySecondVariable = myVariable = 57;
```

What happens in this statement is that the literal value 57 is assigned to the variable myVariable. The value of that assignment (57) is then assigned to the second variable, mySecondVariable. Thus, the value 57 is assigned to both variables. You can assign a value to any number of variables with one statement using the assignment operator (=), as in the following:

```
int a,b,c,d,e;
a = b = c = d = e = 20;
```

Whitespace

In the C# language, spaces, tabs, and newlines are considered to be *whitespace* (so named because you see only the white of the underlying "page"). Extra whitespace is generally ignored in C# statements. Thus, you can write:

```
myVariable = 5;
```

or:

```
myVariable            =              5     ;
```

and the compiler will treat the two statements as identical. The key is to use whitespace to make the program more readable to the programmer; the compiler is indifferent.

The exception to this rule is that whitespace within a string is treated as literal; it is not ignored. If you write:

```
Console.WriteLine("Hello World")
```

each space between "Hello" and "World" is treated as another character in the string. (In this case, there is only one space character.)

Problems arise only when you do not leave space between logical program elements that require it. For instance, the expression:

```
int              myVariable    =              5          ;
```

is the same as:

```
int myVariable=5;
```

but it is *not* the same as:

```
intmyVariable =5;
```

The compiler knows that the whitespace on either side of the assignment operator is extra, but at least some whitespace between the type declaration int and the variable name myVariable is *not* extra; it is required.

This is not surprising; the whitespace allows the compiler to *parse* the keyword int rather than some unknown term intmyVariable. You are free to add as much or as little whitespace between int and myVariable as you care to, but there must be at least one whitespace character (typically a space or tab).

 Visual Basic programmers take note: in C#, the end-of-line has no special significance. Statements are ended with semicolons, not newline characters. There is no line continuation character because none is needed.

Summary

- A complete program instruction is called a statement. Each statement ends with a semicolon (;).
- All objects, constants, and variables must have a specific type.
- Most of the intrinsic types are used for working with numeric values. You will commonly use int for whole numbers and double or float for fractional values.
- The char type is used for holding a single character.
- The bool type can only hold the value true or false.
- A variable is an instance of an intrinsic type. You initialize a variable by creating it with an assigned value.
- A constant is similar to a variable, but the value cannot be changed while the program is running.
- An enumeration is a value type that consists of a set of named constants.
- You can cast a value from one type to another as long as either the compiler knows how to turn the original type into the cast-to type, or you provide a method in your class definition that tells the compiler how to make the cast.
- If no information can be lost, you may cast from one type to another implicitly.
- If information may be lost (such as when casting from a long to an integer), you must cast explicitly.
- A string object holds a series of characters (such as a word or sentence).
- String objects are immutable; when you appear to be changing a string's value, you are actually creating a new string.
- Expressions are statements that evaluate to a value.
- Extra whitespace (spaces, tabs, and newline characters) that is not within a string, is ignored by the compiler.

Quiz

Question 3-1. What values can a bool type have?

Question 3-2. What is the difference between an int and an Int32?

Question 3-3. Which of the following code statements will compile?

```
int myInt = 25;
long myLong = myInt;
int newInt = myLong;
```

Question 3-4. What is the difference between an int and a uint?

Question 3-5. What is the difference between a float and a double?

Question 3-6. Explain definite assignment.

Question 3-7. Given the following declaration, how would you refer to the constant for LightJacketWeather and what would its value be?

```
enum Temperatures
{
    WickedCold = 0,
    FreezingPoint = 32,
    LightJacketWeather,
    SwimmingWeather = 72,
    BoilingPoint = 212,
}
```

Question 3-8. What is an expression?

Exercises

Exercise 3-1. Write a short program creating and initializing each of the following types of variables: int, float, double, char, and then outputting the values to the console.

Exercise 3-2. Modify the program in Exercise 3-1 to change the values of variables and output the values to the console a second time.

Exercise 3-3. Modify the program in Exercise 3-2 to declare a constant float Pi equal to 3.14159. Then assign a new value to pi (3.1) and output its value with the other variables. What happens when you try to compile this program?

CHAPTER 4

Operators

An *operator* is a symbol (such as =, +, or >) that causes C# to take an action. That action might be an assignment of a value to a variable, the addition of two values, a comparison of two values, and so forth.

In the previous chapter, you saw the assignment operator used. The single equals sign (=) is used to assign a value to a variable; in this case, the value 15 to the variable myVariable:

```
myVariable = 15;
```

C# has many different operators that you'll learn about in this chapter. There's a full set of mathematical operators, and a related set of operators just for incrementing and decrementing in integral values by one, which actually are quite useful for controlling loops, as you'll see in Chapter 5. There are also operators available for comparing two values, which are used in the branching statements, as I'll demonstrate in the next chapter.

The Assignment Operator (=)

The assignment operator causes the operand on the left side of the operator to have its value changed to whatever is on the right side of the operator. The following expression assigns the value 15 to myVariable:

```
myVariable = 15;
```

The assignment operator also allows you to *chain* assignments, assigning the same value to multiple variables, as follows:

```
myOtherVariable = myVariable = 15;
```

The previous statement assigns 15 to myVariable, and then also assigns the value (15) to myOtherVariable. This works because the statement:

```
myVariable = 15;
```

is an expression; it evaluates to the value assigned. That is, the expression:

```
myVariable = 15;
```

itself evaluates to 15, and it is this value (15) that is then assigned to myOtherVariable.

 It is important not to confuse the assignment operator (=) with the equality, or equals, operator (==), which has two equals signs and is described later in the chapter. The assignment operator does not test for equality; it assigns a value.

Mathematical Operators

C# uses five mathematical operators: four for standard calculations and one to return the remainder when dividing integers. The following sections consider the use of these operators.

Simple Arithmetical Operators (+, -, *, /)

C# offers four operators for simple arithmetic: the addition (+), subtraction (-), multiplication (*), and division (/) operators work as you might expect, with the possible exception of integer division.

When you divide two integers, C# divides like a child in the third grade: it throws away any fractional remainder. Thus, dividing 17 by 4 returns a value of 4 (with C# discarding the remainder of 1).

This limitation is specific to *integer* division. If you do not want the fractional part thrown away, you can use one of the types that support decimal values, such as float or double. Division between two floats (using the / operator) returns a decimal answer. Integer and floating-point division is illustrated in Example 4-1.

Example 4-1. Integer and float division

```
using System;
public class Tester
{
 public static void Main( )
 {
 int smallInt = 5;
 int largeInt = 12;
 int intQuotient;
 intQuotient = largeInt / smallInt;
 Console.WriteLine("Dividing integers. {0} / {1} = {2}",
 largeInt, smallInt, intQuotient);

 float smallFloat = 5;
 float largeFloat = 12;
 float FloatQuotient;
 FloatQuotient = largeFloat / smallFloat;
```

Example 4-1. Integer and float division (continued)

```
Console.WriteLine("Dividing floats. {0} / {1} = {2}",
largeFloat, smallFloat, FloatQuotient);

  }
}
Output:
Dividing integers. 12 / 5 = 2
Dividing floats. 12 / 5 = 2.4
```

The modulus Operator (%)

C# provides a special operator, modulus (%), to retrieve the remainder from integer division. For example, the statement 17%4 returns 1 (the remainder after integer division).

 You read that statement as, "Seventeen modulo four equals 1."

Example 4-2 demonstrates the effect of division on integers, floats, doubles, and decimals.

Example 4-2. Modulus operator

```
using System;
class Values
{
    static void Main( )
    {
        int firstInt, secondInt;
        float firstFloat, secondFloat;
        double firstDouble, secondDouble;
        decimal firstDecimal, secondDecimal;

        firstInt = 17;
        secondInt = 4;
        firstFloat = 17;
        secondFloat = 4;
        firstDouble = 17;
        secondDouble = 4;
        firstDecimal = 17;
        secondDecimal = 4;
        Console.WriteLine( "Integer:\t{0}\nfloat:\t\t{1}",
        firstInt / secondInt, firstFloat / secondFloat );
        Console.WriteLine( "double:\t\t{0}\ndecimal:\t{1}",
        firstDouble / secondDouble, firstDecimal / secondDecimal );
        Console.WriteLine( "\nRemainder(modulus) from integer division:\t{0}",
        firstInt % secondInt );

    }
}
```

The output looks like this:

```
Integer:           4
float:             4.25
double:            4.25
decimal:           4.25

Remainder(modulus) from integer division:        1
```

> The modulus operator is more than a curiosity; it greatly simplifies finding every nth value, as you'll see in Chapter 5.

Increment and Decrement Operators

A common requirement is to add a value to a variable, subtract a value from a variable, or otherwise change the mathematical value, and then to assign that new value back to the original variable. C# provides several operators for these calculations.

Calculate and Reassign Operators

Suppose you want to increment the mySalary variable by 5,000. You can do this by writing:

```
mySalary = mySalary + 5000;
```

In simple arithmetic, this would make no sense, but in C#, this line means, "Add 5,000 to the value in mySalary, and assign the sum back to mySalary." Thus, after this operation completes, mySalary will have been incremented by 5,000. You can perform this kind of assignment with any mathematical operator:

```
mySalary = mySalary * 5000;
mySalary = mySalary - 5000;
```

and so forth.

The need to perform this kind of manipulation is so common that C# includes special operators for self-assignment. Among these operators are +=, -=, *=, /=, and %=, which, respectively, combine addition, subtraction, multiplication, division, and modulus, with self-assignment. Thus, you can write the previous examples as:

```
mySalary += 5000;
mySalary *= 5000;
mySalary -= 5000;
```

These three instructions, respectively, increment mySalary by 5,000, multiply mySalary by 5,000, and subtract 5,000 from the mySalary variable.

Increment or Decrement by 1

Because incrementing and decrementing by exactly 1 is a very common need, C# provides two additional special operators for these purposes: increment (++) and decrement (--).

Thus, if you want to increment the variable myAge by 1, you can write:

```
myAge++;
```

This is equivalent to writing:

```
myAge += 1;
```

The Prefix and Postfix Operators

To complicate matters further, you might want to increment a variable and assign the results to a second variable:

```
resultingValue = originalValue++;
```

The question arises: do you want to assign before you increment the value or after? In other words, if originalValue starts out with the value 10, do you want to end with both resultingValue and originalValue equal to 11, or do you want resultingValue to be equal to 10 (the original value) and originalValue to be equal to 11?

C# offers two specialized ways to use the increment and decrement operators: prefix and postfix. The way you use the ++ operator determines the order in which the increment/decrement and assignment take place. The semantics of the prefix increment operator is "increment the original value and then assign the incremented value to result" while the semantics of the postfix increment operator is "assign the original value to result, and then increment original."

To use the prefix operator to increment, place the ++ symbol before the variable name; to use the postfix operator to increment, place the ++ symbol after the variable name:

```
result = ++original; // prefix
result = original++; // postfix
```

It is important to understand the different effects of prefix and postfix, as illustrated in Example 4-3. Note the output.

Example 4-3. Prefix and postfix operators

```
using System;
class Values
{
    static void Main( )
    {
        int original = 10;
        int result;

        // increment then assign
        result = ++original;
        Console.WriteLine( "After prefix: {0}, {1}", original, result );

        // assign then increment
        result = original++;
        Console.WriteLine( "After postfix: {0}, {1}", original, result );
    }
}
```

The output looks like this:

```
After prefix: 11, 11
After postfix: 12, 11
```

The prefix and postfix operators can be applied, with the same logic, to the decrement operators, as shown in Example 4-4. Again, note the output.

Example 4-4. Decrementing prefix and postfix

```
using System;
class Values
{
    static void Main( )
    {
        int original = 10;
        int result;

        // increment then assign
        result = --original;
        Console.WriteLine( "After prefix: {0}, {1}", original,
        result );
```

Example 4-4. Decrementing prefix and postfix (continued)

```
    // assign then increment
    result = original--;
    Console.WriteLine( "After postfix: {0}, {1}",
    original, result );
  }
}
```

The output looks like this:

```
After prefix: 9, 9
After postfix: 8, 9
```

Relational Operators

Relational operators compare two values and then return a Boolean value (true or false). The greater than operator (>), for example, returns true if the value on the left of the operator is greater than the value on the right. Thus, 5>2 returns the value true, while 2>5 returns the value false.

The relational operators for C# are shown in Table 4-1. This table assumes two variables: bigValue and smallValue, in which bigValue has been assigned the value 100, and smallValue the value 50.

Table 4-1. C# relational operators (assumes bigValue = 100 and smallValue = 50)

Name	Operator	Given this statement	The expression evaluates to
Equals	==	bigValue == 100 bigValue == 80	True False
Not Equals	!=	bigValue != 100 bigValue != 80	False True
Greater than	>	bigValue > smallValue	True
Greater than or equal to	>=	bigValue >= smallValue smallValue >= bigValue	True False
Less than	<	bigValue < smallValue	False
Less than or equal to	<=	smallValue <= bigValue bigValue <= smallValue	True False

Each of these relational operators acts as you might expect. Notice that most of these operators are composed of two characters. For example, the greater than or equal to operator (>=) is created with the greater than symbol (>) and the equals sign (=). Notice also that the equals operator is created with two equals signs (==) because the single equals sign alone (=) is reserved for the assignment operator.

It is not uncommon to confuse the assignment operator (=) with the equals operator (==). Just remember that the latter has two equals signs, and the former only one.

The C# equals operator (==) tests for equality between the objects on either side of the operator. This operator evaluates to a Boolean value (true or false). Thus, the statement:

```
myX == 5;
```

evaluates to true if and only if the myX variable has a value of 5.

Use of Logical Operators with Conditionals

As you program, you'll often want to test whether a condition is true; for example, using the if statement, which you'll see in the next chapter. Often you will want to test whether two conditions are both true, only one is true, or neither is true. C# provides a set of logical operators for this, shown in Table 4-2.

Table 4-2. Logical operators

Name	Operator	Given this statement	The expression evaluates to	Logic
And	&&	(x == 3) && (y == 7)	False	Both must be true.
Or	||	(x == 3) || (y == 7)	True	Either or both must be true.
Not	!	! (x == 3)	True	Expression must be false.

The examples in this table assume two variables, x and y, in which x has the value 5 and y has the value 7.

The *and* operator tests whether two statements are both true. The first line in Table 4-2 includes an example that illustrates the use of the and operator:

```
(x == 3) && (y == 7)
```

The entire expression evaluates false because one side (x == 3) is false. (Remember that x has the value 5 and y has the value 7.)

With the *or* operator, either or both sides must be true; the expression is false only if both sides are false. So, in the case of the example in Table 4-2:

```
(x == 3) || (y == 7)
```

the entire expression evaluates true because one side (y==7) is true.

With a *not* operator, the statement is true if the expression is false, and vice versa. So, in the accompanying example:

```
! (x == 3)
```

the entire expression is true because the tested expression (x==3) is false. (The logic is: "it is true that it is not true that x is equal to 3.")

The Conditional Operator

Although most operators are unary (they require one term, such as myValue++) or binary (they require two terms, such as a+b), there is one *ternary* operator, which requires three terms: the conditional operator (?:):

```
cond-expr ? expression1 : expression2
```

This operator evaluates a *conditional* expression (an expression that returns a value of type bool) and then invokes either *expression1* if the value returned from the conditional expression is true, or *expression2* if the value returned is false. The logic is: "if this is true, do the first; otherwise do the second." Example 4-5 illustrates this concept.

Example 4-5. The ternary operator

```
using System;
class Values
{
    static void Main( )
    {
        int valueOne = 10;
        int valueTwo = 20;

        int maxValue = valueOne > valueTwo ? valueOne : valueTwo;

        Console.WriteLine( "ValueOne: {0}, valueTwo: {1}, maxValue: {2}",
        valueOne, valueTwo, maxValue );

    }
}
```

The output looks like this:

```
ValueOne: 10, valueTwo: 20, maxValue: 20
```

In Example 4-5, the ternary operator is being used to test whether valueOne is greater than valueTwo. If so, the value of valueOne is assigned to the integer variable maxValue; otherwise, the value of valueTwo is assigned to maxValue.

Operator Precedence

The compiler must know the order in which to evaluate a series of operators. For example, if I write:

```
myVariable = 5 + 7 * 3;
```

there are three operators for the compiler to evaluate (=, +, and *). It could, for example, operate left to right, which would assign the value 5 to myVariable, then add 7 to the 5 (12) and multiply by 3 (36)—but of course, then it would throw that 36 away. This is clearly not what is intended.

The rules of precedence tell the compiler which operators to evaluate first. As is the case in algebra, multiplication has higher precedence than addition, so 5+7*3 is equal to 26 rather than 36. Both addition and multiplication have higher precedence than assignment, so the compiler will do the math and then assign the result (26) to myVariable only after the math is completed.

In C#, parentheses are also used to change the order of precedence much as they are in algebra. Thus, you can change the result by writing:

```
myVariable = (5+7) * 3;
```

Grouping the elements of the assignment in this way causes the compiler to add 5+7, multiply the result by 3, and then assign that value (36) to myVariable.

Table 4-3 summarizes operator precedence in C#, using x and y as possible terms to be operated upon.[*]

Table 4-3. Precedence

Category	Operators
Primary	(x) x.y x->y f(x) a[x] x++ x-- new typeof sizeof checked unchecked stackalloc
Unary	+ - ! ~ ++x --x (T)x *x &x
Multiplicative	* / %
Additive	+ -
Shift	<< >>
Relational	< > <= >= is as
Equality	== !=
Logical AND	&
Logical XOR	^
Logical OR	|
Conditional AND	&&
Conditional OR	||
Conditional	?:
Assignment	= *= /= %= += -= <<= >>= &= ^= |=

[*] This table includes operators that are so esoteric as to be beyond the scope of this book. For a fuller explanation of each, please see *Programming C#*, Fourth Edition, by Jesse Liberty (O'Reilly, 2005).

The operators are listed in precedence order according to the category in which they fit. That is, the primary operators (such as x++) are evaluated before the unary operators (such as !). Multiplication is evaluated before addition.

In some complex equations, you might need to nest parentheses to ensure the proper order of operations. For example, assume I want to know how many seconds my family wastes each morning. The adults spend 20 minutes over coffee each morning and 10 minutes reading the newspaper. The children waste 30 minutes dawdling and 10 minutes arguing.

Here's my algorithm:

```
(((minDrinkingCoffee + minReadingNewspaper )* numAdults ) +
((minDawdling + minArguing) * numChildren)) * secondsPerMinute.
```

 An *algorithm* is a well-defined series of steps to accomplish a task.

Although this works, it is hard to read and hard to get right. It's much easier to use interim variables:

```
wastedByEachAdult = minDrinkingCoffee + minReadingNewspaper;
wastedByAllAdults = wastedByEachAdult * numAdults;
wastedByEachKid = minDawdling + minArguing;
wastedByAllKids = wastedByEachKid * numChildren;
wastedByFamily = wastedByAllAdults + wastedByAllKids;
totalSeconds = wastedByFamily * 60;
```

The latter example uses many more interim variables, but it is far easier to read, understand, and (most importantly) debug. As you step through this program in your debugger, you can see the interim values and make sure they are correct. See Chapter 9 for more information.

Summary

- An operator is a symbol that causes C# to take an action.
- The assignment operator (=) assigns a value to an object or variable.
- C# includes four simple arithmetic operators: +, -, *, and /, and numerous variations such as +=, which increments a variable on the left side of the operator by the value on the right side.
- When you divide integers, C# discards any fractional remainder.
- The modulus operator (%) returns the remainder from integer division.
- C# includes numerous special operators such as the self-increment (++) and self-decrement (--) operators.

- To increment a value before assigning it, you use the prefix operator (++x); to increment the value after assigning it, use the postfix operator (x++).
- The relational operators compare two values and return a Boolean. These operators are often used in conditional statements.
- The conditional operator (?:) is the one ternary operator found in C#. It invokes the expression to the left of the colon if the tested condition evaluates true, and the expression to the right of the colon if the tested condition evaluates false.
- The compiler evaluates operators according to a series of precedence rules, and parentheses have the "highest" precedence.
- It is good programming practice to use parentheses to make your order of precedence explicit if there may be any ambiguity.

Quiz

Question 4-1. What is the output of these operations?

```
4 * 8
(4 + 8) / (4 - 2)
4 + 8 / 4 - 2
```

Question 4-2. Set x = 25 and y = 5. What do these expressions evaluate to?

```
(x >= y)
(x >= y * 5)
(x == y)
(x = y)
(x >= y) && (y <= x)
```

Question 4-3. Describe the difference between the prefix and postfix operators.

Question 4-4. Arrange these operators in order of precedence:

```
&
!=
?:
&&
++
```

Exercises

Exercise 4-1. Write a program that assigns the value 25 to variable x, and 5 to variable y. Output the sum, difference, product, quotient, and modulus of x and y.

Exercise 4-2. What will be the output of the following method?

```
static void Main( )
{
    int varA = 5;
    int varB = ++varA;
    int varC = varB++;
    Console.WriteLine( "A: {0}, B: {1}, C: {2}", varA, varB, varC );
}
```

Exercise 4-3. Write a program that demonstrates the difference between the prefix and postfix operators.

CHAPTER 5
Branching

All the statements in your program execute in order. Unfortunately, that's not very useful, unless you want your program to do exactly the same thing every time you run it. In fact, often you won't want to execute all the code, but rather you'll want the program to do one thing if a variable has a certain value, and something different if the variable has another value. That means you need to be able to cause your program to pick and choose which statements to execute based on conditions that change as the program runs. This process is called *branching*, and there are two ways to accomplish it: unconditionally or conditionally.

As the name implies, unconditional branching happens every time the branch point is reached. An unconditional branch happens, for example, whenever the compiler encounters a new method call. The compiler stops execution in the current method and branches to the newly called method. When the newly called method *returns* (completes its execution), execution picks up in the original method on the line just below the branch point (the line where the new method was called).

Conditional branching is more complicated. Methods can branch based on the evaluation of certain conditions that occur at runtime. For instance, you might create a branch that will calculate an employee's federal withholding tax only when their earnings are greater than the minimum taxable by law. C# provides a number of statements that support conditional branching, such as if, else, and switch. The use of these statements is discussed later in this chapter.

A second way that methods break out of their mindless step-by-step processing of instructions is by looping. A loop causes the method to repeat a set of steps until some condition is met ("Keep asking for input until the user tells you to stop or until you receive ten values"). C# provides many statements for looping, including for, while, and do...while, which are also discussed in this chapter.

Unconditional Branching Statements

The most simple example of an unconditional branch is a method call. When a method call is reached, there is no test made to evaluate the state of the object; the program execution branches immediately (and unconditionally) to the start of the new method.

You call a method by writing its name; for example:

```
UpdateSalary(); // invokes the method UpdateSalary
```

As I explained earlier in the chapter, when the compiler encounters a method call, it stops execution of the current method and branches to the new method. When that new method completes its execution, the compiler picks up where it left off in the original method. This process is illustrated schematically in Figure 5-1.

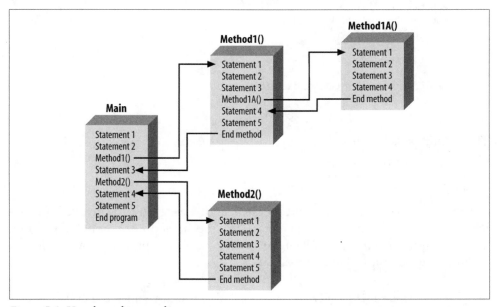

Figure 5-1. How branching works

As Figure 5-1 suggests, it is actually quite common for there to be unconditional branching several methods deep. In Figure 5-1, execution begins in a method called Main( ). Statement1 and Statement2 execute; then the compiler sees a call to Method1( ). Program execution branches unconditionally to the first line of Method1( ), where its first three statements are executed. At the call to Method1A( ), execution again branches, this time to the start of Method1A( ).

The four statements in Method1A( ) are executed, and Method1A( ) returns. Execution resumes on the first statement after the method call in Method1( ) (Statement4). Execution continues until Method1( ) ends, at which time execution resumes back in

Main( ) at Statement3. At the call to Method2( ), execution again branches; all the statements in Method2( ) execute, and then Main( ) resumes at Statement4. When Main( ) ends, the program itself ends.

You can see the effect of method calls in Example 5-1. Execution begins in Main( ), but branches to a method named SomeMethod( ). The WriteLine( ) statements in each method assist you in seeing where you are in the code as the program executes.

Example 5-1. Branching to a method

```
using System;
class Functions
{
    static void Main( )
    {
        Console.WriteLine( "In Main! Calling SomeMethod( )..." );
        SomeMethod( );
        Console.WriteLine( "Back in Main( )." );

    }
    static void SomeMethod( )
    {
        Console.WriteLine( "Greetings from SomeMethod!" );
    }
}
```

The output looks like this:

```
In Main! Calling SomeMethod( )...
Greetings from SomeMethod!
Back in Main( ).
```

Program flow begins in Main( ) and proceeds until SomeMethod( ) is invoked. (Invoking a method is sometimes referred to as *calling* the method.) At that point, program flow branches to the method. When the method completes, program flow resumes at the next line after the call to that method.

 You can instead create an unconditional branch by using one of the unconditional branch keywords: goto, break, continue, return, or throw. The first four of these are discussed later in this chapter, while the final statement, throw, is discussed in Chapter 16.

Methods and their parameters and return values are discussed in detail in Chapter 8.

Conditional Branching Statements

Although methods branch unconditionally, often you will want to branch within a method depending on a condition that you evaluate while the program is running.

This is known as *conditional branching*. Conditional branching statements allow you to write logic such as, "If you are over 25 years old, then you may rent a car."

C# provides a number of constructs that allow you to write conditional branches into your programs; these constructs are described in the following sections.

if Statements

The simplest branching statement is if. An if statement says, "if a particular condition is true, then execute the statement; otherwise, skip it." The condition is a Boolean expression. An expression is a statement that evaluates to a value, and a Boolean expression evaluates to either true or false.

The formal description of an if statement is:

```
if (expression)
    Statement1
```

This is the kind of description of the if statement you are likely to find in your compiler documentation. It shows you that the if statement takes an expression (a statement that returns a value) in parentheses, and executes Statement1 if the expression evaluates true. Note that Statement1 can actually be a block of statements within braces, as illustrated in Example 5-2.

Example 5-2. The if statement

```
using System;
namespace Branching
{
   class Test
   {
      static void Main()
      {
         int valueOne = 10;
         int valueTwo = 20;
         int valueThree = 30;

         Console.WriteLine( "Testing valueOne against valueTwo..." );
         if ( valueOne > valueTwo )
         {
            Console.WriteLine(
            "ValueOne: {0} larger than ValueTwo: {1}",
            valueOne, valueTwo );
         }

         Console.WriteLine( "Testing valueThree against valueTwo..." );
         if ( valueThree > valueTwo )
         {
            Console.WriteLine(
            "ValueThree: {0} larger than ValueTwo: {1}",
            valueThree, valueTwo );
         }    // end if
```

Example 5-2. The if statement (continued)

```
    }          // end Main
  }            // end class
}              // end namespace
```

 Just about anywhere in C# that you are expected to provide a statement, you can instead provide a block of statements within braces. (See the sidebar, "Brace Styles," later in this chapter.)

In this simple program, you declare three variables, valueOne, valueTwo, and valueThree, with the values 10, 20, and 30, respectively. In the first if statement, you test whether valueOne is greater than valueTwo:

```
if ( valueOne > valueTwo )
{
   Console.WriteLine(
   "ValueOne: {0} larger than ValueTwo: {1}",
   valueOne, valueTwo );
}
```

Because valueOne (10) is less than valueTwo (20), this if statement fails (the condition returns false), and thus the body of the if statement (the statements within the braces) doesn't execute.

You then test whether valueThree is greater than valueTwo:

```
if ( valueThree > valueTwo )
{
   Console.WriteLine(
   "ValueThree: {0} larger than ValueTwo: {1}",
   valueThree, valueTwo );
} // end if
```

Because valueThree (30) *is* greater than valueTwo (20), the test returns true, and thus the statement executes. The statement in this case is the block in which you call the WriteLine( ) method, shown in bold. The output reflects that the first if fails but the second succeeds:

```
Testing valueOne against valueTwo...
Testing valueThree against valueTwo...
ValueThree: 30 larger than ValueTwo: 20
```

Single-Statement if Blocks

Notice that the if statement blocks shown in Example 5-2 each contain only a single statement, one call to WriteLine( ). In such cases, you can leave out the braces enclosing the if block. Thus, you might rewrite Example 5-2, as shown in Example 5-3.

Example 5-3. Single statements with if

```
using System;

namespace Branching
{
   class Test
   {
      static void Main( )
      {
         int valueOne = 10;
         int valueTwo = 20;
         int valueThree = 30;

         Console.WriteLine( "Testing valueOne against valueTwo..." );
         if ( valueOne > valueTwo )
            Console.WriteLine(
            "ValueOne: {0} larger than ValueTwo: {1}",
            valueOne, valueTwo );

         Console.WriteLine( "Testing valueThree against valueTwo..." );
         if ( valueThree > valueTwo )
            Console.WriteLine(
            "ValueThree: {0} larger than ValueTwo: {1}",
            valueThree, valueTwo );

      }  // end Main
   }     // end class
}        // end namespace
```

It is generally a good idea, however, to use the braces even when your if block has only a single statement. There are two reasons for this advice. First, the code is somewhat easier to read and understand with the braces. Code that is easier to read is easier to maintain.

 When programmers talk about *maintaining* code, they mean either adding to the code as requirements change or fixing the code as bugs arise.

The second reason for using braces is to avoid a common error: adding a second statement to the if and forgetting to add the braces. Consider the code shown in Example 5-4. The programmer has changed the value of valueThree to 10 and added a second statement to the second if block, as shown in bold.

Example 5-4. Adding a second statement to if

```
using System;

namespace Branching
{
   class Test
```

Example 5-4. Adding a second statement to if (continued)

```
{
   static void Main( )
   {
      int valueOne = 10;
      int valueTwo = 20;               .
      int valueThree = 10;

      Console.WriteLine( "Testing valueOne against valueTwo..." );
      if ( valueOne > valueTwo )
         Console.WriteLine(
         "ValueOne: {0} larger than ValueTwo: {1}",
         valueOne, valueTwo );

      Console.WriteLine( "Testing valueThree against valueTwo..." );
      if ( valueThree > valueTwo )
         Console.WriteLine(
         "ValueThree: {0} larger than ValueTwo: {1}",
         valueThree, valueTwo );
      Console.WriteLine( "Good thing you tested again!" );

   } // end Main
 }      // end class
}        // end namespace
```

Now, before reading any further, review the code and decide for yourself what the output should be. Don't cheat by looking past this paragraph. Then, when you think you know what the output will be, take a look at this:

```
Testing valueOne against valueTwo...
Testing valueThree against valueTwo...
Good thing you tested again!
```

Were you surprised?

The programmer was fooled by the lack of braces and the indentation. Remember that indentation is whitespace and is ignored by the compiler. From the perspective of the programmer, the second statement ("Good thing...") is part of the if block:

```
if ( valueThree > valueTwo )
    Console.WriteLine(
    "ValueThree: {0} larger than ValueTwo: {1}",
    valueThree, valueTwo);
    Console.WriteLine("Good thing you tested again!");
```

The compiler, however, considers only the first statement after the if test to be part of the if statement. The second statement is not part of the if statement. To the compiler, the if statement looks like this:

```
if ( valueThree > valueTwo )
    Console.WriteLine(
    "ValueThree: {0} larger than ValueTwo: {1}",
    valueThree, valueTwo);

Console.WriteLine("Good thing you tested again!");
```

If you want the second statement to be part of the if statement, you must use braces, as in the following:

```
if ( valueThree > valueTwo )
{
    Console.WriteLine(
    "ValueThree: {0} larger than ValueTwo: {1}",
    valueThree, valueTwo);
    Console.WriteLine("Good thing you tested again!");
}
```

Because of this potential for confusion, many C# programmers use braces with every if statement, even if the statement is only one line.

Brace Styles

There are many ways you can form braces around an if statement (and around other blocks of code), but most C# programmers will use one of three styles:

```
if (condition)
{
 // statement
}

if (condition)
 {
 // statement
 }

if (condition){
 // statement
}
```

The first style, used throughout this book, is to put the braces under the keyword if and to indent the contents of the if block. The second style, which is not very popular anymore, is to indent the braces with the contents of the if block. The third style is to put the opening brace on the same line as the if statement and the closing brace under the if statement.

The third style is called K&R style, after Kernighan and Ritchie, the authors of the seminal book *The C Programming Language* (Prentice Hall, 1988). Their book was so influential that many programmers feel a strong commitment to this style of braces. Although it does save room in a book, the K&R style is a bit less clear, and so this book will use the first style.

Short-Circuit Evaluation

Consider the following code snippet:

```
int x = 8;
int y = 15;
if ((x == 8) || (y == 12))
```

The if statement here is a bit complicated. The entire if statement is in parentheses, as are all if statements in C#. Thus, everything within the outer set of parentheses must evaluate true for the if statement to be true.

Within the outer parentheses are two expressions, (x == 8) and (y == 12), which are separated by an or operator (||). Because x is 8, the first term (x == 8) evaluates true. There is no need to evaluate the second term (y == 12). It doesn't matter whether y is 12; the entire expression will be true. Similarly, consider this snippet:

```
int x = 8;
int y = 12;
if ((x == 5) && (y == 12))
```

Again, there is no need to evaluate the second term. Because the first term is false, the and must fail. (Remember, for an and statement to evaluate true, both tested expressions must evaluate true.)

In cases such as these, the C# compiler will short-circuit the evaluation; the second test will never be performed. This allows you to create if statements in which you first check a value before you take action on it, avoiding the possibility of an exception. Here's a short example:

```
public bool QuotientOverTwenty(float dividend, float divisor)
{
    if ( divisor != 0 && dividend / divisor > 20 )
    {
        return true;
    }
    return false;
}
```

In this code, we only want to decide if the quotient is greater than 20, but we must first make sure we are not dividing by zero (division by zero causes the system to throw an exception). With short circuiting, the second part of the if statement (the division) will never occur if the first part is false (that is, if the divisor is zero), and this code is terser and perhaps easier to understand than writing.

```
public bool QuotientOverTwenty(float dividend, float divisor)
{
    bool retVal = false;
    if ( divisor != 0 )
    {
        if ( dividend / divisor > 20 )
```

```
                retVal = true;
        }
        return retVal;
    }
```

if . . . else Statements

Often, you will find that you want to take one set of actions when the condition tests true and a different set of actions when the condition tests false. This allows you to write logic such as, "If you are over 25 years old, then you may rent a car; *otherwise*, you must take the train."

The *otherwise* portion of the logic is executed in the else statement. For example, you can modify Example 5-2 to print an appropriate message whether or not valueOne is greater than valueTwo, as shown in Example 5-5.

Example 5-5. The else statement

```
using System;

namespace Branching
{
    class Test
    {
        static void Main( )
        {
            int valueOne = 10;
            int valueTwo = 20;

            Console.WriteLine( "Testing valueOne against valueTwo..." );
            if ( valueOne > valueTwo )
            {
                Console.WriteLine(
                "ValueOne: {0} larger than ValueTwo: {1}",
                valueOne, valueTwo );
            } // end if
            else
            {
                Console.WriteLine(
                "Nope, ValueOne: {0} is NOT larger than ValueTwo: {1}",
                valueOne, valueTwo );
            } // end else

        } // end Main
    }    // end class
}        // end namespace
```

The output looks like this:

```
Testing valueOne against valueTwo...
Nope, ValueOne: 10 is NOT larger than ValueTwo: 20
```

Because the test in the if statement fails (valueOne is *not* larger than valueTwo), the body of the if statement is skipped and the body of the else statement is executed. Had the test succeeded, the if statement body would execute and the else statement would be skipped.

Nested if Statements

It is possible, and not uncommon, to nest if statements to handle complex conditions. For example, suppose you need to write a program to evaluate the temperature and specifically to return the following types of information:

- If the temperature is 32 degrees or lower, the program should warn you about ice on the road.
- If the temperature is exactly 32 degrees, the program should tell you that there may be ice patches.
- If the temperature is higher than 32 degrees, the program should assure you that there is no ice.

There are many good ways to write this program. Example 5-6 illustrates one approach using nested if statements.

Example 5-6. Nested if statements

```
using System;
class Values
{
   static void Main( )
   {
      int temp = 32;

      if ( temp <= 32 )
      {
         Console.WriteLine( "Warning! Ice on road!" );
         if ( temp == 32 )
         {
            Console.WriteLine("Temp exactly freezing, beware of water." );
         }
         else
         {
            Console.WriteLine( "Watch for black ice! Temp: {0}", temp );
         }
      }

   }
}
```

The logic of Example 5-6 is that it tests whether the temperature is less than or equal to 32. If so, it prints a warning:

```
if (temp <= 32)
{
    Console.WriteLine("Warning! Ice on road!");
```

The program then checks whether the temp is equal to 32 degrees. If so, it prints one message; if not, the temp must be less than 32 and the program prints the next message. Notice that this second if statement is nested within the first if, so the logic of the else statement is: "because it has been established that the temp is less than or equal to 32, and it isn't equal to 32, it must be less than 32."

Another way of chaining together more than one possibility with if statements is the else if idiom that some C# programmers use. The program tests the condition in the first if statement. If that first statement is false, control passes to the else statement, which is immediately followed by another if that tests a different condition. For example, you could rewrite Example 5-6 to test if the temperature is greater than, less than, or exactly equal to freezing with three tests, as shown in Example 5-7.

Example 5-7. Using else if

```
using System;
class Values
{
    static void Main( )
    {
        int temp = 32;

        if ( temp < 32 )
        {
            Console.WriteLine( "Warning! Ice on road!" );
        }
        else if ( temp == 32 )
        {
            Console.WriteLine("Temp exactly freezing, beware of water." );
        }
        else
        {
            Console.WriteLine( "Watch for black ice! Temp: {0}", temp );
        }
    }
}
```

In this case, the condition in the first if statement tests whether temp is less than 32, not less than or equal. Because temp is hard-wired to exactly 32, the first expression is false, and control passes to the else if statement. The second statement is true, so the third case, the else statement, never executes. Please note, however, that this code is *identical* (as far as the compiler is concerned) to the following:

```
using System;
class Values
```

```
{
    static void Main( )
    {
        int temp = 32;

        if ( temp < 32 )
        {
            Console.WriteLine( "Warning! Ice on road!" );
        }
        else
        {
            if ( temp == 32 )
            {
                Console.WriteLine("Temp exactly freezing, beware of water." );
            }
            else
            {
                Console.WriteLine( "Watch for black ice! Temp: {0}", temp );
            }
        }
    }
}
```

In any case, if you do use the else if idiom, be sure to use an else, (not an else if), as your final test, making it the default case that will execute even if nothing else does.

switch Statements

Nested if statements are hard to read, hard to get right, and hard to debug. When you have a complex set of choices to make, the switch statement is a more powerful alternative. The logic of a switch statement is this: "Pick a matching value and act accordingly."

```
switch (expression)
{
 case constant-expression:
 statement
 jump-statement
 [default: statement]
}
```

The expression you are "switching on" is put in parentheses in the head of the switch statement. Each case statement compares a constant value with the expression. The constant expression can be a literal, symbolic, or enumerated constant.

The compiler starts with the first case statement and works its way down the list, looking for a value that matches the expression. If a case is matched, the statement (or block of statements) associated with that case is executed.

The case block must end with a jump statement. Typically, the jump statement is break, which abruptly ends the entire switch statement. When you execute a break in a switch statement, execution continues after the closing brace of the switch statement. (We'll consider the use of the optional default keyword later in this section.)

In the next, somewhat whimsical listing (Example 5-8), the user is asked to choose his political affiliation among Democrat, Republican, or Progressive. To keep the code simple, I'll hardwire the choice to be Democrat.

Example 5-8. Using a switch statement

```
using System;


class Values
{
    enum Party
    {
        Democrat,
        Republican,
        Progressive
    }
    static void Main()
    {

        // hard wire to Democratic
        Party myChoice = Party.Democrat;

        // switch on the value of myChoice
        switch ( myChoice )
        {
            case Party.Democrat:
                Console.WriteLine( "You voted Democratic." );
                break;
            case Party.Republican:
                Console.WriteLine( "You voted Republican." );
                break;
            case Party.Progressive:
                Console.WriteLine( "You voted Progressive." );
                break;

        }
        Console.WriteLine( "Thank you for voting." );
    }
}
```

The output looks like this:

```
You voted Democratic.
Thank you for voting.
```

Rather than using a complicated if statement, Example 5-8 uses a switch statement. The user's choice is evaluated in the head of the switch statement, and the block of statements that gets executed depends on whatever case matches (in this instance, Democrat).

The statements between the case statement and the break are executed in series. You can have more than one statement here without braces; in effect, the case statement and the closing break statement act as the braces.

It is possible that the user will not make a choice among Democrat, Republican, and Progressive. You may want to provide a default case that will be executed whenever no valid choice has been made. You can do that with the default keyword, as shown in Example 5-9.

Example 5-9. A default statement

```
using System;

class Values
{
    enum Party
    {
        Democrat,
        Republican,
        Progressive
    }
    static void Main()
    {

        // hard wire to Democratic
        Party myChoice = Party.Democrat;

        // switch on the value of myChoice
        switch ( myChoice )
        {
            case Party.Democrat:
                Console.WriteLine( "You voted Democratic." );
                break;
            case Party.Republican:
                Console.WriteLine( "You voted Republican." );
                break;
            case Party.Progressive:
                Console.WriteLine( "You voted Progressive." );
                break;
            default:
                Console.WriteLine( "You did not make a valid choice." );
                break;

        }
        Console.WriteLine( "Thank you for voting." );
    }
}
```

The output looks like this:

```
You did not make a valid choice.
Thank you for voting.
```

If the user does not choose one of the values that correspond to a case statement, the default statements will execute. In this case, a message is simply printed telling the user he did not make a valid choice; in production code, you would put all this in a while loop, re-prompting the user until a valid choice is made (or the user elects to quit).

Falling-Through and Jumping-to Cases

If two cases will execute the same code, you can create what's known as a "fall through" case, grouping the case statements together with the same code, as shown here:

```
case CompassionateRepublican:
case Republican:
    Console.WriteLine("You voted Republican.\n");
    Console.WriteLine("Don't you feel compassionate?");
    break;
```

In this example, if the user chooses either CompassionateRepublican or Republican, the same set of statements will be executed.

Note that you can only fall through if the first case executes no code. In this example, the first case, CompassionateRepublican, meets that criteria. Thus, you can fall through to the second case.

If, however, you want to execute a statement with one case and then fall through to the next, you must use the goto keyword to jump to the next case you want to execute.

 The goto keyword is an unconditional branch. When the compiler sees this word, it immediately transfers the flow (jumps) to wherever the goto points to. Thus, even within this conditional branching statement, you've inserted an unconditional branch.

For example, if you create a NewLeft party, you might want the NewLeft voting choice to print a message and then fall through to Democrat (that is, continue on with the statements in the Democrat case). You might (incorrectly) try writing the following:

```
case NewLeft:
    Console.WriteLine("The NewLeft members are voting Democratic.");
case Democrat:
    Console.WriteLine("You voted Democratic.\n");
    break;
```

This code will not compile; it will fail with the error:

```
Control cannot fall through from one case label (case '4:') to another
```

This is a potentially misleading error message. Control *can* fall through from one case label to another, but only if there is no code in the first case label.

 Notice that the error displays the name of the case with its numeric value (4) rather than its symbolic value (NewLeft). Remember that NewLeft is just the name of the constant:

```
const int Democrat = 0;
const int CompassionateRepublican = 1;
const int Republican = 2;
const int Progressive = 3;
const int NewLeft = 4;
```

Because the NewLeft case has a statement, the WriteLine( ) method, you must use a goto statement to fall through:

```
case NewLeft:
    Console.WriteLine("The NewLeft members are voting Democratic.");
    goto case Democrat;
case Democrat:
    Console.WriteLine("You voted Democratic.\n");
    break;
```

This code will compile and execute as you expect.

 The goto can jump over labels; you do not need to put NewLeft just above Democrat. In fact, you can put NewLeft last in the list (just before default), and it will continue to work properly.

Switch on string Statements

In the previous example, the switch value was an integral constant. C# also offers the ability to switch on a string. Thus, you can rewrite Example 5-9 to switch on the string "NewLeft," as in Example 5-10.

Example 5-10. Switching on a string

```
using System;

class Values
{
    static void Main( )
    {
        String myChoice = "NewLeft";

        // switch on the string value of myChoice
        switch ( myChoice )
        {
            case "NewLeft":
                Console.WriteLine(
                "The NewLeft members are voting Democratic." );
                goto case "Democrat";
```

Example 5-10. Switching on a string (continued)

```
        case "Democrat":
            Console.WriteLine( "You voted Democratic.\n" );
            break;
        case "CompassionateRepublican": // fall through
        case "Republican":
            Console.WriteLine( "You voted Republican.\n" );
            Console.WriteLine( "Don't you feel compassionate?" );
            break;
        case "Progressive":
            Console.WriteLine( "You voted Progressive.\n" );
            break;
        default:
            Console.WriteLine( "You did not make a valid choice." );
            break;
    }
    Console.WriteLine( "Thank you for voting." );
  }
}
```

Iteration (Looping) Statements

There are many situations in which you will want to do the same thing again and again, perhaps slightly changing a value each time you repeat the action. This is called *iteration*, or looping. Typically, you'll iterate (or loop) over a set of items, taking the same action on each item in the collection. This is the programming equivalent of an assembly line. On an assembly line, you might take a hundred car bodies and put a windshield on each one as it comes by. In an iterative program, you might work your way through a collection of text boxes on a form, retrieving the value from each in turn and using those values to update a database.

C# provides an extensive suite of iteration statements, including for and while, and also do...while and foreach loops. You can also create a loop by using the goto statement. The remainder of this chapter considers the use of goto, for, while, and do... while. However, we'll postpone coverage of foreach until Chapter 10.

Creating Loops with goto

The goto statement was used earlier in this chapter as an unconditional branch in a switch statement. The more common use of goto, however, is to create a loop. In fact, the goto statement is the seed from which all other looping statements have been germinated. Unfortunately, it is a semolina seed, producer of "spaghetti code" (see the following sidebar) and endless confusion.

Spaghetti Code

Goto can cause your method to loop back and forth in ways that are difficult to follow. If you were to try to draw the flow of control in a program that makes extensive use of goto statements, the resulting morass of intersecting and overlapping lines might look like a plate of spaghetti—hence the term "spaghetti code."

Spaghetti code is a contemptuous epithet; no one *wants* to write spaghetti code, and so most experienced programmers avoid using goto to create loops.

Because of the problems created by the goto statement, it is rarely used in C# outside of switch statements, but in the interest of completeness, here's how you create goto loops:

1. Create a label.
2. goto that label.

The *label* is an identifier followed by a colon. You place the label in your code, and then you use the goto keyword to jump to that label. The goto command is typically tied to an if statement, as illustrated in Example 5-11.

Example 5-11. Using goto

```
using System;
public class Tester
{

   public static void Main( )
   {
      int counterVariable = 0;

   repeat: // the label

      Console.WriteLine(
      "counterVariable: {0}", counterVariable );

      // increment the counter
      counterVariable++;

      if ( counterVariable < 10 )
         goto repeat; // the dastardly deed
   }
}
```

The output looks like this:

```
counterVariable: 0
counterVariable: 1
counterVariable: 2
```

```
counterVariable: 3
counterVariable: 4
counterVariable: 5
counterVariable: 6
counterVariable: 7
counterVariable: 8
counterVariable: 9
```

This code is not terribly complex; you've used only a single goto statement. However, with multiple such statements and labels scattered through your code, tracing the flow of execution becomes very difficult.

It was the phenomenon of spaghetti code that led to the creation of alternatives, such as the while loop.

The while Loop

The semantics of the while loop are "while this condition is true, do this work." The syntax is:

```
while (Boolean expression) statement
```

As usual, a Boolean expression is any statement that evaluates to true or false. The statement executed within a while statement can of course be a block of statements within braces. Example 5-12 illustrates the use of the while loop.

Example 5-12. The while loop

```
using System;
public class Tester
{
   public static void Main( )
   {
      int counterVariable = 0;

      // while the counter variable is less than 10
      // print out its value
      while ( counterVariable < 10 )
      {
         Console.WriteLine( "counterVariable: {0}", counterVariable );
         counterVariable++;
      }
   }
}
```

The output looks like this:

```
counterVariable: 0
counterVariable: 1
counterVariable: 2
counterVariable: 3
counterVariable: 4
counterVariable: 5
```

```
counterVariable: 6
counterVariable: 7
counterVariable: 8
counterVariable: 9
```

The code in Example 5-12 produces results identical to the code in Example 5-11, but the logic is a bit more clear. The while statement is nicely self-contained, and it reads like an English sentence: "while counterVariable is less than 10, print this message and increment counterVariable."

Notice that the while loop tests the value of counterVariable before entering the loop. This ensures that the loop will not run if the condition tested is false. Thus, if counterVariable is initialized to 11, the loop will never run.

The do . . . while Loop

There are times when a while loop might not serve your purpose. In certain situations, you might want to reverse the semantics from "run while this is true" to the subtly different "do this, while this condition remains true." In other words, take the action, and then, after the action is completed, check the condition. Such a loop will *always* run at least once.

To ensure that the action is taken before the condition is tested, use a do...while loop:

```
do statement while (boolean-expression);
```

The syntax is to write the keyword do, followed by your statement (or block), the while keyword, and the condition to test in parentheses. End the statement with a semicolon.

Example 5-13 rewrites Example 5-12 to use a do...while loop.

Example 5-13. The do...while loop

```
using System;
public class Tester
{
   public static void Main( )
   {
      int counterVariable = 11;

      // display the message and then test that the value is
      // less than 10
      do
      {
         Console.WriteLine( "counterVariable: {0}", counterVariable );
         counterVariable++;
      } while ( counterVariable < 10 );
   }
}
```

The output looks like this:

```
counterVariable: 11
```

In Example 5-13, counterVariable is initialized to 11 and the while test fails, but only after the body of the loop has run once.

The for Loop

A careful examination of the while loop in Example 5-12 reveals a pattern often seen in iterative statements: initialize a variable (counterVariable=0), test the variable (counterVariable<10), execute a series of statements, and increment the variable (counterVariable++). The for loop allows you to combine all these steps in a single statement. You write a for loop with the keyword for, followed by the for header, using the syntax:

```
for ([initializers]; [expression]; [iterators]) statement
```

The first part of the header is the *initializer*, in which you initialize a variable. The second part is the Boolean expression to test. The third part is the *iterator*, in which you update the value of the counter variable. All of this is enclosed in parentheses.

A simple for loop is shown in Example 5-14.

Example 5-14. A for loop

```
using System;
public class Tester
{

    public static void Main()
    {
        for ( int counter = 0; counter < 10; counter++ )
        {
            Console.WriteLine(
            "counter: {0} ", counter );
        }
    }
}
```

The output looks like this:

```
counter: 0
counter: 1
counter: 2
counter: 3
counter: 4
counter: 5
counter: 6
counter: 7
counter: 8
counter: 9
```

The counter variable is initialized to zero in the initializer:

```
for (int counter=0; counter<10; counter++)
```

The value of counter is tested in the expression part of the header:

```
for (int counter=0; counter<10; counter++)
```

Finally, the value of counter is incremented in the iterator part of the header:

```
for (int counter=0; counter<10; counter++)
```

The initialization part runs only once, when the for loop begins. The integer value counter is created and initialized to zero, and the test is then executed. Because counter is less than 10, the body of the for loop runs and the value is displayed.

After the loop completes, the iterator part of the header runs and counter is incremented. The value of the counter is tested, and, if the test evaluates true, the body of the for statement is executed again.

 Your iterator doesn't just have to be ++. You can use --, or any other expression that changes the value of the counter variable, as the needs of your program dictate. Also, for the purposes of a for loop, counter++ and ++counter will have the same result.

The logic of the for loop is as if you said, "For every value of counter that I initialize to zero, take this action if the test returns true, and after the action, update the value of counter."

Controlling a for loop with the modulus operator

The modulus operator really comes into its own in controlling for loops. When you perform modulus *n* on a number that is a multiple of *n*, the result is zero. Thus, 80%10=0 because 80 is an even multiple of 10. This fact allows you to set up loops in which you take an action every *n*th time through the loop by testing a counter to see whether %n is equal to zero, as illustrated in Example 5-15.

Example 5-15. Using modulus to find the tenth iteration

```
using System;
public class Tester
{

    public static void Main( )
    {
        for ( int counter = 1; counter <= 100; counter++ )
        {
            Console.Write( "{0} ", counter );

            if ( counter % 10 == 0 )
            {
                Console.WriteLine( "\t{0}", counter );
```

Example 5-15. Using modulus to find the tenth iteration (continued)

```
        }       // end if
    }           // end for
}               // end Main
}               // end namespace
```

The output looks like this:

```
1 2 3 4 5 6 7 8 9 10      10
11 12 13 14 15 16 17 18 19 20     20
21 22 23 24 25 26 27 28 29 30     30
31 32 33 34 35 36 37 38 39 40     40
41 42 43 44 45 46 47 48 49 50     50
51 52 53 54 55 56 57 58 59 60     60
61 62 63 64 65 66 67 68 69 70     70
71 72 73 74 75 76 77 78 79 80     80
81 82 83 84 85 86 87 88 89 90     90
91 92 93 94 95 96 97 98 99 100    100
```

In Example 5-15, the value of the counter variable is incremented each time through the loop. Within the loop, the value of counter is compared with the result of modulus 10 (counter % 10). When this evaluates to zero, the value of counter is evenly divisible by 10, and the value is printed in the righthand column.

Breaking out of a for loop

It is possible to exit from a for loop even before the test condition has been fulfilled. To end a for loop prematurely, use the unconditional branching statement break.

The break statement halts the for loop, and execution resumes after the for loop statement (or closing brace), as in Example 5-16.

Example 5-16. Using break to exit a for loop

```
using System;
public class Tester
{
    public static void Main()
    {
        for ( int counter = 0; counter < 10; counter++ )
        {
            Console.WriteLine(
            "counter: {0} ", counter );

            // if condition is met, break out.
            if ( counter == 5 )
            {
                {
                    Console.WriteLine( "Breaking out of the loop" );
                    break;
                }
            }
        }
```

Example 5-16. Using break to exit a for loop (continued)

```
        Console.WriteLine( "For loop ended" );
      }
   }
}
```

The output looks like this:

```
counter: 0
counter: 1
counter: 2
counter: 3
counter: 4
counter: 5
Breaking out of the loop
For loop ended
```

In this for loop, you test whether the value counter is equal to 5. If that value is found (and in this case, it always will be), you break out of the loop.

The continue statement

Rather than breaking out of a loop, you may at times want the semantics of saying, "Don't execute any more statements in this loop, but start the loop again from the top of the next iteration." To accomplish this, use the unconditional branching statement continue.

 Break and continue create multiple exit points and make for hard-to-understand, and thus hard-to-maintain, code. Use them with care.

Example 5-17 illustrates the mechanics of both continue and break. This code, suggested to me by one of my technical reviewers, Donald Xie, is intended to create a traffic signal processing system.

Example 5-17. Break and continue

```
using System;
public class Tester
{
   public static int Main( )
   {
      string signal = "0"; // initialize to neutral
      while ( signal != "X" ) // X indicates stop
      {
         Console.Write( "Enter a signal. X = stop. A = Abort: " );
         signal = Console.ReadLine( );

         // do some work here, no matter what signal you
         // receive
         Console.WriteLine( "Received: {0}", signal );
```

Example 5-17. Break and continue (continued)

```
        if ( signal == "A" )
        {
           // faulty - abort signal processing
           // Log the problem and abort.
           Console.WriteLine( "Fault! Abort\n" );
           break;
        }

        if ( signal == "0" )
        {
           // normal traffic condition
           // log and continue on
           Console.WriteLine( "All is well.\n" );
           continue;
        }

        // Problem. Take action and then log the problem
        // and then continue on
        Console.WriteLine( "{0} -- raise alarm!\n", signal );
     }
     return 0;
  }
}
```

The signals are simulated by entering numerals and uppercase characters from the keyboard, using the Console.ReadLine( ) method, which reads a line of text from the keyboard. ReadLine( ) reads a line of text into a string variable. The string ends when you press A.

The algorithm is simple: receipt of a "0" (zero) means normal conditions, and no further action is required except to log the event. (In this case, the program simply writes a message to the console; a real application might enter a time-stamped record in a database.)

On receipt of an Abort signal (simulated with an uppercase "A"), the problem is logged and the process is ended. Finally, for any other event, an alarm is raised, perhaps notifying the police. (Note that this sample does not actually notify the police, though it does print out a harrowing message to the console.) If the signal is "X," the alarm is raised but the while loop is also terminated.

Here's one sample output:

```
Enter a signal. X = stop. A = Abort: 0
Received: 0
All is well.
Enter a signal. X = stop. A = Abort: 1
Received: 1
1 -- raise alarm!
Enter a signal. X = stop. A = Abort: X
Received: X
X -- raise alarm!
```

Here's a second sample output:

```
Enter a signal. X = stop. A = Abort: A
Received: A
Fault! Abort
```

The point of this exercise is that when the A signal is received, the action in the if statement is taken and then the program breaks out of the loop, without raising the alarm. When the signal is 0, it is also undesirable to raise the alarm, so the program continues from the top of the loop.

 Be sure to use uppercase letters for X and A. To keep the code simple, there is no code to check for lowercase letters or other inappropriate input.

Optional for loop header elements

You will remember that the for loop header has three parts—initialization, expression, and iteration—and the syntax is as follows:

```
for ([initializers]; [expression]; [iterators]) statement
```

Each part of the for loop header is optional. You can, for example, initialize the value outside the for loop, as shown in Example 5-18.

Example 5-18. No initialization with for loop

```
using System;
public class Tester
{

    public static void Main( )
    {
        int counter = 0;
        // some work here
        counter = 3;
        // more work here

        for ( ; counter < 10; counter++ )
        {
            Console.WriteLine(
            "counter: {0} ", counter );
        }
    }
}
```

The output looks like this:

```
counter: 3
counter: 4
counter: 5
counter: 6
counter: 7
```

```
counter: 8
counter: 9
```

In this example, the counter variable was initialized and modified before the for loop began. Notice that a semicolon is used to hold the place of the missing initialization statement.

You can also leave out the iteration step if you have reason to increment the counter variable inside the loop, as shown in Example 5-19.

Example 5-19. Leaving out the iterator step

```
using System;
public class Tester
{

   public static void Main( )
   {

      for ( int counter = 0; counter < 10; ) // no increment
      {
         Console.WriteLine(
         "counter: {0} ", counter );

         // do more work here

         counter++; // increment counter
      }
   }
}
```

You can mix and match which statements you leave out of a for loop.

 If you create a for loop with no initializer or incrementer, like this:
> for (; counter < 10 ;)

you have a while loop in for loop's clothing; and of course that construct is silly, and thus not used very often.

It is even possible to leave *all* the statements out, creating what is known as a *forever* loop:

```
for ( ;; )
```

You can create the exact same effect with a while(true) loop
> while (true)

You break out of a forever (or while(true)) loop with a break statement. A forever loop is shown in Example 5-20.

Example 5-20. A forever loop

```
using System;
public class Tester
{
    public static void Main( )
    {
        int counterVariable = 0; // initialization

        for ( ; ; )  // forever
        {
            Console.WriteLine(
            "counter: {0} ", counterVariable++ ); // increment

            if ( counterVariable > 10 ) // test
                break;
        }
    }
}
```

The output looks like this:

```
counter: 0
counter: 1
counter: 2
counter: 3
counter: 4
counter: 5
counter: 6
counter: 7
counter: 8
counter: 9
counter: 10
```

Use a forever loop to indicate that the "normal" case is to continue the loop indefinitely; for example, if your program is waiting for an event to occur somewhere in the system. The conditions for breaking out of the loop would then be exceptional and managed inside the body of the loop.

Although it is possible to use a forever loop to good effect, Example 5-20 is a degenerate case. The initialization, increment, and test would be done more cleanly in the header of the for loop, and the program would then be easier to understand. It is shown here to illustrate that a forever loop is possible.

The while (true) construct

You can accomplish exactly the same semantics of a forever loop using the while (true) construct, as shown in Example 5-21.

Example 5-21. The while (true) construct

```
using System;
public class Tester
{
    public static void Main( )
    {
        int counterVariable = 0; // initialization

        while ( true )
        {
            Console.WriteLine(
            "counter: {0} ", counterVariable++ ); // increment

            if ( counterVariable > 10 ) // test
                break;
        }
    }
}
```

The output looks like this:

```
counter: 0
counter: 1
counter: 2
counter: 3
counter: 4
counter: 5
counter: 6
counter: 7
counter: 8
counter: 9
counter: 10
```

Example 5-21 is identical to Example 5-20, except that the forever construct:

```
for ( ;; )
```

is replaced with a:

```
while (true)
```

statement. Of course, the keyword true always returns the Boolean value true; so like the forever loop, this while loop runs until the break statement is executed.

Summary

- Branching causes your program to depart from a top-down statement-by-statement execution.

- A method call is the most common form of *unconditional* branching. When the method completes, execution returns to the point where it left off.

- Conditional branching enables your program to branch based on runtime conditions, typically based on the value or relative value of one or more objects or variables.
- The `if` construct executes a statement if a condition is true and skips it otherwise.
- When the condition in an `if` statement is actually two conditions joined by an `or` operator, if the first condition evaluates to `true`, the second condition will not be evaluated at all. This is called short-circuiting.
- The `if/else` construct lets you take one set of actions if the condition tested evaluates true, and a different set of actions if the condition tested evaluates false.
- `if` statements can be nested to evaluate more complex conditions.
- The `switch` statement lets you compare the value of an expression with several constant values (either integers, enumerated constants, or strings), and take action depending on which value matches.
- It is good programming practice for `switch` statements to include a default statement that executes if no other matches are found.
- Iteration, or looping, allows you to take the same action several times consecutively. Iterations are typically controlled by a conditional expression.
- The `goto` statement is used to redirect execution to another point in the program, and its use is typically discouraged.
- The `while` loop executes a block of code while the tested condition evaluates true. The condition is tested before each iteration.
- The `do...while` loop is similar to the `while` loop, but the condition is evaluated at the end of the iteration, so that the iterated statement is guaranteed to be executed at least once.
- The `for` loop is used to execute a statement a specific number of times. The header of the `for` loop can be used to initialize one or more variables, test a logical condition, and modify the variables. The typical use of a `for` loop is to initialize a counter once, test that a condition is using that counter before each iteration, and modify the counter after each iteration.

Quiz

Question 5-1. What statements are generally used for conditional branching?

Question 5-2. True or false: an `if` statement's condition must evaluate to an expression.

Question 5-3. Why should you use braces when there is only one statement following the `if`?

Question 5-4. What kind of expression can be placed in a switch statement?

Question 5-5. True or false: you can never fall through in a switch statement.

Question 5-6. Name two uses of goto.

Question 5-7. What is the difference between while and do...while?

Question 5-8. What does the keyword continue do?

Question 5-9. What are two ways to create a loop that never ends until you hit a break statement?

Exercises

Exercise 5-1. Create a method that counts from 1–10 using each of the while, do...while, and for statements.

Exercise 5-2. Create a program that evaluates whether a given input is odd or even; a multiple of 10, or too large (over 100) by using four levels of if statement. Then expand the program to do the same work with a switch statement.

Exercise 5-3. Create a program that initializes a variable i at 0 and counts up, and initializes a second variable j at 25 and counts down. Use a for loop to increment i and decrement j simultaneously. When i is greater than j, end the loop and print out the message "Crossed over!"

CHAPTER 6
Object-Oriented Programming

Windows and web programs are enormously complex programs that present information to users in graphically rich ways, offering complicated user interfaces, complete with drop-down and pop-up menus, buttons, listboxes, and so forth. Behind these interfaces, programs model complex business relationships, such as those among customers, products, orders, and inventory. You can interact with such a program in hundreds, if not thousands, of different ways, and the program must respond appropriately every time.

To manage this enormous complexity, programmers have developed a technique called *object-oriented programming*. It is based on a very simple premise: you manage complexity by modeling its essential aspects. The closer your program models the problem you are trying to solve, the easier it is to understand (and thus to write and to maintain) that program.

Programmers refer to the problem you are trying to solve and all the information you know that relates to your problem as the *problem domain*. For example, if you are writing a program to manage the inventory and sales of a company, the problem domain would include everything you know about how the company acquires and manages inventory, makes sales, handles the income from sales, tracks sales figures, and so forth. The sales manager and the stock room manager would be problem domain experts who can help you understand the problem domain.

A well-designed object-oriented program is filled with *objects* (things) from the problem domain. For example, if the problem domain is an Automatic Teller Machine for banking, the *things* (objects) in your domain might include *customers, accounts, monthly statements,* and so forth.

At the first level of design, you'll think about how these objects interact and what their state, capabilities, and responsibilities are:

State
> A programmer refers to the current conditions and values of an object as that object's state. For example, you might have an object representing a customer.

The customer's state includes the customer's address, phone number, and email, as well as the customer's credit rating, recent purchase history, and so forth.

Capabilities

The customer has many capabilities, but a developer cares only about modeling those that are relevant to the problem domain. Thus, a customer object might be able to make a deposit, transfer funds, withdraw cash, and so forth.

Responsibilities

Along with capabilities come responsibilities. The customer object is responsible for managing its own address. In a well-designed program, no other object needs to know the details of the customer's address. The address might be stored as data within the customer object, or it might be stored in a database, but it is up to the customer object to know how to retrieve and update his own address. (The *monthly-statement* object should not know the customer's address, though it might ask the *customer* object for the customer address. This way, when the customer moves, the responsibility for knowing the new address is located in a single object: the *customer*.) This ability for an object to own responsibility for its own internal state and actions is known as *encapsulation*.

Of course, all of the objects in your program are just *metaphors* for the objects in your problem domain.

Metaphors

Many of the concepts used throughout this book, and any book on programming, are actually metaphors. We get so used to the metaphors that we forget they *are* metaphors. You are used to talking about a window in your program, but of course there is no such thing; there is just a rectangle with text and images in it. It looks like a window into your document, so we call it a window. Of course, you don't actually have a document either, just bits in memory. No folders, no buttons—these are all just metaphors.

There are many levels to these metaphors. When you see a window on the screen, the window metaphor is enhanced by an image drawn on your monitor. That image is created by lighting tiny dots, called pixels. These pixels are lit in response to instructions written in your C# program. Each C# instruction is itself a metaphor; there is just a series of 1s and 0s. Of course, the 1s and 0s are just metaphors for electricity in wires. When two wires meet, we measure the amount of electricity, and if there is a threshold amount, we call it 1; otherwise, we call it 0. Of course, electricity is a metaphor, as are electrons, as is quantum physics. You get the idea.

Good metaphors can be very powerful. The art of object-oriented programming is really the art of conceiving good metaphors to simplify solving complex problems.

Creating Models

Humans are model-builders. We create models of the world to manage complexity and to help us understand problems we're trying to solve. You see models all the time. Maps are models of roadways. Globes are models of the Earth. Atomic models are models of the interaction of subatomic particles.

Models are simplifications. There is little point to a model that is as complex as the object in the problem domain. If you had a map of the United States that had every rock, blade of grass, and bit of dirt in the entire country, the map would have to be as big as the country itself.* Your road atlas of the U.S. eschews all sorts of irrelevant detail, focusing only on those aspects of the problem domain (such as the country's roads) that are important to solving the problem (getting from place to place). If you want to drive from Boston to New York City, you don't care where the trees are; you care where the exits and interchanges are located. Therefore, the network of roads is what appears in the atlas.

Albert Einstein once said: "Things should be made as simple as possible, but not any simpler." A model must be faithful to those aspects of the problem domain that are relevant. For example, a road map must provide accurate relative distances. The distance from Boston to New York must be proportional to the actual driving distance. If one inch represents 25 miles at the start of the trip, it must represent 25 miles throughout the trip, or the map will be unusable.†

A good object-oriented design is an accurate model of the problem you are trying to solve. Your design choices influence not only how you solve the problem, but in fact they influence how you think about the problem. A good design, like a good model, allows you to examine the relevant details of the problem without confusion or distraction.

Classes and Objects

We perceive the world to be composed of things. Look at your computer. You do not see various bits of plastic and glass amorphously merging with the surrounding environment. You naturally and inevitably see distinct things: a computer, a keyboard, a monitor, speakers, pens, paper. Things.

---

* Steven Wright joke: "I have a model of the United States. One inch equals one inch. I live at E5."

† Okay, not strictly true. When you flatten a globe into a map, something has to be distorted. The Mercator projection represents the lines of longitude as straight vertical lines, at the cost of grossly distorting size near the poles, and thus are of use to their intended audience (sailors). Unfortunately, these maps are ubiquitous in school rooms, leading generations of children to believe that Greenland is bigger than the United States (when, in fact, the U.S. is more than four times as large).

More importantly, even before you decide to do it, you've categorized these things. You immediately classify the computer on your desk as a specific instance of a type of thing: this computer is one of the type computer. This particular pen in my pocket is an instance of a more general type of thing, pens. It is so natural you can't avoid it, and yet the process is so subtle, it's difficult to articulate. When I see my dog Milo, I can't help also seeing him *as a dog*, not just as an individual entity.

The theory behind object-oriented programming is that for computer programs to accurately model the world, the programs should reflect this human tendency to think about individual things and types of things. In C#, you do that by creating a class to define a type and creating an object to model a thing.

A *class* defines a new type of thing. The class defines the common characteristics of every object of that new type. For example, you might define a class Car. Every car will share certain characteristics (wheels, brake, accelerator, and so forth). Your car and my car both belong to the class of Cars; they are of type Car.

An *object* is an individual instance of a class. Each individual car (your particular car, my particular car) is an instance of the class Car, and thus is an object. An object is just a thing.

Defining a Class

When you define a class, you describe the characteristics and behavior of objects of that type. In C#, you describe characteristics with *member fields*.

```
class Dog
{
 private int weight; // member field
 private String name; // member field
```

Member fields are used to hold each object's state. For example, the state of the Dog is defined by its current weight and name. The state of an Employee might be defined by (among other things) her current salary, management level, and performance rating. Chapter 8 includes a full discussion of member fields.

You define the behavior of your new type with *methods*. Methods contain code to perform an action:

```
class Dog
{
 private int weight;
 private String name;
 public void Bark()     // member method
 {
 // code here to bark
 }
```

The keywords public and private are known as *access modifiers*, which are used to specify what methods of which classes can access particular members. For instance, public members can be called from methods in any class, while private members are visible only to the methods of the class defining the member. Thus, objects of any class can call Bark on an instance of Dog, but only methods of the Dog class have access to the weight and name of a Dog. Access modifiers are discussed in Chapter 8.

A class typically defines a number of methods to do the work of that class. A Dog class might contain methods for barking, eating, napping, and so forth. An Employee class might contain methods for adjusting salary, submitting annual reviews, and evaluating performance objectives.

Methods can manipulate the state of the object by changing the values in member fields, or a method could interact with other objects of its own type or with objects of other types. This interaction among objects is crucial to object-oriented programming.

For example, a method in Dog might change the state of the Dog (for example, a *Feed* method might change the Dog's weight), interact with other Dogs (*Bark* and *Sniff*), or interact with People (*BegForFood*). A Product object might interact with a Customer object, and a Video object might interact with an EditingWindow object.

Designing a good C# program is not unlike forming a good team; you look for players—or objects, in the case of a program—with different skills to whom you can delegate the various tasks you must accomplish. Those players cooperate with one another to get the job done.

In a good object-oriented program, you will design objects that represent things in your problem domain. You will then divide the work of the program among your objects, assigning responsibility to objects based on their ability.

Class Relationships

The heart of object-oriented design is establishing relationships among the classes. Classes interact and relate to one another in various ways.

The simplest interaction is when a method in one class is used to call a method in a second class. For example, the Manager class might have a method that calls the UpdateSalary method on an object of type Employee. We then say that the Manager class and the Employee class are *associated*. Association among classes simply means they interact.

Some complicated types are *composed* of other types. For example, an automobile might be composed of wheels, engine, transmission, and so forth. You might model this by creating a Wheel class, an Engine class, and a Transmission class. You could then create an Automobile class, and each automobile would have four instances of the Wheel class and one instance each of the Engine and Transmission class. This is commonly called the *has-a* relationship. Another way to view this relationship is to say that the Automobile class *aggregates* the Wheel, Engine, and Transmission classes, or that the Car class is *composed of* Wheel, Engine, and Transmission objects.

 Some programming languages (such as C++) distinguish between the *is-composed-of* (composition) and the *has-a* (aggregation) relationships, but this distinction does not apply in C#, and they are treated as equivalent.

This process of aggregation (or composition) allows you to build very complex classes by assembling and combining relatively simple classes. The .NET Framework provides a String class to handle text strings. You might create your own Address class out of five text strings (address line 1, address line 2, city, state, and zip). You might then create a second class, Employee, which has as one of its members an instance of Address.

The Three Pillars of Object-Oriented Programming

Object-oriented programming is built on three pillars: *encapsulation*, *specialization*, and *polymorphism*.

Each class should be fully encapsulated; that is, it should fully define the state and responsibilities of that type. Specialization allows you to establish hierarchical relationships among your classes. Polymorphism allows you to treat a group of hierarchically related objects in a similar way and have the objects sort out how to implement the programming instructions.

Encapsulation

The first pillar of object-oriented programming is encapsulation. The idea behind encapsulation is that you want to keep each type or class discreet and self-contained, so that you can change the implementation of one class without affecting any other class.

A class that provides a method that other classes can use is called a *server*. A class that uses that method is called a *client*. Encapsulation allows you to change the details of how a server does its work without breaking anything in the implementation of the client.

This is accomplished by drawing a bright and shining line between the *public interface* of a class and its *private implementation*. The public interface is a contract issued by your class that consists of two parts. The first part says, "I promise to be able to do this work." Specifically, you'll see that a public interface says, "call this method, with these parameters, and I'll do this work, and return this value." The second part says "You are allowed to access these values (and no others)." C# implements this second part of the interface through *properties* (discussed in Chapter 7).

A client can rely on a public interface not to change. If the public interface does change, then the client must be recompiled and perhaps redesigned.

On the other hand, the private implementation is, as its name implies, private to the server. The designer of the server class is free to change *how* it does the work promised in the public interface, so long as it continues to fulfill the terms of its implicit contract: it must take the given parameters, do the promised work, and return the promised value and allow access to the public properties.

For example, you might have a public method `NetPresentValue( )` that promises as follows: "Give me a dollar amount and a number of years, and I'll return the net present value." How you compute that amount is your business; as long as you return the net present value given a dollar amount and number of years, the client doesn't care if you look it up in a table, compute the value, or ask your friend who is really good at math.

You might implement your Net Present Value interface initially by keeping a table of values. Some time later, you might change your program to compute the net present value using the appropriate algebra. That is encapsulated within your class, and it does not affect the client. As long as you don't change the public interface (that is, as long as you don't change the number or type of parameters expected, or change the type of the return value), your clients will not break when you change the implementation.

Specialization

The second pillar of object-oriented programming, specialization, is implemented in C# through inheritance; specifically by declaring that a new class derives from an existing class. The specialized class *inherits* the characteristics of the more general class. The specialized class is called a *derived* class, while the more general class is known as a *base* class.

The specialization relationship is referred to as the *is-a* relationship. A dog *is a* mammal; a car *is a* vehicle. (Dog would be derived from the base class Mammal and Car from the base class Vehicle.)

For example, a Manager is a special type of Employee. The Manager adds new capabilities (hiring, firing, rewarding, praising) and a new state (annual objectives, management level, etc.). The Manager, however, also inherits the characteristics and capabilities common to all Employees. Thus, a Manager has an address, a name, and an employee ID, and Managers can be given raises, can be laid off, and so forth.

Specialization allows you to create a family of objects. In Windows, a button is a control. A listbox is a control. Controls have certain characteristics (color, size, location) and certain abilities (can be drawn, can be selected). These characteristics and abilities are inherited by all of their derived types, which allows for a very powerful form of reuse. Rather than cutting and pasting code from one type to another, the derived type inherits the shared fields and methods. If you change how a shared ability is implemented in the base class, you do not have to update code in every derived type; they inherit the changes.

You'll see specialization at work in Chapter 11.

Polymorphism

Polymorphism, the third pillar of object-oriented programming, is closely related to inheritance. The prefix *poly* means "many;" *morph* means "form." Thus, polymorphism refers to the ability of a single type or class to take many forms.

There are times that you will know you have a collection of a general type—for example, a collection of controls—but you do not know (or care) what the specific subtype each of your controls is (one may be a button, another a listbox). The important thing is that you know they all inherit shared abilities (such as the draw method) and that you can treat them all as controls. If you write a programming instruction that tells each control to draw itself, the Draw( ) method is implemented properly on a per-control basis (buttons draw as buttons, listboxes draw as listboxes). You do not need to know how each subtype accomplishes this; you only need to know that each type is defined to be able to draw.

Polymorphism allows you to treat a collection of disparate derived types (buttons, listboxes) as a group. You treat the general group of controls the same way, and each individual control does the right thing according to its specific type. Chapter 11 provides details and examples.

Object-Oriented Analysis and Design

Before you program anything, other than a trivial demonstration program, you need to take two steps: analysis and design. Analysis is the process of understanding and detailing the problem you are trying to solve. Design is the actual planning of your solution.

With trivial problems (such as computing the Fibonacci series), you may not need an extensive analysis period, but with complex business problems, the analysis process can take weeks, or even months. One powerful analysis technique is to create what are called *use-case scenarios*, in which you describe in some detail how the system will be used. Among the other considerations in the analysis period are determining your success factors (how do you know if your program works?) and writing a specification of your program's requirements.

The Fibonacci Series

The Fibonacci series is the values 0,1,1,2,3,5,8,13.... The series is named for Fibonacci (Leonardo Pisano), who in 1202 investigated how fast rabbits could breed under ideal circumstances. To simplify, you derive the series by writing 0,1,1 and then adding the previous two numbers to get the next (thus the seventh value in the series, 8, is the sum of the previous two values: 5 + 3). The ratio of consecutive Fibonacci numbers converges to the "golden ratio" Φ (phi), and Φ in turn has implications in many natural phenomena (the number of petals in flowers, the ratio of spirals in Sunflowers, the ratio of parts of your finger, and more). See the Internet for much more on the Fibonacci series.

Once you've analyzed the problem, you design the solution. Imagining the classes you will use and their inter-relationships is key to the design process. You might design a simple program on the fly, without this careful planning; but in any serious business application, you will want to take some time to think through the issues.

There are many powerful design techniques you might use. How much time you put into design[*] before you begin coding will depend on the philosophy of the organization you work for, the size of your team, and your background, experience, and training.[†]

 My personal approach to managing complexity is to keep team size very small. I have worked on large development teams, and over the years I've come to agree with one of the best developers I've ever met, Ed Belove, that the ideal size for a team of developers is three. Three highly skilled programmers can be incredibly productive, and with three, you don't need a manager. Three people can have only one conversation at a time. Three people can never be evenly split on a decision. One day I'll write a book on programming in teams of three, but this isn't it, so we'll stay focused on C# programming, rather than on design debates.

---

[*] See *The Unified Modelling Language User Guide*, Second Edition, by Grady Booch, Ivar Jacobson, and James Rumbaugh (Addison Wesley, 2005).

[†] See *Agile Software Development Principles, Patterns, and Practices* by Robert C. Martin (Prentice Hall, 2003).

About the Examples in This Book

Object-oriented programming is designed to help you manage complex programs. Unfortunately, it is very difficult to show complex problems and their solutions in a primer on C#. The complexity of these problems gets in the way of what you're trying to learn about. Because of necessity, the examples in this book will be extremely simple. The simplicity may hide some of the motivation for the technique, but it makes the technique clearer. You'll have to take it on faith, for now, that these techniques scale up well to very complex problems.

Most of the chapters of this book focus on the syntax of C#. You need the syntax of the language to be able to write a program at all, but it's important to keep in mind that the syntax of any language is less important than its semantics. The meaning of what you are writing and why you're writing it are the real focus of object-oriented programming, and thus of this book.

Don't let concern with syntax get in the way of understanding the semantics. The compiler can help you get the syntax right (if only by complaining when you get it wrong), and the documentation can remind you of the syntax, but understanding the semantics—meaning of the construct—is the hard part. Throughout this book, I work hard to explain not only *how* you do something, but *why* and *when* you do it.

Summary

- Object-oriented programming helps programmers manage complexity by modeling essential aspects of the real-world problem.

- A class defines a new type in your program and is typically used as a representation for a type of thing in the problem domain.

- An object is an instance of a class.

- State is the current condition of an object.

- Many classes define member fields, which are typically private variables visible to every method of the class.

- The behavior of the class is defined with methods, which contain code to perform an action. Methods can manipulate the state of the object and interact with other objects.

- The three pillars of object-oriented programming are encapsulation, specialization, and polymorphism.

- Encapsulation requires that each class should be discrete and self-contained. Each class should "know" and/or "do" one discreet thing or set of things. Specialization is implemented by deriving more specific classes from generalized (base) classes through inheritance.

- Polymorphism allows you to treat a collection of objects of types all derived from a common base as if they were each instances of that base type.
- Analysis is the process of detailing the problem you're trying to solve.
- Design is the planning of the solution to the problem.

Quiz

Question 6-1. How do you create a user-defined type in C#?

Question 6-2. What is the difference between a class and an object?

Question 6-3. Why should member fields be private?

Question 6-4. What is encapsulation?

Question 6-5. What is specialization and how is it implemented in C#?

Question 6-6. What is polymorphism?

Question 6-7. What is the difference between the *is-a* and the *has-a* relationship?

Question 6-8. What are access modifiers?

Question 6-9. Describe the differences between state, capabilities, and responsibilities.

Question 6-10. What is a use-case scenario?

Exercises

Exercise 6-1. Draw a class diagram for a class named "vehicle," and show how the classes "car," "truck," and "motorcycle" derive from it.

Exercise 6-2. Define a class Book, in which a book has a title, author, and ISBN, and the book can be read or shelved.

CHAPTER 7

Classes and Objects

Chapter 3 discusses the intrinsic types, built into the C# language. As you may recall, these simple types allow you to hold and manipulate numeric values and strings. The true power of C#, however, lies in its capacity to let the programmer define new types to suit particular problems. It is this ability to create new types that characterizes an object-oriented language. You specify new types in C# by declaring and defining classes.

Particular instances of a class are called *objects*. The difference between a class and an object is the same as the difference between the concept of a Dog and the particular dog who is sitting at your feet as you read this. You can't play fetch with the definition of a Dog, only with an instance.

A Dog class describes what dogs are like; they have weight, height, eye color, hair color, disposition, and so forth. They also have actions they can take, such as eat, walk, bark, and sleep. A particular dog (such as my dog, Milo) will have a specific weight (62 pounds), height (22 inches), eye color (black), hair color (yellow), disposition (angelic), and so forth. He is capable of all the actions—*methods*, in programming parlance—of any dog (though if you knew him, you might imagine that eating is the only method he implements).

The huge advantage of classes in object-oriented programming is that classes encapsulate the characteristics and capabilities of a type in a single, self-contained unit.

Suppose, for instance, you want to sort the contents of an instance of a Windows listbox control. The listbox control is defined as a class. One of the properties of that class is that it knows how to sort itself. Sorting is *encapsulated* within the class, and the details of how the listbox sorts itself are not made visible to other classes. If you want a listbox sorted, you just tell the listbox to sort itself, and it takes care of the details.

So, you simply write a method that tells the listbox to sort itself—and that's what happens. How it sorts is of no concern; that it does so is all you need to know.

As noted in Chapter 6, this is called encapsulation, which, along with polymorphism and specialization, is one of three cardinal principles of object-oriented programming. Chapter 11 discusses polymorphism and inheritance.

An old programming joke asks, how many object-oriented programmers does it take to change a light bulb? Answer: none, you just tell the light bulb to change itself. This chapter explains the C# language features that are used to specify new classes. The elements of a class—its behaviors and its state—are known collectively as its *class members*.

Class behavior is created by writing methods (sometimes called member functions). A method is a routine that every object of the class can execute. For example, a Dog class might have a Bark method, and a listbox class might have a Sort method.

Class state is maintained by *fields* (sometimes called member variables). Fields may be primitive types (an int to hold the age of the dog or a set of strings to hold the contents of the listbox), or fields may be objects of other classes (for example, an Employee class may have a field of type Address).

Finally, classes may also have *properties*, which act like methods to the creator of the class, but look like fields to clients of the class. A *client* is any object that interacts with instances of the class.

Defining Classes

When you define a new class, you define the characteristics of all objects of that class, as well as their behaviors. For example, if you create your own windowing operating system, you might want to create screen widgets (known as *controls* in Windows). One control of interest might be a listbox, a control that is very useful for presenting a list of choices to the user and enabling the user to select from the list.

Listboxes have a variety of characteristics: height, width, location, and text color, for example. Programmers have also come to expect certain behaviors of listboxes—they can be opened, closed, sorted, and so on.

Object-oriented programming allows you to create a new type, ListBox, which encapsulates these characteristics and capabilities.

To define a new type or class, you first declare it and then define its methods and fields. You declare a class using the class keyword. The complete syntax is:

```
[attributes] [access-modifiers] class identifier [:base-class]
{class-body}
```

Attributes are used to provide special metadata about a class (that is, information about the structure or use of the class). You will not need attributes for routine C# programming.

Access modifiers are discussed later in this chapter. (Typically, your classes will use the keyword public as an access modifier.)

The *identifier* is the name of the class that you provide. Typically, C# classes are named with nouns (Dog, Employee, ListBox). The naming convention (not required, but strongly encouraged) is to use Pascal notation. In Pascal notation, you don't use underbars or hyphens, but if the name has two words (Golden Retriever), you push the two words together, each word beginning with an uppercase letter (GoldenRetriever).

As mentioned earlier, inheritance is one of the pillars of object-oriented programming. The optional *base class* is explained when inheritance is discussed in Chapter 11.

The member definitions that make up the *class-body* are enclosed by open and closed curly braces ({}):

```
class Dog
{
 int age; // the dog's age
 int weight; // the dog's weight
 Bark() { //... }
 Eat() { // ... }
}
```

Methods within the class definition of Dog describe all the things a dog can do. The fields (member variables) such as age and weight describe all the dog's attributes or state.

Instantiating Objects

To make an actual instance, or *object*, of the Dog class, you must declare the object and allocate memory for the object. These two steps combined are necessary to create, or *instantiate*, the object. Here's how you do it.

First, you declare the object by writing the name of the class (Dog) followed by an identifier (name) for the object or instance of that class:

```
Dog milo; // declare milo to be an instance of Dog
```

This is not unlike the way you create a local variable; you declare the type (in this case, Dog), followed by the identifier (milo). Notice also that (as with variables) by convention, the identifier for the object uses Camel notation. Camel notation is just like Pascal notation except that the very first letter is lowercase. Thus, a variable or object name might be myDog, designatedDriver, or plantManager.

The declaration alone doesn't actually create an instance, however. To create an instance of a class, you must also allocate memory for the object using the keyword new.

```
milo = new Dog(); // allocate memory for milo
```

You can combine the declaration of the Dog type with the memory allocation into a single line:

```
Dog milo = new Dog( );
```

This code declares milo to be an object of type Dog and also creates a new instance of Dog. You'll see what the parentheses are for later in this chapter in the discussion of the constructor.

In C#, *everything* happens within a class. No methods can run outside of a class, not even Main( ). The Main( ) method is the entry point for your program; it is called by the operating system, and it is where execution of your program begins. Typically, you'll create a small class to house Main( ), because like every method, Main( ) must live within a class. Some of the examples in this book use a class named Tester to house Main( ):

```
public class Tester
{
 public static void Main( )
 {
 //...
 }
}
```

Even though Tester was created to house the Main( ) method, you've not yet instantiated any objects of type Tester. To do so, you would write:

```
Tester myTester = new Tester( ); // instantiate an object of type Tester
```

As you'll see later in this chapter, creating an instance of the Tester class allows you to call other methods on the object you've created (myTester).

Creating a Time Class

Now consider a class to keep track of and display the time of day. The internal state of the class must be able to represent the current year, month, date, hour, minute, and second. You probably would also like the class to display the time in a variety of formats.

 The .NET Framework provides a fully functional DateTime class. The creation of a simplified Time class here is used only to illustrate how such a class might be designed and implemented.

You might implement such a class by defining a single method and six variables, as shown in Example 7-1.

Classes Versus Objects

One way to understand the difference between a class and an instance (object) is to consider the distinction between the type int and a variable of type int.

You can't assign a value to a type:

```
int = 5; // error
```

Instead, you assign a value to an object of that type (in this case, a variable of type int):

```
int myInteger;
myInteger = 5; // ok
```

Similarly, you can't assign values to fields in a class; you must assign values to fields in an object. Thus, you can't write:

```
Dog.Weight = 5;
```

This is not meaningful. It isn't true that every dog's weight is five pounds. You must instead write:

```
milo.Weight = 5;
```

This says that a particular dog's weight (Milo's weight) is five pounds.

Example 7-1. The Time class

```csharp
using System;

public class Time
{
    // private variables
    private int year;
    private int month;
    private int date;
    private int hour;
    private int minute;
    private int second;

    // public methods
    public void DisplayCurrentTime( )
    {
        Console.WriteLine( "stub for DisplayCurrentTime" );
    }
}

public class Tester
{
    static void Main( )
    {
        Time timeObject = new Time( );
        timeObject.DisplayCurrentTime( );
    }

}
```

This code creates a new user-defined type: Time. The Time class definition begins with the declaration of a number of member variables: Year, Month, Date, Hour, Minute, and Second.

The keyword private indicates that these values can only be called by methods of this class. The private keyword is an access modifier, explained later in this chapter.

 Many C# programmers prefer to put all of the member fields together, either at the very top or the very bottom of the class declaration, though that is not required by the language.

The only method declared within the Time class is the method DisplayCurrentTime(). The DisplayCurrentTime() method is defined to return void; that is, it will not return a value to the method that invokes it. For now, the body of this method has been "stubbed out."

Stubbing out a method is a temporary measure you might use when you first write a program to allow you to think about the overall structure without filling in every detail when you create a class. When you stub out a method body, you leave out the internal logic and just mark the method, perhaps with a message to the console:

```
public void DisplayCurrentTime( )
{
 Console.WriteLine(
 "stub for DisplayCurrentTime");
}
```

After the closing brace, a second class, Tester, is defined. Tester contains our now familiar Main( ) method. In Main( ), an instance of Time is created, named timeObject:

```
Time timeObject = new Time( );
```

 Technically, an unnamed instance of Time is created on the heap and a reference to that object is returned and used to initialize the Time reference named timeObject. Because that is cumbersome, we'll simply say that a Time instance named timeObject was created.

Because timeObject is an instance of Time, Main( ) can make use of the DisplayCurrentTime( ) method available with objects of that type and call it to display the time:

```
timeObject.DisplayCurrentTime( );
```

You invoke a method on an object by writing the name of the object (timeObject) followed by the dot operator (.), the method name (DisplayCurrentTime), and the parameter list in parentheses (in this case, empty). You'll see how to pass in values to initialize the member variables in the discussion of constructors, later in this chapter.

Access Modifiers

An access modifier determines which class methods—including methods of other classes—can see and use a member variable or method within a class. Table 7-1 summarizes the C# access modifiers.

Table 7-1. Access modifiers

Access modifier	Restrictions
public	No restrictions. Members that are marked `public` are visible to any method of any class.
private	The members in class A that are marked `private` are accessible only to methods of class A.
protected	The members in class A that are marked `protected` are accessible to methods of class A and also to methods of classes derived from class A. The `protected` access modifier is used with derived classes, as explained in Chapter 11.
internal	The members in class A that are marked `internal` are accessible to methods of any class in A's assembly. An *assembly* is a collection of files that appear to the programmer as a single executable or DLL.
protected internal	The members in class A that are marked `protected internal` are accessible to methods of class A, to methods of classes derived from class A, and also to any class in A's assembly. This is effectively protected *or* internal; there is no concept of protected *and* internal.

Public methods are part of the class's public interface: they define how this class behaves. Private methods are "helper methods" used by the public methods to accomplish the work of the class. Because the internal workings of the class are private, helper methods need not (and should not) be exposed to other classes.

The `Time` class and its method `DisplayCurrentTime()` are both declared `public` so that any other class can make use of them. If `DisplayCurrentTime()` had been `private`, it would not be possible to invoke `DisplayCurrentTime()` from any method of any class other than methods of `Time`. In Example 7-1, `DisplayCurrentTime()` was invoked from a method of `Tester` (not `Time`), and this was legal because both the class (`Time`) and the method (`DisplayCurrentTime`) were marked `public`.

 It is good programming practice to explicitly set the accessibility of all methods and members of your class. Although you can rely on the fact that class members are declared `private` by default, making their access explicit indicates a conscious decision and is self-documenting.

Method Arguments

The behavior of a class is defined by the methods of that class. To make your methods as flexible as possible, you can define *parameters*: information passed into the method when the method is invoked. Thus, rather than having to write one method when you want to sort your listbox from A to Z and a second method when you want to sort it from Z to A, you define a more general Sort( ) method and pass in a parameter specifying the order of the sort.

Methods can take any number of parameters. The parameter list follows the method name and is enclosed in parentheses. Each parameter's type is identified before the name of the parameter.

 The terms "argument" and "parameter" are often used interchangeably, though some programmers insist on differentiating between the parameter declaration and the arguments passed in when the method is invoked.

For example, the following declaration defines a method named MyMethod( ) that returns void (that is, it returns no value at all) and takes two parameters (an int and a Button):

```
void MyMethod (int firstParam, Button secondParam)
{
    // ...
}
```

Within the body of the method, the parameters act as local variables, as if you had declared them in the body of the method and initialized them with the values passed in. Example 7-2 illustrates how you pass values into a method; in this case, values of type int and float.

Example 7-2. Passing parameters

```
using System;

public class MyClass
{
    public void SomeMethod( int firstParam, float secondParam )
    {
        Console.WriteLine("Here are the parameters received: {0}, {1}",
        firstParam, secondParam );
    }

}

public class Tester
{
    static void Main( )
    {
        int howManyPeople = 5;
        float pi = 3.14f;
        MyClass mc = new MyClass( );
        mc.SomeMethod( howManyPeople, pi );
    }
}
```

Here is the output:

```
Here are the parameters received: 5, 3.14
```

 Note that when you pass in a float with a decimal part (3.14), you must append the letter f (3.14f) to signal to the compiler that the value is a float and not a double.

The method SomeMethod( ) takes two parameters, firstParam and secondParam, and displays them using Console.WriteLine( ). FirstParam is an int, and secondParam is a float. These parameters are treated as local variables within SomeMethod( ). You can manipulate these values within the method, but they go out of scope and are destroyed when the method ends.

In the calling method (Main), two local variables (howManyPeople and pi) are created and initialized. These variables are passed as the parameters to SomeMethod( ). The compiler maps howManyPeople to firstParam and pi to secondParam, based on their relative positions in the parameter list.

Constructors

In Example 7-1, notice that the statement that creates the Time object looks as though it is invoking a Time( ) method:

```
Time timeObject = new Time( );
```

In fact, a member method *is* invoked whenever you instantiate an object. This method is called a *constructor*. Each time you define a class, you are free to define your own constructor, but if you don't, the compiler will provide one for you invisibly and automatically.

The job of a constructor is to create an instance of the object specified by a class and to put it into a valid state. Before the constructor runs, the object is just a blob of memory; after the constructor completes, the memory holds a valid instance of the class.

The Time class of Example 7-2 does not define a constructor, so the compiler implicitly provides one. The constructor provided by the compiler creates the object but takes no other action.

 Any constructor that takes no arguments is called a *default constructor*. The constructor provided by the compiler takes no arguments, and hence is a default constructor. This terminology has caused a great deal of confusion. You can create your own default constructor, and if you do not create a constructor at all, the compiler will create a default constructor for you, by default.

If you do not explicitly initialize your member variables, they are initialized to innocuous values (integers to 0, strings to the empty string, etc.). Table 7-2 lists the default values assigned to various types.

Table 7-2. Primitive types and their default values

Type	Default value
Numeric (int, long, etc.)	0
bool	False
char	'\0' (null)
enum	0
Reference	Null

Typically, you'll want to define your own constructor and provide it with arguments, so that the constructor can set the initial state for your object. In Example 7-3, you want to pass in the current year, month, date, and so forth, so that the object is created with meaningful data.

You declare a constructor like any other member method, except:

- The name of the constructor must be the same as the name of the class.
- Constructors have no return type (not even void).

If there are arguments to be passed, you define an argument list just as you would for any other method. Example 7-3 declares a constructor for the Time class that accepts six arguments, one each for the year, month, date, hour, minute, and second for the new Time object you are creating.

Example 7-3. Creating a constructor

```
using System;

public class Time
{
   // private member variables
   int year;
   int month;
   int date;
   int hour;
   int minute;
   int second;

   // public method
   public void DisplayCurrentTime( )
   {
      System.Console.WriteLine( "{0}/{1}/{2} {3}:{4}:{5}",
      month, date, year, hour, minute, second );
   }
```

Example 7-3. Creating a constructor (continued)

```csharp
    // constructor
    public Time( int theYear, int theMonth, int theDate,
    int theHour, int theMinute, int theSecond )
    {
        year = theYear;
        month = theMonth;
        date = theDate;
        hour = theHour;
        minute = theMinute;
        second = theSecond;
    }
}

public class Tester
{
    static void Main( )
    {
        Time timeObject = new Time( 2008, 8, 1, 9, 35, 20 );
        timeObject.DisplayCurrentTime( );
    }
}
```

The output looks like this:

```
8/1/2008 9:35:20
```

In this example, the constructor takes a series of integer values and initializes all the member variables based on these parameters.

 In this, as in virtually all the demonstration code, we've taken out all the error checking to simplify the presentation. Of course, this allows you to create a date such as July 45th 2005 at 29:32 a.m. Don't do that.

When the constructor finishes, the Time object exists and the values have been initialized. When DisplayCurrentTime( ) is called in Main( ), the values are displayed.

Try commenting out one of the assignments and running the program again. You'll find that each member variable that isn't assigned-to by you is initialized by the compiler to zero. Integer member variables are set to zero if you don't otherwise assign them. Remember that value types (such as integers) must be initialized; if you don't tell the constructor what to do, it sets innocuous values.

Initializers

It is possible to initialize the values of member variables in an *initializer*, instead of having to do so in the constructor. You create an initializer by assigning an initial value to a class member:

```csharp
    private int Second = 30; // initializer
```

Assume that the semantics of the Time object are such that no matter what time is set, the seconds are always initialized to 30. You might rewrite your Time class to use an initializer so that the value of Second is always initialized, as shown in Example 7-4.

Example 7-4. Using an initializer

```
using System;

public class Time
{
   // private member variables
   int year;
   int month;
   int date;
   int hour;
   int minute;
   int second = 30;

   // public method
   public void DisplayCurrentTime( )
   {
      System.Console.WriteLine( "{0}/{1}/{2} {3}:{4}:{5}",
      month, date, year, hour, minute, second );
   }

   // constructor
   public Time( int theYear, int theMonth, int theDate,
   int theHour, int theMinute )
   {
      year = theYear;
      month = theMonth;
      date = theDate;
      hour = theHour;
      minute = theMinute;
   }
}

public class Tester
{
   static void Main( )
   {
      Time timeObject = new Time( 2008, 8, 1, 9, 35 );
      timeObject.DisplayCurrentTime( );
   }
}
```

The output looks like this:

```
8/1/2008 9:35:30
```

If you do not provide a specific initializer, the constructor initializes each integer member variable to zero (0). In the case shown, however, the Second member is initialized to 30:

```
private int Second = 30; // initializer
```

Later in this chapter, you will see that you can have more than one constructor. If you assign 30 to Second in more than one of these, you can avoid the problem of having to keep all the constructors consistent with one another by initializing the Second member, rather than assigning 30 in each of the constructors.

The this Keyword

The keyword this refers to the current instance of an object. The this reference is a hidden parameter in every nonstatic method of a class (static methods are discussed later in this chapter). There are three ways in which the this reference is typically used. The first way is to qualify instance members that have the same name as parameters, as in the following:

```
public void SomeMethod (int hour)
{
 this.hour = newHour;
}
```

In this example, SomeMethod( ) takes a parameter (hour) with the same name as a member variable of the class. The this reference is used to resolve the ambiguity. While this.hour refers to the member variable, hour refers to the parameter.

You can, for example, use the this reference to make assigning to a field more explicit:

```
public void SetTime(
    year, month, date, newHour, newMinute, newSecond)
{
    this.year = year;       // use of "this" required
    this.month = month;     // required
    this.date = date;       // required
    this.hour = hour;       // use of "this" optional
    this.minute = newMinute; // optional
    second = newSecond;     // also ok
}
```

If the name of the parameter is the same as the name of the member variable, then you *must* use the this reference to distinguish between the two, but if the names are different (such as newMinute and newSecond), then the use of the this reference is optional.

The argument in favor of naming the argument to a method the same as the name of the member is that the relationship between the two is made explicit. The counterargument is that using the same name for both the parameter and the member variable can be confusing as to which one you are referring to at any given moment.

The second use of the this reference is to pass the current object as a parameter to another method, as in the following code:

```
Class SomeClass
{
    public void FirstMethod(OtherClass otherObject)
    {
        otherObject.SecondMethod(this);
    }
    // ...
}
```

This code snippet establishes two classes, SomeClass and OtherClass. SomeClass has a method named FirstMethod( ), and OtherClass has a method named SecondMethod( ).

Inside FirstMethod( ), we'd like to invoke SecondMethod( ), passing in the current object (an instance of SomeClass) for further processing. To do so, you pass in the this reference, which refers to the current instance of SomeClass.

The third use of this is with indexers, which are covered in Chapter 12.

Static and Instance Members

The fields, properties, and methods of a class can be either *instance members* or *static members*. Instance members are associated with instances of a type, while static members are associated with the class and not with any particular instance. Methods are instance methods unless you explicitly mark them with the keyword static.

The vast majority of methods will be instance methods. The semantics of an instance method are that you are taking an action on a specific object. From time to time, however, it is convenient to be able to invoke a method without having an instance of the class, and for that, you will use a static method.

You access a static member through the name of the class in which it is declared. For example, suppose you have a class named Button and have instantiated objects of that class named btnUpdate and btnDelete.

Suppose that the Button class has an instance method Draw( ) and a static method GetButtonCount( ). The job of Draw( ) is to draw the current button, and the job of GetButtonCount( ) is to return the number of buttons currently visible on the form.

You access an instance method through an instance of the class—that is, through an object:

```
btnUpdate.SomeMethod( );
```

You access a static method through the class name, not through an instance:

```
Button.GetButtonCount( );
```

Invoking Static Methods

Static methods are said to operate on the class, rather than on an instance of the class. They do not have a this reference, as there is no instance to point to.

Static methods cannot directly access nonstatic members. You will remember that Main( ) is marked static. For Main( ) to call a nonstatic method of any class, including its own class, it must instantiate an object.

For the next example, use Visual Studio 2005 to create a new console application named StaticTester. VS.NET creates a namespace StaticTester and a class named Program. Rename Program to Tester. Get rid of all the comments and the attribute [STATThread] that Visual Studio .NET puts above Main( ). Delete the args parameter to Main( ). When you are done, your source code should look like this:

```
using System;
namespace StaticTester
{
    class Tester
    {
        static void Main( )
        {
        }
    }
}
```

That is a good starting point. Until now, you've always done all the work of the program right in the Main( ) method, but now you'll create an instance method, Run( ). The work of the program will now be done in the Run( ) method, rather than in the Main( ) method.

Within the class, but not within the Main( ) method, declare a new instance method named Run( ). When you declare a method, you write the accessor (public), followed by the return type, the identifier, and then parentheses:

```
public void Run( )
```

The parentheses will hold parameters, but Run( ) won't have any parameters, so you can just leave the parentheses empty. Create braces for the method, and within the braces, just print "Hello World" to the console:

```
public void Run( )
{
 Console.WriteLine("Hello world");
}
```

Run( ) is an instance method. Main( ) is a static method and cannot invoke Run( ) directly. You will therefore create an instance of the Tester class and call Run( ) on that instance:

```
Tester t = new Tester( );
```

When you type the keyword new, IntelliSense tries to help you with the class name. You'll find that Tester is in the list; it is a legitimate class like any other.

On the next line, invoke Run( ) on your Tester object t. When you type t followed by the dot operator, IntelliSense presents all the public methods of the Tester class, as shown in Figure 7-1.

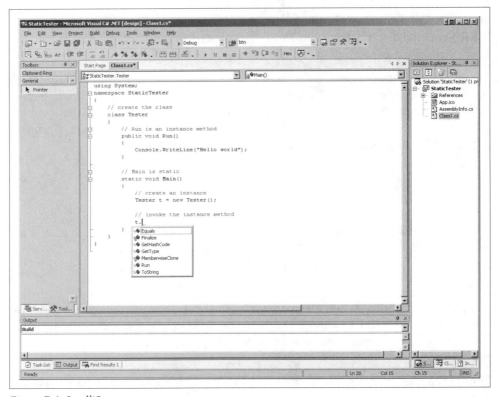

Figure 7-1. IntelliSense

 Notice that the Tester class has a number of methods you did not create (Equals, Finalize, and others). Every class in C# is an object, and these methods are part of the Object class. This is covered in Chapter 11.

When your program is complete, it looks like Example 7-5.

Example 7-5. Instance methods

```
using System;
namespace StaticTester
{
    // create the class
    class Tester
    {
        // Run is an instance method
        public void Run( )
        {
            Console.WriteLine( "Hello world" );
        }

        // Main is static
        static void Main( )
        {
            // create an instance
            Tester t = new Tester( );

            // invoke the instance method
            t.Run( );
        }
    }
}
```

The output looks like this:

```
Hello world
```

This is the model you'll use from now on in most console applications. The Main( ) method will be limited to instantiating an object and then invoking the Run( ) method.

Using Static Fields

A common use of static member variables, or fields, is to keep track of the number of instances/objects that currently exist for your class. In the next example, you create a Cat class. The Cat class might be used in a pet-store simulation.

For this example, the Cat class has been stripped to its absolute essentials. The complete listing is shown in Example 7-6. An analysis follows the example.

Example 7-6. Static fields

```
using System;

namespace Test
{

    // declare a Cat class
    // stripped down
    public class Cat
```

Example 7-6. Static fields (continued)

```
{
    // a private static member to keep
    // track of how many Cat objects have
    // been created
    private static int instances = 0;
    private int weight;
    private String name;

    // cat constructor
    // increments the count of Cats
    public Cat( String name, int weight )
    {
        instances++;
        this.name = name;
        this.weight = weight;
    }

    // Static method to retrieve
    // the current number of Cats
    public static void HowManyCats( )
    {
        Console.WriteLine( "{0} cats adopted", instances );
    }
    public void TellWeight( )
    {
        Console.WriteLine( "{0} is {1} pounds", name, weight );
    }
}

class Tester
{

    public void Run( )
    {
        Cat.HowManyCats( );
        Cat frisky = new Cat( "Frisky", 5 );
        frisky.TellWeight( );
        Cat.HowManyCats( );
        Cat whiskers = new Cat( "Whisky", 7 );
        whiskers.TellWeight( );
        Cat.HowManyCats( );
    }

    static void Main( )
    {
        Tester t = new Tester( );
        t.Run( );
    }
}
}
```

Here is the output:

```
0 cats adopted
Frisky is 5 pounds
1 cats adopted
Whisky is 7 pounds
2 cats adopted
```

The Cat class begins by defining a static member variable, instances, that is initialized to zero. This static member field will keep track of the number of Cat objects created. Each time the constructor runs (creating a new object), the instances field is incremented.

The Cat class also defines two instance fields: name and weight. These track the name and weight of each individual Cat object.

The Cat class defines two methods: HowManyCats( ) and TellWeight( ). HowManyCats( ) is static. The number of Cats is not an attribute of any given Cat; it is an attribute of the entire class. TellWeight( ) is an instance method. The name and weight of each cat is per instance (each Cat has his own name and weight).

The Main( ) method accesses the static HowManyCats( ) method directly, through the class:

```
Cat.HowManyCats( );
```

Main( ) then creates an instance of Cat and accesses the instance method, TellWeight( ), through the instance of Cat:

```
Cat frisky = new Cat( )
frisky.TellWeight( );
```

Each time a new Cat is created, HowManyCats( ) reports the increase.

Destroying Objects

Unlike many other programming languages (C, C++, Pascal, etc.), C# provides *garbage collection*. Your objects are destroyed after you are done with them. You do not need to worry about cleaning up after your objects unless you use unmanaged or scarce resources. An unmanaged resource is an operating-system feature outside of the .NET Framework; a scarce resource is a resource that you have in limited quantity, perhaps because of licensing limitations (such as database connections).

If you do control an unmanaged resource, you need to explicitly free that resource when you are done with it. Implicit control over this resource is provided with a *destructor*, which is called by the garbage collector when your object is destroyed.

 This material is fairly advanced and is included here for completeness. Feel free to skip this section and come back if and when you need it. It's your book; you paid for it. (You did, right?)

You declare a C# destructor with a tilde, as follows:

```
~MyClass(){}
```

This syntax is actually translated by the compiler into:

```
protected override void Finalize()
{
    try
    {
        // do work here
    }
    finally
    {
        base.Finalize();
    }
}
```

For this reason, some programmers refer to the destructor as a *finalizer*.

It is not legal to call a destructor explicitly—your destructor (finalizer) will be called by the garbage collector. If you do handle precious unmanaged resources (such as file handles) that you want to close and dispose of as quickly as possible, you ought to implement the IDisposable interface. (You will learn more about interfaces in Chapter 13.)

The IDisposable interface requires you to create a method named Dispose(), which will be called by your clients.

If you provide a Dispose() method, you should stop the garbage collector from calling your object's destructor. To stop the garbage collector, call the static method GC.SuppressFinalize(), passing in the this reference for your object. Your destructor can then call your Dispose() method. Thus, you might write:

```
using System;
class Testing : IDisposable
{
    bool is_disposed = false;
    protected virtual void Dispose( bool disposing )
    {
      if ( !is_disposed ) // only dispose once!
      {
        if ( disposing )
        {
          Console.WriteLine( "Not in destructor,
          OK to reference other objects" );
        }
        // perform cleanup for this object
        Console.WriteLine( "Disposing..." );
      }
      this.is_disposed = true;
    }

    public void Dispose()
    {
```

```
      Dispose( true );
      // tell the GC not to finalize
      GC.SuppressFinalize( this );
   }

   ~Testing( )
   {
      Dispose( false );
      Console.WriteLine( "In destructor." );
   }
}
```

For some objects, you'd rather have your clients call the Close( ) method. (For example, Close( ) makes more sense than Dispose( ) for file objects.) You can implement this by creating a private Dispose( ) method and a public Close( ) method and having your Close( ) method invoke Dispose( ).

Because you cannot be certain that your user will call Dispose( ) reliably, and because finalization is nondeterministic (that is, you can't control when the garbage collector will run), C# provides a using statement to ensure that Dispose( ) is called at the earliest possible time. The idiom is to declare which objects you are using and then to create a scope for these objects with curly braces. When the close brace is reached, the Dispose( ) method will be called on the object automatically, as illustrated here:

```
using System.Drawing;
class Tester
{
 public static void Main( )
 {
     using (Font theFont = new Font("Arial", 10.0f))
     {
     // use the font
     }
 }
}
```

Because Windows only lets you have a small number of Font objects, we want to dispose of it at the earliest opportunity. In this code snippet, the Font object is created within the using statement. When the using statement ends, Dispose( ) is guaranteed to be called on the Font object.

Memory Allocation: The Stack Versus the Heap

Objects created within methods are called *local variables*. They are local to the method, as opposed to belonging to the object, as member variables do. The object is created within the method, used within the method, and then destroyed when the method ends. Local objects are not part of the object's state—they are temporary value holders, useful only within the particular method.

Local variables of intrinsic types such as int are created on a portion of memory known as *the stack*. The stack is allocated and de-allocated as methods are invoked. When you start a method, all the local variables are created on the stack. When the method ends, local variables are destroyed.

These variables are referred to as local because they exist (and are visible) only during the lifetime of the method. They are said to have *local scope*. When the method ends, the variable goes *out of scope* and is destroyed.

C# divides the world of types into value types and reference types. *Value types* are created on the stack. All the intrinsic types (int, long) are value types (as are structs, discussed later in the chapter), and thus are created on the stack.

Classes, on the other hand, are *reference types*. Reference types are created on an undifferentiated block of memory known as *the heap*. When you declare an instance of a reference type, what you are actually declaring is a *reference*, which is a variable that refers to another object. The reference acts like an alias for the object.

That is, when you write:

```
Dog milo = new Dog( );
```

the new operator creates a Dog object on the heap and returns a reference to it. That reference is assigned to milo. Thus, milo is a reference object that refers to a Dog object on the heap. It is common to say that milo is a reference to a dog, or even that milo is a Dog object, but technically that is incorrect. milo is actually a reference object that refers to an (unnamed) Dog object on the heap.

The reference milo acts as an alias for that unnamed object. For all practical purposes, however, you can treat milo as if it were the Dog object itself.

The implication of using references is that you can have more than one reference to the same object. To see this difference between creating value types and reference types, examine Example 7-7. A complete analysis follows the output.

Example 7-7. Creating value types and reference types

```
using System;

namespace heap
{
    public class Dog
    {
        public int weight;
    }

    class Tester
    {
        public void Run( )
        {
            // create an integer
            int firstInt = 5;
```

Example 7-7. Creating value types and reference types (continued)

```
        // create a second integer
        int secondInt = firstInt;

        // display the two integers
        Console.WriteLine( "firstInt: {0} secondInt: {1}",
        firstInt, secondInt );

        // modify the second integer
        secondInt = 7;

        // display the two integers
        Console.WriteLine( "firstInt: {0} secondInt: {1}",
        firstInt, secondInt );

        // create a dog
        Dog milo = new Dog( );

        // assign a value to weight
        milo.weight = 5;

        // create a second reference to the dog
        Dog fido = milo;

        // display their values
        Console.WriteLine( "Milo: {0}, fido: {1}",
        milo.weight, fido.weight );

        // assign a new weight to the second reference
        fido.weight = 7;

        // display the two values
        Console.WriteLine( "Milo: {0}, fido: {1}",
        milo.weight, fido.weight );
    }

    static void Main( )
    {
        Tester t = new Tester( );
        t.Run( );
    }
}
}
```

The output looks like this:

```
firstInt: 5 secondInt: 5
firstInt: 5 secondInt: 7
Milo: 5, fido: 5
Milo: 7, fido: 7
```

The program begins by creating an integer, firstInt, and initializing it with the value 5. The second integer, secondInt, is then created and initialized with the value in firstInt. Their values are displayed as output:

```
firstInt: 5 secondInt: 5
```

These values are identical. Because int is a value type, a copy of the firstInt value is made and assigned to secondInt; secondInt is an independent second variable, as illustrated in Figure 7-2.

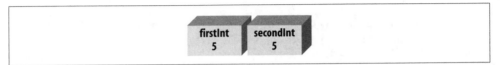

Figure 7-2. secondInt is a copy of firstInt

Then the program assigns a new value to secondInt:

```
secondInt = 7;
```

Because these variables are value types, independent of one another, the first variable is unaffected. Only the copy is changed, as illustrated in Figure 7-3.

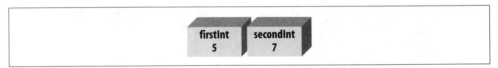

Figure 7-3. Only the copy is changed

When the values are displayed, they are different:

```
firstInt: 5 secondInt: 7
```

Your next step is to create a simple Dog class with only one member variable (field) called weight. Note that this field is given a keyword, public, which specifies that any method of any class can access this field. public is what is known as an *access modifier*. (Generally, you will not make member variables public. The weight field was made public to simplify this example.) Access modifiers are covered in detail later in this chapter.

You instantiate a Dog object and save a reference to that dog in the reference milo.

```
Dog milo = new Dog( );
```

You assign the value 5 to milo's weight field:

```
milo.weight = 5;
```

You commonly say that you've set milo's weight to 5, but actually you've set the weight of the unnamed object on the heap to which milo refers, as shown in Figure 7-4.

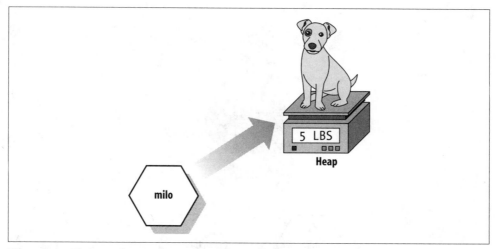

Figure 7-4. milo is a reference to an unnamed Dog object

Next, you create a second reference to Dog and initialize it by setting it equal to milo. This creates a new reference to the same object on the heap.

```
Dog fido = milo;
```

Notice that this is syntactically similar to creating a second int variable and initializing it with an existing int, as you did before:

```
int secondInt = firstInt;
Dog fido = milo;
```

The difference is that Dog is a reference type, so fido is not a copy of milo—it is a second reference to the same object to which milo refers. That is, you now have an object on the heap with two references to it, as illustrated in Figure 7-5.

When you change the weight of that object through the fido reference:

```
fido.weight = 7;
```

you change the weight of the same object to which milo refers. The output reflects this:

```
Milo: 7, fido: 7
```

It isn't that fido is changing milo; it is that by changing the (unnamed) object on the heap to which fido refers, you simultaneously change the value of milo because they refer to the same unnamed object.

 If you had used the keyword new when creating fido, you'd have created a new instance of Dog on the heap, and fido and milo would not point to the same Dog object.

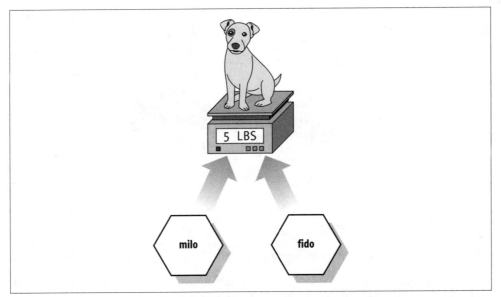

Figure 7-5. fido is a second reference to the Dog object

If you need a class that acts as a value object, you can create a *struct* (see the "Structs" sidebar). The use of structs is so unusual that they are not covered beyond the sidebar for the rest of this book. In five years of professional C# programming, my principal use of structs has been to teach what they are, not to actually use them.

Summary

- When you define a new class, you declare its name with the class keyword, and then define its methods, fields, delegates, events, and properties.

- To instantiate an object, you declare the name of the class, followed by an identifier for the object, much as you would a local variable. You then need to allocate memory for the actual (unnamed) object that will be created on the heap; you do so with the keyword new.

- You can define a reference to an existing object by declaring the class and an identifier and then assigning to that identifier an existing object; the two identifiers now both refer to the same (unnamed) object on the heap.

- You invoke a method on an object by writing the name of the object, followed by the dot operator, and the method name followed by parentheses. Parameters, if any, are placed within the parentheses.

- Access modifiers dictate which methods can see and use a variable or method within a class. All members of the class are visible to all methods of the class.

Structs

Structs are value types, but they are similar to classes in that they can contain constructors, properties, methods, fields, and operators, all explained in this chapter. Structs can also support indexers (see Chapter 12).

On the other hand, structs don't support inheritance or destructors (see Chapter 11) or field initialization. You define a struct almost exactly like you define a class:

```
[attributes] [access-modifiers] struct identifier
[:interface-list] { struct-members }
```

Structs implicitly derive from Object (as do all types in C#, including the built-in types) but cannot inherit from any other class or struct (as classes can). Structs are also implicitly *sealed* (that is, no class or struct can derive from a struct) (see Chapter 11); this is not true for classes.

The goal of structs is to be "lightweight"—requiring little memory overhead— but their use is so constrained, and the savings are so minimal, that most programmers make little use of them.

C++ programmers *beware*: structs in C++ are identical to classes (except for visibility)—that is not true in C#.

- Members marked public have no restrictions, and are visible to methods of any class.

- Members marked private are only visible to methods within the same class.

- Members marked protected are visible to methods within the same class, and methods in derived classes.

- A constructor is a special method invoked when a new object is created. If you do not define any constructors at all for your class, the compiler will provide a default constructor that does nothing. A default constructor is a constructor that takes no parameters. You are free to create your own default constructor for your class.

- You can initialize the values of your member variables when you define them in your class.

- The this keyword is used to refer to the current instance of an object.

- Every non-static method of a class has an implicit "this" variable passed into the method.

- Static members are associated with the class itself, not with a particular instance. Static members are declared with the keyword static, and are invoked through the class name. Static methods do not have a this parameter because there is no instance to refer to.

- C# does not specifically require a destructor method in your classes because the framework will destroy any object that is not in use.
- You should provide a Dispose( ) method if your class uses unmanaged resources.
- Local value type variables are created on the stack. When the method ends, these variables go out of scope and are destroyed.
- Objects are references types, and are created on the heap. When you declare an instance of a reference type, you are actually creating a reference to that object's location in memory. If you declare a reference to an object on the heap within a method, when the method ends, that reference is destroyed. If there are no remaining references to the object on the heap, the object itself is destroyed by the garbage collector.

Quiz

Question 7-1. What is the difference between a class and an object?

Question 7-2. Where are reference types created?

Question 7-3. Where are value types created?

Question 7-4. What does the keyword private do?

Question 7-5. What does the keyword public do?

Question 7-6. What method is called when you create an object?

Question 7-7. What is a default constructor?

Question 7-8. What types can a constructor return?

Question 7-9. How do you initialize the value of a member variable in a class?

Question 7-10. What does the keyword this refer to?

Question 7-11. What is the difference between a static method and an instance method?

Question 7-12. What does the using statement do?

Exercises

Exercise 7-1. Write a program with a Math class that has four methods: Add, Subtract, Multiply, and Divide, each of which takes two parameters. Call each method from Main( ).

Exercise 7-2. Modify the program from Exercise 7-1 so that you do not have to create an instance of Math to call the four methods.

CHAPTER 8

Inside Methods

In Chapter 7, you saw that classes consist of fields and methods. Fields hold the state of the object, and methods define the object's behavior.

In this chapter, you'll explore how methods work in more detail. You've already seen how to create methods, and in this chapter, you'll learn about method *overloading*, a technique that allows you to create more than one method with the same name. This enables your clients to invoke the method with different parameter types.

This chapter also introduces *properties*. To clients of your class, properties look like member variables, but properties are implemented as methods. This allows you to maintain good data-hiding, while providing your clients with convenient access to the state of your class.

Chapter 7 described the difference between value types (such as int and long) and reference types. The most common value types are the "built-in" or "primitive" types (as well as structs), while the most common reference types are the user-defined types. This chapter explores the implications of passing value types to methods and shows how you can pass value types *by reference*, allowing the called method to act on the original object in the calling method.

Overloading Methods

Often you'll want to have more than one method with the same name. The most common example of this is to have more than one constructor with the same name, which allows you to create the object with different types of parameters, or a different number of parameters. For example, if you were creating a Time object, you might have circumstances where you want to create the Time object by passing in the date, hours, minutes, and seconds. Other times, you might want to create a Time object by passing in an existing Time object. Still other times, you might want to pass in just a date, without hours and minutes. Overloading the constructor allows you to provide these various options.

Chapter 7 explained that your constructor is automatically invoked when your object is created. Let's return to the Time class created in that chapter, to the client who could create a Time object by passing in a DateTime object to the constructor.

 The DateTime object is an object that's built into the System library, with many of the same data members as your custom Time class. In short, having DateTime means you probably won't ever create your own Time class, but we're using our custom Time class as an example of many of the issues that arise in creating classes.

It would be convenient also to allow the client to create a new Time object by passing in year, month, date, hour, minute, and second values. Some clients might prefer one or the other constructor; you can provide both, and the client can decide which better fits the situation.

In order to overload your constructor, you must make sure that each constructor has a unique *signature*. The signature of a method is composed of its name and its parameter list. Two methods differ in their signatures if they have different names or different parameter lists. Parameter lists can differ by having different numbers or types of parameters. The following four lines of code show how you might distinguish methods by signature:

```
void MyMethod(int p1);
void MyMethod(int p1, int p2);     // different number
void MyMethod(int p1, string s1); // different types
void SomeMethod(int p1);           // different name
```

The first three methods are all overloads of the MyMethod( ) method. The first differs from the second and third in the number of parameters. The second closely resembles the third version, but the second parameter in each is a different type. In the second method, the second parameter (p2) is an integer; in the third method, the second parameter (s1) is a string. These changes to the number or type of parameters are sufficient changes in the signature to allow the compiler to distinguish the methods.

The fourth method differs from the other three methods by having a different name. This is not method overloading, just different methods, but it illustrates that two methods can have the same number and type of parameters if they have different names. Thus, the fourth method and the first have the same parameter list, but their names are different.

A class can have any number of methods, as long as each one's signature differs from that of all the others. Example 8-1 illustrates a Time class with two constructors: one that takes a DateTime object and one that takes six integers.

Example 8-1. Overloading a method

```
using System;

namespace MethodOverloading
{
   public class Time
   {
      // private member variables
      private int Year;
      private int Month;
      private int Date;
      private int Hour;
      private int Minute;
      private int Second;

      // public accessor methods
      public void DisplayCurrentTime( )
      {
         System.Console.WriteLine( "{0}/{1}/{2} {3}:{4}:{5}",
         Month, Date, Year, Hour, Minute, Second );
      }

      // constructors
      public Time( System.DateTime dt )
      {
         Year = dt.Year;
         Month = dt.Month;
         Date = dt.Day;
         Hour = dt.Hour;
         Minute = dt.Minute;
         Second = dt.Second;
      }

      public Time( int Year, int Month, int Date,
      int Hour, int Minute, int Second )
      {
         this.Year = Year;
         this.Month = Month;
         this.Date = Date;
         this.Hour = Hour;
         this.Minute = Minute;
         this.Second = Second;
      }
   }

   class Tester
   {
      public void Run( )
      {
         System.DateTime currentTime = System.DateTime.Now;

         Time time1 = new Time( currentTime );
         time1.DisplayCurrentTime( );
```

Example 8-1. Overloading a method (continued)

```
        Time time2 = new Time( 2000, 11, 18, 11, 03, 30 );
        time2.DisplayCurrentTime( );
    }

    static void Main( )
    {
        Tester t = new Tester( );
        t.Run( );
    }
  }
}
```

The output looks like this:

```
7/10/2008 16:17:32
11/18/2000 11:3:30
```

> Note that the minutes in the second output show as 3 rather than 03.
> You can fix this by formatting the output string, left as an exercise for
> the user.

If a function's signature consisted only of the function name, the compiler would not know which constructors to call when constructing the new Time objects, time1 and time2. However, because the signature includes the parameters and their types, the compiler is able to match the constructor call for time1 with the constructor whose signature requires a DateTime object:

```
System.DateTime currentTime = System.DateTime.Now;
Time time1 = new Time(currentTime);
public Time(System.DateTime dt)
```

Likewise, the compiler is able to associate the time2 constructor call with the constructor whose signature specifies six integer arguments.

```
Time time2 = new Time(2000,11,18,11,03,30);
public Time(int Year, int Month, int Date, int Hour, int Minute, int Second)
```

> When you overload a method, you must change the signature (the
> name, number, or type of the parameters). You are free, as well, to
> change the return type, but this is optional. Changing only the return
> type does not overload the method, and creating two methods with
> the same signature but differing return types generates a compile error.

Encapsulating Data with Properties

It is generally desirable to designate the member variables of a class as private. This means that only member methods of that class can access their value. When you prevent methods outside the class from directly accessing member variables, you're enforcing *data hiding*, which is part of the encapsulation of a class.

Object-oriented programmers are told that member variables should be private. That's fine, but how do you provide access to this data to your clients? The answer for C# programmers is *properties*. Properties allow clients to access class state as if they were accessing member fields directly, while actually implementing that access through a class method.

This solution is ideal. The client wants direct access to the state of the object. The class designer, however, wants to hide the internal state of the class in class fields and provide indirect access through a method. The property provides both the illusion of direct access for the client, and the reality of indirect access for the class developer.

By decoupling the class state from the method that accesses that state, the designer is free to change the internal state of the object as needed. When the Time class is first created, the Hour value might be stored as a member variable. When the class is redesigned, the Hour value might be computed or retrieved from a database. If the client had direct access to the original Hour member variable, changing how that value is resolved would break the client. By decoupling and forcing the client to go through a property, the Time class can change how it manages its internal state without breaking client code.

In short, properties provide the data hiding required by good object-oriented design. Example 8-2 creates a property called Hour, which is then discussed in the paragraphs that follow.

Example 8-2. Properties

```
using System;

namespace Properties
{
    public class Time
    {

        // private member variables
        private int year;
        private int month;
        private int date;
        private int hour;
        private int minute;
        private int second;

        // create a property
        public int Hour
        {
            get
            {
```

Example 8-2. Properties (continued)

```
        return hour;
    }

    set
    {
        hour = value;
    }
}

// public accessor methods
public void DisplayCurrentTime( )
{
    System.Console.WriteLine(
    "Time: {0}/{1}/{2} {3}:{4}:{5}",
    month, date, year, hour, minute, second );
}


// constructors
public Time( System.DateTime dt )
{
    year = dt.Year;
    month = dt.Month;
    date = dt.Day;
    hour = dt.Hour;
    minute = dt.Minute;
    second = dt.Second;
}


}
class Tester
{
    public void Run( )
    {
        System.DateTime currentTime = System.DateTime.Now;
        Time t = new Time( currentTime );
        t.DisplayCurrentTime( );

        // access the hour to a local variable
        int theHour = t.Hour;

        // display it
        System.Console.WriteLine( "Retrieved the hour: {0}",
        theHour );

        // increment it
        theHour++;

        // reassign the incremented value back through
        // the property
        t.Hour = theHour;
```

Example 8-2. Properties (continued)

```
        // display the property
        System.Console.WriteLine( "Updated the hour: {0}", t.Hour );
    }

    [STAThread]
    static void Main( )
    {
        Tester t = new Tester( );
        t.Run( );
    }
  }
}
```

The output should look something like this:

```
Time : 7/10/2008 12:7:43
Retrieved the hour: 12
Updated the hour: 13
```

You create a property by writing the property type and name followed by a pair of braces. Within the braces, you can declare the get and set accessors. These accessors are very similar to methods, but they are actually part of the property itself. The purpose of these accessors is to provide the client with simple ways to retrieve and change the value of the private member hour, as you'll see.

Neither of these accessors has explicit parameters, though the set accessor has an *implicit* parameter called value, which is used to set the value of the member variable.

 By convention, property names are written in Pascal notation (initial uppercase).

In Example 8-2, the declaration of the Hour property creates both get and set accessors:

```
public int Hour
{
    get
    {
        return hour;
    }

  set
    {
        hour = value;
    }
}
```

Each accessor has an *accessor-body*, which does the work of retrieving or setting the property value. The property value might be stored in a database (in which case, the accessor would do whatever work is needed to interact with the database), or it might just be stored in a private member variable (in this case, hour):

```
private int hour;
```

The get Accessor

The body of the get accessor is similar to a class method that returns an object of the type of the property. In Example 8-2, the accessor for the Hour property is similar to a method that returns an int. It returns the value of the private member variable hour in which the value of the property has been stored:

```
get
{
    return hour;
}
```

In this example, the value of a private int member variable is returned, but you could just as easily retrieve an integer value from a database or compute it on the fly.

 Remember, this description is from the perspective of the author of the Time class. To the client (user) of the Time class, Hour is a property, and how the Time class returns its hour is encapsulated within the Time class—the client doesn't know or care.

Whenever you need to retrieve the value (other than to assign to it), the get accessor is invoked. For example, in the following code, the value of the Time object's Hour property is assigned to a local variable.

To the client, the local variable theHour is assigned the value of the Hour property of t (the Time object). To the creator of the Time object, however, the get accessor is called, which, in this case, returns the value of the hour member variable:

```
Time t = new Time(currentTime);
int theHour = t.Hour;
```

The set Accessor

The set accessor sets the value of a property. When you define a set accessor, you must use the value keyword to represent the argument whose value is assigned to the property:

```
set
{
    hour = value;
}
```

Here, again, a private member variable is used to store the value of the property, but the set accessor could write to a database or update other member variables as needed.

When you assign a value to the property, the set accessor is automatically invoked, and the implicit parameter value is set to the value you assign:

```
theHour++;
t.Hour = theHour;
```

The first line increments a local variable named theHour. As far as the client is concerned, that new value is assigned to the Hour property of the local time object t. To the author of the Time class, however, the local variable theHour is passed in to the set accessor as the implicit parameter value and assigned (in this case) to the local member variable hour.

The advantage of this approach is that the client can interact with the properties directly, without sacrificing the data hiding and encapsulation sacrosanct in good object-oriented design.

 You can create a read-only property by not implementing the set part of the property. Similarly, you can create a write-only property by not implementing the get part.

Returning Multiple Values

Methods can return only a single value, but this isn't always convenient. Let's return to the Time class. It would be great to create a GetTime( ) method to return the hour, minutes, and seconds. You can't return all three of these as return values, but perhaps you can pass in three parameters, let the GetTime( ) method modify the parameters, and then examine the result in the calling method—in this case, Run( ). Example 8-3 is a first attempt.

Example 8-3. Retrieving multiple values, first attempt

```
using System;

namespace PassByRef
{
    public class Time
    {
        // private member variables
        private int Year;
        private int Month;
        private int Date;
        private int Hour;
        private int Minute;
        private int Second;

        // public accessor methods
        public void DisplayCurrentTime()
        {
```

Example 8-3. Retrieving multiple values, first attempt (continued)

```csharp
        System.Console.WriteLine( "{0}/{1}/{2} {3}:{4}:{5}",
        Month, Date, Year, Hour, Minute, Second );
    }

    public void GetTime(
        int theHour,
        int theMinute,
        int theSecond )
    {
        theHour = Hour;
        theMinute = Minute;
        theSecond = Second;
    }

    // constructor
    public Time( System.DateTime dt )
    {

        Year = dt.Year;
        Month = dt.Month;
        Date = dt.Day;
        Hour = dt.Hour;
        Minute = dt.Minute;
        Second = dt.Second;
    }


}

class Tester
{
    public void Run()
    {
        System.DateTime currentTime = System.DateTime.Now;
        Time t = new Time( currentTime );
        t.DisplayCurrentTime();

        int theHour = 0;
        int theMinute = 0;
        int theSecond = 0;
        t.GetTime( theHour, theMinute, theSecond );
        System.Console.WriteLine( "Current time: {0}:{1}:{2}",
        theHour, theMinute, theSecond );

    }

    static void Main()
    {
        Tester t = new Tester();
        t.Run();
    }
}
}
```

The output will look something like this:

```
7/1/2008 12:22:19
Current time: 0:0:0
```

Notice that the "Current time" in the output is 0:0:0. Clearly, this first attempt did not work. The problem is with the parameters. You pass in three integer parameters to GetTime( ), and you modify the parameters in GetTime( ), but when the values are accessed back in Run( ), they are unchanged. This is because integers are value types.

Passing Value Types by Reference

As discussed in Chapter 7, C# divides the world of types into value types and reference types. All intrinsic types (such as int and long) are value types. Instances of classes (objects) are reference types.

When you pass a value type (such as an int) into a method, a copy is made. When you make changes to the parameter, you make changes to the copy. Back in the Run( ) method, the original integer variables—theHour, theMinute, and theSecond—are unaffected by the changes made in GetTime( ).

What you need is a way to pass in the integer parameters by reference so that changes made in the method are made to the original object in the calling method. When you pass an object by reference, the parameter refers to the same object. Thus when you make changes in GetTime( ), the changes are also made to the original variables in Run( ).

 Please ignore this note as it is advanced, confusing, and put here just to cut down on my email. *Technically*, when you pass a reference type, it is in fact passed by value; but the copy that is made is a copy of a reference, and thus that copy points to the same (unnamed) object on the heap as did the original reference object. That is how you achieve the semantics of "pass by reference" in C# using pass by value.

This is the last time I'll point out this esoteric idea as it is perfectly reasonable to consider the reference to be the object. It takes too long to refer to Fido as a "reference to an unnamed Dog object on the heap"; it is easier to say Fido is a Dog object, and it is reasonable to imagine that Fido is passed by reference, even though (technically) we know better.

Not only is this shorthand reasonable, it is how most professional programmers think and talk about it. In most cases, it comes down to a distinction without a meaningful difference.

This requires two small modifications to the code in Example 8-3. First, change the parameters of the GetTime( ) method to indicate that the parameters are ref (reference) parameters:

```
public void GetTime(
    ref int theHour,
```

```
        ref int theMinute,
        ref int theSecond )
    {
        theHour = Hour;
        theMinute = Minute;
        theSecond = Second;
    }
```

Second, modify the call to GetTime( ) to pass the arguments as references:

```
t.GetTime(ref theHour, ref theMinute, ref theSecond);
```

 If you leave out the second step of marking the arguments with the keyword ref, the compiler will complain that the argument cannot be converted from an int to a ref int.

These changes are shown in Example 8-4.

Example 8-4. Passing by reference

```
using System;

namespace PassByRef
{

    public class Time
    {
        // private member variables
        private int Year;
        private int Month;
        private int Date;
        private int Hour;
        private int Minute;
        private int Second;


        // public accessor methods
        public void DisplayCurrentTime()
        {
            System.Console.WriteLine( "{0}/{1}/{2} {3}:{4}:{5}",
            Month, Date, Year, Hour, Minute, Second );
        }

        // takes references to ints
        public void GetTime(
            ref int theHour,
            ref int theMinute,
            ref int theSecond )
        {
            theHour = Hour;
            theMinute = Minute;
            theSecond = Second;
        }
```

Example 8-4. Passing by reference (continued)

```
    // constructor
    public Time( System.DateTime dt )
    {

        Year = dt.Year;
        Month = dt.Month;
        Date = dt.Day;
        Hour = dt.Hour;
        Minute = dt.Minute;
        Second = dt.Second;

    }


}

class Tester
{
    public void Run()
    {
        System.DateTime currentTime = System.DateTime.Now;
        Time t = new Time( currentTime );
        t.DisplayCurrentTime();

        int theHour = 0;
        int theMinute = 0;
        int theSecond = 0;

        // pass the ints by reference
        t.GetTime( ref theHour, ref theMinute, ref theSecond );

        System.Console.WriteLine( "Current time: {0}:{1}:{2}",
        theHour, theMinute, theSecond );

    }

    static void Main()
    {
        Tester t = new Tester();
        t.Run();
    }
}
}
```

This time, the output looks like this:

```
7/1/2008 12:25:41
Current time: 12:25:41
```

The results now show the correct time.

By declaring these parameters to be ref parameters, you instruct the compiler to pass them by reference. Instead of a copy being made, the parameters in GetTime( ) are references to the corresponding variables (theHour, theMinute, theSecond) that were created in Run( ). When you change these values in GetTime( ), the change is reflected in Run( ).

Keep in mind that ref parameters are references to the actual original value—it is as if you said, "here, work on this one." Conversely, value parameters are copies—it is as if you said, "here, work on one *just like* this."

out Parameters and Definite Assignment

As noted in Chapter 4, C# imposes *definite assignment*, which requires that all variables be assigned a value before they are used. In Example 8-4, you initialize theHour, theMinute, and theSecond before you pass them as parameters to GetTime( ), yet the initialization merely sets their values to 0 before they are passed to the method:

```
int theHour = 0;
int theMinute = 0;
int theSecond = 0;
t.GetTime( ref theHour, ref theMinute, ref theSecond);
```

It seems silly to initialize these values because you immediately pass them by reference into GetTime( ) where they'll be changed, but if you don't, the following compiler errors are reported:

```
Use of unassigned local variable 'theHour'
Use of unassigned local variable 'theMinute'
Use of unassigned local variable 'theSecond'
```

C# provides the out modifier for situations like this, in which initializing a parameter is only a formality. The out modifier removes the requirement that a reference parameter be initialized. The parameters to GetTime( ), for example, provide no information to the method; they are simply a mechanism for getting information out of it. Thus, by marking all three as out parameters using the out keyword, you eliminate the need to initialize them outside the method.

Within the called method, the out parameters must be assigned a value before the method returns. Here are the altered parameter declarations for GetTime( ):

```
public void GetTime(
    out int theHour,
    out int theMinute,
    out int theSecond )
{
    theHour = Hour;
    theMinute = Minute;
    theSecond = Second;
}
```

Here is the new invocation of the method in Main( ):

```
int theHour;
int theMinute;
int theSecond;
t.GetTime( out theHour, out theMinute, out theSecond);
```

The keyword out implies the same semantics as the keyword ref, except that it also allows you to use the variable without first initializing it in the calling method.

Summary

- Overloading is the act of creating two or more methods with the same name, but that differ in the number and/or type of parameters.
- Properties appear to clients to be members, but appear to the designer of the class to be methods. This allows the designer to modify how the property retrieves its value without breaking the semantics of the client program.
- Properties include get and set accessors that are used to retrieve and modify a member field, respectively. The set accessor has an implicit parameter named value that represents the value to be assigned through the property.
- When you "pass by reference," the called method affects the object referred to in the calling method. When you pass by value, the changes in the called method are not reflected in the calling method. You can pass value types by reference by using either the ref or the out keyword.
- The out parameter eliminates the requirement to initialize a variable before passing it to a method.

Quiz

Question 8-1. What is method overloading and how must the overloaded methods differ?

Question 8-2. What is the signature of a method?

Question 8-3. What are properties?

Question 8-4. How do you create a read-only property?

Question 8-5. How do you retrieve more than one return value from a method?

Question 8-6. Where must you use the keyword ref?

Question 8-7. What is the keyword out used for?

Exercises

Exercise 8-1. Write a program with an overloaded method for doubling the value of the argument. One version of the method should double an int value, and the other version should double a float value. Call both methods to demonstrate that they work.

Exercise 8-2. Write a program with one method that takes an int value, and returns both double and triple that value. You'll need to use reference parameters.

Exercise 8-3. Modify the program from Exercise 8-2 so that you don't need to initialize the variables that will hold the doubled and tripled values before calling the method.

CHAPTER 9
Basic Debugging

The debugger is your friend. There is simply no tool more powerful than a debugger for learning C# and for writing quality C# programs. Put simply, the debugger is a tool that helps you understand what is really going on when your program is running. It is the x-ray of software development, allowing you to see inside programs and diagnose potential problems.

Without a debugger, you are guessing; with a debugger, you are seeing. It is as simple as that. Whatever time you invest in learning to use your debugger is time well spent.

The debugger is also a powerful tool for understanding code written by others. By putting someone else's code into the debugger and stepping through it, you can see exactly how the methods work and what data they manipulate.

 This book assumes you are working with Visual Studio 2005 (in one form or another).

The Visual Studio debugger provides a number of windows for watching and interacting with your program while it executes. Getting comfortable with the debugger can make the difference between quickly finding bugs and struggling for hours or days.

Setting a Breakpoint

To get started with the debugger, return to Example 8-1. You'll be putting a *breakpoint* on the first line of Main( ) to see how this code actually works. A breakpoint is an instruction to the debugger to stop running. You set a breakpoint, run the program, and the debugger runs the program up until the breakpoint. Then you have the opportunity to examine the value of your variables at this point in the execution. Examining your program as it runs can help you untangle otherwise impenetrable problems. It is common to set multiple breakpoints, which allows you to skip through your program, examining the state of your object at selected locations.

You can set a breakpoint in many different ways. The easiest is to click in the far-left margin. This causes a red dot to appear in the margin next to the relevant line of code, which is also highlighted in red, as shown in Figure 9-1. Notice that as you hover over the breakpoint, it tells you the line on which the breakpoint appears.

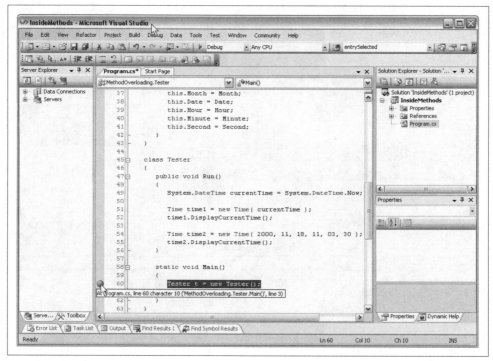

Figure 9-1. Setting a breakpoint

You are now ready to run the program to the breakpoint. To do so, you must be sure to run in debug mode, which you can do by clicking the Start button or by choosing the Start Debugging item from the Debug menu. In any case, the program starts and runs to the breakpoint, as shown in Figure 9-2.

The program stops just before executing the statement with the breakpoint, and that statement is highlighted. There are a number of helpful windows open as well, which we'll examine in a moment.

The most useful feature of the debugger is the ability to *step into* the code, or execute the program one line at a time, watching the changes that happen with each line. To step into the code, press the F11 function key twice. With the first keypress, the Tester object is created. The second keypress moves you to the next line in the

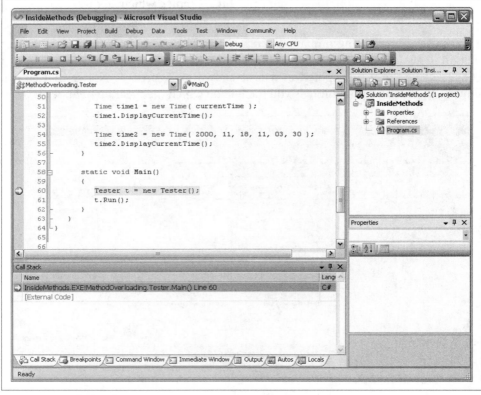

Figure 9-2. At the breakpoint

code, which calls the Run( ) method. Press the key once more to *step inside* the code for the Run( ) method where the program assigns the value of System.DateTime.Now to the currentTime variable.

> F11 and F10 are the step commands. The difference is that F10 steps over method calls, while F11 steps into them.
>
> With F10, the methods are executed, but you don't see each step within the method in the debugger; the highlighting jumps to the next statement after the method call. When you step into the method call with F11, on the other hand, the highlighting will move to the first line of the called method.
>
> If you use F11 to step into a method you actually meant to step over, Shift-F11 will step you out. The method you stepped into will run to completion, and you'll break on the first line back in the calling method.

Using the Debug Menu to Set Your Breakpoint

Instead of clicking in the margin to set your breakpoint, you can use the New Breakpoint item on the Debug menu (or use the keyboard shortcut for the menu item, Ctrl-D, N). This brings up the New Breakpoint dialog box, as shown in Figure 9-3. In this dialog box, you can specify the name of the method where you want to break, and even the line and character within the method, if you know it.

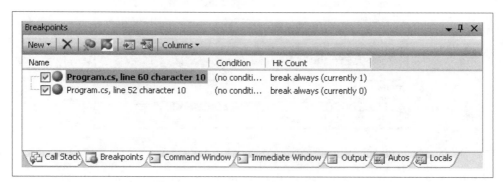

Figure 9-3. The New Breakpoint dialog

You can also examine and manipulate all the breakpoints together in the Breakpoints window, as shown in Figure 9-4.

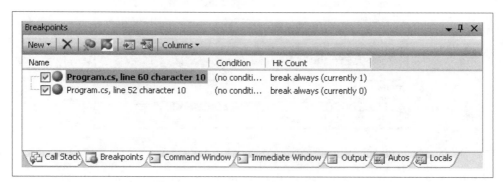

Figure 9-4. Breakpoints window

Setting Conditions and Hit Counts

The default behavior is for the breakpoint to cause the program to break every time you pass that line of code. Sometimes you only want to break (for example) every 20th time it passes that line of code, or only if the value of some variable is greater than, for example, 0. You can set conditions on the breakpoint by right clicking on it in the Editor window or in the Breakpoints window, as shown in Figure 9-5.

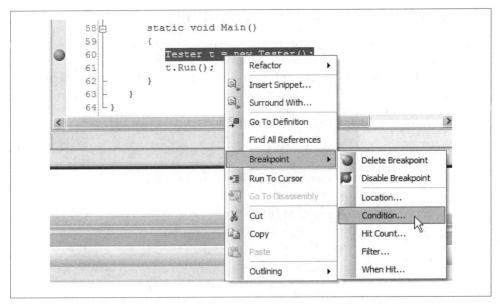

Figure 9-5. Breakpoint menu

Choose either Hit Count or Condition. If you choose Hit Count, you are offered variations such as "when the hit count is a multiple of…," as shown in Figure 9-6.

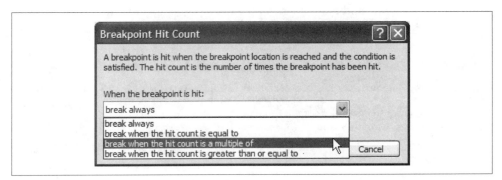

Figure 9-6. Breakpoint Hit Count dialog

If you choose Condition, an open-ended condition text box is provided. In Figure 9-7, I have typed in the Value > 20 as an example.

Examining Values: The Autos and Locals Windows

Look at the tabs below the code window; you'll find a Locals window and an Autos window. Both of these display your local variables. The difference is that the Autos window shows variables used in the current statement and the previous statement. (The current statement is the statement at the current execution location, which is

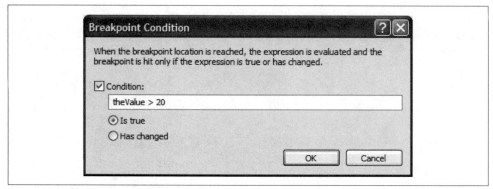

Figure 9-7. Breakpoint Condition dialog

highlighted *automatically* in the debugger—thus, the window's name.) The Locals window displays all the variables in the current method, including parameters, as shown in Figure 9-8, along with each variable's current value and type.

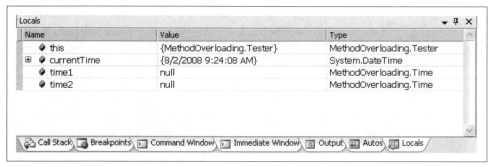

Figure 9-8. Locals window

 The debugger stacks the Autos and Locals windows together with other tabs, as shown in Figure 9-8. You are free to separate these windows or to move them to be tabbed with other windows. You can simply drag and drop the windows where you want them. When you drop one window on another, the two windows are tabbed together.

To see how this works, put a break point on the first line of the Run( ) method and run the program. When the program stops, click F10 to step over the creation of the new DateTime object. The Autos window shows you that the current time has been set to the current date, as shown in Figure 9-9.

Because the value of currentTime has just been set, it is shown in red. Notice the plus sign (+) next to the currentTime variable. This variable is of type System.DateTime, which is a type with many members. Expanding the plus sign reveals the state of this object, as shown in Figure 9-10.

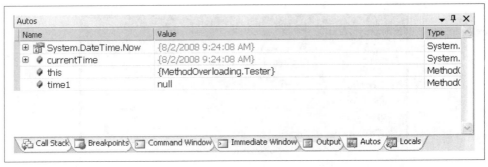

Figure 9-9. Autos variables window

Figure 9-10. Expanding the variable

Press F11 again to step into the Time class constructor. When you step into the Time constructor, the Autos window changes to show you the new values, appropriate to the current line of code.

As mentioned earlier, the Locals window lets you look at all the variables in the current method simultaneously. In this series of examples, clicking on the Locals window reveals the local variables dt (the parameter) and this (the current object). Expand the this variable, and you'll see the Time object, with its members uninitialized. Press F11 to progress through the assignment of values to the member variables of the Time class. As you hit the F11 key, the update is reflected in the Locals window, as shown in Figure 9-11.

Explore the Locals and Autos windows as you step through the program. When you want to stop, choose the Stop debugging item from the Debug menu to stop processing and return to the editor.

Set Your Watch

When you're debugging a program with many local variables, you usually don't want to watch all of them; you only need to keep track of a few. You can track specific variables and objects in the Watch window. You can have up to four Watch windows at a

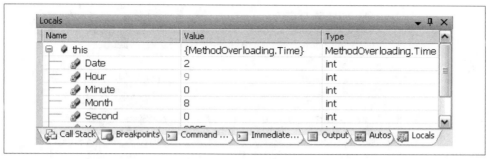

Figure 9-11. Watching assignment

time. Watch windows are like by-invitation versions of the Locals window; they list the objects you ask the debugger to keep an eye on, and you can see their values change as you step through the program, as illustrated in Figure 9-12.

Name	Value	Type
⊟ ● currentTime	{8/2/2008 9:24:08 AM}	System.DateTime
⊞ 🔧 Date	{8/2/2008 12:00:00 AM}	System.DateTime
🔧 Day	2	int
🔧 DayOfWeek	Tuesday	System.DayOfWeek
🔧 DayOfYear	214	int
🔧 Hour	9	int
🔧 Kind	Local	System.DateTimeKind
🔧 Millisecond	148	int
🔧 Minute	24	int
🔧 Month	8	int
🔧 Second	8	int
🔧 Ticks	632585714481486250	long
⊞ 🔧 TimeOfDay	{09:24:08.1486250}	System.TimeSpan

Call Stack | Breakpoints | Command Window | Immediate Window | Output | Autos | Watch 1 | Locals

Figure 9-12. A Watch window

The Watch windows are usually tabbed with the Locals window. You can create more than one Watch window to organize the variables you keep an eye on, by selecting Watch 1 through Watch 4 from the Debug menu. You can add a watch by right-clicking on a variable and choosing Add Watch, or just drag the variable to the Watch window. The variable will be added to your Watch window. To remove a variable that you've added to your Watch window, right click on it in the Watch list, and select Delete.

If you just need to peek at a variable, and perhaps to experiment with manipulating its value, you can right-click on it and choose QuickWatch, which opens a dialog box with watch information about a single object, as shown in Figure 9-13.

You can enter any expression into the Expression field and evaluate it from within the QuickWatch window. For example, suppose you had integer variables named varOne and varTwo:

```
int varOne = 5;
int varTwo = 7;
```

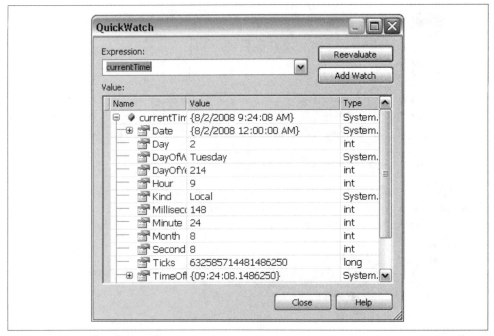

Figure 9-13. QuickWatch window

If you want to know the impact of multiplying them, enter:

```
varOne * varTwo
```

into the Expression window and click Reevaluate. The value is shown in the Value window, as in Figure 9-14.

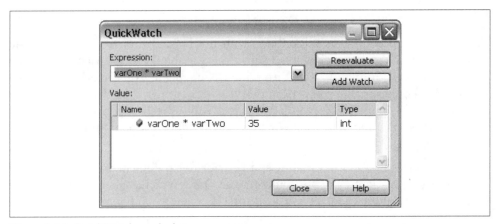

Figure 9-14. QuickWatch recalculation

If you decide that you want to add the variable to a Watch window after all, click the Add Watch button.

The Call Stack

As you step in and out of methods, the Call Stack window keeps track of the order and hierarchy of method calls. Figure 9-15 shows a close-up picture of the Call Stack window. You can see that the Time constructor was called by the Run( ) method, while the Run( ) method was in turn called by Main( ).

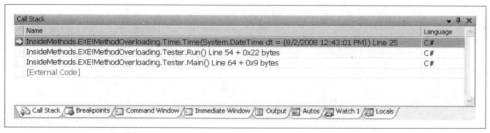

Figure 9-15. The Call Stack window

In this case, if you double-click on the second line in the Call Stack window, the debugger shows you the line in Run( ) that called the Time constructor, as shown in Figure 9-16. Notice that the debugger puts a curved arrow on the line in the call stack you've double-clicked on, and a matching arrow in the editor to the line that corresponds to that call. This way, if you're debugging a method, and you think that the data causing the problem came from outside the method, you can quickly find where the method call came from, and check the values at that point.

Summary

- Visual Studio 2005 includes a powerful debugger that lets you step through your program and examine the value of variables and objects as methods execute.
- You can set breakpoints in your code, which causes execution to stop when it reaches that point. Break points can be set to stop every time, every nth time, or when a particular condition is true.
- Press F11 to step into called methods, and F10 to skip over method calls.
- The Autos window displays the values of the variables used in the current statement and the previous statement. The Locals window shows the values of all the variables in the current method.
- The Watch window allows you to keep an eye on variables or objects as your method executes, revealing not only their value, but with complex objects allowing you to "drill down" into their internal state.

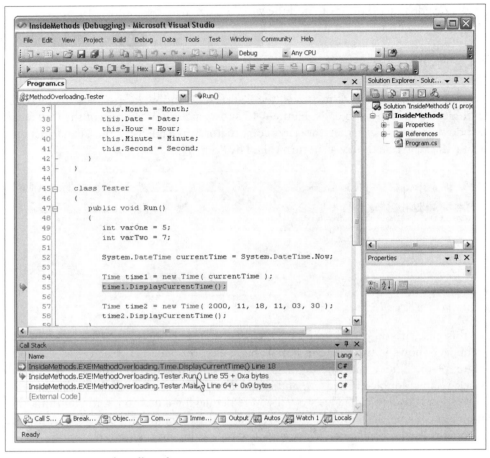

Figure 9-16. Tracing the call stack

- The QuickWatch window displays information about a single object, and allows you to manipulate that object without changing the value of the object in the running program.
- The Call Stack window shows you the method that called your currently executing method, and the method that invoked *that* method, and so forth, so that you can see how you arrived at the currently executing method.

Quiz

Question 9-1. What is the easiest way to set a breakpoint?

Question 9-2. How do you step over or into a method?

Question 9-3. How can you disable breakpoints, and set conditions on breakpoints?

Question 9-4. What is the difference between the Locals window and the Autos window?

Question 9-5. What is the easiest way to set a watch on a variable?

Question 9-6. How do you open a QuickWatch window?

Question 9-7. What does the call stack show and why is it useful?

Exercises

Exercise 9-1. You'll use the following program for this exercise. Either type it into Visual Studio, or copy it from this book's web site. Note that this is spaghetti code— you'd never write method calls like this, but that's why this is the debugging chapter.

```
using System;

namespace Debugging
{

    class Tester
    {
        public void Run( )
        {

            int myInt = 42;
            float myFloat = 9.685f;

            System.Console.WriteLine("Before starting: \n value of myInt: {0} \n
            value of myFloat: {1}", myInt, myFloat);

            // pass the variables by reference
            Multiply( ref myInt, ref myFloat );

            System.Console.WriteLine("After finishing: \n value of myInt: {0} \n
            value of myFloat: {1}", myInt, myFloat);

        }

        private static void Multiply (ref int theInt, ref float theFloat)
        {
            theInt = theInt * 2;
            theFloat = theFloat *2;

            Divide( ref theInt, ref theFloat);
        }
```

```
private static void Divide (ref int theInt, ref float theFloat)
{
    theInt = theInt / 3;
    theFloat = theFloat / 3;

    Add(ref theInt, ref theFloat);
}

public static void Add(ref int theInt, ref float theFloat)
{
    theInt = theInt + theInt;
    theFloat = theFloat + theFloat;
}

static void Main( )
{
    Tester t = new Tester( );
    t.Run( );
}
    }
}
```

1. Place a breakpoint in Run( ) on the following line:

```
System.Console.WriteLine("Before starting: \n value of myInt: {0} \n
                value of myFloat: {1}", myInt, myFloat);
```

2. Step into the Multiply( ) method, up to the call to Divide( ). What are the values of theInt and theFloat at this point?

3. Run the program again, and when it reaches the breakpoint in Run( ), set a watch on myInt. Step through the methods. When does the value of myInt change?

4. Set another breakpoint in Add( ) at this line:

```
theInt = theInt + theInt;
```

Run the program. How many calls are in the call stack when the program reaches this breakpoint?

Exercise 9-2. The program in this exercise is similar to the first, but it has a logic error. Type this program into Visual Studio, or download it from this book's web site.

```
using System;

namespace Debugging
{

    class Tester
    {
        public void Run( )
        {

            int myInt = 42;
            float myFloat = 9.685f;
```

```
System.Console.WriteLine("Before starting: \n value of myInt: {0} \n
value of myFloat: {1}", myInt, myFloat);

// pass the variables by reference
Multiply( ref myInt, ref myFloat );

System.Console.WriteLine("After finishing: \n value of myInt: {0} \n
value of myFloat: {1}", myInt, myFloat);

}

private static void Multiply (ref int theInt, ref float theFloat)
{
    theInt = theInt * 2;
    theFloat = theFloat *2;
    Divide( ref theInt, ref theFloat);
}

private static void Divide (ref int theInt, ref float theFloat)
{
    theInt = theInt * 3;
    theFloat = theFloat * 3;
    Add(ref theInt, ref theFloat);
}

public static void Add(ref int theInt, ref float theFloat)
{
    theInt = theInt - theInt;
    theFloat = theFloat - theFloat;
}

static void Main( )
{
    Tester t = new Tester( );
    t.Run( );
}
    }
}
```

If you run this program, you will not get the same results as you did in the previous
example. Use the debugging tools you just learned about to find the error. Correct
the error, and then run the program again to see if the results are correct.

CHAPTER 10

Arrays

Most of the examples in previous chapters have dealt with one object at a time. In many applications, however, you want to work with a *collection* of objects all at the same time. The simplest collection in C# is the array, the only collection type for which C# provides built-in support. The other collection types, such as stack and queue, are not part of the language; they are part of the Framework Class Library. The collection classes are covered in detail in Chapter 14. In this chapter, you will learn to work with three types of arrays: one-dimensional arrays, multidimensional rectangular arrays, and jagged arrays.

Using Arrays

Before we get to generic syntax, it makes sense to begin with the simplest collection: the array. An *array* is an indexed collection of objects, all of the same type (all ints, all strings, and so on). C# provides native syntax for the declaration of arrays. To picture a one-dimensional array, imagine a series of mailboxes, all lined up one after the other, as shown in Figure 10-1. Each mailbox can hold exactly one object (letter, box, and so on). Each mailbox also has a number, so you can identify which item is in which box. Unlike real-world mailboxes, though, all the mailboxes must hold the same kind of object; you declare the type of object that the mailboxes will hold when you declare the array.

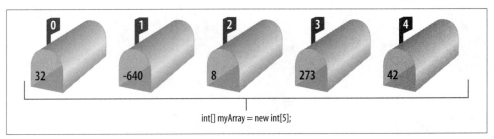

Figure 10-1. An array of five integers

The important thing about arrays is that you can treat the entire array (the set of mailboxes) as a single entity, with a single name. As you'll see, using loops, you can easily perform an operation on every element within an array in turn.

Declaring Arrays

Declare a C# array with the following syntax:

```
type[] array-name;
```

For example:

```
int[] myIntArray;
```

 You are not actually declaring an array. Technically, you are declaring a variable (myIntArray) that will hold a reference to an array of integers. As always, we'll use the shorthand and refer to myIntArray as the array, knowing that what we really mean is that it is a variable that holds a reference to an (unnamed) array.

The square brackets ([]) tell the C# compiler that you are declaring an array, and the type specifies the type of the elements it will contain. In the previous example, myIntArray is an array of integers.

Instantiate an array using the new keyword. For example:

```
myIntArray = new int[5];
```

This statement creates and intializes an array of five integers, all of which are initialized to the value zero.

It is important to distinguish between the array itself (which is a collection) and the elements held in the array (which can be of any type, so long as all the elements in the array are the same type). myIntArray is the array (or, more accurately, the variable that holds the reference to the array); its elements are the five integers it holds.

C# arrays are reference types, created on the heap. Thus, the array to which the variable myIntArray refers is allocated on the heap. The *elements* of an array are allocated based on their own type. Because integers are value types, the elements in myIntArray will be value types, and thus all the elements will be created inside the block of memory allocated for the array.

The block of memory allocated to an array of reference types will contain references to the actual elements, which are themselves created on the heap in memory separate from that allocated for the array.

Understanding Default Values

When you create an array of value types, each element initially contains the default value for the type stored in the array (see Table 3-1). The statement:

```
myIntArray = new int[5];
```

creates an array of five integers, each of whose value is set to 0, which is the default value for integer types.

Unlike arrays of value types, the reference types in an array are not initialized to their default value. Instead, the references held in the array are initialized to null. If you attempt to access an element in an array of reference types before you have specifically initialized the elements, you will generate an exception.

Assume you have created a Button class. Declare an array of Button objects with the following statement:

```
Button[] myButtonArray;
```

and instantiate the actual array like this:

```
myButtonArray = new Button[3];
```

You can shorten this to:

```
Button[] myButtonArray = new Button[3];
```

This statement does *not* create an array with references to three Button objects. Instead, this creates the array myButtonArray with three null references. To use this array, you must first construct and assign the Button objects for each reference in the array. You can construct the objects in a loop that adds them one by one to the array, as you'll see later in the chapter.

Accessing Array Elements

You can access the elements of an array using the index operator ([ ]). Arrays are zero-based, which means that the index of the first element is always zero—in this case, myArray[0].

The Length property of the array tells you how many objects the array holds. Therefore, objects are indexed from 0 to Length-1.

Example 10-1 illustrates the array concepts covered so far. In this example, a class named Tester creates an array of Employees and an array of integers, populates the Employee array, and then prints the values of both.

Example 10-1. Working with an array

```
using System;
namespace Learning_CSharp
{
```

Example 10-1. Working with an array (continued)

```
// a simple class to store in the array
public class Employee
{

    public Employee(int empID)
    {
        this.empID = empID;
    }
    public override string ToString()
    {
        return empID.ToString();
    }
    private int empID;
}
public class Tester
{
    static void Main()
    {
        int[] intArray;
        Employee[] empArray;
        intArray = new int[5];
        empArray = new Employee[3];

        // populate the arrays
        for (int i = 0;i<intArray.Length;i++)
        {
            intArray[i] = i*2;
        }

        for (int i = 0;i<empArray.Length;i++)
        {
            empArray[i] = new Employee(i+1005);
        }

        // output array values
        Console.WriteLine("intArray values:");
        for (int i = 0;i<intArray.Length;i++)
        {
            Console.WriteLine(intArray[i].ToString());
        }

        Console.WriteLine("\nemployee IDs:");
        for (int i = 0;i<empArray.Length;i++)
        {
            Console.WriteLine(empArray[i].ToString());
        }
    }
}
}
```

The output looks like this:

```
intArray values:
0
2
4
6
8

employee IDs:
1005
1006
1007
```

The example starts with the definition of an `Employee` class that implements a constructor that takes a single integer parameter. `Employee` implements the `ToString()` method to print the value of the `Employee` object's employee ID.

The test method declares and then instantiates a pair of arrays. Initially, the integer array is automatically filled with integers whose value is set to 0, but then you populate it with a `for` loop. The loop has a counter, `i`, and you *iterate* through the loop by setting each element of the array as the index value (`i`) increases. You set the value in `intArray` with this statement:

```
intArray[i] = i*2;
```

The first time through the loop, `i` is equal to 0, and `intArray[0]` is set to 0*2, which is 0. The next time through, `i` is 1, and the second element (`intArray[1]`) is set to the value 2 (1*2). The loop runs until `i` is equal to `intArray.Length`, at which point it stops. Note that `i` is equal to `intArray.Length - 1` on the last time through the loop, which is the index of the last element in the array.

It's not hard to remember that arrays start at 0, but it can be tricky to remember that the highest index is actually *one less* than `Length`. When you use a loop to iterate through your array, always make sure that your condition for ending the loop is `counter < Array.Length`, not `counter <= Array.Length`.

C# is smarter than its C++ and C ancestors; if you do try to write past the end of the array, rather than trampling on random memory, you'll get an "IndexOutOfRange" exception, which will help you find the error quickly and reliably.

In any case, you want always to be on the lookout for what programmers call the "off-by-one" error. A famous example of this is the fencepost error. Imagine you are building a picket fence, where each horizontal board is one foot long. How many uprights do you need to build a 10-foot fence?*

---

* It is tempting to say 10 uprights for a 10-foot fence. But how many do you need for a one-foot fence? You need two, one on each end of the one-foot board. For a two-foot fence, you need three. You always need that extra upright, and so for a 10-foot fence, you need 11 uprights. Watch out for off-by-one errors; they come up a lot.

The Employee array contents must be constructed by hand, because the values of reference types are not initialized when the array is created (the array is filled with null values). You assign values to the elements of empArray the same way you did intArray, with a for loop. This time, though, you have to create a new Employee object to add to each index in the array

Finally, the contents of the arrays are displayed to ensure that they are filled as intended, using the same for loop technique. The five integers print their value first, followed by the three Employee objects.

The foreach Statement

The foreach statement allows you to iterate through all the items in an array or other collection, examining each item in turn. The syntax for the foreach statement is:

> foreach (*type identifier* in *expression*) *statement*

You can update Example 10-1 to replace the final two for statements (that iterate over the contents of the populated array) with foreach statements, as shown in Example 10-2.

Example 10-2. Using foreach

```
foreach ( int i in intArray )
{
   Console.WriteLine( i.ToString() );
}
foreach ( Employee e in empArray )
{
   Console.WriteLine( e.ToString() );
}
```

The output will be identical.

Initializing Array Elements

You can initialize the contents of an array at the time it is instantiated by providing a list of values delimited by curly brackets ({}). C# provides a longer and a shorter syntax:

```
int[] myIntArray = new int[5] { 2, 4, 6, 8, 10 };
int[] myIntArray = { 2, 4, 6, 8, 10 };
```

In the shorter syntax, C# automatically creates an array of the proper size for the number of elements in the brackets. There is no practical difference between these two statements, and most programmers will use the shorter syntax.

The params Keyword

The params keyword allows you to pass in a variable number of parameters of the same type to a method. What the method receives is an array of that type.

In the next example, you create a method, DisplayVals( ), that takes a variable number of integer arguments:

```
public void DisplayVals(params int[] intVals)
```

You are free to iterate over the array as you would over any other array of integers:

```
foreach (int i in intVals)
{
    Console.WriteLine("DisplayVals {0}",i);
}
```

The calling method, however, need not explicitly create an array: it can simply pass in integers, and the compiler will assemble the parameters into an array for the DisplayVals( ) method:

```
t.DisplayVals(5,6,7,8);
```

You are free to pass in an array if you prefer:

```
int [] explicitArray = new int[5] {1,2,3,4,5};
t.DisplayVals(explicitArray);
```

 You can only use one params argument for each method you create, and the params argument must be the last argument in the method's signature.

Example 10-3 illustrates using the params keyword.

Example 10-3. Using the params keyword

```
using System;

namespace UsingParams
{
    public class Tester
    {
        static void Main( )
        {
            Tester t = new Tester();
            t.DisplayVals(5,6,7,8);
            int [] explicitArray = new int[] {1,2,3,4,5};
            t.DisplayVals(explicitArray);
        }

        public void DisplayVals(params int[] intVals)
        {
            foreach (int i in intVals)
            {
```

Example 10-3. Using the params keyword (continued)

```
            Console.WriteLine("DisplayVals {0}",i);
        }
    }
  }
}
```

The output looks like this:

```
DisplayVals 5
DisplayVals 6
DisplayVals 7
DisplayVals 8
DisplayVals 1
DisplayVals 2
DisplayVals 3
DisplayVals 4
DisplayVals 5
```

Multidimensional Arrays

Arrays can be thought of as long rows of slots into which values can be placed. Once you have a picture of a row of slots, imagine 10 rows, one on top of another. This is the classic two-dimensional array of rows and columns. The rows run across the array and the columns run up and down the array, as shown in Figure 10-2.

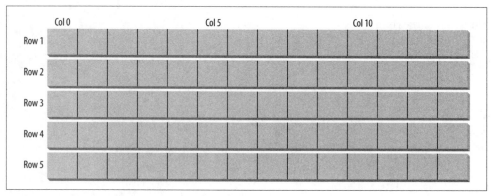

Figure 10-2. Rows and columns create a multidimensional array

A third dimension is a bit harder to imagine. Okay, now imagine four dimensions. Now imagine 10.

Those of you who are not string-theory physicists have probably given up, as have I. Multidimensional arrays are useful, however, even if you can't quite picture what they would look like.

C# supports two types of multidimensional arrays: rectangular and jagged. In a rectangular array, every row is the same length. A jagged array, however, is an array of arrays, each of which can be a different length.

Rectangular Arrays

A *rectangular array* is an array of two (or more) dimensions. In the classic two-dimensional array, the first dimension is the number of rows and the second dimension is the number of columns.

To declare a two-dimensional array, use the following syntax:

```
type [,] array-name
```

For example, to declare and instantiate a two-dimensional rectangular array named myRectangularArray that contains two rows and three columns of integers, you would write:

```
int [,] myRectangularArray = new int[2,3];
```

Example 10-4 declares, instantiates, initializes, and prints the contents of a two-dimensional array. In this example, a for loop is used to initialize the elements of the array.

Example 10-4. Rectangular arrays

```
using System;

namespace RectangularArray
{
    public class Tester
    {
        static void Main( )
        {
            const int rows = 4;
            const int columns = 3;

            // declare a 4x3 integer array
            int[,] rectangularArray = new int[rows, columns];

            // populate the array
            for ( int i = 0; i < rows; i++ )
            {
                for ( int j = 0; j < columns; j++ )
                {
                    rectangularArray[i, j] = i + j;
                }
            }

            // report the contents of the array
            for ( int i = 0; i < rows; i++ )
            {
                for ( int j = 0; j < columns; j++ )
```

Example 10-4. Rectangular arrays (continued)

```
        {
            Console.WriteLine( "rectangularArray[{0},{1}] = {2}",
                i, j, rectangularArray[i, j] );
        }
    }
  }
 }
}
```

The output looks like this:

```
rectangularArray[0,0] = 0
rectangularArray[0,1] = 1
rectangularArray[0,2] = 2
rectangularArray[1,0] = 1
rectangularArray[1,1] = 2
rectangularArray[1,2] = 3
rectangularArray[2,0] = 2
rectangularArray[2,1] = 3
rectangularArray[2,2] = 4
rectangularArray[3,0] = 3
rectangularArray[3,1] = 4
rectangularArray[3,2] = 5
```

The brackets in the `int[,]` declaration indicate that the type is an array of integers, and the comma indicates the array has two dimensions (two commas would indicate three dimensions, and so on). The actual instantiation of `rectangularArray` with `new int[rows, columns]` sets the size of each dimension. Here, the declaration and instantiation have been combined.

The program fills the rectangle with a pair of nested for loops, iterating through each column in each row. Thus, the first element filled is `rectangularArray[0,0]`, followed by `rectangularArray[0,1]` and `rectangularArray[0,2]`. Once this is done, the program moves on to the next rows: `rectangularArray[1,0]`, `rectangularArray[1,1]`, `rectangularArray[1,2]`, and so forth, until all the columns in all the rows are filled.

Just as you can initialize a one-dimensional array using bracketed lists of values, you can initialize a two-dimensional array using similar syntax. Example 10-5 declares a two-dimensional array (`rectangularArray`), initializes its elements using bracketed lists of values, and then prints out the contents.

Example 10-5. Initializing a multidimensional array

```
using System;

namespace InitializingMultiDimensionalArray
{
    public class Tester
    {
        static void Main( )
        {
```

Example 10-5. Initializing a multidimensional array (continued)

```
        const int rows = 4;
        const int columns = 3;

        // imply a 4x3 array
        int[,] rectangularArray =
        {
            {0,1,2}, {3,4,5}, {6,7,8}, {9,10,11}
        };

        for ( int i = 0; i < rows; i++ )
        {
            for ( int j = 0; j < columns; j++ )
            {
                Console.WriteLine( "rectangularArray[{0},{1}] = {2}",
                    i, j, rectangularArray[i, j] );
            }
        }
    }
  }
}
```

The output looks like this:

```
rectangularArrayrectangularArray[0,0] = 0
rectangularArrayrectangularArray[0,1] = 1
rectangularArrayrectangularArray[0,2] = 2
rectangularArrayrectangularArray[1,0] = 3
rectangularArrayrectangularArray[1,1] = 4
rectangularArrayrectangularArray[1,2] = 5
rectangularArrayrectangularArray[2,0] = 6
rectangularArrayrectangularArray[2,1] = 7
rectangularArrayrectangularArray[2,2] = 8
rectangularArrayrectangularArray[3,0] = 9
rectangularArrayrectangularArray[3,1] = 10
rectangularArrayrectangularArray[3,2] = 11
```

The preceding example is very similar to Example 10-4, but this time you *imply* the exact dimensions of the array by how you initialize it:

```
int[,] rectangularArrayrectangularArray =
{
    {0,1,2}, {3,4,5}, {6,7,8}, {9,10,11}
};
```

Assigning values in four bracketed lists, each consisting of three elements, implies a 4 (rows) by 3 (columns) array.

Had you written this as:

```
int[,] rectangularArrayrectangularArray =
{
    {0,1,2,3}, {4,5,6,7}, {8,9,10,11}
};
```

you would instead have implied a 3 by 4 array.

You can see that the C# compiler understands the implications of the way you grouped the input values, because it is able to access the objects with the appropriate offsets, as illustrated in the output.

C# arrays are "smart" and they keep track of their bounds. When you imply a 4×3 array, you must treat it as such, and not as a 3×4 array, or just an array of 12 integers (as you can with some other C-family languages).

Jagged Arrays

A *jagged array* is an array of arrays. It is called "jagged" because each of the rows need not be the same size as all the others, and thus a graphical representation of the array would not be square.

When you create a jagged array, you declare the number of rows in your array. Each row will hold an array, which can be of any length. These arrays must each be declared. You can then fill in the values for the elements in these "inner" arrays.

In a jagged array, each dimension is a one-dimensional array. To declare a jagged array, use the following syntax, where the number of brackets indicates the number of dimensions of the array:

```
type [] []...
```

For example, you would declare a two-dimensional jagged array of integers named myJaggedArray, as follows:

```
int [] [] myJaggedArray;
```

Access the fifth element of the third array by writing myJaggedArray[2][4].

 Remember that in all arrays, the first element is at offset 0 and the nth element is at offset n − 1; thus, the seventh element is at offset 6.

Example 10-6 creates a jagged array named myJaggedArray, initializes its elements, and then prints their content. To save space, the program takes advantage of the fact that integer array elements are automatically initialized to zero, and it initializes the values of only some of the elements.

Example 10-6. Working with a jagged array

```
using System;
namespace JaggedArray
{
    public class Tester
    {
        static void Main( )
        {
            const int rows = 4;
```

Example 10-6. Working with a jagged array (continued)

```
// declare the jagged array as 4 rows high
int[][] jaggedArray = new int[rows][];

// the first row has 5 elements
jaggedArray[0] = new int[5];

// a row with 2 elements
jaggedArray[1] = new int[2];

// a row with 3 elements
jaggedArray[2] = new int[3];

// the last row has 5 elements
jaggedArray[3] = new int[5];

// Fill some (but not all) elements of the rows
jaggedArray[0][3] = 15;
jaggedArray[1][1] = 12;
jaggedArray[2][1] = 9;
jaggedArray[2][2] = 99;
jaggedArray[3][0] = 10;
jaggedArray[3][1] = 11;
jaggedArray[3][2] = 12;
jaggedArray[3][3] = 13;
jaggedArray[3][4] = 14;

for ( int i = 0; i < 5; i++ )
{
   Console.WriteLine( "jaggedArray[0][{0}] = {1}",
      i, jaggedArray[0][i] );
}

for ( int i = 0; i < 2; i++ )
{
   Console.WriteLine( "jaggedArray[1][{0}] = {1}",
      i, jaggedArray[1][i] );
}

for ( int i = 0; i < 3; i++ )
{
   Console.WriteLine( "jaggedArray[2][{0}] = {1}",
      i, jaggedArray[2][i] );
}
for ( int i = 0; i < 5; i++ )
{
   Console.WriteLine( "jaggedArray[3][{0}] = {1}",
      i, jaggedArray[3][i] );
}
   }
  }
}
```

The output looks like this:

```
jaggedArray[0][0] = 0
jaggedArray[0][1] = 0
jaggedArray[0][2] = 0
jaggedArray[0][3] = 15
jaggedArray[0][4] = 0
jaggedArray[1][0] = 0
jaggedArray[1][1] = 12
jaggedArray[2][0] = 0
jaggedArray[2][1] = 9
jaggedArray[2][2] = 99
jaggedArray[3][0] = 10
jaggedArray[3][1] = 11
jaggedArray[3][2] = 12
jaggedArray[3][3] = 13
jaggedArray[3][4] = 14
```

In this example, a jagged array is created with four rows:

```
int[][] jaggedArray = new int[rows][];
```

Notice that the second dimension is not specified. This is set by creating a new array for each row. Each of these arrays can have a different size:

```
// the first row has 5 elements
jaggedArray[0] = new int[5];

// a row with 2 elements
jaggedArray[1] = new int[2];

// a row with 3 elements
jaggedArray[2] = new int[3];

// the last row has 5 elements
jaggedArray[3] = new int[5];
```

Once an array is specified for each row, you need only populate the various members of each array and then print out their contents to ensure that all went as expected.

Another way of outputting the values would be to use two nested for loops, and use the Length property of the array to control the loop:

```
for (int i = 0; i < jaggedArray.Length; i++ )
{
    for (int j = 0; j < jaggedArray[i].Length; j++)
    {
        Console.WriteLine("jaggedArray[{0}][{1}] = {2}",
        i, j, jaggedArray[i][j]);
    }
}
```

In this case, the "outer" for loop iterates over the rows in the array. The "inner" loop outputs each column in the given row. Because you're using Length to control how many times the loop runs, it doesn't matter that each row is a different length.

Notice that when you access the members of the rectangular array, you put the indexes all within one set of square brackets:

```
rectangularArrayrectangularArray[i,j]
```

while with a jagged array, you need a pair of brackets:

```
jaggedArray[i][j]
```

You can keep this straight by thinking of the first as a single array of more than one dimension and the jagged array as an array *of arrays*.

Array Methods

Although you've been using arrays as built-in types throughout this chapter, an array is actually an object of type System.Array.* Arrays in C# thus provide you with the best of both worlds: easy-to-use syntax underpinned with an actual class definition so that instances of an array have access to the methods and properties of System. Array. You've seen the Length property of arrays used several times already. Some of the other important methods and properties appear in Table 10-1.

Table 10-1. System.Array methods and properties

Method or property	Purpose
BinarySearch( )	Overloaded public static method that searches a one-dimensional sorted array
Clear( )	Public static method that sets a range of elements in the array either to zero or to a null reference
Copy( )	Overloaded public static method that copies a section of one array to another array
CreateInstance ( )	Overloaded public static method that instantiates a new instance of an array
IndexOf( )	Overloaded public static method that returns the index (offset) of the first instance of a value in a one-dimensional array
LastIndexOf( )	Overloaded public static method that returns the index of the last instance of a value in a one-dimensional array
Reverse( )	Overloaded public static method that reverses the order of the elements in a one-dimensional array
Sort( )	Overloaded public static method that sorts the values in a one-dimensional array
Length	Public property that returns the length of the array
GetEnumerator( )	Public method that returns an IEnumerator

---

* Of course, when you create an array with int[] myArray = new int[5], what you actually create in the IL code is an instance of System.int32[]. Because this derives from the Abstract Base Class System.Array, however, it is fair to say you've created an instance of a System.Array.

Sorting Arrays

Two useful static methods from Table 10-1 that deserve a closer look are Sort( ) and
Reverse( ). These methods do what you think they would: Reverse( ) reverses the
order of elements in the array, and Sort( ) sorts the elements in order. These are fully
supported for arrays of the built-in C# types, such as string, so sorting an array of
strings puts the elements in alphabetical order, and sorting an array of ints puts them
in numeric order. Making the Sort( ) method work with your own classes is a bit
trickier, as you must implement the IComparable interface (see Chapter 13 for more
on interfaces). Example 10-7 demonstrates the use of these two methods to manipulate String objects.

Example 10-7. Using Array.Sort and Array.Reverse

```
using System;

namespace ArraySortAndReverse
{
    public class Tester
    {
        public static void PrintMyArray( string[] theArray )
        {

            foreach ( string str in theArray )
            {
                Console.WriteLine( "Value: {0}", str );
            }
            Console.WriteLine( "\n" );
        }

        static void Main( )
        {
            String[] myArray =
                {
                    "Proust", "Faulkner", "Mann", "Hugo"
                };

            PrintMyArray( myArray );
            Array.Reverse( myArray );
            PrintMyArray( myArray );

            String[] myOtherArray =
                {
                    "We", "Hold", "These", "Truths",
                    "To", "Be", "Self","Evident",
                };
```

Example 10-7. Using Array.Sort and Array.Reverse (continued)

```
        PrintMyArray( myOtherArray );
        Array.Sort( myOtherArray );
        PrintMyArray( myOtherArray );

    }
  }
}
```

The output looks like this:

```
Value: Proust
Value: Faulkner
Value: Mann
Value: Hugo

Value: Hugo
Value: Mann
Value: Faulkner
Value: Proust

Value: We
Value: Hold
Value: These
Value: Truths
Value: To
Value: Be
Value: Self
Value: Evident

Value: Be
Value: Evident
Value: Hold
Value: Self
Value: These
Value: To
Value: Truths
Value: We
```

The example begins by creating myArray, an array of strings with the words:

```
"Proust", "Faulkner", "Mann", "Hugo"
```

This array is printed, and then passed to the Array.Reverse( ) method, where it is printed again to see that the array itself has been reversed:

```
Value: Hugo
Value: Mann
Value: Faulkner
Value: Proust
```

Similarly, the example creates a second array, myOtherArray, containing the words:

```
"We", "Hold", "These", "Truths",
"To", "Be", "Self", "Evident",
```

This is passed to the Array.Sort( ) method. Then Array.Sort( ) happily sorts them alphabetically:

```
Value: Be
Value: Evident
Value: Hold
Value: Self
Value: These
Value: To
Value: Truths
Value: We
```

 Array.Sort( ) and Array.Reverse( ) are static methods, meaning you call them on the class, not the object, as discussed in Chapter 7. That means you don't call myArray.Reverse( ) to reverse the elements; instead, you call the static method and pass in the array as an argument, like this:

```
Array.Reverse(myArray);
```

Summary

- An array is an indexed collection of objects, all of the same type.
- You declare an array by giving the type of objects the array contains, followed by the square bracket operator ([ ]), followed by the name of the array. You then instantiate the array with the new keyword and the number of elements the array will contain.
- The index of the first element in the array is always zero, and the index of the last element in the array is always Length-1.
- You can use a for loop to iterate through the array, by using the loop's counter as the index to the array.
- The foreach statement allows you to iterate through the items in the array (or any other collection) without the need for a counter.
- The elements of an array can be initialized when the array is created by providing the values of the members in curly braces ({}).
- The params keyword lets you pass an arbitrary number of parameters of the same type into a method; the method will treat the parameters as a single array.
- Arrays can contain more than one dimension. A two-dimensional array has two indexes, which you can think of as rows and columns.

- A rectangular array is a two-dimensional array in which all the rows have the same number of columns.
- A jagged array is an array of arrays—the rows do not need to be all the same length.
- The Length property of an array returns the total number of elements in the array.
- The array class contains a number of methods for searching, sorting, and manipulating the elements.

Quiz

Question 10-1. What is the index of the seventh member of an array?

Question 10-2. Are arrays type-safe?

Question 10-3. Are arrays reference or value types? And where are they created?

Question 10-4. Where are the elements of the array created?

Question 10-5. What are the two ways to initialize an array of three values?

Question 10-6. What does the params keyword do?

Question 10-7. What are the two types of multidimensional arrays and what is the difference between them?

Exercises

Exercise 10-1. Declare a Dog class with two private members: weight (an int), and name (a string). Be sure to add properties to access the members. Then create an array that holds three Dog objects (Milo, 26 pounds; Frisky, 10 pounds; and Laika, 50 pounds). Output each dog's name and weight.

Exercise 10-2. Create an array of 10 integers. Populate the array by having the user enter integers at the console (use Console.Readline). Don't worry about error-checking for this exercise. Output the integers sorted from greatest to least.

Exercise 10-3. Extend Exercise 10-1 by creating a two-dimensional array that represents a collection of strings that indicate the awards each dog has won at dog shows. Each dog may have a different number of awards won. Output the contents of the array to check its validity.

Exercise 10-4. Create a two-dimensional array that represents a chessboard (an 8×8 array). Each element in the array should contain either the string "black" or "white," depending on where it is on the board. Create a method that initializes the array with the strings. Then create a method that asks the reader to enter two integers for the coordinates of a square, and returns whether that square is black or white.

CHAPTER 11

Inheritance and Polymorphism

In Chapter 7, you learned how to create new types by declaring classes, and in Chapter 6, you saw a discussion of the principle object relationships of association, aggregation, and specialization. This chapter focuses on *specialization*, which is implemented in C# through *inheritance*. This chapter also explains how instances of more specialized classes can be treated as if they were instances of more general classes, a process known as *polymorphism*. This chapter ends with a consideration of *sealed classes*, which cannot be specialized, and a discussion of the root of all classes, the Object class.

Specialization and Generalization

Classes and their instances (objects) do not exist in a vacuum, but rather in a network of interdependencies and relationships, just as we, as social animals, live in a world of relationships and categories.

One of the most important relationships among objects in the real world is specialization, which can be described as the *is-a* relationship. When we say that a dog *is a* mammal, we mean that the dog is a specialized kind of mammal. It has all the characteristics of any mammal (it bears live young, nurses with milk, has hair), but it specializes these characteristics to the familiar characteristics of *canis domesticus*. A cat is also a mammal. As such, we expect it to share certain characteristics with the dog that are generalized in Mammal, but to differ in those characteristics that are specialized in cats.

The specialization and generalization relationships are both reciprocal and hierarchical. Specialization is just the other side of the generalization coin: Mammal generalizes what is common between dogs and cats, and dogs and cats specialize mammals to their own specific subtypes.

These relationships are hierarchical because they create a relationship tree, with specialized types branching off from more generalized types. As you move "up" the hierarchy, you achieve greater generalization. You move up toward Mammal to generalize that dogs, cats, and horses all bear live young. As you move "down" the hierarchy you specialize. Thus, the cat specializes Mammal in having claws (a characteristic) and purring (a behavior).

Similarly, when you say that ListBox and Button *are* Windows, you indicate that there are characteristics and behaviors of Windows that you expect to find in both of these types. In other words, Window generalizes the shared characteristics of both ListBox and Button, while each specializes its own particular characteristics and behaviors.

The Unified Modeling Language (UML) is a standardized language for describing an object-oriented system. The UML has many different visual representations, but in this case, all you need to know is that classes are represented as boxes. The name of the class appears at the top of the box, and (optionally) methods and members can be listed in the sections within the box.

In the UML, you model specialization relationships, as shown in Figure 11-1. Note that the arrow points from the more specialized class up to the more general class. In the figure, the more specialized Button and ListBox classes point up to the more general Window class.

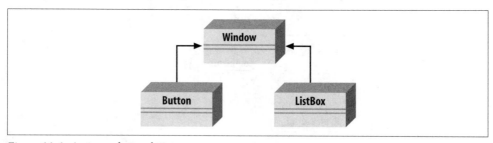

Figure 11-1. An is-a relationship

It is not uncommon for two classes to share functionality. When this occurs, you can *factor out* these commonalities into a shared base class, which is more general than the specialized classes. This provides you with greater reuse of common code and gives you code that is easier to maintain, because the changes are located in a single class rather than scattered among numerous classes.

For example, suppose you started out creating a series of objects, as illustrated in Figure 11-2. After working with RadioButtons, CheckBoxes, and Command buttons for a while, you realize that they share certain characteristics and behaviors that are more specialized than Window, but more general than any of the three. You might factor these common traits and behaviors into a common base class, Button, and rearrange your inheritance hierarchy, as shown in Figure 11-3. This is an example of how generalization is used in object-oriented development.

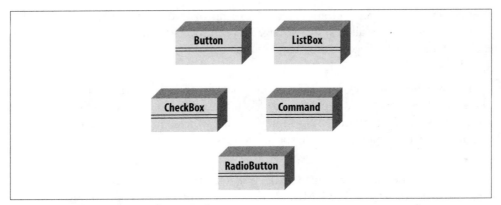

Figure 11-2. Objects deriving from Window

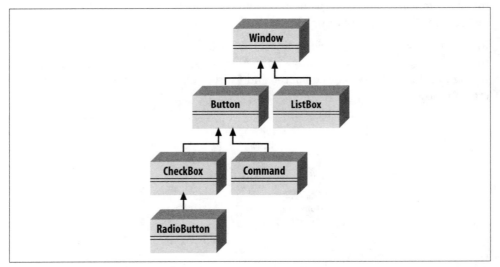

Figure 11-3. Factoring a Button class

The UML diagram in Figure 11-3 depicts the relationship among the factored classes and shows that both ListBox and Button derive from Window, and that Button is specialized into CheckBox and Command. Finally, RadioButton derives from Check-Box. You can thus say that RadioButton is a CheckBox, which in turn is a Button, and that Buttons are Windows.

This is not the only, or even necessarily the best, organization for these objects, but it is a reasonable starting point for understanding how these types (classes) relate to one another.

Actually, although this discussion might reflect how some widget hierarchies are organized, I am very skeptical of any system in which the model does not reflect how I perceive reality, and when I find myself saying that a RadioButton is a CheckBox, I have to think long and hard about whether that makes sense. I suppose a RadioButton *is* a kind of CheckBox. It is a checkbox that supports the idiom of mutually exclusive choices. That said, it is a bit of a stretch and might be a sign of a shaky design.

Inheritance

In C#, the specialization relationship is implemented using a principle called *inheritance*. This is not the only way to implement specialization, but it is the most common and most natural way to implement this relationship.

Saying that ListBox inherits from (or derives from) Window indicates that it specializes Window. Window is referred to as the *base* class, and ListBox is referred to as the *derived* class. That is, ListBox derives its characteristics and behaviors from Window and then specializes to its own particular needs.

You'll often see the immediate base class referred to as the *parent* class, and the derived class referred to as the *child* class, while the topmost class, Object, is called the *root* class.

Implementing Inheritance

In C#, you create a derived class by adding a colon after the name of the derived class, followed by the name of the base class:

```
public class ListBox : Window
```

This code declares a new class, ListBox, that derives from Window. You can read the colon as "derives from."

The derived class inherits all the members of the base class (both member variables and methods), and methods of the derived class have access to all the public and protected members of the base class. The derived class is free to implement its own version of a base class method. This is called *hiding* the base class method and is accomplished by marking the method with the keyword new. (Many C# programmers advise never hiding base class methods as it is unreliable, hard to maintain, and confusing.)

This is a different use of the keyword new than you've seen earlier in this book. In Chapter 7, new was used to create an object on the heap; here, new is used to replace the base class method. Programmers say the keyword new is overloaded, which means that the word has more than one meaning or use.

The new keyword indicates that the derived class has intentionally hidden and replaced the base class method, as shown in the Example 11-1. (The new keyword is also discussed in the section "Versioning with new and override," later in this chapter.)

Example 11-1. Deriving a new class

```
using System;

public class Window
{
    // constructor takes two integers to
    // fix location on the console
    public Window( int top, int left )
    {
        this.top = top;
        this.left = left;
    }

    // simulates drawing the window
    public void DrawWindow( )
    {
        Console.WriteLine( "Drawing Window at {0}, {1}",
        top, left );
    }

    // these members are private and thus invisible
    // to derived class methods; we'll examine this
    // later in the chapter
    private int top;
    private int left;
}

// ListBox derives from Window
public class ListBox : Window
{
    // constructor adds a parameter
    public ListBox( int top, int left, string theContents ) :
    base( top, left ) // call base constructor
    {
        mListBoxContents = theContents;
    }

    // a new version (note keyword) because in the
    // derived method we change the behavior
    public new void DrawWindow( )
```

Example 11-1. Deriving a new class (continued)

```
    {
        base.DrawWindow( ); // invoke the base method
        Console.WriteLine( "Writing string to the listbox: {0}",
        mListBoxContents );
    }
    private string mListBoxContents; // new member variable
}

public class Tester
{
    public static void Main( )
    {
        // create a base instance
        Window w = new Window( 5, 10 );
        w.DrawWindow( );

        // create a derived instance
        ListBox lb = new ListBox( 20, 30, "Hello world" );
        lb.DrawWindow( );
    }
}
```

The output looks like this:

```
Drawing Window at 5, 10
Drawing Window at 20, 30
Writing string to the listbox: Hello world
```

Example 11-1 starts with the declaration of the base class Window. This class implements a constructor and a simple DrawWindow( ) method. There are two private member variables, top and left. The program is analyzed in detail in the following sections.

Calling Base Class Constructors

In Example 11-1, the new class ListBox derives from Window and has its own constructor, which takes three parameters. The ListBox constructor invokes the constructor of its parent by placing a colon (:) after the parameter list and then invoking the base class constructor with the keyword base:

```
public ListBox( int theTop,  int theLeft, string theContents):
    base(theTop, theLeft) // call base constructor
```

Because classes cannot inherit constructors, a derived class must implement its own constructor and can only make use of the constructor of its base class by calling it explicitly.

If the base class has an accessible default constructor, the derived constructor is not required to invoke the base constructor explicitly; instead, the default constructor is called implicitly as the object is constructed. However, if the base class does *not* have a default constructor, every derived constructor *must* explicitly invoke one of the base class constructors using the base keyword. The keyword base identifies the base class for the current object.

 As discussed in Chapter 7, if you do not declare a constructor of any kind, the compiler creates a default constructor for you. Whether you write it yourself or you use the one provided by the compiler, a default constructor is one that takes no parameters. Note, however, that once you do create a constructor of any kind (with or without parameters), the compiler does *not* create a default constructor for you.

Controlling Access

You can restrict the visibility of a class and its members through the use of access modifiers, such as public, private, and protected. (See Chapter 8 for a discussion of access modifiers.)

As you've seen, public allows a member to be accessed by the member methods of other classes, while private indicates that the member is visible only to member methods of its own class. The protected keyword extends visibility to methods of derived classes.

Classes, as well as their members, can be designated with any of these accessibility levels. If a class member has a different access designation than the class, the more restricted access applies. Thus, if you define a class, myClass, as follows:

```
public class MyClass
{
 // ...
 protected int myValue;
}
```

the accessibility for myValue is protected even though the class itself is public. A public class is one that is visible to any other class that wishes to interact with it. If you create a new class, myOtherClass, that derives from myClass, like this:

```
public class MyClass : MyOtherClass
{
   Console.WriteLine("myInt: {0}", myValue);
}
```

MyOtherClass can access myValue, because MyOtherClass derives from MyClass, and myValue is protected. Any class that doesn't derive from MyClass would not be able to access myValue.

 It is more common to make properties and methods protected than it is to make member variables protected. Member variables are almost always private.

Polymorphism

There are two powerful aspects to inheritance. One is code reuse. When you create a ListBox class, you're able to reuse some of the logic in the base (Window) class.

What is arguably more powerful, however, is the second aspect of inheritance: *polymorphism*. *Poly* means many and *morph* means form. Thus, polymorphism refers to being able to use many forms of a type without regard to the details.

When the phone company sends your phone a ring signal, it does not know what type of phone is on the other end of the line. You might have an old-fashioned Western Electric phone that energizes a motor to ring a bell, or you might have an electronic phone that plays digital music.

As far as the phone company is concerned, it knows only about the "base type" *phone* and expects that any "derived" instance of this type knows how to ring. When the phone company tells your phone to ring, it, effectively, calls your phone's ring method, and old fashioned phones ring, digital phones trill, and cutting-edge phones announce your name. The phone company doesn't know or care what your individual phone does; it treats your telephone polymorphically.

Creating Polymorphic Types

Because a ListBox *is a* Window and a Button *is a* Window, you expect to be able to use either of these types in situations that call for a Window. For example, a form might want to keep a collection of all the derived instances of Window it manages (buttons, lists, and so on), so that when the form is opened, it can tell each of its Windows to draw itself. For this operation, the form does not want to know which elements are ListBoxes and which are Buttons; it just wants to tick through its collection and tell each one to "draw." In short, the form wants to treat all its Window objects polymorphically.

You implement polymorphism in two steps:

1. Create a base class with virtual methods.
2. Create derived classes that override the behavior of the base class's virtual methods.

To create a method in a base class that supports polymorphism, mark the method as virtual. For example, to indicate that the method DrawWindow( ) of class Window in Example 11-1 is polymorphic, add the keyword virtual to its declaration, as follows:

```
public virtual void DrawWindow( )
```

Each derived class is free to inherit and use the base class's DrawWindow( ) method as is or to implement its own version of DrawWindow( ). If a derived class does override the DrawWindow( ) method, that overridden version will be invoked for each instance of the derived class. You override the base class virtual method by using the keyword override in the derived class method definition, and then add the modified code for that overridden method.

Example 11-2 shows how to override virtual methods.

Example 11-2. Virtual methods

```
using System;

public class Window
{
   // constructor takes two integers to
   // fix location on the console
   public Window( int top, int left )
   {
      this.top = top;
      this.left = left;
   }

   // simulates drawing the window
   public virtual void DrawWindow( )
   {
      Console.WriteLine( "Window: drawing Window at {0}, {1}",
      top, left );
   }

   // these members are protected and thus visible
   // to derived class methods. We'll examine this
   // later in the chapter. (Typically, these would be private
   // and wrapped in protected properties, but the current approach
   // keeps the example simpler.)
   protected int top;
   protected int left;

} // end Window

// ListBox derives from Window
public class ListBox : Window
{
   // constructor adds a parameter
   // and calls the base constructor
   public ListBox(
   int top,
   int left,
   string contents ) : base( top, left )
   {
      listBoxContents = contents;
   }

   // an overridden version (note keyword) because in the
   // derived method we change the behavior
   public override void DrawWindow( )
   {
      base.DrawWindow( ); // invoke the base method
```

Example 11-2. Virtual methods (continued)

```
        Console.WriteLine( "Writing string to the listbox: {0}",
        listBoxContents );
    }

    private string listBoxContents; // new member variable
} // end ListBox

public class Button : Window
{
    public Button(
    int top,
    int left ) : base( top, left )
    {}

    // an overridden version (note keyword) because in the
    // derived method we change the behavior
    public override void DrawWindow()
    {
        Console.WriteLine( "Drawing a button at {0}, {1}\n",
        top, left );
    }
} // end Button

public class Tester
{
    static void Main()
    {
        Window win = new Window( 1, 2 );
        ListBox lb = new ListBox( 3, 4, "Stand alone list box" );
        Button b = new Button( 5, 6 );
        win.DrawWindow();
        lb.DrawWindow();
        b.DrawWindow();

        Window[] winArray = new Window[3];
        winArray[0] = new Window( 1, 2 );
        winArray[1] = new ListBox( 3, 4, "List box in array" );
        winArray[2] = new Button( 5, 6 );

        for ( int i = 0; i < 3; i++ )
        {
            winArray[i].DrawWindow();
        }   // end for
    }   // end Main
}       // end Tester
```

The output looks like this:

```
    Window: drawing Window at 1, 2
    Window: drawing Window at 3, 4
    Writing string to the listbox: Stand alone list box
    Drawing a button at 5, 6
```

```
Window: drawing Window at 1, 2
Window: drawing Window at 3, 4
Writing string to the listbox: List box in array
Drawing a button at 5, 6
```

In Example 11-2, ListBox derives from Window and implements its own version of DrawWindow( ):

```
public override void DrawWindow( )
{
    base.DrawWindow( ); // invoke the base method
    Console.WriteLine ("Writing string to the listbox: {0}",
    listBoxContents);
}
```

The keyword override tells the compiler that this class has intentionally overridden how DrawWindow( ) works. Similarly, you'll override DrawWindow( ) in another class that derives from Window: the Button class.

In the body of the example, you create three objects: a Window, a ListBox, and a Button. Then you call DrawWindow( ) on each:

```
Window win = new Window(1,2);
ListBox lb = new ListBox(3,4,"Stand alone list box");
Button b = new Button(5,6);
win.DrawWindow( );
lb.DrawWindow( );
b.DrawWindow( );
```

This works much as you might expect. The correct DrawWindow( ) method is called for each. So far, *nothing polymorphic has been done* (after all, you called the Button version of DrawWindow on a Button object). The real magic starts when you create an array of Window objects.

Because a ListBox *is a* Window, you are free to place a ListBox into an array of Windows. Similarly, you can add a Button to a collection of Windows, because a Button *is a* Window.

```
Window[] winArray = new Window[3];
winArray[0] = new Window(1,2);
winArray[1] = new ListBox(3,4,"List box in array");
winArray[2] = new Button(5,6);
```

The first line of code declares an array named winArray that will hold three Window objects. The next three lines add new Window objects to the array. The first adds an object of type Window. The second adds an object of type ListBox (which is a Window because ListBox derives from Window), and the third adds an object of type Button, which is also a type of Window.

What happens when you call DrawWindow( ) on each of these objects?

```
for (int i = 0; i < winArray.Length-1; i++)
{
    winArray[i].DrawWindow();
}
```

This code uses i as a counter variable. It calls DrawWindow() on each element in the array in turn. The value i is evaluated each time through the loop, and that value is used as an index into the array.

All the compiler knows is that it has three Window objects and that you've called DrawWindow() on each. If you had not marked DrawWindow() as virtual, Window's original DrawWindow() method would be called three times.

However, because you did mark DrawWindow() as virtual, and because the derived classes override that method, when you call DrawWindow() on the array, the right thing happens for each object in the array. Specifically, the compiler determines the *runtime type* of the actual objects (a Window, a ListBox, and a Button) and calls the right method on each. This is the essence of polymorphism.

The runtime type of an object is the actual (derived) type. At compile time, you do not have to decide what kind of objects will be added to your collection, so long as they all derive from the declared type (in this case, Window). At runtime, the actual type is discovered and the right method is called. This allows you to pick the actual type of objects to add to the collection while the program is running.

Note that throughout this example, the overridden methods are marked with the keyword override:

```
public override void DrawWindow()
```

The compiler now knows to use the overridden method when treating these objects polymorphically. The compiler is responsible for tracking the real type of the object and for handling the late binding, so that ListBox.DrawWindow() is called when the Window reference really points to a ListBox object.

Versioning with new and override

In C#, the programmer's decision to override a virtual method is made explicit with the override keyword. This helps you release new versions of your code; changes to the base class will not break existing code in the derived classes. The requirement to use the override keyword helps prevent that problem.

Here's how: assume for a moment that Company A wrote the Window base class in Example 11-2. Suppose also that the ListBox and RadioButton classes were written by programmers from Company B using a purchased copy of the Company A Window class as a base. The programmers in Company B have little or no control over the design of the Window class, including future changes that Company A might choose to make.

Now suppose that one of the programmers for Company B decides to add a Sort( ) method to ListBox:

```
public class ListBox : Window
{
 public virtual void Sort() {...}
}
```

This presents no problems until Company A, the author of Window, releases Version 2 of its Window class, and the programmers in Company A also add a Sort( ) method to their public class Window:

```
public class Window
{
 // ...
 public virtual void Sort() {...}
}
```

In other object-oriented languages (such as C++), the new virtual Sort( ) method in Window would now act as a base virtual method for the Sort( ) method in ListBox, which is not what the developer of ListBox intended.

C# prevents this confusion. In C#, a virtual function is always considered to be the *root of virtual dispatch;* that is, once C# finds a virtual method, it looks no further up the inheritance hierarchy. If a new virtual Sort( ) function is introduced into Window, the runtime behavior of ListBox is unchanged.

When ListBox is compiled again, however, the compiler generates a *warning*:

```
...\class1.cs(54,24): warning CS0114: 'ListBox.Sort()' hides
inherited member 'Window.Sort()'.
To make the current member override that implementation,
add the override keyword. Otherwise add the new keyword.
```

 Never ignore warnings. Treat them as errors until you have satisfied yourself that you understand the warning and that it is not only innocuous but that there is nothing you can do to eliminate the warning. Your goal, (almost) always, is to compile warning-free code.

To remove the warning, the programmer must indicate what she intends.* She can mark the ListBox Sort( ) method new to indicate that it is *not* an override of the virtual method in Window:

```
public class ListBox : Window
{
 public new virtual void Sort() {...}
}
```

* In standard English, one uses "he" when the pronoun might refer either to a male or a female. Nonetheless, this assumption has such profound cultural implications, especially in the male-dominated programming profession, that I will use the term "she" for the unknown programmer from time to time. I apologize if this causes you to falter a bit when reading; consider it an opportunity to reflect on the linguistic implications of a patriarchal society.

This action removes the warning. If, on the other hand, the programmer does want to override the method in Window, she need only use the override keyword to make that intention explicit:

```
public class ListBox : Window
{
public override void Sort() {...}
```

 To avoid this warning, it might be tempting to add the new keyword to all your virtual methods. This is a *bad* idea. When new appears in the code, it ought to document the versioning of code. It points a potential client to the base class to see what it is that you are intentionally not overriding. Using new scattershot undermines this documentation and reduces the utility of a warning that exists to help identify a real issue.

If the programmer now creates any new classes that derive from ListBox, those derived classes will inherit the Sort() method from ListBox, not from the base Window class.

Abstract Classes

Each type of Window has a different shape and appearance. Drop-down listboxes look very different from buttons. Clearly, every subclass of Window *should* implement its own DrawWindow() method—but so far, nothing in the Window class enforces that they must do so. To require subclasses to implement a method of their base, you need to designate that method as *abstract*.

An abstract method has no implementation. It creates a method name and signature that must be implemented in all derived classes. Furthermore, making at least one method of any class abstract has the side effect of making the class abstract.

Abstract classes establish a base for derived classes, but it is not legal to instantiate an object of an abstract class. Once you declare a method to be abstract, you prohibit the creation of any instances of that class.

Thus, if you were to designate DrawWindow() as an abstract method in the Window class, the Window class itself would become abstract. Then you could derive from Window, but you could not create any Window instances. If the Window class is an abstraction, there is no such thing as a simple Window object, only objects derived from Window.

Making Window.DrawWindow() abstract means that each class derived from Window would have to implement its own DrawWindow() method. If the derived class failed to implement the abstract method, that derived class would also be abstract, and again no instances would be possible.

The Idea Behind Abstraction

Abstract classes should not just be an implementation trick; they should represent the idea of an abstraction that establishes a "contract" for all derived classes. In other words, abstract classes mandate the public methods of the classes that will implement the abstraction.

The idea of an abstract Window class ought to lay out the common characteristics and behaviors of all windows, even though you never intend to instantiate the abstraction Window itself.

The idea of an abstract class is implied in the word "abstract." It serves to implement the abstraction "Window" that will be manifest in the various concrete instances of Window, such as browser window, frame, button, listbox, drop-down, and so forth. The abstract class establishes what a Window is, even though we never intend to create a "Window" per se. An alternative to using abstract is to define an interface, as described in Chapter 13.

Designating a method as abstract is accomplished by placing the abstract keyword at the beginning of the method definition:

```
abstract public void DrawWindow( );
```

(Because the method can have no implementation, there are no braces, only a semicolon.)

If one or more methods are abstract, the class definition must also be marked abstract, as in the following:

```
abstract public class Window
```

Example 11-3 illustrates the creation of an abstract Window class and an abstract DrawWindow( ) method.

Example 11-3. Abstract methods

```
using System;

public abstract class Window
{
   // constructor takes two integers to
   // fix location on the console
   public Window( int top, int left )
   {
      this.top = top;
      this.left = left;
   }

   // simulates drawing the window
   // notice: no implementation
   public abstract void DrawWindow( );
```

Example 11-3. Abstract methods (continued)

```
    protected int top;
    protected int left;
}      // end class Window

// ListBox derives from Window
public class ListBox : Window
{
    // constructor adds a parameter
    public ListBox(
    int top,
    int left,
    string contents ) :  base( top, left ) // call base constructor
    {

        listBoxContents = contents;
    }

    // an overridden version implementing the
    // abstract method
    public override void DrawWindow( )
    {
        Console.WriteLine( "Writing string to the listbox: {0}",
        listBoxContents );
    }
    private string listBoxContents; // new member variable
}      // end class ListBox

public class Button : Window
{
    public Button(
    int top,
    int left ) : base( top, left ) { }

    // implement the abstract method
    public override void DrawWindow( )
    {
        Console.WriteLine( "Drawing a button at {0}, {1}\n",
        top, left );
    }
}          // end class Button

public class Tester
{
    static void Main( )
    {
        Window[] winArray = new Window[3];
        winArray[0] = new ListBox( 1, 2, "First List Box" );
        winArray[1] = new ListBox( 3, 4, "Second List Box" );
        winArray[2] = new Button( 5, 6 );

        for ( int i = 0; i < 3; i++ )
        {
```

Example 11-3. Abstract methods (continued)

```
        winArray[i].DrawWindow( );
    }        // end for loop
  }          // end main
}            // end class Tester
```

The output looks like this:

```
Writing string to the listbox: First List Box
Writing string to the listbox: Second List Box
Drawing a button at 5, 6
```

In Example 11-3, the Window class has been declared abstract and therefore cannot be instantiated. If you replace the first array member:

```
winArray[0] = new ListBox(1,2,"First List Box");
```

with this code:

```
winArray[0] = new Window(1,2);
```

the program generates the following error at compile time:

```
Cannot create an instance of the abstract class or interface 'Window'
```

You can instantiate the ListBox and Button objects because these classes override the abstract method, thus making the classes *concrete* (that is, not abstract).

Often an abstract class will include non-abstract methods. Typically, these will be marked virtual, providing the programmer who derives from your abstract class the choice of using the implementation provided in the abstract class, or overriding it. Once again, however, all abstract methods must, eventually, be overridden in order to make an instance of the (derived) class.

Sealed Classes

The opposite side of the design coin from abstract is *sealed*. In contrast to an abstract class, which is intended to be derived from and to provide a template for its subclasses to follow, a sealed class does not allow classes to derive from it at all. The sealed keyword placed before the class declaration precludes derivation. Classes are most often marked sealed to prevent accidental inheritance.

If you changed the declaration of Window in Example 11-3 from abstract to sealed (eliminating the abstract keyword from the DrawWindow( ) declaration as well), the program fails to compile. If you try to build this project, the compiler returns the following error message:

```
'ListBox' cannot inherit from sealed type 'Window'
```

among many other complaints (such as that you cannot create a new protected member in a sealed class).

Microsoft recommends using sealed when you know that you won't need to create derived classes, and also when your class consists of nothing but static methods and properties.

The Root of All Classes: Object

All C# classes, of any type, ultimately derive from a single class: Object. Object is the base class for all other classes.

A base class is the immediate "parent" of a derived class. A derived class can be the base to further derived classes, creating an inheritance *tree* or hierarchy. A *root* class is the topmost class in an inheritance hierarchy. In C#, the root class is Object. The nomenclature is a bit confusing until you imagine an upside-down tree, with the root on top and the derived classes below. Thus, the base class is considered to be "above" the derived class.

Object provides a number of methods that subclasses can override. These include Equals( ), which determines if two objects are the same, and ToString( ), which returns a string to represent the current object. Specifically, ToString( ) returns a string with the name of the class to which the object belongs. Table 11-1 summarizes the methods of Object.

Table 11-1. The Object class

Method	What it does
Equals( )	Evaluates whether two objects are equivalent
GetHashCode( )	Allows objects to provide their own hash function for use in collections (see Chapter 14)
GetType( )	Provides access to the Type object
ToString( )	Provides a string representation of the object
Finalize( )	Cleans up nonmemory resources; implemented by a destructor (finalizer)

In Example 11-4, the Dog class overrides the ToString( ) method inherited from Object, to return the weight of the Dog.

Example 11-4. Overriding ToString

```
using System;

public class Dog
{
   private int weight;

   // constructor
   public Dog( int weight )
   {
      this.weight = weight;
   }
```

Example 11-4. Overriding ToString (continued)

```
    // override Object.ToString
    public override string ToString( )
    {
        return weight.ToString( );
    }
}

public class Tester
{
    static void Main( )
    {
        int i = 5;
        Console.WriteLine( "The value of i is: {0}", i.ToString( ) );

        Dog milo = new Dog( 62 );
        Console.WriteLine( "My dog Milo weighs {0} pounds", milo);
    }
}
```

```
Output:
The value of i is: 5
My dog Milo weighs 62 pounds
```

Some classes (such as Console) have methods that expect a string (such as Write-Line( )). These methods will call the ToString( ) method on your class if you've over-ridden the inherited ToString( ) method from Object. This lets you pass a Dog to Console.WriteLine, and the correct information will display.

This example also takes advantage of the startling fact that intrinsic types (int, long, etc.) can also be treated as if they derive from Object, and thus you can call ToString( ) on an int variable! Calling ToString( ) on an intrinsic type returns a string representation of the variable's value.

The documentation for Object.ToString( ) reveals its signature:

```
    public virtual string ToString( );
```

It is a public virtual method that returns a string and takes no parameters. All the built-in types, such as int, derive from Object and so can invoke Object's methods.

 The Console class's Write( ) and WriteLine( ) methods call ToString( ) for you on objects that you pass in for display. Thus, by overriding ToString( ) in the Dog class, you did not have to pass in milo.ToString( ) but rather could just pass in milo!

If you comment out the overridden function, the base method will be invoked. The base class default behavior is to return a string with the name of the class itself. Thus, the output would be changed to the meaningless:

```
    My dog Milo weighs Dog pounds
```

Classes do not need to declare explicitly that they derive from Object; the inheritance is implicit.

Boxing and Unboxing Types

Boxing and *unboxing* are the processes that enable value types (such as, integers) to be treated as reference types (objects). The value is "boxed" inside an Object and subsequently "unboxed" back to a value type. It is this process that allowed you to call the ToString( ) method on the integer in Example 11-4.

Boxing Is Implicit

Boxing is an implicit conversion of a value type to the type Object. Boxing a value allocates an instance of Object and copies the value into the new object instance, as shown in Figure 11-4.

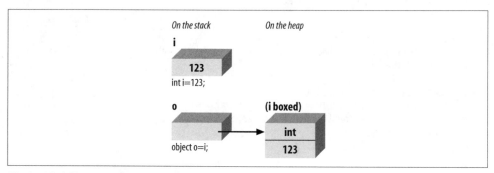

Figure 11-4. Boxing value types

Boxing is implicit when you provide a value type where a reference is expected. The runtime notices that you've provided a value type and silently boxes it within an object. You can, of course, first cast the value type to a reference type, as in the following:

```
int myIntegerValue = 5;
object myObject = myIntegerValue; // cast to an object
myObject.ToString();
```

This is not necessary, however, as the compiler boxes the value for you silently and with no action on your part:

```
int myIntegerValue = 5;
myIntegerValue.ToString(); // myIntegerValue is boxed
```

Unboxing Must Be Explicit

To return the boxed object back to a value type, you must explicitly unbox it. For the unboxing to succeed, the object being unboxed must really be of the type you indicate when you unbox it.

You should accomplish unboxing in two steps:

1. Make sure the object instance is a boxed value of the given value type.
2. Copy the value from the instance to the value-type variable.

Example 11-5 illustrates boxing and unboxing.

Example 11-5. Boxing and unboxing

```
using System;
public class UnboxingTest
{
   public static void Main( )
   {
      int myIntegerVariable = 123;

      //Boxing
      object myObjectVariable = myIntegerVariable;
      Console.WriteLine( "myObjectVariable: {0}",
      myObjectVariable.ToString( ) );

      // unboxing (must be explicit)
      int anotherIntegerVariable = (int)myObjectVariable;
      Console.WriteLine( "anotherIntegerVariable: {0}",
      anotherIntegerVariable );
   }
}

Output:
myObjectVariable: 123
anotherIntegerVariable: 123
```

Figure 11-5 illustrates unboxing.

Example 11-5 creates an integer myIntegerVariable and implicitly boxes it when it is assigned to the object myObjectVariable; then, to exercise the newly boxed object, its value is displayed by calling ToString( ).

The object is then explicitly unboxed and assigned to a new integer variable, anotherIntegerVariable, whose value is displayed to show that the value has been preserved.

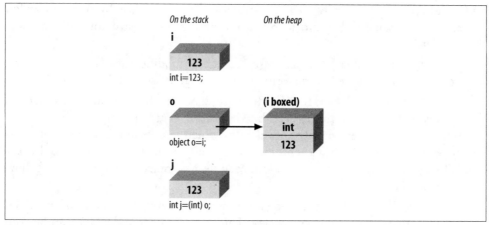

Figure 11-5. Unboxing

Avoiding Boxing with Generics

The most common place that value types were boxed in C# 1.*x* was in collections that expected Objects. Now that C# supports generics, collections that hold integers need not box and unbox them, and that can increase performance when you have a very large collection. Generics are discussed in more detail in the Chapter 14.

Summary

- Specialization is described as the *is-a* relationship; the reverse of specialization is generalization.

- Specialization and generalization are reciprocal and hierarchical—that is, specialization is reciprocal to generalization, and each class can have any number of specialized derived classes but only one parent class that it specializes: thus creating a branching hierarchy.

- C# implements specialization through inheritance.

- The inherited class derives the public and protected characteristics and behaviors of the base class, and is free to add or modify its own characteristics and behaviors.

- You implement inheritance by adding a colon after the name of the derived class, followed by the name of its base class.

- A derived class can invoke the constructor of its base class by placing a colon after the parameter list and invoking the base class constructor with the keyword base.

- Classes, like members, can also use the access modifiers public, private, and protected, though the vast majority of non-nested classes will be public.

- A method marked as virtual in the base class can be overridden by derived classes if the derived classes use the keyword override in their method definition. This is the key to polymorphism in which you have a collection of references to a base class but each object is actually an instance of a derived class. When you call the virtual method on each derived object, the overridden behavior is invoked.

- A derived class can break the polymorphism of a derived method but must signal that intent with the keyword new. This is unusual, complex and can be confusing, but is provided to allow for versioning of derived classes. Typically, you will use the keyword overrides (rather than new) to indicate that you are modifying the behavior of the base class's method.

- A method marked as abstract has no implementation—instead, it provides a virtual method name and signature that all derived classes *must* override. Any class with an abstract method is an abstract class, and cannot be instantiated.

- Any class marked as sealed cannot be derived from.

- In C#, all classes (and built-in types) are ultimately derived from the Object class, implicitly, and thus inherit a number of useful methods such as ToString.

- When you pass a value type to a method or collection that expects a reference type, the value type is "boxed" and must be explicitly "unboxed" when retrieved.

- Generics make boxing and unboxing less common, and well-designed code will have little or no boxing or unboxing.

Quiz

Question 11-1. What is the relationship between specialization and generalization?

Question 11-2. How is specialization implemented in C#?

Question 11-3. What is the syntax for inheritance in C#?

Question 11-4. How do you implement polymorphism?

Question 11-5. What are the two meanings of the keyword new?

Question 11-6. How do you call a base class constructor from a derived class?

Question 11-7. What is the difference between public, protected, and private?

Question 11-8. What is an abstract method?

Question 11-9. What is a sealed class?

Question 11-10. What is the base class of Int32?

Question 11-11. What is the base class of any class you create if you do not otherwise indicate a base class?

Question 11-12. What is boxing?

Question 11-13. What is unboxing?

Exercises

Exercise 11-1. Create a base class, Telephone, and derive a class ElectronicPhone from it. In Telephone, create a protected string member phonetype, and a public method Ring( ) that outputs a text message like this: "Ringing the <phonetype>." In ElectronicPhone, the constructor should set the phonetype to "Digital." In the Run( ) method, call Ring( ) on the ElectronicPhone to test the inheritance.

Exercise 11-2. Extend Exercise 11-1 to illustrate a polymorphic method. Have the derived class override the Ring( ) method to display a different message.

Exercise 11-3. Change the Telephone class to abstract, and make Ring( ) an abstract method. Derive two new classes from Telephone: DigitalPhone and TalkingPhone. Each derived class should set the phonetype, and override the Ring( ) method.

CHAPTER 12

Operator Overloading

One of the goals of C# is to allow you to create new classes that have all the functionality of built-in types such as integer (int) and Boolean (bool). (See Chapter 3 for a discussion of these intrinsic types.) For example, suppose you define a type (Fraction) to represent fractional numbers. The following constructors establish two Fraction objects, the first representing 1/2 and the second representing 3/4:

```
Fraction firstFraction = new Fraction(1,2); // create 1/2
Fraction secondFraction = new Fraction(3,4); // create 3/4
```

The assumption here, of course, is that the first parameter will represent the numerator, and the second parameter will represent the denominator.

Ensuring that the Fraction class has all the functionality of the built-in types means that you must be able to perform arithmetic on instances of your fractions (add two fractions, multiply, and so on) and to convert fractions to and from built-in types such as int.

Hypothetically, you could implement methods for each of these operations. For example, for your Fraction type, you might create an Add( ) method and invoke it by writing a statement such as:

```
// add 1/2 and 3/4
Fraction theSum = firstFraction.Add(secondFraction);
```

Although this will work, it is ugly and not how the built-in types are used. It would be much better to be able to write:

```
// add 1/2 and 3/4 using + operator
Fraction theSum = firstFraction + secondFraction;
```

Statements that use operators (in this case, the plus sign) are intuitive and easy to use. Equally important, this use of operators is consistent with how built-in types are added, multiplied, and so forth.

In this chapter, you will learn techniques for adding standard operators to be used with your user-defined types. When you create an operator for a class, you say you have "overloaded" that operator, much as you might overload a member method (discussed in Chapter 8). The C# syntax for overloading an operator is to write the keyword operator followed by the operator to overload. The next section demonstrates how you might do this for the Fraction class.

The chapter also discusses the special case of overloading the equals operator, which is used to test whether two objects are equal. Overriding this operator also requires you to override the class's Equals( ) method.

Later in the chapter, you will learn how to add conversion operators to your user-defined types so that they can be implicitly and explicitly converted to other types.

Using the operator Keyword

In C#, operators are static methods. The return value of an operator represents the result of an operation. The operator's parameters are the operands.

Thus, to create an addition operator for a Fraction class, you use the C# syntax of combining the operator keyword with the plus sign (+) operator combined with the keyword static. For example, the overloaded addition operator (the operator+ method) takes two Fraction objects (the fractions you want to add) as parameters and returns a reference to another Fraction object representing the sum of the two parameters. Here is its signature:

```
public static Fraction operator+(Fraction lhs, Fraction rhs)
```

And here's what you can do with it. Assume, for instance, you've defined two fractions representing the portion of a pie you've eaten for breakfast and lunch, respectively. (You love pie.)

```
Fraction pieIAteForBreakfast = new Fraction(1,2); // 1/2 of a pie
Fraction pieIAteForLunch = new Fraction(1,3);     // 1/3 of a pie
```

The overloaded operator+ allows you to figure out how much pie you've eaten in total. (And there's still 1/6 of a pie left over for dinner!) You write:

```
Fraction totalPigOut = pieIAteForBreakfast + pieIAteForLunch;
```

The compiler takes the first operand (pieIAteForBreakfast) and passes it to operator+ as the parameter lhs; it passes the second operand (pieIAteForLunch) as rhs. These two Fractions are then added, and the result is returned and assigned to the Fraction object named totalPigOut.

 It is my convention to name the parameters to a binary operator lhs and rhs. A binary operator is an operator that takes two operands. The parameter name lhs stands for "lefthand side" and reminds me that the first parameter represents the lefthand side of the operation. Similarly, rhs stands for "righthand side."

To see how this works, you'll create a Fraction class, as described previously. The complete listing is shown in Example 12-1, followed by a detailed analysis.

Example 12-1. Implementing operator+ for Fraction

```
using System;

public class Fraction
{
    private int numerator;
    private int denominator;

    // create a fraction by passing in the numerator
    // and denominator
    public Fraction( int numerator, int denominator )
    {
        this.numerator = numerator;
        this.denominator = denominator;
    }

    // overloaded operator + takes two fractions
    // and returns their sum
    public static Fraction operator+( Fraction lhs, Fraction rhs )
    {
        // like fractions (shared denominator) can be added
        // by adding their numerators
        if ( lhs.denominator == rhs.denominator )
        {
            return new Fraction( lhs.numerator + rhs.numerator,
            lhs.denominator );
        }

        // simplistic solution for unlike fractions
        // 1/2 + 3/4 == (1*4) + (3*2) / (2*4) == 10/8
        // this method does not reduce.
        int firstProduct = lhs.numerator * rhs.denominator;
        int secondProduct = rhs.numerator * lhs.denominator;
        return new Fraction(
        firstProduct + secondProduct,
        lhs.denominator * rhs.denominator
        );
    }

    // return a string representation of the fraction
    public override string ToString()
    {
        String s = numerator.ToString() + "/" +
        denominator.ToString();
        return s;
    }
}
```

Example 12-1. Implementing operator+ for Fraction (continued)

```
public class Tester
{
    public void Run( )
    {
        Fraction firstFraction = new Fraction( 3, 4 );
        Console.WriteLine( "firstFraction: {0}", firstFraction.ToString( ) );

        Fraction secondFraction = new Fraction( 2, 4 );
        Console.WriteLine( "secondFraction: {0}", secondFraction.ToString( ) );

        Fraction sumOfTwoFractions = firstFraction + secondFraction;
        Console.WriteLine(
            "firstFraction + secondFraction = sumOfTwoFractions: {0}",
            sumOfTwoFractions.ToString( ) );

    }
    static void Main( )
    {
        Tester t = new Tester( );
        t.Run( );
    }
}
```

The output looks like this:

```
firstFraction: 3/4
secondFraction: 2/4
firstFraction + secondFraction = sumOfTwoFractions: 5/4
```

In Example 12-1, you start by creating a Fraction class. The private member data is the numerator and denominator, stored as integers:

```
public class Fraction
{
 private int numerator;
 private int denominator;
```

The constructor just initializes these values. The overloaded addition operator takes two Fraction objects, returns a Fraction, and is marked static:

```
public static Fraction operator+(Fraction lhs, Fraction rhs)
{
```

If the denominators for the fractions are the same, you add the numerators and return a new Fraction object created by passing in the sum of the numerators as the new numerator and the shared denominator as the new denominator:

```
if (lhs.denominator == rhs.denominator)
{
    return new Fraction(lhs.numerator+rhs.numerator,
    lhs.denominator);
}
```

The Fraction objects firstFraction and secondFraction are passed in to the overloaded addition operator as lhs and rhs, respectively. The new Fraction is created on the heap, and a reference is returned to the calling method, Run( ), where it is assigned to sumOfTwoFractions:

```
Fraction sumOfTwoFractions = firstFraction + secondFraction;
Console.WriteLine( "firstFraction + secondFraction = sumOfTwoFractions: {0}",
    sumOfTwoFractions.ToString() );
```

Back in the implementation of the operator, if the denominators are different, you cross-multiply before adding. This allows you to add like Fractions.

```
int firstProduct = lhs.numerator * rhs.denominator;
int secondProduct = rhs.numerator * lhs.denominator;
return new Fraction(
  firstProduct + secondProduct,
  lhs.denominator * rhs.denominator
);
```

The two local variables, firstProduct and secondProduct, are temporary; they are destroyed when the method returns. The new Fraction created, however, is not temporary; it is created on the heap, and a reference is returned as previously.

 A good Fraction class would, no doubt, implement all the arithmetic operators (addition, subtraction, multiplication, division). To overload the multiplication operator, you would write operator*; to overload the division operator, you would write operator/.

The Fraction class overrides the ToString( ) method (inherited from Object) to allow you to display the fractions by passing them to Console.WriteLine( ). (For more information about overloading methods, see Chapter 8.)

Creating Useful Operators

Operator overloading can make your code more intuitive and enable it to act more like the built-in types. However, if you break the common idiom for the use of operators, operator overloading can make your code unmanageably complex and obtuse. Therefore you should always resist the temptation to use operators in new and idiosyncratic ways.

For example, although it might be tempting to overload the increment operator (++) on an employee class to invoke a method incrementing the employee's pay level, this can create tremendous confusion. The increment operator normally means "increase this scalar value by one." Giving it the new meaning of "increase this employee's pay level" will be obvious to the person implementing the operator, but may be very confusing to you or other programmers who have to maintain the code. It is best to use operator overloading sparingly, and only when its meaning is clear and consistent with how the built-in classes operate.

The Equals Operator

The Object class (which is the root of every class in C#) offers a virtual method called Equals( ). (Virtual methods are discussed in Chapter 11.) If you overload the equals operator (==), it is recommended that you also override the Equals( ) method.

Overriding the Equals( ) method allows your class to be compatible with other .NET languages that do not overload operators (but do support method overloading).

The Object class implements the Equals( ) method with this signature:

```
public virtual bool Equals(object o)
```

From this signature, you can see that your override of this method will take an object as a parameter, and return a bool (true if the two objects are equal, where "equality" is defined by the creator of the class).

By overriding this method, you allow your Fraction class to act polymorphically with all other objects. For example, anywhere you can call Equals( ) on two Objects, you can call Equals( ) on two Fractions.

Inside the body of Equals( ), you need to ensure that you are comparing one Fraction object with another Fraction object. If the other object is not a fraction, they cannot be equal, and you'll return false.

```
public override bool Equals(object o)
{
    if ( ! (o is Fraction) )
    {
        return false;
    }
    return this == (Fraction) o;
}
```

The is operator is used to check whether the runtime type of an object is compatible with the operand (in this case, Fraction). Thus o is Fraction evaluates true if o is, in fact, a Fraction or a type derived from Fraction.

If you are comparing two Fractions, you can delegate the decision as to their equality to the overloaded operator (operator==) that you've already written. This allows you to avoid duplicate code.

```
public override bool Equals(object o)
{
    if (! (o is Fraction) )
    {
        return false;
    }
    return this == (Fraction) o;
}
```

In this way, the Equals( ) method determines only that you do in fact have two fractions. If so, it delegates deciding if the two fractions are truly equal to the already implemented operator ==.

The complete modification of the Fraction class is shown in Example 12-2, followed by the analysis.

Example 12-2. Implementing equality operators

```
using System;

public class Fraction
{
    private int numerator;
    private int denominator;

    // create a fraction by passing in the numerator
    // and denominator
    public Fraction( int numerator, int denominator )
    {
        this.numerator = numerator;
        this.denominator = denominator;
    }

    // overloaded operator+ takes two fractions
    // and returns their sum
    public static Fraction operator +( Fraction lhs, Fraction rhs )
    {
        // like fractions (shared denominator) can be added
        // by adding thier numerators
        if ( lhs.denominator == rhs.denominator )
        {
            return new Fraction( lhs.numerator + rhs.numerator,
            lhs.denominator );
        }

        // simplistic solution for unlike fractions
        // 1/2 + 3/4 == (1*4) + (3*2) / (2*4) == 10/8
        // this method does not reduce.
        int firstProduct = lhs.numerator * rhs.denominator;
        int secondProduct = rhs.numerator * lhs.denominator;
        return new Fraction(
        firstProduct + secondProduct,
        lhs.denominator * rhs.denominator
        );
    }

    // test whether two Fractions are equal
    public static bool operator ==( Fraction lhs, Fraction rhs )
    {
        if ( lhs.denominator == rhs.denominator &&
        lhs.numerator == rhs.numerator )
        {
```

Example 12-2. Implementing equality operators (continued)

```
            return true;
        }
        // code here to handle unlike fractions
        return false;
    }
    // delegates to operator ==
    public static bool operator !=( Fraction lhs, Fraction rhs )
    {
        return !( lhs == rhs );
    }
    // tests for same types, then delegates
    public override bool Equals( object o )
    {
        if ( !( o is Fraction ) )
        {
            return false;
        }
        return this == (Fraction)o;
    }
    // return a string representation of the fraction
    public override string ToString()
    {
        String s = numerator.ToString() + "/" +
        denominator.ToString();
        return s;
    }
}


public class Tester
{
    public void Run()
    {
        Fraction f1 = new Fraction( 3, 4 );
        Console.WriteLine( "f1: {0}", f1.ToString() );

        Fraction f2 = new Fraction( 2, 4 );
        Console.WriteLine( "f2: {0}", f2.ToString() );

        Fraction f3 = f1 + f2;
        Console.WriteLine( "f1 + f2 = f3: {0}", f3.ToString() );

        Fraction f4 = new Fraction( 5, 4 );
        if ( f4 == f3 )
        {
            Console.WriteLine( "f4: {0} == F3: {1}",
            f4.ToString(),
            f3.ToString() );
        }

        if ( f4 != f2 )
        {
```

Example 12-2. Implementing equality operators (continued)

```
            Console.WriteLine( "f4: {0} != F2: {1}",
            f4.ToString( ),
            f2.ToString( ) );
      }


   if ( f4.Equals( f3 ) )
   {
      Console.WriteLine( "{0}.Equals({1})",
      f4.ToString( ),
      f3.ToString( ) );
   }


}
static void Main( )
{
   Tester t = new Tester( );
   t.Run( );
}
}
```

The output looks like this:

```
f1: 3/4
f2: 2/4
f1 + f2 = f3: 5/4
f4: 5/4 == F3: 5/4
f4: 5/4 != F2: 2/4
5/4.Equals(5/4)
```

Example 12-2 starts by implementing the overloaded equals operator, operator==. If the fractions have the same denominator, you test whether the numerators are equal. If they are, you return true; otherwise, you return false.

 This is a mathematical simplification to keep the example readable. Testing for true equality (such as 3/4 = 6/8) is left as an exercise for the reader.

```
public static bool operator ==( Fraction lhs, Fraction rhs )
{
   if ( lhs.denominator == rhs.denominator &&
   lhs.numerator == rhs.numerator )
   {
      return true;
   }
   // code here to handle unlike fractions
   return false;
}
```

This method is invoked in the Run( ) method when you write:

```
if (f4 == f3)
```

The `if` statement expects a Boolean value, which is what `operator==` returns.

It is quite common to overload the equals operator (==) to test whether two objects are equal. C# insists that if you overload the equals operator, you must also over-load the not-equals operator (!=). Similarly, the less than (<) and greater than (>) operators must be paired, as must the less than or equal to (<=) and greater than or equal to (>=) operators.

It is good programming practice to have the inequality operator delegate its work to the equality operator, so that if you change the definition of equality, you are assured that the inequality operator will use the new definition.

```
public static bool operator !=(Fraction lhs, Fraction rhs)
{
    return !(lhs==rhs);
}
```

This operator is invoked in `Run( )` when you write:

```
if (f4 != f2)
```

Put a breakpoint on this line of code and run to this line in Visual Studio .NET, as shown in Figure 12-1. (For more about breakpoints, see Chapter 9.)

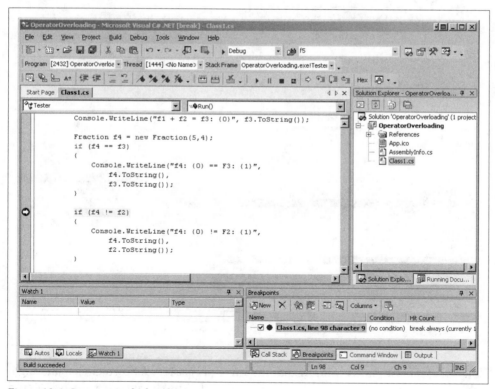

Figure 12-1. Running to the breakpoint

Press F11 to step into the method call—you'll step into the != operator at the return statement. Press F11 again and step into the == operator. Whatever value is returned by the == operator is negated when it is returned by the != operator. If false is returned by ==, then true is returned by !=.

You can make the reversal of equality explicit by adding a temporary Boolean variable named "equality." Rewrite the != operator as follows:

```
public static bool operator !=(Fraction lhs, Fraction rhs)
{
    bool equality = lhs == rhs;
    return !(equality);
}
```

You can now put a breakpoint on the second line of this method and examine the value returned by operator==, as shown in Figure 12-2.

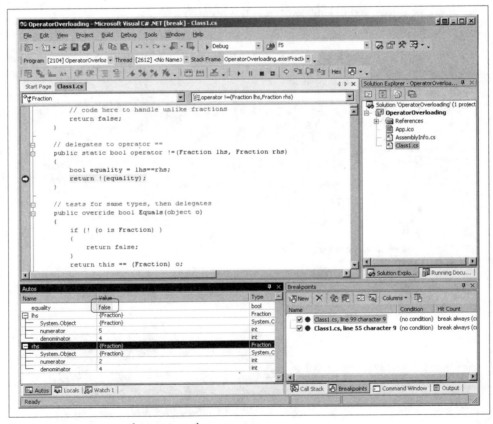

Figure 12-2. Examining the interim value

You can see in the Autos window that the value of equality (shown circled and highlighted) is false. The fractions have been expanded to show their values (5/4 and

2/4), and they are not equal. The value returned by the != operator is the opposite of false; that is, true.

In addition to implementing the == and != operator, you implement the Equals() method, for the reasons explained previously.

```
public override bool Equals( object o )
{
    if ( !( o is Fraction ) )
    {
        return false;
    }
    return this == (Fraction)o;
}
```

If the two objects are not both Fractions, you return false; otherwise, you delegate to the == operator, casting o to a Fraction type. Put a breakpoint on the return line, and you'll find that you step back into operator==. The value returned by operator== is the value returned by the Equals() method if both objects are fractions.

The Meaning of Equality

It is up to you, as the class designer, to decide what it means for two instances of your class to be equal. Two employees might be equal if they have the same name, or you might decide they are only equal if they have the same Employee ID.

Conversion Operators

C# will convert (for example) an int to a long *implicitly* but will only allow you to convert a long to an int *explicitly*. The conversion from int to long is implicit because you know that any int will fit into the memory representation of a long without losing any information. The reverse operation, from long to int, must be explicit (using a cast) because it is possible to lose information in the conversion:

```
int myInt = 5;
long myLong;
myLong = myInt;         // implicit
myInt = (int) myLong;   // explicit
```

You want to be able to convert your Fraction objects to intrinsic types (such as int) and back. Given an int, you can support an implicit conversion to a fraction because any whole value is equal to that value over 1 (15 == 15/1).

Given a fraction, you might want to provide an explicit conversion back to an integer, understanding that some information might be lost. Thus, you might convert 9/4 to the integer value 2 (truncating to the nearest whole number).

A more sophisticated Fraction class might not truncate, but rather round to the nearest whole number. This idea is left, as they say, as an exercise for the reader, to keep this example simple.

You use the keyword implicit when the conversion is guaranteed to succeed and no information will be lost; otherwise, you use explicit. implicit and explicit are actually operators, often called cast or casting operators because their job is to cast from one type to another (int to Fraction or Fraction to int).

Example 12-3 illustrates how you might implement implicit and explicit conversions; detailed analysis follows.

Example 12-3. Conversion operators

```
using System;

public class Fraction
{
    private int numerator;
    private int denominator;

    // create a fraction by passing in the numerator
    // and denominator
    public Fraction( int numerator, int denominator )
    {
        this.numerator = numerator;
        this.denominator = denominator;
    }

    // overload the constructor to create a
    // fraction from a whole number
    public Fraction( int wholeNumber )
    {
        Console.WriteLine( "In constructor taking a whole number" );
        numerator = wholeNumber;
        denominator = 1;
    }

    // convert ints to Fractions implicitly
    public static implicit operator Fraction( int theInt )
    {
        Console.WriteLine( "Implicitly converting int to Fraction" );
        return new Fraction( theInt );
    }

    // convert Fractions to ints explicitly
    public static explicit operator int( Fraction theFraction )
    {
        Console.WriteLine( "Explicitly converting Fraction to int" );
        return theFraction.numerator / theFraction.denominator;
    }
```

Example 12-3. Conversion operators (continued)

```
// overloaded operator + takes two fractions
// and returns their sum
public static Fraction operator +( Fraction lhs, Fraction rhs )
{
    // like fractions (shared denominator) can be added
    // by adding their numerators
    if ( lhs.denominator == rhs.denominator )
    {
        return new Fraction( lhs.numerator + rhs.numerator,
        lhs.denominator );
    }

    // simplistic solution for unlike fractions
    // 1/2 + 3/4 == (1*4) + (3*2) / (2*4) == 10/8
    // this method does not reduce.
    int firstProduct = lhs.numerator * rhs.denominator;
    int secondProduct = rhs.numerator * lhs.denominator;
    return new Fraction(
    firstProduct + secondProduct,
    lhs.denominator * rhs.denominator
    );
}

// test whether two Fractions are equal
public static bool operator ==( Fraction lhs, Fraction rhs )
{
    if ( lhs.denominator == rhs.denominator &&
    lhs.numerator == rhs.numerator )
    {
        return true;
    }
    // code here to handle unlike fractions
    return false;
}

// delegates to operator ==
public static bool operator !=( Fraction lhs, Fraction rhs )
{
    bool equality = lhs == rhs;
    return !( equality );
}

// tests for same types, then delegates
public override bool Equals( object o )
{
    if ( !( o is Fraction ) )
    {
        return false;
    }
    return this == (Fraction)o;
}
```

Example 12-3. Conversion operators (continued)

```
    // return a string representation of the fraction
    public override string ToString( )
    {
        String s = numerator.ToString( ) + "/" +
        denominator.ToString( );
        return s;
    }
}


public class Tester
{
    public void Run( )
    {
        Fraction f1 = new Fraction( 3, 4 );
        Fraction f2 = new Fraction( 2, 4 );
        Fraction f3 = f1 + f2;

        Console.WriteLine( "adding f3 + 5..." );
        Fraction f4 = f3 + 5;
        Console.WriteLine( "f3 + 5 = f4: {0}", f4.ToString( ) );

        Console.WriteLine( "\nAssigning f4 to an int..." );
        int truncated = (int)f4;
        Console.WriteLine( "When you truncate f4 you get {0}",
        truncated );
    }
    static void Main( )
    {
        Tester t = new Tester( );
        t.Run( );
    }
}
```

```
Output:
adding f3 + 5...
Implicitly converting int to Fraction
In constructor taking a whole number
f3 + 5 = f4: 25/4

Assigning f4 to an int...
Explicitly converting Fraction to int
When you truncate f4 you get 6
```

In Example 12-3, you add a second constructor that takes a whole number and creates a Fraction:

```
    public Fraction(int wholeNumber)
    {
        Console.WriteLine("In constructor taking a whole number");
        numerator = wholeNumber;
        denominator = 1;
    }
```

Notice that in this and the following code samples, you add WriteLine( ) statements to indicate when you've entered the method. This is an alternative to stepping through in a debugger. While using the debugger is usually more effective, this kind of output can help you trace the execution of your program for review at a later time.

You want to be able to convert Fractions to and from ints. To do so, create the conversion operators. As discussed previously, converting from a Fraction to an int requires truncating the value, and so must be explicit:

```
public static explicit operator int(Fraction theFraction)
{
    Console.WriteLine("Explicitly converting Fraction to int");
    return theFraction.numerator /
    theFraction.denominator;
}
```

Note the use of the explicit keyword, indicating that this requires an explicit cast from a Fraction to an int. You see the cast in the Run( ) method:

```
int truncated = (int) f4;
```

The cast from an int to a Fraction, on the other hand, is perfectly safe, so it can be implicit:

```
Fraction f4 = f3 + 5;
```

Notice that there is no explicit cast (in parentheses). When you add the int to the Fraction, the int is implicitly cast to a Fraction. The implementation of this is to create a new Fraction object and to return it:

```
public static implicit operator Fraction(int theInt)
{
    Console.WriteLine("Implicitly converting int to Fraction");
    return new Fraction(theInt);
}
```

Calling the implicit cast operator causes the constructor to be invoked:

```
public Fraction(int wholeNumber)
{
    Console.WriteLine("In constructor taking a whole number");
    numerator = wholeNumber;
    denominator = 1;
}
```

You see this sequence of events represented in the output:

```
Implicitly converting int to Fraction
In constructor taking a whole number
```

Summary

- You can overload operators in much the same way that you would overload methods.
- To overload an operator, use the `static` keyword with the `operator` keyword, and the name of the operator you're overloading.
- It is good programming practice to be parsimonious in your use of operator overloading, and to be sure that the meaning of the overload is obvious and intuitive.
- When you overload the equals (`==`) operator, you should also overload the `Equals( )` method for compatibility with other .NET languages.
- If you overload the `==` operator, you must also overload the `!=` operator. Similarly, the `<` and `>` operators are paired, as are the `<=` and `>=` operators.
- You can also overload conversion operators to allow one type to be implicitly or explicitly cast to another type. When doing so, you must use the keyword `implicit` when the conversion is guaranteed to succeed without loss of information, and `explicit` when there is a risk that information might be lost.

Quiz

Question 12-1. What is operator overloading?

Question 12-2. Are operators implemented as properties, static methods, or instance methods?

Question 12-3. How does the compiler translate:

```
Fraction f3 = f2 + f1;
```

assuming that `f2` and `f1` are `Fraction` objects and you have overloaded the `+` operator for the `Fraction` class?

Question 12-4. What should you also do if you overload the `==` operator?

Question 12-5. What is the difference between implicit and explicit conversion?

Exercises

Exercise 12-1. Create a class Invoice, that has a string property vendor and a double property amount. Overload the addition operator so that if the vendor properties match, the amount properties of the two invoices are added together in a new invoice. If the vendor properties do not match, the new invoice is blank.

Exercise 12-2. Modify the Invoice class so that two invoices are considered equal if the vendor and amount properties match. Test your methods.

CHAPTER 13

Interfaces

There are times when you may not want to create a new type, but you do want to describe a set of behaviors that any number of types might implement. For example, you might want to describe what it means to be *storable* (capable of being written to disk) or *printable*.

Such a description is called an *interface*. An interface is a contract. When you design an interface, you're saying "if you want to provide this capability, you must implement these methods, provide these properties and indexers, and support these events." The *implementer* of the interface agrees to the contract and implements the required elements.

 See Chapter 8 for information about methods and properties, Chapter 17 for information about events, and Chapter 14 for coverage of indexers.

When specifying interfaces, it is easy to get confused about who is responsible for what. There are three concepts to keep clear:

The interface
> This is the contract. By convention, interface names begin with a capital I, so your interface might have a name such as IPrintable. The IPrintable interface might require, among other things, a Print( ) method. This states that any class that wants to implement IPrintable must implement a Print( ) method, but it does *not* specify how that method works. That is up to the designer of the implementing class.

The implementing class
> This is the class that agrees to the contract described by the interface. For example, Document might be a class that implements IPrintable and thus implements the Print( ) method in whatever way the designer of the Document class thinks is appropriate.

The client class

The client calls methods on the implementing class. For example, you might have an Editor class that has a collection of IPrintable objects (every object in the class is an instance of a type that implements IPrintable). The client can expect to be able to call Print( ) on each, and while each may implement the method differently, each will do so appropriately and without complaint.

Interfaces Versus Abstract Base Classes

Programmers learning C# often ask about the difference between an interface and an abstract base class. The key difference is that an abstract base class serves as the base class for a family of derived classes, while an interface is meant to be mixed in with other inheritance trees. That is, a class can only inherit from a single parent class, but it can implement multiple interfaces.

Inheriting from an abstract class implements the *is-a* relationship, introduced in Chapter 6. Implementing an interface defines a different relationship, one you've not seen until now: the *implements* relationship. These two relationships are subtly different. A car *is a* vehicle, but it might *implement* the CanBeBoughtWithABigLoan capability (as can a house, for example).

Interfaces are a critical addition to any framework, and they are used extensively throughout .NET. For example, the collection classes (stacks, queues, dictionaries) are defined, in large measure, by the interfaces they implement. (The collection classes are reviewed in detail in Chapter 14.)

In this chapter, you will learn how to create, implement, and use interfaces. You'll learn how one class can implement multiple interfaces, and you will also learn how to make new interfaces by combining or deriving from existing interfaces. Finally, you will learn how to test whether a class has implemented an interface.

Implementing an Interface

The syntax for defining an interface is very similar to the syntax for defining a class:

```
[attributes] [access-modifier] interface interface-name [:base-list] {interface-body}
```

The optional *attributes* are well beyond the scope of this book (however, see the sidebar, "Attributes").

Access modifiers (public, private, etc.) work just as they do with classes. (See Chapter 7 for more about access modifiers.) The interface keyword is followed by an identifier (the interface name). It is common (but not required) to begin the name of your interface with a capital I (IStorable, ICloneable, IGetNoKickFromChampagne, etc.). The optional base list is discussed later in this chapter.

Attributes

Every .NET application contains code, data, and metadata. Attributes are objects that are embedded in your program (invisible at run time) that contain metadata—that is, data about your classes and about your program. Attributes can be made visible with ILDasm—the tool for looking at the Microsoft Intermediate Language (MSIL) that the C# compiler produces.

The element to which an attribute is attached is referred to as the *target* of that attribute. For example, the attribute:

```
[NoIDispatch]
```

is associated with a class or an interface to indicate that the target should derive from IUnknown rather than IDispatch when exporting to COM.

Attributes are most often used in one of two ways: either for interacting with legacy COM objects or for creating controls that will be fully recognized by the Visual Studio development environment. You *can* create your own custom attributes, but this is unusual and not covered in this book (for more on this, see *Programming C#*, Fourth Edition [O'Reilly, 2005]). Now suppose you are the author of a Document class, which specifies that Document objects can be stored in a database. You decide to have Document implement the IStorable interface. It isn't required that you do so, but by implementing the IStorable interface, you signal to potential clients that the Document class can be used just like any other IStorable object. This will, for example, allow your clients to add your Document objects to an array of Notes

```
IStorable[] myStorableArray = new IStorable[3];
```

and to otherwise interact with your Document in this very general and well-understood way.

To implement the IStorable interface, use the same syntax as if the new Document class were inheriting from IStorable—a colon (:) followed by the interface name:

```
public class Document : IStorable
```

You can read this as "define a public class named Document that implements the IStorable interface." The compiler distinguishes whether the colon indicates inheritance or implementation of an interface by checking to see if IStorable is defined, and whether it is an interface or base class.

If you derive from a base class and you also implement one or more interfaces, you use a single colon and separate the base class and the interfaces by commas. The base class must be listed first; the interfaces may be listed in any order.

```
public MyBigClass : TheBaseClass, IPrintable, IStorable,
    IClaudius, IAndThou
```

In this declaration, the new class MyBigClass derives from TheBaseClass and implements four interfaces.

Your definition of the Document class that implements the IStorable interface might look like this:

```
public class Document : IStorable
{
    public void Read() {...}
    public void Write(object obj) {...}
    // ...
}
```

It is now your responsibility, as the author of the Document class, to provide a meaningful implementation of the IStorable methods. Having designated Document as implementing IStorable, you must implement all the IStorable methods, or you will generate an error when you compile. Example 13-1 illustrates defining and implementing the IStorable interface.

Example 13-1. Document class implementing IStorable

```
using System;

namespace InterfaceDemo
{

    interface IStorable
    {
        void Read( );
        void Write( object obj );
        int Status { get; set; }

    }

    public class Document : IStorable
    {
        // store the value for the IStorable required property
        private int status = 0;

        public Document( string s )
        {
            Console.WriteLine( "Creating document with: {0}", s );
        }

#region IStorable
```

Example 13-1. Document class implementing IStorable (continued)

```
    public void Read( )
    {
        Console.WriteLine(
        "Implementing the Read Method for IStorable" );
    }

    public void Write( object o )
    {
        Console.WriteLine(
        "Implementing the Write Method for IStorable" );
    }

    public int Status
    {
        get { return status; }
        set { status = value; }
    }
#endregion

    }

    class Tester
    {
        public void Run( )
        {
            Document doc = new Document( "Test Document" );
            doc.Status = -1;
            doc.Read( );
            Console.WriteLine( "Document Status: {0}", doc.Status );
        }

        static void Main( )
        {
            Tester t = new Tester( );
            t.Run( );
        }
    }
}
```

The output looks like this:

```
Creating document with: Test Document
Implementing the Read Method for IStorable
Document Status: -1
```

Defining the Interface

In Example 13-1, the first few lines define an interface, IStorable, which has two methods (Read( ) and Write( )) and a property (Status) of type int:

```
interface IStorable
    {
```

```
        void Read( );
        void Write(object obj);
        int Status { get; set; }
}
```

Notice that the IStorable method declarations for Read( ) and Write( ) do not include access modifiers (public, protected, internal, private). In fact, providing an access modifier generates a compile error. Interface methods are implicitly public because an interface is a contract meant to be used by other classes. In addition, you must declare these methods to be public, and not static, when you implement the interface.

In the interface declaration, the methods are otherwise defined just like methods in a class: you indicate the return type (void), followed by the identifier (Write), followed by the parameter list (object obj), and, of course, you end all statements with a semicolon.

An interface can also require that the implementing class provide a property (see Chapter 8 for a discussion of properties). Notice that the declaration of the Status property does not provide an implementation for get( ) and set( ), but simply designates that there *is* a get( ) and a set( ):

```
    int Status { get; set; }
```

Implementing the Interface on the Client

Once you've defined the IStorable interface, you can define classes that implement your interface. Keep in mind that you cannot create an instance of an interface; instead, you instantiate a class that implements the interface.

 You can make a reference to an interface, but you must assign an actual implementing object to that reference:

```
        IStorable myStorable = new Document( );
```

The class implementing the interface must fulfill the contract exactly and completely. Thus, your Document class must provide both a Read( ) and a Write( ) method and the Status property.

```
    public class Document : IStorable
    {
```

This statement defines Document as a class that defines IStorable. I also like to separate the implementation of an interface in a *region*—this is a Visual Studio 2005 convenience that allows you to collapse and expand the code within the region to make reading the code easier:

```
    #region IStorable
      //...
    #endregion
```

Within the region, you place the code that implements the two required methods and the required property. Exactly how your Document class fulfills the requirements of the interface, however, is entirely up to you.

Although IStorable dictates that Document must have a Status property, it does not know or care whether Document stores the actual status as a member variable or looks it up in a database. Example 13-1 implements the Status property by returning (or setting) the value of a private member variable, status. Another class that implements IStorable could provide the Status property in an entirely different manner (such as by looking it up in a database).

Implementing More than One Interface

Classes can derive from only one class (and if it doesn't explicitly derive from a class, then it implicitly derives from Object).

 Some languages, such as C++, support implementation from multiple base classes (called Multiple Inheritance or MI). In 10 years of working with C++, I never used MI except to demonstrate that it could be done, and in 6 years of working with C#, I've never missed MI.

When you design your class, you can choose not to implement any interfaces, you can implement a single interface, or you can implement two or more interfaces. For example, in addition to IStorable, you might have a second interface, ICompressible, for files that can be compressed to save disk space. If your Document class can be stored and compressed, you might choose to have Document implement both the IStorable and ICompressible interfaces.

 Both IStorable and ICompressible are interfaces created for this book and are not part of the standard .NET Framework.

Example 13-2 shows the complete listing of the new ICompressible interface and demonstrates how you modify the Document class to implement the two interfaces.

Example 13-2. IStorable and ICompressible, implemented by Document

```
using System;

namespace InterfaceDemo
{
    interface IStorable
    {
        void Read( );
        void Write( object obj );
        int Status { get; set; }
```

```
}

// here's the new interface
interface ICompressible
{
   void Compress();
   void Decompress();
}


public class Document : IStorable, ICompressible
{
   private int status = 0;

   public Document( string s )
   {
      Console.WriteLine( "Creating document with: {0}", s );
   }

   #region IStorable

   public void Read()
   {
      Console.WriteLine(
      "Implementing the Read Method for IStorable" );
   }

   public void Write( object o )
   {
      Console.WriteLine(
      "Implementing the Write Method for IStorable" );
   }

   public int Status
   {
      get { return status; }
      set { status = value; }
   }

   #endregion      // IStorable

   #region ICompressible

   public void Compress()
   {
      Console.WriteLine( "Implementing Compress" );
   }

   public void Decompress()
   {
      Console.WriteLine( "Implementing Decompress" );
   }
```

```
    #endregion  // ICompressible
}


class Tester
{
    public void Run( )
    {
        Document doc = new Document( "Test Document" );
        doc.Status = -1;
        doc.Read( );           // invoke method from IStorable
        doc.Compress( );       // invoke method from ICompressible
        Console.WriteLine( "Document Status: {0}", doc.Status );
    }

    static void Main( )
    {
        Tester t = new Tester( );
        t.Run( );
    }
}
}
```

The output looks like this:

```
Creating document with: Test Document
Implementing the Read Method for IStorable
Implementing Compress
Document Status: -1
```

As Example 13-2 shows, you declare the fact that your Document class will implement two interfaces by adding the second interface to the declaration (in the base list), separating the two interfaces with commas:

```
public class Document : IStorable, ICompressible
```

Once you've done this, the Document class must also implement the methods specified by the ICompressible interface. ICompressible has only two methods, Compress( ) and Uncompress( ), which are specified as:

```
interface ICompressible
{
    void Compress( );
    void Decompress( );
}
```

In this simplified example, Document implements these two methods as follows, printing notification messages to the console:

```
public void Compress( )
{
 Console.WriteLine("Implementing the Compress Method");
}
```

```
public void Decompress()
{
  Console.WriteLine("Implementing the Decompress Method");
}
```

Casting to an Interface

You can access the members of an interface through an object of any class that implements the interface. For example, because Document implements IStorable, you can access the IStorable methods and property through any Document instance:

```
Document doc = new Document("Test Document");
doc.Status = -1;
doc.Read();
```

At times, though, you won't know that you have a Document object; you'll only know that you have objects that implement IStorable, for example, if you have an array of IStorable objects. You can create a reference of type IStorable, and assign that to each member in the array, accessing the IStorable methods and property (but not the Document-specific methods, because all the compiler knows is that you have an IStorable, not a Document).

You *cannot* instantiate an interface directly; that is, you cannot write:

```
IStorable isDoc = new IStorable;
```

You can, however, create an instance of the implementing class and then assign that object to a reference to any of the interfaces it implements:

```
Document myDoc = new Document(//...);
IStorable myStorable = myDoc;
```

You can read this line as "assign the IStorable-implementing object myDoc to the IStorable reference myStorable."

You are now free to use the IStorable reference to access the IStorable methods and properties of the document:

```
myStorable.Status = 0;
myStorable.Read();
```

Notice that the IStorable reference myStorable has access to the IStorable property Status, but *not* to the Document's private member variable status, even though the IStorable reference was instantiated as a reference to the Document. The IStorable reference only knows about the IStorable interface, not about the Document's internal members.

Thus far, you have assigned the Document object (myDoc) to an IStorable reference.

The is and as Operators

There may be times, however, in which you do not know at compile time whether or not an object supports a particular interface. For instance, given a List of IStorable objects, you might not know whether any given object in the collection also implements ICompressible (some do, some do not). Let's set aside the question of whether this is a good design, and move on to how we solve the problem.

Any time you see casting, you must question the design of the program. It is common for casting to be the result of poor or lazy design. That said, there are times that casting is unavoidable, especially when dealing with nongeneric collections that you did not create.

You could cast each member blindly to ICompressible, and then catch the exception that will be thrown for those that are not ICompressible, but this is ugly, and there are two better ways to do so: the is and the as operators.

The is operator lets you query whether an object implements an interface (or derives from a base class). The form of the is operator is:

```
if ( myObject is ICompressible )
```

The is operator evaluates true if the *expression* (which must be a reference type, such as an instance of a class) can be safely cast to *type* without throwing an exception.[*]

The as operator tries to cast the object to the type, and if an exception would be thrown, it instead returns null:

```
ICompressible myCompressible = myObject as ICompressible
if ( myCompressible != null )
```

The is operator is slightly less efficient than using as, so the as operator is slightly preferred over the is operator, except when you want to do the test but not actually do the cast (a rare situation).

Example 13-3 illustrates the use of both the is and the as operators by creating two classes. The Note class implements IStorable. The Document class derives from Note (and thus inherits the implementation of IStorable) and adds a property (ID) along with an implementation of ICompressible.

In this example, you'll create an array of Note objects and then, if you want to access either ICompressible or the ID, you'll need to test the Note to see if it is of the correct type. Both the is and the as operators are demonstrated. The entire program is documented fully immediately after the source code.

---

[*] Historical footnote: "It depends on what the meaning of the word 'is' is. If the—if he—if 'is' means is and never has been, that is not—that is one thing."—But not in C#.

Example 13-3. The is and as operators

```
using System;

namespace InterfaceDemo
{
    interface IStorable
    {
        void Read( );
        void Write( object obj );
        int Status { get; set; }
    }

    interface ICompressible
    {
        void Compress( );
        void Decompress( );
    }

    public class Note : IStorable
    {
        private int status = 0; // IStorable
        private string myString;

        public Note( string theString )
        {
            myString = theString;
        }

        public override string ToString( )
        {
            return myString;
        }

        #region IStorable

        public void Read( )
        {
            Console.WriteLine(
            "Implementing the Read Method for IStorable" );
        }

        public void Write( object o )
        {
            Console.WriteLine(
            "Implementing the Write Method for IStorable" );
        }

        public int Status
        {
            get { return status; }
            set { status = value; }
        }
```

Example 13-3. The is and as operators (continued)

```
        #endregion // IStorable

}

public class Document : Note, ICompressible
{
    private int documentID;
    public int ID
    {
        get { return this.documentID; }
    }

    public Document( string docString, int documentID )
        :
    base( docString )
    {
        this.documentID = documentID;
    }

    #region ICompressible

    public void Compress()
    {
        Console.WriteLine( "Compressing..." );
    }
    public void Decompress()
    {
        Console.WriteLine( "Decompressing..." );
    }
    #endregion  // ICompressible

}   // end Document class

class Tester
{
    public void Run()
    {
        string testString = "String ";
        Note[] myNoteArray = new Note[3];

        for ( int i = 0; i < 3; i++ )
        {
            string docText = testString + i.ToString();
            if ( i % 2 == 0 )
            {
                Document myDocument = new Document( docText, ( i + 5 ) * 10 );
                myNoteArray[i] = myDocument;
            }
            else
            {
                Note myNote = new Note( docText );
                myNoteArray[i] = myNote;
```

Example 13-3. The is and as operators (continued)

```
        }
    }

    foreach ( Note theNote in myNoteArray )
    {
        Console.WriteLine( "\nTesting {0} with IS", theNote );

        theNote.Read();     // all notes can do this
        if ( theNote is ICompressible )
        {
            ICompressible myCompressible = theNote as ICompressible;
            myCompressible.Compress();
        }
        else
        {
            Console.WriteLine( "This storable object is not compressible." );
        }

        if ( theNote is Document )
        {
            Document myDoc = theNote as Document;

            // clean cast
            myDoc = theNote as Document;
            Console.WriteLine( "my documentID is {0}", myDoc.ID );

            // old fashioned cast!
            Console.WriteLine( "My documentID is {0}",
              ( ( Document ) theNote ).ID );
        }
    }

    foreach ( Note theNote in myNoteArray )
    {
        Console.WriteLine( "\nTesting {0} with AS", theNote );
        ICompressible myCompressible = theNote as ICompressible;
        if ( myCompressible != null )
        {
            myCompressible.Compress();
        }
        else
        {
            Console.WriteLine( "This storable object is not compressible." );
        }    // end else

        Document theDoc = theNote as Document;
        if ( theDoc != null )
        {
            Console.WriteLine( "My documentID is {0}",
                ( ( Document ) theNote ).ID );
        }
        else
```

Example 13-3. The is and as operators (continued)

```
            {
                Console.WriteLine( "Not a document." );
            }
        }
    }

    static void Main( )
    {
        Tester t = new Tester( );
        t.Run( );
    }
    }            // end class Tester
}            // end Namespace InterfaceDemo
```

The output looks like this:

```
Testing String 0 with IS
Implementing the Read Method for IStorable
Compressing...
my documentID is 50
My documentID is 50

Testing String 1 with IS
Implementing the Read Method for IStorable
This storable object is not compressible.

Testing String 2 with IS
Implementing the Read Method for IStorable
Compressing...
my documentID is 70
My documentID is 70

Testing String 0 with AS
Compressing...
My documentID is 50

Testing String 1 with AS
This storable object is not compressible.
Not a document.

Testing String 2 with AS
Compressing...
My documentID is 70
```

The best way to understand this program is to take it apart piece by piece.

Within the namespace, we declare two interfaces, IStorable and ICompressible, and then three classes: Note, which implements IStorable; and Document, which derives from Note (and thus inherits the implementation of IStorable) and which also implements ICompressible). Finally, we add the class Tester to test the program.

Within the Run( ) method of the Tester class, we create an array of Note objects, and we add to that array two Document and one Note instances (using the expedient that each time through the for loop, we check whether the counter variable i is even, and if so, we create a Document; otherwise, we create a Note).

We then iterate through the array, extract each Note in turn, and use the is operator to test first if the Note can safely be assigned to an ICompressible reference and then to check if the Note can safely be cast to a Document. In the case shown, these tests amount to the same thing, but you can imagine that we could have a collection with many types derived from Note, some of which implement ICompressible and some of which do not.

We have a choice as to how we cast to a document. The old-fashioned way is to use the C-style cast:

```
myDoc = (Document) theNote;
```

The preferred way is to use the as operator:

```
myDoc = theNote as Document;
```

The advantage of the latter is that it will return null (rather than throwing an exception) if the cast fails, and it may be a good idea to get in the habit of using this new form of casting.

In any case, you can use the interim variable:

```
myDoc = theNote as Document;
 Console.WriteLine( "my documentID is {0}", myDoc.ID );
```

Or you can cast and access the property all in one ugly but effective line:

```
Console.WriteLine( "My documentID is {0}",
    ( ( Document ) theNote ).ID );
```

The extra parentheses are required to ensure that the cast is done before the attempt at accessing the property.

The second foreach loop uses the as operator to accomplish the same work, and the results are identical. (If you bother to look at the actual IL code, you'll see that the second foreach loop actually generates less code, and thus is slightly more efficient.)

Extending Interfaces

It is possible to extend an existing interface to add new methods or members. For example, you might extend ICompressible with a new interface, ILoggedCompressible, which extends the original interface with methods to keep track of the bytes saved. One such method might be called LogSavedBytes( ). The following code creates a new interface named ILoggedCompressible that is identical to ICompressible except that it adds the method LogSavedBytes:

```
interface ILoggedCompressible : ICompressible
{
  void LogSavedBytes();
}
```

Classes are now free to implement either ICompressible or ILoggedCompressible, depending on whether they need the additional functionality. If a class does implement ILoggedCompressible, it must implement all the methods of both ILoggedCompressible and also ICompressible. Objects of that type can be cast either to ILoggedCompressible or to ICompressible.

Example 13-4 extends ICompressible to create ILoggedCompressible, and then casts the Document first to be of type IStorable, then to be of type ILoggedCompressible. Finally, the example casts the Document object to ICompressible. This last cast is safe because any object that implements ILoggedCompressible must also have implemented ICompressible (the former is a superset of the latter). This is the same logic that says you can cast any object of a derived type to an object of a base type (that is, if Student derives from Human, then all Students are Human, even though not all Humans are Students).

Example 13-4. Extending interfaces

```
using System;

namespace ExtendingInterfaces
{
    interface ICompressible
    {
        void Compress();
        void Decompress();
    }

    // extend ICompressible to log the bytes saved
    interface ILoggedCompressible : ICompressible
    {
        void LogSavedBytes();
    }

    public class Document :  ILoggedCompressible
    {

        public Document( string s )
        {
            Console.WriteLine( "Creating document with: {0}", s );
        }


        #region
```

Example 13-4. Extending interfaces (continued)

```
      public void Compress( )
      {
         Console.WriteLine( "Implementing Compress" );
      }

      public void Decompress( )
      {
         Console.WriteLine( "Implementing Decompress" );
      }


      public void LogSavedBytes( )
      {
         Console.WriteLine( "Implementing LogSavedBytes" );
      }

      #endregion //ILoggedCompressible

   }

   class Tester
   {
      public void Run( )
      {
         Document doc = new Document( "Test Document" );

         ILoggedCompressible myLoggedCompressible = doc as ILoggedCompressible;
         if ( myLoggedCompressible != null )
         {
            Console.Write( "\nCalling both ICompressible and " );
            Console.WriteLine( "ILoggedCompressible methods..." );
            myLoggedCompressible.Compress( );
            myLoggedCompressible.LogSavedBytes( );
         }
         else
         {
            Console.WriteLine( "Something went wrong! Not ILoggedCompressible" );
         }
      }

      static void Main( )
      {
         Tester t = new Tester( );
         t.Run( );
      }
   }
}
```

The output looks like this:

```
Creating document with: Test Document

Calling both ICompressible and ILoggedCompressible methods...
Implementing Compress
Implementing LogSavedBytes
```

Example 13-4 starts by creating the ILoggedCompressible interface, which extends the ICompressible interface:

```
// extend ICompressible to log the bytes saved
interface ILoggedCompressible : ICompressible
{
    void LogSavedBytes( );
}
```

Notice that the syntax for extending an interface is the same as that for deriving from a class. This extended interface defines only one new method (LogSavedBytes( )), but any class implementing this interface must also implement the base interface (ICompressible) and all its members. (In this sense, it is reasonable to say that an ILoggedCompressible object *is-a* ICompressible object.)

Combining Interfaces

You can also create new interfaces by combining existing interfaces and optionally adding new methods or properties. For example, you might decide to combine the definitions of IStorable and ICompressible into a new interface called IStorableCompressible. This interface would combine the methods of each of the other two interfaces, but would also add a new method, LogOriginalSize( ), to store the original size of the precompressed item:

```
interface IStorableCompressible : IStorable, ILoggedCompressible
{
 void LogOriginalSize( );
}
```

Having created this interface, you can now modify Document to implement IStorableCompressible:

```
public class Document : IStorableCompressible
```

You now can cast the Document object to any of the four interfaces you've created so far:

```
IStorable isDoc = doc as IStorable;
ILoggedCompressible ilDoc = doc as ILoggedCompressible;
ICompressible icDoc = doc as ICompressible;
IStorableCompressible iscDoc = doc as IStorableCompressible;
```

When you cast to the new combined interface, you can invoke any of the methods of any of the interfaces it extends or combines. The following code invokes four methods on iscDoc (the IStorableCompressible object). Only one of these methods is defined in IStorableCompressible, but all four are methods defined by interfaces that IStorableCompressible extends or combines.

```
if (iscDoc != null)
{
 iscDoc.Read(); // Read( ) from IStorable
 iscDoc.Compress(); // Compress( ) from ICompressible
 iscDoc.LogSavedBytes(); // LogSavedBytes( ) from
 // ILoggedCompressible
 iscDoc.LogOriginalSize(); // LogOriginalSize( ) from
 // IStorableCompressible
}
```

Overriding Interface Implementations

An implementing class is free to mark any or all of the methods from the interface as virtual. Derived classes can then override or provide new implementations, just as they might with any other virtual instance method.

For example, a Document class might implement the IStorable interface and mark its Read( ) and Write( ) methods as virtual. In an earlier example, we created a base class Note, and a derived class Document. While the Note class implements Read( ) and Write( ) to save to a file, the Document class might implement Read( ) and Write( ) to read from and write to a database.

Example 13-5 strips down the complexity of the previous examples and illustrates overriding an interface implementation. Note implements the IStorable-required Read( ) method as a virtual method, and Document overrides that implementation.

 Notice that Note does not mark Write( ) as virtual. You'll see the implications of this decision in the analysis that follows Example 13-5.

The complete listing is shown in Example 13-5.

Example 13-5. Overriding an interface implementation

```
using System;

namespace OverridingAnInterfaceImplementation
{
    interface IStorable
    {
        void Read( );
        void Write( );
    }
```

Example 13-5. Overriding an interface implementation (continued)

```csharp
public class Note : IStorable
{
   public Note( string s )
   {
      Console.WriteLine(
      "Creating Note with: {0}", s );
   }

   // NB: virtual
   public virtual void Read( )
   {
      Console.WriteLine(
      "Note Read Method for IStorable" );
   }

   // NB: Not virtual!
   public void Write( )
   {
      Console.WriteLine(
      "Note Write Method for IStorable" );
   }
}

public class Document : Note
{
   public Document( string s ):
   base( s )
   {
      Console.WriteLine(
      "Creating Document with: {0}", s );
   }

   // override the Read method
   public override void Read( )
   {
      Console.WriteLine(
      "Overriding the Read method for Document!" );
   }

   // implement my own Write method
   public new void Write( )
   {
      Console.WriteLine(
      "Implementing the Write method for Document!" );
   }
}

class Tester
{
   public void Run( )
   {
      Note theNote = new Document( "Test Document" );
```

Example 13-5. Overriding an interface implementation (continued)

```
         theNote.Read( );
         theNote.Write( );

         Console.WriteLine( "\n" );

         IStorable isStorable = theNote as IStorable;
         if ( isStorable != null )
         {
            isStorable.Read( );
            isStorable.Write( );
         }
         Console.WriteLine( "\n" );

         // This time create a reference to the derived type
         Document theDoc = new Document( "Second Test" );

         theDoc.Read( );
         theDoc.Write( );
         Console.WriteLine( "\n" );

         IStorable isStorable2 = theDoc as IStorable;
         if ( isStorable != null )
         {
            isStorable2.Read( );
            isStorable2.Write( );
         }
      }

   static void Main( )
   {
      Tester t = new Tester( );
      t.Run( );
   }
   }
}
```

The output looks like this:

```
Creating Note with: Test Document
Creating Document with: Test Document
Overriding the Read method for Document!
Note Write Method for IStorable


Overriding the Read method for Document!
Note Write Method for IStorable


Creating Note with: Second Test
Creating Document with: Second Test
Overriding the Read method for Document!
Implementing the Write method for Document!
```

```
Overriding the Read method for Document!
Note Write Method for IStorable
```

In Example 13-5, the IStorable interface is simplified for clarity's sake:

```
interface IStorable
{
 void Read( );
 void Write( );
}
```

The Note class implements the IStorable interface:

```
public class Note : IStorable
```

The designer of Note has opted to make the Read( ) method virtual but not to make the Write( ) method virtual:

```
public virtual void Read( )
public void Write( )
```

 In a real-world application, you would almost certainly mark both methods as virtual, but I've differentiated them to demonstrate that the developer is free to pick and choose which methods are made virtual.

The new class, Document, derives from Note:

```
public class Document : Note
```

It is not necessary for Document to override Read( ), but it is free to do so and has done so here:

```
public override void Read( )
```

To illustrate the implications of marking an implementing method as virtual, the Run( ) method calls the Read( ) and Write( ) methods in four ways:

- Through the Note class reference to a Document object
- Through an interface created from the Note class reference to the Document object
- Through a Document object
- Through an interface created from the Document object

Virtual implementations of interface methods are polymorphic, just like the virtual methods of classes.

When you call the non-polymorphic Write( ) method on the IStorable interface cast from the derived Document, you actually get the Note's Write method, because Write( ) is implemented in the base class and is non-virtual.

To see polymorphism at work with interfaces, you'll create a reference to the Note class and initialize it with a new instance of the derived Document class:

```
Note theDocument = new Document("Test Document");
```

Invoke the Read and Write methods:

```
theDocument.Read( );
theDocument.Write( );
```

The output reveals that the (virtual) Read( ) method is called polymorphically—that is, the Document class overrides the Note class's Read( ), while the non-virtual Write( ) method of the Note class is invoked because it was not made virtual.

```
Overriding the Read method for Document!
Note Write Method for IStorable
```

The overridden method of Read( ) is called because you've created a new Document object:

```
Note theDocument = new Document("Test Document");
```

The non-virtual Write method of Note is called because you've assigned theDocument to a reference to a Note:

```
Note theDocument = new Document("Test Document");
```

To illustrate calling the methods through an interface that is created from the Note class reference to the Document object, create an interface reference named isDocument. Use the as operator to cast the Note (theDocument) to the IStorable reference:

```
IStorable isDocument = theDocument as IStorable;
```

Then invoke the Read( ) and Write( ) methods for theDocument through that interface:

```
if (isDocument != null)
{
 isDocument.Read( );
 isDocument.Write( );
}
```

The output is the same: once again, the virtual Read( ) method is polymorphic, and the non-virtual Write( ) method is not:

```
Overriding the Read method for Document
Note Write Method for IStorable
```

Next, create a second Document object, this time assigning its address to a reference to a Document, rather than a reference to a Note. This will be used to illustrate the final cases (a call through a Document object and a call through an interface created from the Document object):

```
Document Document2 = new Document("Second Test");
```

Call the methods on the Document object:

```
Document2.Read( );
Document2.Write( );
```

Again, the virtual Read( ) method is polymorphic, and the non-virtual Write( ) method is not, but this time you get the Write( ) method for Document because you are calling the method on a Document object:

```
Overriding the Read method for Document!
Implementing the Write method for Document!
```

Finally, cast the Document object to an IStorable reference and call Read( ) and Write( ):

```
IStorable isDocument2 = Document2 as IStorable;
if (isDocument != null)
{
 isDocument2.Read( );
 isDocument2.Write( );
}
```

The Read( ) method is called polymorphically, but the Write( ) method for Note is called because Note implements IStorable, and Write( ) is not polymorphic:

```
Overriding the Read method for Document!
Note Write Method for IStorable
```

Explicit Interface Implementation

In the implementation shown so far, the class that implements the interface (Document) creates a member method with the same signature and return type as the method detailed in the interface. It is not necessary to explicitly state that Document is implementing IStorable, for example; the compiler understands this implicitly.

What happens, however, if the class implements two interfaces, each of which has a method with the same signature? This might happen if the class implements interfaces defined by two different organizations or even two different programmers. The next example creates two interfaces: IStorable and ITalk. ITalk implements a Read( ) method that reads a book aloud. Unfortunately, this conflicts with the Read( ) method in IStorable.

Because both IStorable and ITalk have a Read( ) method, the implementing Document class must use *explicit implementation* for at least one of the methods. With explicit implementation, the implementing class (Document) explicitly identifies the interface for the method:

```
void ITalk.Read( )
```

Marking the Read( ) method as a member of the ITalk interface resolves the conflict between the identical Read( ) methods. There are some additional aspects you should keep in mind.

First, the explicit implementation method cannot have an access modifier:

```
void ITalk.Read( )
```

This method is implicitly public. In fact, a method declared through explicit implementation cannot be declared with the abstract, virtual, override, or new keywords.

Most importantly, you cannot access the explicitly implemented method through the object itself. When you write:

```
theDoc.Read( );
```

the compiler assumes you mean the implicitly implemented interface for IStorable. The only way to access an explicitly implemented interface is through a cast to the interface:

```
ITalk itDoc = theDoc as ITalk;
if (itDoc != null)
{
  itDoc.Read( );
}
```

Explicit implementation is demonstrated in Example 13-6. Note that there is no need to use explicit implementation with the other method of ITalk:

```
public void Talk( )
```

Because there is no conflict, this can be declared as usual.

Example 13-6. Explicit implementation

```
using System;

namespace OverridingInterfaces
{
    interface IStorable
    {
        void Read( );
        void Write( );
    }

    interface ITalk
    {
        void Talk( );
        void Read( );
    }


    // Modify Document to also implement ITalk
    public class Document : IStorable, ITalk
    {
        // the document constructor
        public Document( string s )
        {
            Console.WriteLine(
            "Creating document with: {0}", s );
        }
```

Example 13-6. Explicit implementation (continued)

```csharp
        // Implicit implementation
        public virtual void Read( )
        {
            Console.WriteLine(
            "Document Read Method for IStorable" );
        }

        public void Write( )
        {
            Console.WriteLine(
            "Document Write Method for IStorable" );
        }

        // Explicit implementation
        void ITalk.Read( )
        {
            Console.WriteLine( "Implementing ITalk.Read" );
        }

        public void Talk( )
        {
            Console.WriteLine( "Implementing ITalk.Talk" );
        }
    }

    class Tester
    {
        public void Run( )
        {
            // Create a Document object
            Document theDoc = new Document( "Test Document" );
            IStorable isDoc = theDoc as IStorable;
            if ( isDoc != null )
            {
                isDoc.Read( );
            }

            // Cast to an ITalk interface
            ITalk itDoc = theDoc as ITalk;
            if ( itDoc != null )
            {
                itDoc.Read( );
            }

            theDoc.Read( );
            theDoc.Talk( );
        }

        [STAThread]
        static void Main( )
        {
```

Example 13-6. Explicit implementation (continued)

```
        Tester t = new Tester( );
        t.Run( );
    }
  }
}
```

The output looks like this:

```
Creating document with: Test Document
Document Read Method for IStorable
Implementing ITalk.Read
Document Read Method for IStorable
Implementing ITalk.Talk
```

Summary

- An interface is a contract through which a class guarantees that it will implement certain methods, provide certain properties and indexers, and support certain events, all of which are specified in the interface definition.

- You declare an interface much like you would a class, but using the keyword interface. You can apply access modifiers to the interface, as you would with a class.

- In the interface definition, the method declarations cannot have access modifiers.

- To implement an interface on a class, you use the colon operator, followed by the name of the interface, similar to the syntax for inheritance.

- Classes can derive from zero or one class, and can implement any number of interfaces. If a class has a base class and one or more interface, the base class must be listed first (after the colon). Separate base classes and implementation names by commas.

- When you define a class that implements an interface, you must then implement all the required members of that interface.

- In situations where you don't know what type of object you have, just that the object implements a specific interface, you can create a reference to the interface, and assign the object to that reference, providing you with access to the implemented interface methods.

- You can use the is operator to determine if an object derives from a base class or implements an interface. The is operator returns a Boolean value indicating whether or not the cast is valid, but it does not perform the cast.

- The as operator attempts to cast a reference to a base type or an interface, and returns null if the cast is not valid.

- You can extend an interface to add new methods or members. In the new interface definition, use the colon operator followed by the name of the original interface. This is very similar to derivation in classes.

- The extended interface subsumes the original interface, so any class that implements the extended interface must also implement the original interface as well.

- A class that implements an interface may mark any of the interface methods as virtual. These methods may then be overridden by derived classes.

- When a class implements two or more interfaces with methods that have the same name, you resolve the conflict by prefixing the method name with the name of the interface and the dot operator (for example, IStorable.Write( )).

Quiz

Question 13-1. What is the difference between an interface and a class that implements an interface?

Question 13-2. What is the difference between an interface and an abstract base class?

Question 13-3. How do you indicate that class MyClass derives from class MyBase and implements the interfaces ISuppose and IDo?

Question 13-4. What two operators can tell you if an object's class implements an interface?

Question 13-5. What is the difference between the is and as operators?

Question 13-6. What does it mean to "extend" an interface?

Question 13-7. What is the syntax for extending an interface?

Question 13-8. What does it mean to override an interface implementation?

Question 13-9. What is explicit interface implementation and why would you use it?

Exercises

Exercise 13-1. Define an interface IConvertible that indicates that the class can convert a string to C# or VB2005. The interface should have two methods: ConvertToCSharp and ConvertToVB2005. Each method should take a string, and return a string.

Exercise 13-2. Implement that interface and test it by creating a class `ProgramHelper` that implements `IConvertible`. You can use simple string messages to simulate the conversion.

Exercise 13-3. Extend the interface by creating a new interface, `ICodeChecker`. The new interface should implement one new method, `CodeCheckSyntax`, which takes two strings: the string to check, and the language to use. The method should return a bool. Revise the `ProgramHelper` class from Exercise 13-2 to use the new interface.

Exercise 13-4. Demonstrate the use of is and as. Create a new class, `ProgramConverter`, that implements `IConvertible`. `ProgramConverter` should implement the `ConvertToCSharp()` and `ConvertToVB()` methods. Revise `ProgramHelper` so that it derives from `ProgramConverter`, and implements `ICodeChecker`.

CHAPTER 14

Generics and Collections

You saw in Chapter 10 that arrays are useful for when you have a group of objects of the same type, and you need to treat them as a group—as a *collection*. Arrays are the least flexible of the five standard collections used in C# 2005:

- Array
- List
- Stack
- Queue
- Dictionary

This chapter will introduce each of the latter four collections, and will show how the new feature *generics* are used to make these collections type-safe (and why type-safety is important!).

You can also create classes that *act like* collections, and you can provide support for your collection classes so that they support some or all of the behavior expected of collections like the ability to be used in a foreach loop or to access their members using an indexer:

```
Employee joe = MyCompany[EmployeeID]
```

Generics

Until generics, all the collection classes (Array, List, Stack, and Queue) were defined to hold objects of type Object (the root class). Thus, you could add integers and strings to the same class, and when you took items out of the collection, you had to cast them to their "real" type. This was ugly, and it was error-prone (the compiler could not tell if you had a collection of integers and added a string).

With generics, the designer of the class (the person who creates the Stack class) can say, "This class will hold only one type, and that type will be defined by the developer who makes an instance of this class."

The user of the generic Stack class defines an instance of the Stack and the type it will hold, and the compiler can now use this type-safe Stack to ensure that only objects of the designated type are stored in the collection. Much better.

The designer adds a type placeholder (technically called a *type parameter*):

```
class Stack<T>
```

The user of the Stack class puts in the actual type when instantiating the class, like this:

```
class Stack<Employee> = new Stack<Employee>
```

Collection Interfaces

The .NET Framework provides a number of interfaces, such as IEnumerable and ICollection, that the designer of a collection must implement to provide full collection semantics. For example, ICollection allows your collection to be enumerated in a foreach loop.

Creating Your Own Collections

The goal in creating your own collections is to make them as similar to the standard .NET collections as possible. This reduces confusion, and makes for easier-to-use classes and easier-to-maintain code.

One feature you may want to provide is to allow users of your collection to add to or extract from the collection with an indexer, just as is done with arrays.

For example, suppose you create a ListBox control named myListBox that contains a list of strings stored in a one-dimensional array, a private member variable named myStrings. A ListBox control contains member properties and methods in addition to its array of strings, so the ListBox itself is not an array. However, it would be convenient to be able to access the ListBox array with an index, just as if the ListBox itself were an array.[*] For example, such a property would permit statements such as the following:

```
string theFirstString = myListBox[0];
string theLastString = myListBox[Length-1];
```

An *indexer* is a C# construct that allows you to treat a class as if it were an array. In the preceding example, you are treating the ListBox as if it were an array of strings, even though it is more than that. An indexer is a special kind of property, but like all properties, it includes get and set accessors to specify its behavior.

---

[*] The actual ListBox control provided by both Windows forms and ASP.NET has a collection called Items, and it is the Items collection that implements the indexer.

You declare an indexer property within a class using the following syntax:

```
type this [type argument]{get; set;}
```

The return type determines the type of object that will be returned by the indexer, while the type argument specifies what kind of argument will be used to index into the collection that contains the target objects. Although it is common to use integers as index values, you can index a collection on other types as well, including strings. You can even provide an indexer with multiple parameters to create a multidimensional array!

The this keyword is a reference to the object in which the indexer appears. As with a normal property, you also must define get and set accessors, which determine how the requested object is retrieved from or assigned to its collection.

Example 14-1 declares a ListBox control (ListBoxTest) that contains a simple array (myStrings) and a simple indexer for accessing its contents.

Example 14-1. Using a simple indexer

```
using System;

namespace SimpleIndexer
{
    // a simplified ListBox control
    public class ListBoxTest
    {
        private string[] strings;
        private int ctr = 0;

        // initialize the list box with strings
        public ListBoxTest( params string[] initialStrings )
        {
            // allocate space for the strings
            strings = new String[256];

            // copy the strings passed in to the constructor
            foreach ( string s in initialStrings )
            {
                strings[ctr++] = s;
            }
        }

        // add a single string to the end of the list box
        public void Add( string theString )
        {
            if ( ctr >= strings.Length )
            {
                // handle bad index
            }
            else
                strings[ctr++] = theString;
        }
```

Example 14-1. Using a simple indexer (continued)

```csharp
        // allow array-like access

        public string this[int index]
        {
           get
           {
              if ( index < 0 || index >= strings.Length )
              {
                 // handle bad index
              }
              return strings[index];
           }
           set
           {
              // add only through the add method
              if ( index >= ctr )
              {
                 // handle error
              }
              else
                 strings[index] = value;
           }
        }

        // publish how many strings you hold
        public int GetNumEntries()
        {
           return ctr;
        }
    }

    public class Tester
    {
       static void Main()
       {
          // create a new list box and initialize
          ListBoxTest lbt =
             new ListBoxTest( "Hello", "World" );

          // add a few strings
          lbt.Add( "Proust" );
          lbt.Add( "Faulkner" );
          lbt.Add( "Mann" );
          lbt.Add( "Hugo" );

          // test the access
          string subst = "Universe";
          lbt[1] = subst;

          // access all the strings
          for ( int i = 0; i < lbt.GetNumEntries(); i++ )
          {
```

Example 14-1. Using a simple indexer (continued)

```
        Console.WriteLine( "lbt[{0}]: {1}", i, lbt[i] );
    }
  }
}
}
```

The output looks like this:

```
lbt[0]: Hello
lbt[1]: Universe
lbt[2]: Proust
lbt[3]: Faulkner
lbt[4]: Mann
lbt[5]: Hugo
```

To keep Example 14-1 simple, we strip the ListBox control down to the few features we care about. The listing ignores everything having to do with being a user control and focuses only on the list of strings the ListBox maintains, and methods for manipulating them. In a real application, of course, these are a small fraction of the total methods of a ListBox, whose principal job is to display the strings and enable user choice.

The first things to notice in this example are the two private members:

```
private string[] strings;
private int ctr = 0;
```

Our ListBox maintains a simple array of strings, cleverly named strings. The member variable ctr will keep track of how many strings have been added to this array.

Initialize the array in the constructor with the statement:

```
strings = new String[256];
```

The Add( ) method of ListBoxTest does nothing more than append a new string to its internal array (strings), though a more complex object might write the strings to a database or other more complex data structure.

The key method of ListBoxTest, is the indexer. An indexer uses the this keyword:

```
public string this[int index]
```

The syntax of the indexer is very similar to that for properties. There is either a get( ) method, a set( ) method, or both. In the case shown, the get( ) method endeavors to implement rudimentary bounds checking, and assuming the index requested is acceptable, it returns the value requested:

```
get
{
    if (index < 0 || index >= strings.Length)
    {
        // handle bad index
    }
    return strings[index];
}
```

How you handle a bad index is up to you. A common approach is to throw an exception; see the help files for information on the "ArgumentOutOfRange" exception.

The set( ) method checks to make sure that the index you are setting already has a value in the ListBox. If not, it treats the set as an error. (New elements can only be added using Add with this approach.) The set accessor takes advantage of the implicit parameter value that represents whatever is assigned using the index operator:

```
set
{
    if (index >= ctr )
    {
        // handle error
    }
    else
    {
        strings[index] = value;
    }
}
```

Thus, if you write:

```
lbt[5] = "Hello World"
```

the compiler will call the indexer set( ) method on your object and pass in the string Hello World as an implicit parameter named value.

Indexers and Assignment

In Example 14-1, you cannot assign to an index that does not have a value. Thus, if you write:

```
lbt[10] = "wow!";
```

you would trigger the error handler in the set( ) method, which would note that the index you've passed in (10) is larger than the counter (6).

This code is kept simple, and thus is not robust. There are any number of other checks you'll want to make on the value passed in (e.g., checking that you were not passed a negative index and that it does not exceed the size of the underlying strings[ ] array).

In Main( ), you create an instance of the ListBoxTest class named lbt and pass in two strings as parameters:

```
ListBoxTest lbt = new ListBoxTest("Hello", "World");
```

Then call Add( ) to add four more strings:

```
// add a few strings
lbt.Add( "Proust" );
```

```
lbt.Add( "Faulkner" );
lbt.Add( "Mann" );
lbt.Add( "Hugo" );
```

Before examining the values, modify the second value (at index 1):

```
string subst = "Universe";
lbt[1] = subst;
```

Finally, display each value in a loop:

```
for (int i = 0;i<lbt.GetNumEntries();i++)
{
    Console.WriteLine("lbt[{0}]: {1}",i,lbt[i]);
}
```

Indexing on Other Values

C# does not require that you always use an integer value as the index to a collection. When you create a custom collection class and create your indexer, you are free to create indexers that index on strings and other types. In fact, the index value can be overloaded so that a given collection can be indexed, for example, by an integer value and also by a string value, depending on the needs of the client.

Example 14-2 illustrates a string index. The indexer calls FindString( ), which is a helper method that returns a record based on the value of the string provided. Notice that the overloaded indexer and the indexer from Example 14-1 are able to coexist.

Example 14-2. Overloading an index

```
using System;

namespace OverloadedIndexer
{
    // a simplified ListBox control
    public class ListBoxTest
    {
        private string[] strings;
        private int ctr = 0;

        // initialize the list box with strings
        public ListBoxTest( params string[] initialStrings )
        {
            // allocate space for the strings
            strings = new String[256];

            // copy the strings passed in to the constructor
            foreach ( string s in initialStrings )
            {
                strings[ctr++] = s;
            }
        }
```

Example 14-2. Overloading an index (continued)

```csharp
// add a single string to the end of the list box
public void Add( string theString )
{
    if ( ctr >= strings.Length )
    {
        // handle bad index
    }
    else
    {
        strings[ctr++] = theString;
    }
}


// allow array-like access
public string this[int index]
{
    get
    {
        if ( index < 0 || index >= strings.Length )
        {
            // handle bad index
        }
        return strings[index];
    }
    set
    {
        // add only through the add method
        if ( index >= ctr )
        {
            // handle error
        }
        else
            strings[index] = value;
    }
}

private int FindString( string searchString )
{
    for ( int i = 0; i < strings.Length; i++ )
    {
        if ( strings[i].StartsWith( searchString ) )
        {
            return i;
        }
    }
    return -1;
}

// index on string
public string this[string index]
{
```

Example 14-2. Overloading an index (continued)

```
        get
        {
            if ( index.Length == 0 )
            {
                // handle bad index
            }
            return this[FindString( index )];
        }
        set
        {
            // no need to check the index here because
            // find string will handle a bad index value
            strings[FindString( index )] = value;
        }
    }



    // publish how many strings you hold
    public int GetNumEntries( )
    {
        return ctr;
    }
}

public class Tester
{
    static void Main( )
    {
        // create a new list box and initialize
        ListBoxTest lbt =
            new ListBoxTest( "Hello", "World" );

        // add a few strings
        lbt.Add( "Proust" );
        lbt.Add( "Faulkner" );
        lbt.Add( "Mann" );
        lbt.Add( "Hugo" );

        // test the access
        string subst = "Universe";
        lbt[1] = subst;
        lbt["Hel"] = "GoodBye";
        // lbt["xyz"] = "oops";

        // access all the strings
        for ( int i = 0; i < lbt.GetNumEntries( ); i++ )
        {
            Console.WriteLine( "lbt[{0}]: {1}", i, lbt[i] );
        }       // end for
    }           // end main
}               // end tester
}
```

The output looks like this:

```
lbt[0]: GoodBye
lbt[1]: Universe
lbt[2]: Proust
lbt[3]: Faulkner
lbt[4]: Mann
lbt[5]: Hugo
```

Example 14-2 is identical to Example 14-1 except for the addition of an overloaded indexer, which can match a string, and the method FindString, created to support that index.

The FindString method simply iterates through the strings held in myStrings until it finds a string that starts with the target string used in the index. If found, it returns the index of that string; otherwise, it returns the value -1.

You can see in Main( ) that the user passes in a string segment to the index, just as with an integer:

```
lbt["Hel"] = "GoodBye";
```

This calls the overloaded index, which does some rudimentary error-checking (in this case, making sure the string passed in has at least one letter) and then passes the value (Hel) to FindString. It gets back an index and uses that index to index into myStrings:

```
return this[FindString(index)];
```

The set value works in the same way:

```
myStrings[FindString(index)] = value;
```

The careful reader will note that if the string does not match, a value of -1 is returned, which is then used as an index into myStrings. This action then generates an exception (System.NullReferenceException), as you can see by uncommenting the following line in Main( ):

```
lbt["xyz"] = "oops";
```

The proper handling of not finding a string is, as they say, left as an exercise for the reader. You might consider displaying an error message or otherwise allowing the user to recover from the error.

Generic Collection Interfaces

The .NET Framework provides standard interfaces for enumerating and comparing collections. These standard interfaces are type-safe, but the type is *generic*; that is, you can declare an ICollection of any type by substituting the actual type (int, string, or Employee) for the generic type in the interface declaration (<T>).

For example, if you were creating an interface called IStorable, but you didn't know what kind of objects would be stored, you'd declare the interface like this:

```
interface IStorable<T>
{
  // implementation here
}
```

Later on, if you wanted to create a class Document that implemented IStorable to store strings, you'd do it like this:

```
public class Document : IStorable<String>
```

Replacing T with the type you want to apply the interface to (in this case, string).

 Shockingly, perhaps, that is all there is to generics. The creator of the class says, in essence, "This applies to some type <T> to be named later (when the interface or class is used) and the programmer using the interface or collection type replaces <T> with the actual type (e.g., int, string, Employee, etc.)."

The key generic collection interfaces are listed in Table 14-1.[*]

Table 14-1. Generic collection interfaces

Interface	Purpose
ICollection<T>	Base interface for generic collections
IEnumerator<T> IEnumerable<T>	Required for collections that will be enumerated with foreach
IComparer<T> IComparable<T>	Required for collections that will be sorted
IList<T>	Used by indexable collections (see the section "Generic Lists: List<T>")
IDictionary<K,V>	Used for key/value-based collections (see the section "Dictionaries")

The IEnumerable<T> Interface

You can support the foreach statement in ListBoxTest by implementing the IEnumerable<T> interface.

 You read this as "IEnumerable of <T>" or "the generic interface IEnumerable."

---

[*] C# also provides nongeneric interfaces (ICollection, IEnumerator), but we will focus on the generic collections, which should be preferred whenever possible as they are type-safe.

IEnumerable has only one method, GetEnumerator( ), whose job is to return an implementation of IEnumerator<T>. The C# language provides special help in creating the enumerator, using the new keyword yield, as demonstrated in Example 14-3 and explained below.

Example 14-3. Making a ListBox an enumerable class

```
using System;
using System.Collections.Generic;  // for the generic classes

namespace Enumerable
{
    public class ListBoxTest : IEnumerable<String>
    {
        private string[] strings;
        private int ctr = 0;
        // Enumerable classes can return an enumerator
        public IEnumerator<string> GetEnumerator()
        {
            foreach ( string s in strings )
            {
                yield return s;
            }
        }

        // required to fulfill IEnumerable
        System.Collections.IEnumerator System.Collections.IEnumerable.GetEnumerator()
        {
            throw new NotImplementedException();
        }


        // initialize the list box with strings
        public ListBoxTest( params string[] initialStrings )
        {
            // allocate space for the strings
            strings = new String[256];

            // copy the strings passed in to the constructor
            foreach ( string s in initialStrings )
            {
                strings[ctr++] = s;
            }
        }

        // add a single string to the end of the list box
        public void Add( string theString )
        {
            strings[ctr] = theString;
            ctr++;
        }
```

Example 14-3. Making a ListBox an enumerable class (continued)

```csharp
// allow array-like access
public string this[int index]
{
    get
    {
        if ( index < 0 || index >= strings.Length )
        {
            // handle bad index
        }
        return strings[index];
    }
    set
    {
        strings[index] = value;
    }
}

// publish how many strings you hold
public int GetNumEntries()
{
    return ctr;
}

}

public class Tester
{
    static void Main()
    {
        // create a new list box and initialize
        ListBoxTest lbt =
            new ListBoxTest( "Hello", "World" );

        // add a few strings
        lbt.Add( "Proust" );
        lbt.Add( "Faulkner" );
        lbt.Add( "Mann" );
        lbt.Add( "Hugo" );

        // test the access
        string subst = "Universe";
        lbt[1] = subst;

        // access all the strings
        foreach ( string s in lbt )
        {
            if ( s == null )
            {
                break;
            }
```

Example 14-3. Making a ListBox an enumerable class (continued)

```
            Console.WriteLine( "Value: {0}", s );
        }
      }
   }
}
```

The output looks like this:

```
Value: Hello
Value: Universe
Value: Proust
Value: Faulkner
Value: Mann
Value: Hugo
```

The program begins in Main( ), creating a new ListBoxTest object and passing two strings to the constructor. When the object is created, an array of Strings is created with enough room for 256 strings. Four more strings are added using the Add method, and the second string is updated, just as in the previous example.

The big change in this version of the program is that a foreach loop is called, retrieving each string in the ListBox. The foreach loop *automatically* uses the IEnumerable<T> interface, invoking GetEnumerator( ).

The GetEnumerator method is declared to return an IEnumerator of type string:

```
public IEnumerator<string> GetEnumerator( )
```

The implementation iterates through the array of strings, yielding each in turn:

```
foreach ( string s in strings )
{
   yield return s;
}
```

The new keyword yield is used here explicitly to return a value to the enumerator object. By using the yield keyword, all the bookkeeping for keeping track of which element is next, resetting the iterator, and so forth, is provided for you by the framework.

Note that our implementation includes an implementation of the non-generic Get-Enumerator method. This is required by the definition of the generic IEnumerable and is typically defined to just throw an exception, since we don't expect to call it:

```
// required to fulfill IEnumerable
System.Collections.IEnumerator
System.Collections.IEnumerable.GetEnumerator( )
{
   throw new NotImplementedException( );
}
```

Framework Generic Collections

The .NET Framework provides four very useful generic collections, as enumerated earlier (List, Stack, Queue, and Dictionary). The most common case is that rather than writing your own collection, you'll use one of the collection classes provided for you. Each is described in turn in the next few sections.

Generic Lists: List<T>

The classic problem with the Array type is its fixed size. If you do not know in advance how many objects an array will hold, you run the risk of declaring either too small an array (and running out of room) or too large an array (and wasting memory).

The generic List class (which replaces the old non-generic ArrayList) is, essentially, an array whose size is dynamically increased as required. Lists provide a number of useful methods and properties for their manipulation. Some of the most important are shown in Table 14-2.

Table 14-2. List properties and methods

Method or property	Purpose
Capacity	Property to get or set the number of elements the List can contain. This value is increased automatically if count exceeds capacity. You might set this value to reduce the number of reallocations, and you may call Trim( ) to reduce this value to the actual Count.
Count	Property to get the number of elements currently in the list.
Item( )	Gets or sets the element at the specified index. This is the indexer for the List class.[a]
Add( )	Public method to add an object to the List.
AddRange( )	Public method that adds the elements of an ICollection to the end of the List.
BinarySearch( )	Overloaded public method that uses a binary search to locate a specific element in a sorted List.
Clear( )	Removes all elements from the List.
Contains( )	Determines if an element is in the List.
CopyTo( )	Overloaded public method that copies a List to a one-dimensional array.
Exists( )	Determines if an element is in the List.
Find( )	Returns the first occurrence of the element in the List.
FindAll( )	Returns all the specified elements in the List.
GetEnumerator( )	Overloaded public method that returns an enumerator to iterate through a List.
GetRange( )	Copies a range of elements to a new List.
IndexOf( )	Overloaded public method that returns the index of the first occurrence of a value.
Insert( )	Inserts an element into List.
InsertRange( )	Inserts the elements of a collection into the List.
LastIndexOf( )	Overloaded public method that returns the index of the last occurrence of a value in the List.
Remove( )	Removes the first occurrence of a specific object.

Table 14-2. List properties and methods (continued)

Method or property	Purpose
RemoveAt( )	Removes the element at the specified index.
RemoveRange( )	Removes a range of elements.
Reverse( )	Reverses the order of elements in the List.
Sort( )	Sorts the List.
ToArray( )	Copies the elements of the List to a new array.
TrimToSize( )	Sets the capacity to the actual number of elements in the List.

a The idiom in the Framework Class Library is to provide an Item element for collection classes, which is implemented as an indexer in C#.

When you create a List, you do not define how many objects it will contain. You add to the List using the Add( ) method, and the List takes care of its own internal bookkeeping, as illustrated in Example 14-4.

Example 14-4. Working with a List

```
using System;
using System.Collections.Generic;

namespace ListCollection
{
    // a simple class to store in the List
    public class Employee
    {
        private int empID;

        public Employee( int empID )
        {
            this.empID = empID;
        }
        public override string ToString( )
        {
            return empID.ToString( );
        }
        public int EmpID
        {
            get
            {
                return empID;
            }
            set
            {
                empID = value;
            }
        }
    }
    public class Tester
    {
        static void Main( )
        {
```

Example 14-4. Working with a List (continued)

```
        List<Employee> empList = new List<Employee>( );
        List<int> intList = new List<int>( );

        // populate the List
        for ( int i = 0; i < 5; i++ )
        {
            empList.Add( new Employee( i + 100 ) );
            intList.Add( i * 5 );
        }


        // print all the contents
        for ( int i = 0; i < intList.Count; i++ )
        {
            Console.Write( "{0} ", intList[i].ToString( ) );
        }

        Console.WriteLine( "\n" );

        // print all the contents of the Employee List
        for ( int i = 0; i < empList.Count; i++ )
        {
            Console.Write( "{0} ", empList[i].ToString( ) );
        }

        Console.WriteLine( "\n" );
        Console.WriteLine( "empList.Capacity: {0}", empList.Capacity );
    }
  }
}
```

The output looks like this:

```
0 5 10 15 20
100 101 102 103 104
empArray.Capacity: 8
```

The List class has a property, Capacity, which is the number of elements the List is capable of storing; however, this capacity is automatically doubled each time you reach the limit.

Creating objects that can be sorted by the generic list

The List implements the Sort( ) method. You can sort any List that contains objects that implement IComparable. All the built-in types do implement this interface, so you can sort a List<integer> or a List<string>.

On the other hand, if you want to sort a List<Employee>, you must change the Employee class to implement IComparable:

```
public class Employee : IComparable<Employee>
```

As part of the ICompareable interface contract, the Employee object must provide a CompareTo( ) method:

```
public int CompareTo(Employee rhs)
{
    return this.empID.CompareTo(rhs.empID);
}
```

The CompareTo( ) method takes an Employee as a parameter (we know this, because the interface is now generic and we can assume type safety). The Employee object must compare itself to this second Employee object and return -1 if it is smaller than the second Employee, 1 if it is greater, and 0 if the two Employee objects are equal to each other.

It is up to the designer of the Employee class to determine what *smaller than*, *greater than*, and *equal to* mean. In this example, you will delegate the comparison to the empId member. The empId member is an int and uses the default CompareTo( ) method for integer types, which will do an integer comparison of the two values.

To see if the sort is working, you'll add integers and Employee instances to their respective lists with random values. To create the random values, you'll instantiate an object of class Random. To cause your Random instance to generate the random values, you'll call its Next( ) method. One version of the Next( ) method allows you to specify the largest random number you want. In this case, you'll pass in the value 10 to generate a random number between 0 and 10:

```
Random r = new Random( );
r.Next(10);
```

Example 14-5 creates an integer array and an Employee array, populates them both with random numbers, and prints their values. It then sorts both arrays and prints the new values.

Example 14-5. Sorting an integer and an Employee array

```
using System;
using System.Collections.Generic;

namespace IComparable
{
    // a simple class to store in the array
    public class Employee : IComparable<Employee>
    {
        private int empID;

        public Employee( int empID )
        {
            this.empID = empID;
        }

        public override string ToString( )
        {
```

Example 14-5. Sorting an integer and an Employee array (continued)

```
      return empID.ToString( );
   }


   public bool Equals( Employee other )
   {
      if ( this.empID == other.empID )
      {
         return true;
      }
      else
      {
         return false;
      }
   }

   // Comparer delegates back to Employee
   // Employee uses the integer's default
   // CompareTo method

   public int CompareTo( Employee rhs )
   {
      return this.empID.CompareTo( rhs.empID );
   }
}
public class Tester
{
   static void Main( )
   {
      List<Employee> empList = new List<Employee>( );
      List<Int32> intList = new List<Int32>( );

      // generate random numbers for
      // both the integers and the
      // employee id's
      Random r = new Random( );

      // populate the array
      for ( int i = 0; i < 5; i++ )
      {
         // add a random employee id
         empList.Add( new Employee( r.Next( 10 ) + 100 ) );

         // add a random integer
         intList.Add( r.Next( 10 ) );
      }


      // display all the contents of the int array
      Console.WriteLine("List<int> before sorting:");
      for ( int i = 0; i < intList.Count; i++ )
      {
```

Example 14-5. Sorting an integer and an Employee array (continued)

```
            Console.Write( "{0} ", intList[i].ToString( ) );
        }
        Console.WriteLine( "\n" );

        // display all the contents of the Employee array
        Console.WriteLine("List<Employee> before sorting:");
        for ( int i = 0; i < empList.Count; i++ )
        {
            Console.Write( "{0} ", empList[i].ToString( ) );
        }
        Console.WriteLine( "\n" );

        // sort and display the int array
        Console.WriteLine("List<int>after sorting:");
        intList.Sort( );
        for ( int i = 0; i < intList.Count; i++ )
        {
            Console.Write( "{0} ", intList[i].ToString( ) );
        }
        Console.WriteLine( "\n" );

        // sort and display the Employee array
        Console.WriteLine("List<Employee>after sorting:");
        //Employee.EmployeeComparer c = Employee.GetComparer( );
        //empList.Sort(c);

        empList.Sort( );


        // display all the contents of the Employee array
        for ( int i = 0; i < empList.Count; i++ )
        {
            Console.Write( "{0} ", empList[i].ToString( ) );
        }
        Console.WriteLine( "\n" );

    }
  }
}
```

The output looks like this:

```
List<int> before sorting:
6 9 8 3 6
List<Employee> before sorting:
108 103 107 102 109
List<int>after sorting:
3 6 6 8 9
List<Employee>after sorting:
102 103 107 108 109
```

The output shows that the lists of integers and Employees were generated with random numbers (and thus the numbers may be different each time you run the program). When sorted, the display shows the values have been ordered properly.

 Random number generators do not, technically, create true random numbers; they create what computer scientists call pseudo-random numbers. Microsoft notes: "Pseudo-random numbers are chosen with equal probability from a finite set of numbers. The chosen numbers are not completely random because a definite mathematical algorithm is used to select them, but they are sufficiently random for practical purposes." This is certainly sufficient for our example.

Controlling how elements in a generic collection are sorted by implementing IComparer<T>

When you call Sort( ) on the List in Example 14-5, the default implementation of IComparer is called, which uses QuickSort to call the IComparable implementation of CompareTo( ) on each element in the List.

You are free, however, to create your own implementation of IComparer, which you might want to do if you need control over how the sort ordering is defined. In the next example, you will add a second field to Employee: yearsOfSvc. You want to be able to sort the Employee objects in the List either by ID or by years of service, and you want to make that decision at run time.

To accomplish this, you will create a custom implementation of IComparer, which you will pass to the Sort( ) method of List. In this IComparer class, EmployeeComparer will know how to sort Employees.

To simplify the programmer's ability to choose how a given set of Employees are sorted, we'll add a property WhichComparison, of type Employee.EmployeeComparer. ComparisonType (an enumeration):

```
public
Employee.EmployeeComparer.ComparisonType  WhichComparison
{
   get { return whichComparison; }
   set { whichComparison = value; }
}
```

ComparisonType is an enumeration with two values, empID or yearsOfSvc (indicating that you want to sort by employee ID or years of service, respectively):

```
public enum ComparisonType
{
  EmpID,
  YearsOfService
};
```

Before invoking Sort( ), you will create an instance of EmployeeComparer and set its ComparisonType property:

```
Employee.EmployeeComparer c = Employee.GetComparer( );
c.WhichComparison=Employee.EmployeeComparer.ComparisonType.EmpID;
empArray.Sort(c);
```

When you invoke Sort( ), the List will call the Compare( ) method on the Employee-Comparer, which in turn will delegate the comparison to the Employee.CompareTo( ) method, passing in its WhichComparison property:

```
public int Compare( Employee lhs, Employee rhs )
{
    return lhs.CompareTo( rhs, WhichComparison );
}
```

The Employee object must implement a custom version of CompareTo( ), which takes the comparison and compares the objects accordingly:

```
public int CompareTo
    (
    Employee rhs,
    Employee.EmployeeComparer.ComparisonType whichComparison
    )
{
    switch (whichComparison)
    {
        case Employee.EmployeeComparer.ComparisonType.EmpID:
            return this.empID.CompareTo(rhs.empID);
        case Employee.EmployeeComparer.ComparisonType.Yrs:
            return this.yearsOfSvc.CompareTo(rhs.yearsOfSvc);
    }
    return 0;
}
```

The complete source for this example is shown in Example 14-6. The integer array has been removed to simplify the example, and the output of the employee's ToString( ) method has been enhanced to enable you to see the effects of the sort.

Example 14-6. Sorting an array by employees' IDs and years of service

```
using System;
using System.Collections.Generic;

namespace IComparer
{
    public class Employee : IComparable<Employee>
    {
        private int empID;

        private int yearsOfSvc = 1;

        public Employee( int empID )
        {
```

```
      this.empID = empID;
   }


   public Employee( int empID, int yearsOfSvc )
   {
      this.empID = empID;
      this.yearsOfSvc = yearsOfSvc;
   }

   public override string ToString( )
   {
      return "ID: " + empID.ToString( ) +
      ". Years of Svc: " + yearsOfSvc.ToString( );
   }

   public bool Equals( Employee other )
   {
      if ( this.empID == other.empID )
      {
         return true;
      }
      else
      {
         return false;
      }
   }

   // static method to get a Comparer object
   public static EmployeeComparer GetComparer()
   {
      return new Employee.EmployeeComparer( );
   }


   // Comparer delegates back to Employee
   // Employee uses the integer's default
   // CompareTo method
   public int CompareTo( Employee rhs )
   {
      return this.empID.CompareTo( rhs.empID );
   }


   // Special implementation to be called by custom comparer
   public int CompareTo(
      Employee rhs,
      Employee.EmployeeComparer.ComparisonType which )
   {
      switch ( which )
      {
         case Employee.EmployeeComparer.ComparisonType.EmpID:
```

```csharp
                return this.empID.CompareTo( rhs.empID );
            case Employee.EmployeeComparer.ComparisonType.Yrs:
                return this.yearsOfSvc.CompareTo( rhs.yearsOfSvc );
        }
        return 0;

    }

    // nested class which implements IComparer
    public class EmployeeComparer : IComparer<Employee>
    {
        // private state variable
        private Employee.EmployeeComparer.ComparisonType
            whichComparison;

        // enumeration of comparsion types
        public enum ComparisonType
        {
            EmpID,
            Yrs
        };

        public  bool Equals( Employee lhs, Employee rhs )
        {
            return this.Compare( lhs, rhs ) == 0;
        }


        public  int GetHashCode(Employee e)
        {
            return e.GetHashCode( );
        }

        // Tell the Employee objects to compare themselves
        public int Compare( Employee lhs, Employee rhs )
        {
            return lhs.CompareTo( rhs, WhichComparison );
        }

        public Employee.EmployeeComparer.ComparisonType
            WhichComparison
        {
            get{return whichComparison;}
            set{whichComparison = value;}
        }


    }
}
public class Tester
{
    static void Main( )
```

```
{
    List<Employee> empArray = new List<Employee>( );

    // generate random numbers for
    // both the integers and the
    // employee id's
    Random r = new Random( );

    // populate the array
    for ( int i = 0; i < 5; i++ )
    {
        // add a random employee id

        empArray.Add(
            new Employee(
                r.Next( 10 ) + 100, r.Next( 20 )

            )
        );
    }

    // display all the contents of the Employee array
    for ( int i = 0; i < empArray.Count; i++ )
    {
        Console.Write( "\n{0} ", empArray[i].ToString( ) );
    }
    Console.WriteLine( "\n" );


    // sort and display the employee array
    Employee.EmployeeComparer c = Employee.GetComparer( );
    c.WhichComparison =
    Employee.EmployeeComparer.ComparisonType.EmpID;
    empArray.Sort( c );

    // display all the contents of the Employee array
    for ( int i = 0; i < empArray.Count; i++ )
    {
        Console.Write( "\n{0} ", empArray[i].ToString( ) );
    }
    Console.WriteLine( "\n" );


    c.WhichComparison = Employee.EmployeeComparer.ComparisonType.Yrs;
    empArray.Sort( c );

    for ( int i = 0; i < empArray.Count; i++ )
    {
        Console.Write( "\n{0} ", empArray[i].ToString( ) );
```

Example 14-6. Sorting an array by employees' IDs and years of service (continued)

```
        }
        Console.WriteLine( "\n" );



    }
  }
}
```

The output looks like this for one run of the program:

```
ID: 103. Years of Svc: 11
ID: 108. Years of Svc: 15
ID: 107. Years of Svc: 14
ID: 108. Years of Svc: 5
ID: 102. Years of Svc: 0

ID: 102. Years of Svc: 0
ID: 103. Years of Svc: 11
ID: 107. Years of Svc: 14
ID: 108. Years of Svc: 15
ID: 108. Years of Svc: 5

ID: 102. Years of Svc: 0
ID: 108. Years of Svc: 5
ID: 103. Years of Svc: 11
ID: 107. Years of Svc: 14
ID: 108. Years of Svc: 15
```

The first block of output shows the Employee objects as they are added to the List. The employee ID values and the years of service are in random order. The second block shows the results of sorting by the employee ID, and the third block shows the results of sorting by years of service.

Generic Queues

A *queue* represents a first-in, first-out (FIFO) collection. The classic analogy is to a line (or queue, if you are British) at a ticket window. The first person in line ought to be the first person to come off the line to buy a ticket.

A queue is a good collection to use when you are managing a limited resource. For example, you might want to send messages to a resource that can only handle one message at a time. You would then create a message queue so that you can say to your clients: "Your message is important to us. Messages are handled in the order in which they are received."

The Queue class has a number of member methods and properties, the most important of which are shown in Table 14-3.

Table 14-3. Queue methods and properties

Method or property	Purpose
Count	Public property that gets the number of elements in the Queue
Clear( )	Removes all objects from the Queue
Contains( )	Determines if an element is in the Queue
CopyTo( )	Copies the Queue elements to an existing one-dimensional array
Dequeue( )	Removes and returns the object at the beginning of the Queue
Enqueue( )	Adds an object to the end of the Queue
GetEnumerator( )	Returns an enumerator for the Queue
Peek( )	Returns the object at the beginning of the Queue without removing it
ToArray( )	Copies the elements to a new array

Add elements to your queue with the Enqueue command and take them off the queue with Dequeue or by using an enumerator, as shown in Example 14-7.

Example 14-7. Working with a queue

```
using System;
using System.Collections.Generic;

namespace Queue
{
   public class Tester
   {

      static void Main( )
      {

         Queue<Int32> intQueue = new Queue<Int32>( );


         // populate the array
         for ( int i = 0; i < 5; i++ )
         {

            intQueue.Enqueue( i * 5 );

         }

         // Display the Queue.
         Console.Write( "intQueue values:\t" );
         PrintValues( intQueue );

         // Remove an element from the Queue.
         Console.WriteLine(
            "\n(Dequeue)\t{0}", intQueue.Dequeue( ) );
```

Example 14-7. Working with a queue (continued)

```
        // Display the Queue.
        Console.Write( "intQueue values:\t" );
        PrintValues( intQueue );

        // Remove another element from the Queue.
        Console.WriteLine(
            "\n(Dequeue)\t{0}", intQueue.Dequeue( ) );

        // Display the Queue.
        Console.Write( "intQueue values:\t" );
        PrintValues( intQueue );

        // View the first element in the
        // Queue but do not remove.
        Console.WriteLine(
            "\n(Peek)    \t{0}", intQueue.Peek( ) );


        // Display the Queue.
        Console.Write( "intQueue values:\t" );
        PrintValues( intQueue );

    }

    public static void PrintValues(IEnumerable<Int32> myCollection)
    {
        IEnumerator<Int32> myEnumerator =
            myCollection.GetEnumerator( );
        while ( myEnumerator.MoveNext( ) )
            Console.Write( "{0} ", myEnumerator.Current );
        Console.WriteLine( );
    }

  }
}
```

The output looks like this:

```
intQueue values:        0 5 10 15 20

(Dequeue)       0
intQueue values:        5 10 15 20

(Dequeue)       5
intQueue values:        10 15 20

(Peek)          10
intQueue values:        10 15 20
```

I've dispensed with the Employee class to save room, but of course you can enqueue user-defined objects as well. The output shows that queuing objects adds them to the Queue, while Dequeue( ) returns the object and also removes them from the Queue. The

Queue class also provides a Peek( ) method that allows you to see, but not remove, the next element.

Because the Queue class is enumerable, you can pass it to the PrintValues( ) method, which is provided as an IEnumerable interface. The conversion is implicit. In the PrintValues method, you call GetEnumerator, which you will remember is the single method of all IEnumerable classes. This returns an IEnumerator, which you then use to enumerate all the objects in the collection.

Generic Stacks

A *Stack* is a last-in, first-out (LIFO) collection, like a stack of dishes at a buffet table, or a stack of coins on your desk. A dish added on top, is the first dish you take off the stack.

The principal methods for adding to and removing from a stack are Push( ) and Pop( ); Stack also offers a Peek( ) method, very much like Queue. The significant methods and properties for Stack are shown in Table 14-4.

Table 14-4. Stack methods and properties

Method or property	Purpose
Count	Public property that gets the number of elements in the Stack
Clear( )	Removes all objects from the Stack
Contains( )	Determines if an element is in the Stack
CopyTo( )	Copies the Stack elements to an existing one-dimensional array
GetEnumerator( )	Returns an enumerator for the Stack
Peek( )	Returns the object at the top of the Stack without removing it
Pop( )	Removes and returns the object at the top of the Stack
Push( )	Inserts an object at the top of the Stack
ToArray( )	Copies the elements to a new array

The List, Queue, and Stack types contain multiple versions of the CopyTo( ) and ToArray( ) methods for copying their elements to an array. In the case of a Stack, the CopyTo( ) method will copy its elements to an existing one-dimensional array, overwriting the contents of the array beginning at the index you specify. The ToArray( ) method returns a new array with the contents of the Stack's elements. Example 14-8 illustrates several of the Stack methods.

Example 14-8. Working with a Stack

```
using System;
using System.Collections.Generic;

namespace Stack
{
```

Example 14-8. Working with a Stack (continued)

```
public class Tester
{
    static void Main( )
    {
        Stack<Int32> intStack = new Stack<Int32>( );

        // populate the array

        for ( int i = 0; i < 8; i++ )
        {
            intStack.Push( i * 5 );
        }


        // Display the Stack.
        Console.Write( "intStack values:\t" );
        PrintValues( intStack );

        // Remove an element from the Stack.
        Console.WriteLine( "\n(Pop)\t{0}",
        intStack.Pop( ) );

        // Display the Stack.
        Console.Write( "intStack values:\t" );
        PrintValues( intStack );

        // Remove another element from the Stack.
        Console.WriteLine( "\n(Pop)\t{0}",
            intStack.Pop( ) );

        // Display the Stack.
        Console.Write( "intStack values:\t" );
        PrintValues( intStack );

        // View the first element in the
        // Stack but do not remove.
        Console.WriteLine( "\n(Peek)    \t{0}",
            intStack.Peek( ) );


        // Display the Stack.
        Console.Write( "intStack values:\t" );
        PrintValues( intStack );

        // Declare an array object which will
        // hold 12 integers
        int[] targetArray = new int[12];

        for (int i = 0; i < targetArray.Length; i++)
        {
            targetArray[i] = i * 100 + 100;
        }
```

Example 14-8. Working with a Stack (continued)

```
        // Display the values of the target Array instance.
        Console.WriteLine( "\nTarget array:   " );
        PrintValues( targetArray );

        // Copy the entire source Stack to the
        // target Array instance, starting at index 6.
        intStack.CopyTo( targetArray, 6 );


        // Display the values of the target Array instance.
        Console.WriteLine( "\nTarget array after copy:   " );
        PrintValues( targetArray );


    }


    public static void PrintValues(
        IEnumerable<Int32> myCollection )
    {
        IEnumerator<Int32> enumerator =
            myCollection.GetEnumerator();
        while ( enumerator.MoveNext() )
            Console.Write( "{0}  ", enumerator.Current );
        Console.WriteLine();
    }
  }
}
```

The output looks like this:

```
intStack values:       35  30  25  20  15  10  5  0

(Pop)    35
intStack values:       30  25  20  15  10  5  0

(Pop)    30
intStack values:       25  20  15  10  5  0

(Peek)           25
intStack values:       25  20  15  10  5  0

Target array:
100  200  300  400  500  600  700  800  900  1000  1100  1200

Target array after copy:
100  200  300  400  500  600  25  20  15  10  5  0

The new  array:
25  20  15  10  5  0
```

The output reflects that the items pushed onto the Stack were popped in reverse order.

The effect of CopyTo( ) can be seen by examining the target array before and after calling CopyTo( ). The array elements are overwritten beginning with the index specified (6).

Dictionaries

A *dictionary* is a collection that associates a *key* to a *value*. A language dictionary, such as Webster's, associates a word (the key) with its definition (the value).

To see the value of dictionaries, start by imagining that you want to keep a list of the state capitals. One approach might be to put them in an array:

```
string[] stateCapitals = new string[50];
```

The stateCapitals array will hold 50 state capitals. Each capital is accessed as an offset into the array. For example, to access the capital for Arkansas, you need to know that Arkansas is the fourth state in alphabetical order:

```
string capitalOfArkansas = stateCapitals[3];
```

It is inconvenient, however, to access state capitals using array notation. After all, if I need the capital for Massachusetts, there is no easy way for me to determine that Massachusetts is the 21st state alphabetically.

It would be far more convenient to store the capital with the state name. A dictionary allows you to store a value (in this case, the capital) with a key (in this case, the name of the state).

A .NET Framework dictionary can associate any kind of key (string, integer, object) with any kind of value (string, integer, object). Typically, the key is fairly short and the value fairly complex, though in this case, we'll use short strings for both.

The most important attributes of a good dictionary are that it is easy to add values and it is quick to retrieve values. Table 14-5 lists some of the more important methods and properties of the dictionary.

Table 14-5. Dictionary methods and properties

Method or property	Purpose
Count	Public property that gets the number of elements in the Dictionary.
Item( )	The indexer for the Dictionary.
Keys	Public property that gets a collection containing the keys in the Dictionary. (See also Values, later in this table.)
Values	Public property that gets a collection containing the values in the Dictionary. (See also Keys, earlier in this table.)
Add( )	Adds an entry with a specified Key and Value.
Clear( )	Removes all objects from the Dictionary.
ContainsKey( )	Determines whether the Dictionary has a specified key.

Table 14-5. Dictionary methods and properties (continued)

Method or property	Purpose
ContainsValue( )	Determines whether the Dictionary has a specified value.
GetEnumerator( )	Returns an enumerator for the Dictionary.
Remove( )	Removes the entry with the specified Key.

The key in a Dictionary can be a primitive type, or it can be an instance of a user-defined type (an object).

> Objects used as keys for a Dictionary must implement GetHashCode( ) as well as Equals. In most cases, you can simply use the inherited implementation from Object.

Dictionaries implement the IDictionary<TKey,TValue> interface (where TKey is the key type and TValue> is the value type). IDictionary provides a public property Item. The Item property retrieves a value with the specified key.

The Item property is implemented with the index operator ([ ]). Thus, you access items in any Dictionary object using the offset syntax, as you would with an array.

Example 14-9 demonstrates adding items to a Dictionary and then retrieving them with the indexer (which implicitly calls the Dictionary's Item property).

Example 14-9. The Item property as offset operators

```
using System;
using System.Collections.Generic;

namespace Dictionary
{
    public class Tester
    {
        static void Main( )
        {
            // Create and initialize a new Dictionary.
            Dictionary<string, string> dict =
                new Dictionary<string, string>( );

            dict.Add("Alabama", "Montgomery");
            dict.Add("Alaska", "Juneau");
            dict.Add("Arizona", "Phoenix");
            dict.Add("Arkansas", "Little Rock");
            dict.Add("California", "Sacramento");
            dict.Add("Colorado", "Denver");
            dict.Add("Connecticut", "Hartford");
            dict.Add("Delaware", "Dover");
            dict.Add("Florida", "Tallahassee");
            dict.Add("Georgia", "Atlanta");
            dict.Add("Hawaii", "Honolulu");
```

Example 14-9. The Item property as offset operators (continued)

```
        dict.Add("Idaho", "Boise");
        dict.Add("Illinois", "Springfield");
        dict.Add("Indiana", "Indianapolis");
        dict.Add("Iowa", "Des Moines");
        dict.Add("Kansas", "Topeka");
        dict.Add("Kentucky", "Frankfort");
        dict.Add("Louisiana", "Baton Rouge");
        dict.Add("Maine", "Augusta");
        dict.Add("Maryland", "Annapolis");
        dict.Add("Massachusetts", "Boston");
        dict.Add("Michigan", "Lansing");
        dict.Add("Minnesota", "St. Paul");
        dict.Add("Mississippi", "Jackson");
        dict.Add("Missouri", "Jefferson City");
        dict.Add("Montana", "Helena");
        dict.Add("Nebraska", "Lincoln");
        dict.Add("Nevada", "Carson City");
        dict.Add("New Hampshire", "Concord");
        dict.Add("New Jersey", "Trenton");
        dict.Add("New Mexico", "Santa Fe");
        dict.Add("New York", "Albany");
        dict.Add("North Carolina", "Raleigh");
        dict.Add("North Dakota", "Bismarck");
        dict.Add("Ohio", "Columbus");
        dict.Add("Oklahoma", "Oklahoma City");
        dict.Add("Oregon", "Portland");
        dict.Add("Pennsylvania", "Harrisburg");
        dict.Add("Rhode Island", "Providence");
        dict.Add("South Carolina", "Columbia");
        dict.Add("South Dakota", "Pierre");
        dict.Add("Tennessee", "Nashville");
        dict.Add("Texas", "Austin");
        dict.Add("Utah", "Salt Lake City");
        dict.Add("Vermont", "Montpelier");
        dict.Add("Virginia", "Richmond");
        dict.Add("Washington", "Olympia");
        dict.Add("West Virginia", "Charleston");
        dict.Add("Wisconsin", "Madison");
        dict.Add("Wyoming", "Cheyenne");

        // access a state
        Console.WriteLine( "The capital of Massachusetts is {0}",
          dict["Massachusetts"] );
    }        // end main
    }        // end class
}            // end namespace
```

The output looks like this:

```
The capital of Massachusetts is Boston
```

Example 14-9 begins by instantiating a new Dictionary object with the type of the key and of the value declared to be string.

We add 50 key/value pairs. In this example, the state name is the key and the capital is the value (though, in a typical dictionary, the value is almost always larger than the key).

 You must not change the value of the key object once you use it in a dictionary.

Summary

- The .NET Framework provides a number of type-safe (generic) collections, including the list<t>, stack<t>, queue<t>, and dictionary<key><value>.
- You are free to create your own generic collection types as well.
- Generics allow the collection designer to create a single collection without regard to the type of object it will hold, but to allow the collection *user* to define, at compile time, which type the object will hold. This enlists the compiler in finding bugs; if you add an object of the wrong type to a collection, it will be found at compile time, not run time. It also eliminates the need for casting and for boxing and unboxing.
- The .NET Framework provides a number of interfaces that collections must implement if they wish to act like the built-in collections (such as being iterated by a foreach loop).
- An indexer allows you to access or assign objects to and from a collection just as you do with an array (for example, myCollection[5] = "hello").
- Indexers need not be restricted to integers. It is common to create indexers that take a string to assign or retrieve a value.
- All framework collections implement the Sort( ) method. If you want to be able to sort a collection of objects of a user-defined type, however, the defining class must implement the IComparable interface.
- The generic list collection, List<T>, works like an array whose size is increased dynamically as you add elements.
- The Queue<T> class is a first-in, first-out collection.
- The Stack<T> class is a last-in, first-out collection.
- A dictionary<k,v> is a collection that associates a key with a value. Typically, the key is short, and the value is large.

Quiz

Question 14-1. What is the convention for naming an indexer?

Question 14-2. What types can be used in an indexer to index a collection?

Question 14-3. What are the preconditions for calling Sort( ) on an array?

Question 14-4. What is the purpose of generics?

Question 14-5. What is the IEnumerable<T> interface?

Question 14-6. What is the principal difference between a List<T> and an array?

Question 14-7. What is the difference between a List, a Stack, a Queue, and a Dictionary?

Exercises

Exercise 14-1. Create an abstract Animal class that has private members weight and name, and abstract methods Speak( ), Move( ), and ToString( ). Derive from Animal a Cat and Dog class that override the methods appropriately. Create an Animal array, populate it with Dogs and Cats, and then call each member's overridden virtual method.

Exercise 14-2. Replace the array in Exercise 14-1 with a List. Sort the animals by size. You can simplify by just calling ToString( ) before and after the sort. Remember that you'll need to implement IComparable.

Exercise 14-3. Replace the list from Exercise 14-2 with both a Stack and a Queue, and see the difference in the order in which the animals are returned.

Exercise 14-4. Rewrite Exercise 14-2 to allow Animals to be sorted either by weight or alphabetically by name.

CHAPTER 15

Strings

There was a time (long, long ago, when the earth was still molten and I was in high school) when people thought of computers as manipulating numeric values exclusively. Among the first use of computers was to calculate missile trajectories during World War II, and for a very long time, programming was taught in the math department of major universities.

Today, most programs are concerned more with manipulating and displaying strings of characters than with strings of numbers. Typically, these strings are used for word processing, document manipulation, and creation of web pages.

C# provides built-in support for a fully functional string type. More importantly, C# treats strings as objects that encapsulate all the manipulation, sorting, and searching methods normally applied to strings of characters.

The .NET Framework provides a String class (uppercase "S"). The C# language offers an alias to the String class as the string class (lowercase "s"). These class names are interchangeable, and you are free to use either upper- or lowercase.

Complex string manipulation and pattern matching is aided by the use of *regular expressions*.

Regular expressions are a powerful technology for describing and manipulating text. Underlying regular expressions is a technique called *pattern matching*, which involves comparing one string to another, or comparing a series of wildcards that represent a type of string to a literal string. A regular expression is *applied* to a string—that is, to a set of characters. Often, that string is an entire text document. More on regular expressions later in this chapter.

C# combines the power and complexity of regular expression syntax, originally found only in string manipulation languages such as awk and Perl, with a fully object-oriented design.

In this chapter, you will learn to work with the C# string type and the .NET Framework System.String class that it aliases. You will see how to extract sub-strings, manipulate and concatenate strings, and build new strings with the StringBuilder class. In addition, you will find a short introduction to the RegEx class used to match strings based on regular expressions.

Creating Strings

C# treats strings as if they were built-in types (much as it does with arrays). C# strings are flexible, powerful, and easy to use.

In .NET, each string object is an *immutable* sequence of Unicode characters. In other words, methods that appear to change the string actually return a modified copy; the original string remains intact (and if no longer used, is collected by the Garbage Collector).

The declaration of the System.String class is (in part):

```
public sealed class String :
  IComparable, ICloneable, IConvertible, IEnumerable
```

This declaration reveals that the class is sealed, meaning that it is not possible to derive from the String class. The class also implements four system interfaces—IComparable, ICloneable, IConvertible, and IEnumerable—which dictate functionality that System.String shares with other classes in the .NET Framework: the ability to be sorted, copied, converted to other types, and enumerated in foreach loops, respectively.

String Literals

The most common way to create a string is to assign a quoted string of characters, known as a *string literal*, to a user-defined variable of type string. The following code declares a string called newString that contains the phrase "This book teaches C#":

```
string newString = "This book teaches C#";
```

To be precise, newString is a string object that is initialized with the string literal "This book teaches C#". If you pass newString to the WriteLine method of the Console object, the string *This book teaches C#* will be displayed.

Escape Characters

Quoted strings can include *escape characters* (often referred to as "escape sequences"). Escape characters are a way to signal that the letters or characters that follow have a special meaning (for example, the two characters \n do not mean print a slash and then an n, but rather mean print a new-line). You indicate escape characters by preceding a letter or punctuation mark with a backslash (\). The two most common escape characters are \n, which is used to create a new line, and \t, which is used to insert a tab into a string. If you need to include a quotation mark (") within a string, you indicate that this is in the string (rather than ending the string) by escaping it:

```
Console.Writeline("This \"string\" has quotes around it");
```

This will produce the output: This "string" has quotes around it.

If you want to display the backslash character itself, you must escape it with (you guessed it) another backslash. Thus, if you were writing the string c:\myDirectory, you'd write:

```
"c:\\myDirectory"
```

Verbatim Strings

Strings can also be created using *verbatim string literals*, which start with the "at" (@) symbol. This tells the String constructor that the string should be used *as is* (verbatim), even if it spans multiple lines or includes escape characters. In a verbatim string literal, backslashes and the characters that follow them are simply considered additional characters of the string. Thus, the following two definitions are equivalent:

```
string s1 = "My \'favorite\' book is in the directory \\books";
string s2 = @" My 'favorite' book is in the directory \books";
```

In s1, a nonverbatim string literal is used, and so the quote and backslash characters must be *escaped* (preceded by a backslash character). The verbatim string s2 does not require the escape characters. A second example illustrates two ways to specify multiline verbatim strings. The first definition uses a non-verbatim string with a newline escape character (\n) to signal the line break. The second definition uses a verbatim string literal:

```
string s3 = "Line One\nLine Two";
string s4 = @"Line One
Line Two";
```

If you want to use quotation marks in a verbatim string literal, you use two quotation marks, like this:

```
string s5 = @"This string has ""quotation marks"" in it.";
```

Again, these declarations are interchangeable. Which one you use is a matter of convenience and personal style.

The ToString( ) Method

Another common way to create a string is to call the ToString( ) method on an object and assign the result to a string variable. All the built-in types override this method to simplify the task of converting a value (often a numeric value) to a string representation of that value. In the following example, the ToString() method of an integer type is called to store its value in a string:

```
int myInteger = 5;
string integerString = myInteger.ToString();
```

The call to myInteger.ToString() returns a string object that is then assigned to the string variable, integerString.

Manipulating Strings

The String class provides a host of methods for comparing, searching, and manipulating strings, the most important of which are shown in Table 15-1.

Table 15-1. String class properties and methods

Method or property	Explanation
Chars	Property that returns the string indexer
Compare()	Overloaded public static method that compares two strings
Copy()	Public static method that creates a new string by copying another
Equals()	Overloaded public static and instance method that determines if two strings have the same value
Format()	Overloaded public static method that formats a string using a format specification
Length	Property that returns the number of characters in the instance
PadLeft()	Right-aligns the characters in the string, padding to the left with spaces or a specified character
PadRight()	Left-aligns the characters in the string, padding to the right with spaces or a specified character
Remove()	Deletes the specified number of characters
Split()	Divides a string, returning the substrings delimited by the specified characters
StartsWith()	Indicates if the string starts with the specified characters
Substring()	Retrieves a substring
ToCharArray()	Copies the characters from the string to a character array
ToLower()	Returns a copy of the string in lowercase
ToUpper()	Returns a copy of the string in uppercase
Trim()	Removes all occurrences of a set of specified characters from beginning and end of the string
TrimEnd()	Behaves like Trim(), but only at the end
TrimStart()	Behaves like Trim(), but only at the start

Comparing Strings

The Compare() method of String is overloaded. The first version takes two strings and returns a negative number if the first string is alphabetically before the second, a positive number if the first string is alphabetically after the second, and zero if they are equal. The second version works just like the first but is case-insensitive. Example 15-1 illustrates the use of Compare( ).

Example 15-1. Compare() method

```
using System;

namespace StringManipulation
{
    class Tester
    {
        public void Run( )
        {
            // create some strings to work with
            string s1 = "abcd";
            string s2 = "ABCD";
            int result; // hold the results of comparisons

            // compare two strings, case sensitive
            result = string.Compare( s1, s2 );
            Console.WriteLine(
            "compare s1: {0}, s2: {1}, result: {2}\n",
            s1, s2, result );

            // overloaded compare, takes boolean "ignore case"
            //(true = ignore case)
            result = string.Compare( s1, s2, true );
            Console.WriteLine( "Compare insensitive. result: {0}\n",
            result );

        }

        static void Main( )
        {
            Tester t = new Tester();
            t.Run( );
        }
    }
}
```

The output looks like this:

```
compare s1: abcd, s2: ABCD, result: -1
Compare insensitive. result: 0
```

Example 15-1 begins by declaring two strings, s1 and s2, and initializing them with string literals:

```
string s1 = "abcd";
string s2 = "ABCD";
```

Compare( ) is used with many types. A negative return value indicates that the first parameter is less than the second, a positive result indicates the first parameter is greater than the second, and a zero indicates they are equal. In Unicode (as in

ASCII), a lowercase letter has a smaller value than an uppercase letter; with strings identical except for case, lowercase comes first alphabetically. Thus, the output properly indicates that s1 (abcd) is "less than" s2 (ABCD):

```
compare s1: abcd, s2: ABCD, result: -1
```

The second comparison uses an overloaded version of Compare( ), which takes a third Boolean parameter, the value of which determines whether case should be ignored in the comparison. If the value of this "ignore case" parameter is true, the comparison is made without regard to case. This time the result is 0, indicating that the two strings are identical:

```
Compare insensitive. result: 0
```

Concatenating Strings

There are a couple of ways to concatenate strings in C#. You can use the Concat( ) method, which is a static public method of the String class:

```
string s3 = string.Concat(s1,s2);
```

or you can simply use the overloaded concatenation (+) operator:

```
string s4 = s1 + s2;
```

Example 15-2 demonstrates both of these methods.

Example 15-2. Concatenation

```
using System;

namespace StringManipulation
{
   class Tester
   {
      public void Run( )
      {
         string s1 = "abcd";
         string s2 = "ABCD";

         // concatenation method
         string s3 = string.Concat( s1, s2 );
         Console.WriteLine(
         "s3 concatenated from s1 and s2: {0}", s3 );

         // use the overloaded operator
         string s4 = s1 + s2;
         Console.WriteLine(
         "s4 concatenated from s1 + s2: {0}", s4 );
      }

      static void Main( )
      {
         Tester t = new Tester( );
```

Example 15-2. Concatenation (continued)

```
            t.Run( );
        }
    }
}
```

The output looks like this:

```
s3 concatenated from s1 and s2: abcdABCD
s4 concatenated from s1 + s2: abcdABCD
```

In Example 15-2, the new string s3 is created by calling the static Concat( ) method and passing in s1 and s2, while the string s4 is created by using the overloaded concatenation operator (+) that concatenates two strings and returns a string as a result.

Copying Strings

There are two ways to copy strings. 99.9 percent of the time you will just write:

```
oneString = theOtherString;
```

and not worry about what is going on in memory.

There is a second, somewhat awkward way to copy strings:

```
myString = String.Copy(yourString);
```

and this actually does something subtly different. The difference is somewhat advanced, but here it is in a nutshell.

When you use the assignment operator (=), you create a second reference to the same object in memory, but when you use Copy, you create a reference to a new string that is initialized with the value of the first string.

"Huh?" I hear you cry. An example will make it clear (see Example 15-3).

Example 15-3. Copying strings

```
using System;

namespace StringManipulation
{
    class Tester
    {
        public void Run()
        {
            string s1 = "abcd";

            Console.WriteLine( " string s1: {0}",s1 );
            Console.WriteLine( " string s2 = s1; " );
            string s2 = s1;
            Console.WriteLine( "s1: {0} s2: {1}", s1, s2 );
            Console.WriteLine( "s1 == s2? {0}", s1 == s2 );
            Console.WriteLine( "ReferenceEquals(s1,s2): {0}",
                ReferenceEquals( s1, s2 ) );
```

Example 15-3. Copying strings (continued)

```
          Console.WriteLine( " \nstring s2 = string.Copy( s1 ); " );
          string s3 = string.Copy( s1 );
          Console.WriteLine( "s1: {0} s3: {1}", s1, s3 );
          Console.WriteLine( "s1 == s3? {0}", s1 == s3 );
          Console.WriteLine( "ReferenceEquals(s1,s3): {0}",
              ReferenceEquals( s1, s3 ) );

          Console.WriteLine( " \ns2 = \"Hello\"; " );
          s1 = "Hello";
          Console.WriteLine( "s1: {0} s2: {1}", s1, s2 );
          Console.WriteLine( "s1 == s2? {0}", s1 == s2 );
          Console.WriteLine( "ReferenceEquals(s1,s2): {0}",
              ReferenceEquals( s1, s2 ) );

      }

      static void Main()
      {
          Tester t = new Tester();
          t.Run();
      }
    }
}
```

The output looks like this:

```
    string s1: abcd
    string s2 = s1;
    s1: abcd s2: abcd
    s1 == s2? True
    ReferenceEquals(s1,s2): True

    string s2 = string.Copy( s1 );
    s1: abcd s3: abcd
    s1 == s3? True
    ReferenceEquals(s1,s3): False

    s1 = "Hello";
    s1: Hello s2: abcd
    s1 == s2? False
    ReferenceEquals(s1,s2): False
```

In Example 15-3, you start by initializing one string:

```
    string s1 = "abcd";
```

You then assign the value of s1 to s2 using the assignment operator:

```
    s2 = s1;
```

You print their values, as shown in the first section of results, and find that not only do the two string references have the same value, as indicated by using the equality operator (==), but they actually point to the same object in memory, which is why ReferenceEquals returns true.

On the other hand, if you create s3 and assign its value using String.Copy(s1), while the two values are equal (as shown by using the equality operator), they refer to different objects in memory (as shown by the fact that ReferenceEquals returns false).

Now, returning to s1 and s2, which refer to the same object, if you change either one, for example, when you write:

```
s1 = "Hello";
```

s3 goes on referring to the original string, but s1 now refers to a brand new string.

If you later write:

```
S3 = "Goodbye";
```

(not shown in the example), the original string referred to by s1 will no longer have any references to it, and it will be mercifully and painlessly destroyed by the Garbage Collector.

Testing for Equality

The .NET String class provides three ways to test for the equality of two strings. First, you can use the overloaded Equals() method and ask one string (say, s6) directly whether another string (s5) is of equal value:

```
Console.WriteLine( "\nDoes s6.Equals(s5)?: {0}", s6.Equals(s5));
```

You can also pass both strings to String's static method Equals():

```
Console.WriteLine( "Does Equals(s6,s5)?: {0}" string.Equals(s6,s5));
```

Or you can use the String class's overloaded equality operator (==):

```
Console.WriteLine( "Does s6==s5?: {0}", s6 == s5);
```

In each of these cases, the returned result is a Boolean value (true for equal and false for unequal). Example 15-4 demonstrates these techniques.

Example 15-4. Are all strings created equal?

```
using System;

namespace StringManipulation
{
   class Tester
   {
      public void Run( )
      {
         string s1 = "abcd";
         string s2 = "ABCD";

         // the string copy method
         string s5 = string.Copy( s2 );
         Console.WriteLine(
         "s5 copied from s2: {0}", s5 );
```

Example 15-4. Are all strings created equal? (continued)

```
        string s6 = s5;
        Console.WriteLine( "s6 = s5: {0}", s6 );

        // member method
        Console.WriteLine(
        "\nDoes s6.Equals(s5)?: {0}",
        s6.Equals( s5 ) );

        // static method
        Console.WriteLine(
        "Does Equals(s6,s5)?: {0}",
        string.Equals( s6, s5 ) );

        // overloaded operator
        Console.WriteLine(
        "Does s6==s5?: {0}", s6 == s5 );
    }

    static void Main()
    {
        Tester t = new Tester();
        t.Run();
    }
  }
}
```

The output looks like this:

```
s5 copied from s2: ABCD
s6 = s5: ABCD

Does s6.Equals(s5)?: True
Does Equals(s6,s5)?: True
Does s6==s5?: True
```

The equality operator is the most natural of the three methods to use when you have two string objects.

Other Useful String Methods

The String class includes a number of useful methods and properties for finding specific characters or substrings within a string, as well as for manipulating the contents of the string. Example 15-5 demonstrates a few methods, such as locating substrings, finding the index of a substring, and inserting text from one string into another. Following the output is a complete analysis.

Example 15-5. Useful methods of the String class

```
using System;

namespace StringManipulation
{
    class Tester
    {
        public void Run( )
        {
            string s1 = "abcd";
            string s2 = "ABCD";
            string s3 = @"Liberty Associates, Inc.
provides custom .NET development,
on-site Training and Consulting";

            // the string copy method
            string s5 = string.Copy( s2 );
            Console.WriteLine(
            "s5 copied from s2: {0}", s5 );

            // Two useful properties: the index and the length
            Console.WriteLine(
            "\nString s3 is {0} characters long. ",
            s5.Length );

            Console.WriteLine(
            "The 5th character is {0}\n", s3[4] );

            // test whether a string ends with a set of characters
            Console.WriteLine( "s3:{0}\nEnds with Training?: {1}\n",
            s3,
            s3.EndsWith( "Training" ) );
            Console.WriteLine(
            "Ends with Consulting?: {0}",
            s3.EndsWith( "Consulting" ) );

            // return the index of the substring
            Console.WriteLine(
            "\nThe first occurrence of Training " );
            Console.WriteLine( "in s3 is {0}\n",
            s3.IndexOf( "Training" ) );

            // insert the word excellent before "training"
            string s10 = s3.Insert( 73, "excellent " );
            Console.WriteLine( "s10: {0}\n", s10 );

            // you can combine the two as follows:
            string s11 = s3.Insert( s3.IndexOf( "Training" ),
            "excellent " );
            Console.WriteLine( "s11: {0}\n", s11 );
        }
```

Example 15-5. Useful methods of the String class (continued)

```
     static void Main( )
     {
        Tester t = new Tester( );
        t.Run( );
     }
  }
}
```

The output looks like this:

```
s5 copied from s2: ABCD

String s3 is 4 characters long.
The 5th character is r

s3:Liberty Associates, Inc.
 provides custom .NET development,
 on-site Training and Consulting
Ends with Training?: False

Ends with Consulting?: True

The first occurrence of Training
in s3 is 73

s10: Liberty Associates, Inc.
 provides custom .NET development,
 on-site excellent Training and Consulting

s11: Liberty Associates, Inc.
 provides custom .NET development,
 on-site excellent Training and Consulting
```

The Length property returns the length of the entire string, and the index operator ([ ]) is used to access a particular character within a string:

```
Console.WriteLine(
  "\nString s3 is {0} characters long. ",
  s5.Length);

Console.WriteLine(
  "The 5th character is {0}\n", s3[4]);
```

Here's the output:

```
String s3 is 4 characters long.
The 5th character is r
```

The EndsWith( ) method asks a string whether a substring is found at the end of the string. Thus, you might first ask if s3 ends with "Training" (which it does not), and then if it ends with "Consulting" (which it does):

```
Console.WriteLine("s3:{0}\nEnds with Training?: {1}\n",
  s3,
```

```
    s3.EndsWith("Training") );
  Console.WriteLine(
    "Ends with Consulting?: {0}",
    s3.EndsWith("Consulting"));
```

The output reflects that the first test fails and the second succeeds:

```
Ends with Training?: False
Ends with Consulting?: True
```

The IndexOf( ) method locates a substring within a string, and the Insert( ) method inserts a new substring into a copy of the original string. The following code locates the first occurrence of "Training" in s3:

```
Console.WriteLine("\nThe first occurrence of Training ");
Console.WriteLine ("in s3 is {0}\n",
  s3.IndexOf("Training"));
```

The output indicates that the offset is 73:

```
The first occurrence of Training
in s3 is 73
```

Then use that value to insert the word "excellent," followed by a space, into that string. Actually the insertion is into a copy of the string returned by the Insert( ) method and assigned to s10:

```
string s10 = s3.Insert(73,"excellent ");
Console.WriteLine("s10: {0}\n",s10);
```

Here's the output:

```
s10: Liberty Associates, Inc.
  provides custom .NET development,
  on-site excellent Training and Consulting
```

Finally, you can combine these operations to make a more efficient insertion statement:

```
string s11 = s3.Insert(s3.IndexOf("Training"),"excellent ");
Console.WriteLine("s11: {0}\n",s11);
```

with the identical result:

```
s11: Liberty Associates, Inc.
  provides custom .NET development,
  on-site excellent Training and Consulting
```

Finding Substrings

The String class has methods for finding and extracting substrings. For example, the IndexOf( ) method returns the index of the *first* occurrence of a string (or of any character in an array of characters) within a target string. For example, given the definition of the string s1 as:

```
string s1 = "One Two Three Four";
```

you can find the first instance of the characters "hre" by writing:

```
int index = s1.IndexOf("hre");
```

This code sets the int variable index to 9, which is the offset of the letters "hre" in the string s1.

Similarly, the LastIndexOf( ) method returns the index of the *last* occurrence of a string or substring. While the following code:

```
s1.IndexOf("o");
```

returns the value 6 (the first occurrence of the lowercase letter "o" is at the end of the word "Two"), the method call:

```
s1.LastIndexOf("o");
```

returns the value 15 (the last occurrence of "o" is in the word "Four").

The Substring( ) method returns a series of characters. You can ask it for all the characters starting at a particular offset and ending either with the end of the string or with an offset you (optionally) provide. Example 15-6 illustrates the Substring( ) method.

Example 15-6. Finding substrings by index

```csharp
using System;

namespace StringSearch
{
    class Tester
    {
        public void Run( )
        {
            // create some strings to work with
            string s1 = "One Two Three Four";

            int index;

            // get the index of the last space
            index = s1.LastIndexOf( " " );

            // get the last word.
            string s2 = s1.Substring( index + 1 );

            // set s1 to the substring starting at 0
            // and ending at index (the start of the last word)
            // thus s1 has "one two three"
            s1 = s1.Substring( 0, index );

            // find the last space in s1 (after two)
            index = s1.LastIndexOf( " " );

            // set s3 to the substring starting at
            // index, the space after "two" plus one more
            // thus s3 = "three"
            string s3 = s1.Substring( index + 1 );
```

Example 15-6. Finding substrings by index (continued)

```
// reset s1 to the substring starting at 0
// and ending at index, thus the string "one two"
s1 = s1.Substring( 0, index );

// reset index to the space between
// "one" and "two"
index = s1.LastIndexOf( " " );

// set s4 to the substring starting one
// space after index, thus the substring "two"
string s4 = s1.Substring( index + 1 );

// reset s1 to the substring starting at 0
// and ending at index, thus "one"
s1 = s1.Substring( 0, index );

// set index to the last space, but there is
// none so index now = -1
index = s1.LastIndexOf( " " );

// set s5 to the substring at one past
// the last space. there was no last space
// so this sets s5 to the substring starting
// at zero
string s5 = s1.Substring( index + 1 );

Console.WriteLine( "s2: {0}\ns3: {1}", s2, s3 );
Console.WriteLine( "s4: {0}\ns5: {1}\n", s4, s5 );
Console.WriteLine( "s1: {0}\n", s1 );
}

static void Main( )
{
    Tester t = new Tester( );
    t.Run( );
}
}
}
```

The output looks like this:

```
s2: Four
s3: Three
s4: Two
s5: One

s1: One
```

Example 15-6 is not the most elegant solution possible to the problem of extracting words from a string, but it is a good first approximation, and it illustrates a useful technique. The example begins by creating a string, s1:

```
string s1 = "One Two Three Four";
```

The local variable index is assigned the value of the last literal space in the string (which comes before the word "Four"):

```
index=s1.LastIndexOf(" ");
```

The substring that begins one position later is assigned to the new string, s2:

```
string s2 = s1.Substring(index+1);
```

This extracts the characters from index +1 to the end of the line (the string "Four") and assigns the value "Four" to s2.

The next step is to remove the word "Four" from s1; assign to s1 the substring of s1 that begins at 0 and ends at the index:

```
s1 = s1.Substring(0,index);
```

After this line executes, the variable s1 will point to a new string object that will contain the appropriate substring of the string that s1 used to point to. That original string will eventually be destroyed by the garbage collector because no variable now references it.

You reassign index to the last (remaining) space, which points you to the beginning of the word "Three." You then extract the character "Three" into string s3. Continue like this until you've populated s4 and s5. Finally, display the results:

```
s2: Four
s3: Three
s4: Two
s5: One
s1: One
```

Splitting Strings

A more effective solution to the problem illustrated in Example 15-6 would be to use the String class's Split( ) method, which parses a string into substrings. To use Split( ), pass in an array of delimiters (characters that indicate where to divide the words). The method returns an array of substrings (which Example 15-7 illustrates). The complete analysis follows the code.

Example 15-7. The Split() method

```
using System;

namespace StringSearch
{
    class Tester
    {
        public void Run( )
        {
            // create some strings to work with
            string s1 = "One,Two,Three Liberty Associates, Inc.";
```

Example 15-7. The Split() method (continued)

```
        // constants for the space and comma characters
        const char Space = ' ';
        const char Comma = ',';

        // array of delimiters to split the sentence with
        char[] delimiters = new char[]
        {
            Space,
            Comma
        };

        int ctr = 1;

        // split the string and then iterate over the
        // resulting array of strings

        String[] resultArray = s1.Split( delimiters );

        foreach ( String subString in resultArray )
        {
            Console.WriteLine(ctr++ + ":" + subString);
        }
    }

    static void Main( )
    {
        Tester t = new Tester( );
        t.Run( );
    }
}
}
```

The output looks like this:

```
1: One
2: Two
3: Three
4: Liberty
5: Associates
6:
7: Inc.
```

Example 15-7 starts by creating a string to parse:

```
string s1 = "One,Two,Three Liberty Associates, Inc.";
```

The delimiters are set to the space and comma characters. Then call Split( ) on the string, passing in the delimiters:

```
String[] resultArray = s1.Split(delimiters);
```

Split( ) returns an array of the substrings that you can then iterate over using the foreach loop, as explained in Chapter 10:

```
foreach (String subString in resultArray)
```

You can, of course, combine the call to split with the iteration, as in the following:

```
foreach (string subString in s1.Split(delimiters))
```

C# programmers are fond of combining statements like this. The advantage of splitting the statement into two, however, and of using an interim variable like resultArray is that you can examine the contents of resultArray in the debugger.

Start the foreach loop by initializing output to an empty string, and then build up the output string in four steps. Start by concatenating the incremented value of ctr to the output string, using the += operator.

```
output += ctr++;
```

Next add the colon, then the substring returned by Split( ), and then the newline:

```
output += ": ";
output += subString;
output += "\n";
```

With each concatenation, a new copy of the string is made, and all four steps are repeated for each substring found by Split( ).

This repeated copying of string is terribly inefficient. The problem is that the string type is not designed for this kind of operation. What you want is to create a new string by appending a formatted string each time through the loop. The class you need is StringBuilder.

The StringBuilder Class

You can use the System.Text.StringBuilder class for creating and modifying strings. Table 15-2 summarizes the important members of StringBuilder.

Table 15-2. StringBuilder members

Method or property	Explanation
Append( )	Overloaded public method that appends a typed object to the end of the current StringBuilder
AppendFormat( )	Overloaded public method that replaces format specifiers with the formatted value of an object
EnsureCapacity( )	Ensures that the current StringBuilder has a capacity at least as large as the specified value
Capacity	Property that retrieves or assigns the number of characters the StringBuilder is capable of holding
Insert( )	Overloaded public method that inserts an object at the specified position
Length	Property that retrieves or assigns the length of the StringBuilder
MaxCapacity	Property that retrieves the maximum capacity of the StringBuilder

Table 15-2. StringBuilder members (continued)

Method or property	Explanation
Remove( )	Removes the specified range of characters
Replace( )	Overloaded public method that replaces all instances of the specified characters with new characters

Unlike String, StringBuilder is mutable; when you modify an instance of the StringBuilder class, you modify the actual string, not a copy.

Example 15-8 replaces the String object in Example 15-7 with a StringBuilder object.

Example 15-8. The StringBuilder class

```
using System;
using System.Text;

namespace StringSearch
{
    class Tester
    {
        public void Run( )
        {
            // create some strings to work with
            string s1 = "One,Two,Three Liberty Associates, Inc.";

            // constants for the space and comma characters
            const char Space = ' ';
            const char Comma = ',';

            // array of delimiters to split the sentence with
            char[] delimiters = new char[]
            {
                Space,
                Comma
            };

            // use a StringBuilder class to build the
            // output string
            StringBuilder output = new StringBuilder( );
            int ctr = 1;

            // split the string and then iterate over the
            // resulting array of strings
            foreach ( string subString in s1.Split( delimiters ) )
            {
                // AppendFormat appends a formatted string
                output.AppendFormat( "{0}: {1}\n", ctr++, subString );
            }
            Console.WriteLine( output );

        }
```

Example 15-8. The StringBuilder class (continued)

```
    static void Main( )
    {
        Tester t = new Tester( );
        t.Run( );
    }
  }
}
```

Only the last part of the program is modified. Rather than using the concatenation operator to modify the string, use the AppendFormat( ) method of StringBuilder to append new formatted strings as you create them. This is much easier and far more efficient. The output is identical:

```
1: One
2: Two
3: Three
4: Liberty
5: Associates
6:
7: Inc.
```

Because you passed in delimiters of both comma and space, the space after the comma between "Associates" and "Inc." is returned as a word, numbered 6 in the previous code. That is not what you want. To eliminate this, you need to tell Split( ) to match a comma (as between One, Two, and Three), a space (as between Liberty and Associates), or a comma followed by a space. It is that last bit that is tricky and requires that you use a regular expression.

Regular Expressions

As noted earlier, regular expressions provide a very powerful way to describe and manipulate text through pattern matching.

The result of applying a regular expression to a string is either to return a substring or to return a new string representing a modification of some part of the original string. (Remember that string objects are immutable and so cannot be changed by the regular expression.)

By applying a properly constructed regular expression to the following string:

```
One,Two,Three Liberty Associates, Inc.
```

you can return any or all of its substrings (such as "Liberty" or "One") or modified versions of its substrings (such as "LIBeRtY" or "OnE"). What the regular expression does is determined by the syntax of the regular expression itself.

A regular expression consists of two types of characters: *literals* and *metacharacters*. A literal is a character you want to match in the target string. A metacharacter is a special symbol that acts as a command to the regular expression parser. The parser is the engine responsible for understanding the regular expression. For example, if you create a regular expression:

```
^(From|To|Subject|Date):
```

this will match any substring with the letters "From," "To," "Subject," or "Date," so long as those letters start a new line (^) and end with a colon (:).

The caret (^) indicates to the regular expression parser that the string you're searching for must begin a new line. The letters "From" and "To" are literals, and the metacharacters left and right parentheses ((,)) and vertical bar (|) are all used to group sets of literals and indicate that any of the choices should match. Thus, you would read the following line as "match any string that begins a new line, followed by any of the four literal strings From, To, Subject, or Date, and followed by a colon":

```
^(From|To|Subject|Date):
```

 A full explanation of regular expressions is beyond the scope of this book, but all the regular expressions used in the examples are explained. For a complete understanding of regular expressions, I highly recommend *Mastering Regular Expressions*, Second Edition, by Jeffrey E. F. Friedl (O'Reilly, 2002).

The Regex Class

The .NET Framework provides an object-oriented approach to regular expression pattern matching and replacement.

The Framework Class Library namespace `System.Text.RegularExpressions` is the home to all the .NET Framework objects associated with regular expressions. The central class for regular expression support is `Regex`, which provides methods and properties for working with regular expressions, the most important of which are shown in Table 15-3.

Table 15-3. Regex members

Method or property	Explanation
Regex constructor	Overloaded; creates an instance of Regex
Options	Property that returns the options passed in to the constructor
IsMatch( )	Method that indicates whether a match is found in the input string
Match	Searches an input string and returns a match for a regular expression
Matches	Searches an input string and returns all successful matches for a regular expression
Replace	Replaces all occurrences of a pattern with a replacement string
Split	Splits an input string into an array of substrings based on a regular expression

Example 15-9 rewrites Example 15-8 to use regular expressions and thus solve the problem of searching for more than one type of delimiter.

Example 15-9. Regular expressions

```
using System;
using System.Text;
using System.Text.RegularExpressions;

namespace RegularExpressions
{
    class Tester
    {
        public void Run( )
        {
            string s1 =
            "One,Two,Three Liberty Associates, Inc.";
            Regex theRegex = new Regex( " |, |," );
            StringBuilder sBuilder = new StringBuilder( );
            int id = 1;

            foreach ( string subString in theRegex.Split( s1 ) )
            {
                sBuilder.AppendFormat(
                "{0}: {1}\n", id++, subString );
            }
            Console.WriteLine( "{0}", sBuilder );
        }


        static void Main( )
        {
            Tester t = new Tester( );
            t.Run( );
        }
    }
}
```

The output looks like this:

```
1: One
2: Two
3: Three
4: Liberty
5: Associates
6: Inc.
```

Example 15-9 begins by creating a string, s1, identical to the string used in Example 15-8:

```
string s1 = "One,Two,Three Liberty Associates, Inc.";
```

and a regular expression that is used to search the string:

```
Regex theRegex = new Regex(" |,|, ");
```

One of the overloaded constructors for Regex takes a regular expression string as its parameter.

 This can be a bit confusing. In the context of a C# program, which is the regular expression—the text passed in to the constructor or the Regex object itself? It is true that the text string passed to the constructor is a regular expression in the traditional sense of the term. From a C# (that is, object-oriented) point of view, however, the argument to the constructor is just a string of characters; it is the object called the Regex that is the regular expression object.

The rest of the program proceeds like Example 15-8, except that rather than calling the Split() method of String on string s1, the Split() method of Regex is called. theRegex.Split() acts in much the same way as String.Split(), returning an array of strings as a result of matching the regular expression pattern within theRegex. Because it matches a regular expression, rather than using a set of delimiters, you have much greater control over how the string is split.

Summary

- C# strings can be sorted, searched, and otherwise manipulated.
- The String class is sealed, meaning it cannot be derived from. It implements the IComparable, IClonable, IConvertible, and IEnumerable interfaces, indicating that you can compare two strings (to sort them), clone a string (to create a duplicate), convert a string to another type (for example, converting the string "15" to the integer 15), and enumerate over a string using a foreach statement, respectively.
- A string literal is a quoted string of characters assigned to a variable of type string. This is the most common use of strings.
- Escape characters allow you to add special characters to strings that would otherwise not be valid within a string.
- A verbatim string literal starts with an @ symbol and indicates that the string should be used exactly as is. Verbatim strings do not require escape characters.
- You can concatenate strings with the Concat() method or the + operator.
- You can copy strings with the Copy() method or the = operator.
- You can test for equality of two strings with the Equals() method or the == operator.
- The String class also includes methods for finding and extracting substrings, such as IndexOf(), LastIndexOf(), and Substring().
- You can use the Split() method with an array of delimiters to divide a string into substrings.
- Strings are immutable. Every time you appear to modify a string, a copy is made with the modification and the original string is released to the garbage collector.

- The `StringBuilder` class allows you to assemble the contents of a string with greater efficiency and then to call its `ToString()` method to generate the string you need once it is fully assembled.
- Regular expressions provide pattern-matching abilities that enable you to search and manipulate text.

Quiz

Question 15-1. What is the difference between `string` and `String` (lower- and uppercase)?

Question 15-2. Some of the interfaces implemented by the string are: `IComparable`, `ICloneable`, `IConvertible` and `IEnumerable`. What do these guarantee to you as a client of the String class?

Question 15-3. What is a string literal?

Question 15-4. What is the purpose of escape characters? Give two examples.

Question 15-5. What are verbatim strings?

Question 15-6. What does it mean that strings are immutable?

Question 15-7. What does it mean that the `String` class is sealed?

Question 15-8. What are the two ways to concatenate strings?

Question 15-9. What does `Split()` do?

Question 15-10. What is the `StringBuilder` class, why is it used, and how do you create a string with one?

Question 15-11. What are regular expressions?

Exercises

Exercise 15-1. Create the following six strings:
- String 1: "Hello"
- String 2: "World"
- String 3 (a verbatim string): "Come visit us at http://www.LibertyAssociates.com"

- String 4: a concatenation of strings 1 and 2
- String 5: "world"
- String 6: a copy of string 3

Once you have the strings created, do the following:

1. Output the length of each string.
2. Output the third character in each string.
3. Output whether the character "H" appears in each string.
4. Output which strings are the same as string 2.
5. Output which strings are the same as string 2, ignoring case.

Exercise 15-2. Take the following string:

> We hold these truths to be self-evident, that all men are created equal, that they are endowed by their Creator with certain unalienable Rights, that among these are Life, Liberty and the pursuit of Happiness.

and use a regular expression to split the string into words.

CHAPTER 16

Throwing and Catching Exceptions

Things go wrong. Programmers always need to plan for the inevitable problems that might arise while their program is running: networks go down, disks fail, computers exhaust their memory, and so forth.

In C#, you address these problems with *exceptions*. An exception is an object that encapsulates information about an unusual program occurrence. When an exceptional circumstance arises, an exception is "thrown." You might throw an exception in your own methods (for example, if you realize that an invalid parameter has been provided), or an exception might be thrown in a class provided by the Framework Class Library (for example, if you try to write to a read-only file). Many exceptions are thrown by the .NET runtime when the program can no longer continue due to an operating system problem (such as a security violation).

Throwing an exception is sometimes called *raising* an exception.

Your job as programmer is to *try* potentially dangerous code, and if an exception is thrown, you *catch* the exception in your "catch block."

Both try and catch are keywords in C#. Catching an exception is sometimes referred to as *handling* the exception.

Ideally, after the exception is caught, the program can fix the problem and continue. Even if your program can't continue, by catching the exception, you have an opportunity to print a meaningful error message and terminate gracefully.

Bugs, Errors, and Exceptions

It is important to distinguish exceptions from *bugs* and *errors*. A bug is a programmer mistake that should be fixed before the code is shipped. An exception is not the result of a programmer mistake (though such mistakes can also raise exceptions). Rather, exceptions are raised as a result of predictable but unpreventable problems that arise while your program is running (e.g., a network connection is dropped or you run out of disk space).

An error is caused by user action. For example, the user might enter a number where a letter is expected. Once again, an error might cause an exception, but you can prevent that by implementing code to validate user input. Whenever possible, user errors should be anticipated and prevented.

Even if you remove all bugs and anticipate all user errors, you will still run into predictable but unpreventable problems, such as running out of memory or attempting to open a file that no longer exists. These are exceptions. You cannot prevent exceptions, but you can handle them so that they do not bring down your program.

Throwing Exceptions

All exceptions are either of type `System.Exception` or of types derived from `System.Exception`. Microsoft suggests that all the exceptions you use in your program derive from `System.Exception`, though you are also free to derive from `System.ApplicationException` (which was the previous recommended strategy).

The CLR System namespace includes a number of pre-defined exception types that you can use in your own programs. These exception types include `ArgumentNullException`, `InvalidCastException`, and `OverflowException`, as well as many others. You can guess their use based on their name. For example, `ArgumentNull` exception is thrown when an argument to a method is null when that is not an expected (or acceptable) value.

This chapter describes how to write your programs to catch and handle exceptions. This chapter also shows you how to use the properties of the `Exception` class to provide information to the user about what went wrong, and it shows you how to create and use your own custom exception types.

Searching for an Exception Handler

When your program encounters an exceptional circumstance, such as running out of memory, it throws an exception. Exceptions must be handled before the program can continue.

If the currently running function does not handle the exception, the current function terminates and the calling function gets a chance to handle the exception (this is called "unwinding the stack"). If none of the calling functions handles it, the exception ultimately is handled by the Common Language Runtime (CLR), which abruptly terminates your program.

In other words, if function A calls function B, and function B calls function C, these function calls are all placed on the stack. When a programmer talks about "unwinding the stack," what is meant is that you back up from C to B to A, as illustrated in Figure 16-1.

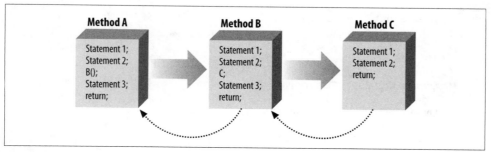

Figure 16-1. Unwinding the stack

If you must unwind the stack from C to B to A to handle the exception, when you are done, you are in A; there is no automatic return to C.

The throw Statement

To signal an abnormal condition in a C# program, throw an exception by using the throw keyword. The following line of code creates a new instance of System. Exception and then throws it:

```
throw new System.Exception();
```

Example 16-1 illustrates what happens if you throw an exception and there is no try/catch block to catch and handle the exception. In this example, you'll throw an exception even though nothing has actually gone wrong, just to illustrate how an exception can bring your program to a halt.

Example 16-1. Unhandled exception

```
using System;

namespace UnhandledException
{
    class Tester
    {

        static void Main()
        {
```

Example 16-1. Unhandled exception (continued)

```
        Console.WriteLine( "Enter Main..." );
        Tester t = new Tester( );
        t.Run( );
        Console.WriteLine( "Exit Main..." );
    }
    public void Run( )
    {
        Console.WriteLine( "Enter Run..." );
        Func1( );
        Console.WriteLine( "Exit Run..." );
    }

    public void Func1( )
    {
        Console.WriteLine( "Enter Func1..." );
        Func2( );
        Console.WriteLine( "Exit Func1..." );
    }

    public void Func2( )
    {
        Console.WriteLine( "Enter Func2..." );
        throw new ApplicationException( );
        // this next line can never execute
        Console.WriteLine( "Exit Func2..." );
    }

    }
}
```

The output looks like this:

```
Enter Main...
Enter Run...
Enter Func1...
Enter Func2...

Unhandled Exception: System.Exception: Exception of type
System.Exception was thrown. at
ExceptionHandling.Tester.Func2( ) in source\exceptions\exceptionhandling\class1.cs:
line 34
 at ExceptionHandling.Tester.Func1( ) in source\exceptions\exceptionhandling\class1.
cs:
line 27
 at ExceptionHandling.Tester.Run( ) in source\exceptions\exceptionhandling\class1.cs:
line 19
 at ExceptionHandling.Tester.Main( ) in source\exceptions\exceptionhandling\class1.cs:
line 13
```

When you run this code, you'll also receive a warning that the following line is unreachable:

```
Console.WriteLine( "Exit Func2..." );
```

That's because the compiler can tell that there's no way this line will ever be reached. In this example, you can ignore the warning, but as noted earlier, you should usually try to write warning-free code.

This simple example writes to the console as it enters and exits each method. Main( ) calls Run( ), which in turn calls Func1( ). After printing out the "Enter Func1" message, Func1( ) immediately calls Func2( ). Func2( ) prints out the first message and throws an object of type System.Exception.

Execution immediately stops, and the CLR looks to see if there is a handler in Func2( ). There is not, and so the runtime unwinds the stack (never printing the exit statement) to Func1( ). Again, there is no handler, and the runtime unwinds the stack back to Main( ). With no exception handler there, the default handler is called, which prints the error message, and terminates the program.

The try and catch Statements

As you saw, the exception in your previous example stopped your program dead. That's usually not the desired behavior. What you need is a way to tell the compiler, "If any exceptions are thrown in this section of code, take this action." That way, your program can continue on from the error, or at least end gracefully. This process is called *handling* the exception. To handle exceptions, take the following steps:

1. Execute any code that you suspect might throw an exception (such as code that opens a file or allocates memory) within a try block.
2. Catch any exceptions that are thrown in a catch block.

A try block is created using the keyword try and is enclosed in braces. The try block is the area of code where you want to watch for exceptions. A catch block holds the code where you take action based on the type of exception thrown. It is created using the keyword catch and is also enclosed in braces. Example 16-2 illustrates these constructs. Note that Example 16-2 is identical to Example 16-1 except that now the program includes a try/catch block.

Example 16-2. Try and catch blocks

```
using System;

namespace TryAndCatchBlocks
{
    class Tester
    {
        static void Main( )
```

Example 16-2. Try and catch blocks (continued)

```csharp
{
    Console.WriteLine( "Enter Main..." );
    Tester t = new Tester( );
    t.Run( );
    Console.WriteLine( "Exit Main..." );
}
public void Run( )
{
    Console.WriteLine( "Enter Run..." );
    Func1( );
    Console.WriteLine( "Exit Run..." );
}


public void Func1( )
{
    Console.WriteLine( "Enter Func1..." );
    Func2( );
    Console.WriteLine( "Exit Func1..." );
}

public void Func2( )
{
    Console.WriteLine( "Enter Func2..." );
    try
    {
        Console.WriteLine( "Entering try block..." );
        throw new ApplicationException( );
        // this code never executes because of the exception
        Console.WriteLine( "Exiting try block..." );
    }
    catch
    {
        Console.WriteLine( "Exception caught and handled!" );
    }
    Console.WriteLine( "Exit Func2..." );
    }
  }
}
```

The output looks like this:

```
Enter Main...
Enter Run...
Enter Func1...
Enter Func2...
Entering try block...
Exception caught and handled!
Exit Func2...
Exit Func1...
Exit Run...
Exit Main...
```

Following the try statement is the catch statement. In a real catch statement, you might silently fix the problem (for example, by retrying a database connection), or you might interact with the user to solve the problem (such as offering the user the opportunity to close other applications and free up memory). In Example 16-2, the catch statement simply reports that the exception has been caught and handled.

Notice that the exit statements are now written. With the exception handled, execution resumes immediately after the catch block.

How the Call Stack Works

Examine the output of Example 16-2 carefully. You see the code enter Main( ), Func1( ), Func2( ), and the try block. You never see it exit the try block, though it does exit Func2( ), Func1( ), and Main( ). What happened?

When the exception is thrown, execution halts immediately and is handed to the catch block. It *never* returns to the original code path. It never gets to the line that prints the exit statement for the try block. The catch block handles the error, and then execution falls through to the code following the catch block.

If there is no exception handler at all, the stack is unwound, returning to the calling method in search of an exception handler. This unwinding continues until the Main( ) method is reached, and if no exception handler is found, the default (ugly) exception handler is invoked and the program terminates.

In this example, because there *is* a catch block, the stack does not need to unwind. The exception is handled, and the program can continue execution. Unwinding the stack becomes a bit more clear if you move the try/catch blocks up to Func1( ), as Example 16-3 shows.

Example 16-3. Unwinding the stack by one level

```
using System;

namespace UnwindingTheStackByOneLevel
{
    class Tester
    {

        static void Main()
        {
            Console.WriteLine( "Enter Main..." );
            Tester t = new Tester();
            t.Run();
            Console.WriteLine( "Exit Main..." );
        }
        public void Run()
        {
            Console.WriteLine( "Enter Run..." );
```

Example 16-3. Unwinding the stack by one level (continued)

```
            Func1();
            Console.WriteLine( "Exit Run..." );
        }

        public void Func1()
        {
            Console.WriteLine( "Enter Func1..." );
            try
            {
                Console.WriteLine( "Entering try block..." );
                Func2();
                Console.WriteLine( "Exiting try block..." );
            }
            catch
            {
                Console.WriteLine( "Exception caught and handled!" );
            }
            Console.WriteLine( "Exit Func1..." );
        }

        public void Func2()
        {
            Console.WriteLine( "Enter Func2..." );
            throw new ApplicationException();
            Console.WriteLine( "Exit Func2..." );
        }
    }
}
```

Now the output looks like this:

```
Enter Main...
Enter Run...
Enter Func1...
Entering try block...
Enter Func2...
Exception caught and handled!
Exit Func1...
Exit Run...
Exit Main...
```

This time the exception is not handled in Func2(); it is handled in Func1(). When Func2() is called, it uses Console.WriteLine() to display its first milestone:

```
Enter Func2...
```

Then Func2() throws an exception and execution halts. The runtime looks for a handler in Func2(), but there isn't one. Then the stack begins to unwind, and the runtime looks for a handler in the calling function: Func1(). There is a catch block in Func1(), so its code is executed. Execution then resumes immediately following the catch statement, printing the exit statement for Func1() and then for Main().

Notice that even though the exception is handled, you are now in Func1, and there is no automatic way to return to where you were in Func2.

If you're not entirely sure why the "Exiting Try Block" statement and the "Exit Func2" statement are not printed, try putting the code into a debugger and then stepping through it.

Creating Dedicated catch Statements

So far, you've been working with generic catch statements only. You can create dedicated catch statements that handle only some exceptions and not others, based on the type of exception thrown. Example 16-4 illustrates how to specify which exception you'd like to handle.

Example 16-4. Three dedicated catch statements

```
using System;

namespace ThreeDedicatedCatchStatements
{
    class Tester
    {

        public void Run( )
        {
            try
            {
                double a = 5;
                double b = 0;
                Console.WriteLine( "Dividing {0} by {1}...", a, b );
                Console.WriteLine( "{0} / {1} = {2}",
                a, b, DoDivide( a, b ) );
            }

            // most specific exception type first
            catch ( DivideByZeroException )
            {
                Console.WriteLine(
                "DivideByZeroException caught!" );
            }

            catch ( ArithmeticException )
            {
                Console.WriteLine(
                "ArithmeticException caught!" );
            }

            // generic exception type last
            catch
            {
                Console.WriteLine(
```

Example 16-4. Three dedicated catch statements (continued)

```
                "Unknown exception caught" );
        }
    }

    // do the division if legal
    public double DoDivide( double a, double b )
    {
        if ( b == 0 )
            throw new DivideByZeroException( );
        if ( a == 0 )
            throw new ArithmeticException( );
        return a / b;
    }

    static void Main( )
    {
        Console.WriteLine( "Enter Main..." );
        Tester t = new Tester( );
        t.Run( );
        Console.WriteLine( "Exit Main..." );
    }
  }
}
```

The output looks like this:

```
Enter Main...
Dividing 5 by 0...
DivideByZeroException caught!
Exit Main...
```

In Example 16-4, the DoDivide( ) method does not let you divide zero by another number, nor does it let you divide a number by zero. If you try to divide by zero, it throws an instance of DivideByZeroException. If you try to divide zero by another number, there is no appropriate exception; dividing zero by another number is a legal mathematical operation and shouldn't throw an exception at all. However, for the sake of this example, assume you don't want to allow division of zero by any number; you will throw an ArithmeticException.

When the exception is thrown, the runtime examines each exception handler in the order in which they appear in the code and matches the first one it can. When you run this program with a=5 and b=7, the output is:

```
5 / 7 = 0.7142857142857143
```

As you'd expect, no exception is thrown. However, when you change the value of a to 0, the output is:

```
ArithmeticException caught!
```

The exception is thrown, and the runtime examines the first exception: DivideByZeroException. Because this does not match, it goes on to the next handler, ArithmeticException, which does match.

In a final pass through, suppose you change a to 7 and b to 0. This throws the DivideByZeroException.

> You have to be particularly careful with the order of the catch statements in this case because the DivideByZeroException is derived from ArithmeticException. If you reverse the catch statements, then the DivideByZeroException matches the ArithmeticException handler and the exception never gets to the DivideByZeroException handler. In fact, if their order is reversed, it is impossible for *any* exception to reach the DivideByZeroException handler. Then the compiler recognizes that the DivideByZeroException handler cannot be reached and reports a compile error!

Typically, a method catches every exception it can anticipate for the code it is running. However, it is possible to distribute your try/catch statements, catching some specific exceptions in one function and more generic exceptions in higher calling functions. Your design goals should dictate exactly where you put each try and catch statement.

Assume you have a Method A that calls another Method B, which in turn calls Method C, which calls Method D, which then calls Method E. Method E is deep in your code, while Methods B and A are higher up. If you anticipate that Method E might throw an exception, you should create a try/catch block deep in your code to catch that exception as close as possible to the place where the problem arises. You might also want to create more general exception handlers higher up in the code in case unanticipated exceptions slip by.

The finally Statement

In some instances, throwing an exception and unwinding the stack can create a problem. For example, if you opened a file or otherwise committed a resource, you might need an opportunity to close the file or flush the buffer.

If there is some action you *must* take regardless of whether an exception is thrown, such as closing a file, you have two strategies to choose from. One approach is to enclose the dangerous action in a try block and then to perform the necessary action (close the file) in both the catch and try blocks. However, this is an ugly duplication of code, and it's error prone. C# provides a better alternative in the finally block.

You create a finally block with the keyword finally, and you enclose the block in braces. The code in the finally block is guaranteed to be executed regardless of whether an exception is thrown. The TestFunc() method in the next listing,

Example 16-5, simulates opening a file as its first action. The method then undertakes some mathematical operations, and then the file is closed.

 A finally block can be created with or without catch blocks, but a finally block requires a try block to execute. It is an error to exit a finally block with break, continue, return, or goto.

It is possible that sometime between opening and closing the file, an exception will be thrown. If this were to occur, it would be possible for the file to remain open. The developer knows that no matter what happens, at the end of this method, the file should be closed, so the file close function call is moved to a finally block, where it is executed regardless of whether an exception is thrown. Example 16-5 uses a finally block.

Example 16-5. Using a finally block

```
using System;

namespace UsingAFinallyBlock
{
    class Tester
    {
        public void Run( )
        {
            try
            {
                Console.WriteLine( "Open file here" );
                double a = 5;
                double b = 0;
                Console.WriteLine( "{0} / {1} = {2}",
                a, b, DoDivide( a, b ) );
                Console.WriteLine(
                "This line may or may not print" );
            }

            // most derived exception type first
            catch ( DivideByZeroException )
            {
                Console.WriteLine(
                "DivideByZeroException caught!" );
            }
            catch
            {
                Console.WriteLine( "Unknown exception caught" );
            }
            finally
            {
                Console.WriteLine( "Close file here." );
            }
        }
```

Example 16-5. Using a finally block (continued)

```
      // do the division if legal
      public double DoDivide( double a, double b )
      {
         if ( b == 0 )
            throw new DivideByZeroException( );
         if ( a == 0 )
            throw new ArithmeticException( );
         return a / b;
      }

      static void Main( )
      {
         Console.WriteLine( "Enter Main..." );
         Tester t = new Tester( );
         t.Run( );
         Console.WriteLine( "Exit Main..." );
      }
   }
}
```

The output looks like this:

```
Enter Main...
Open file here
DivideByZeroException caught!
Close file here.
Exit Main...
```

In Example 16-5, one of the catch blocks from Example 16-4 has been eliminated to save space and a finally block has been added. Whether or not an exception is thrown, the finally block is executed; thus, in both examples, the following message is output:

```
Close file here.
```

Of course, in a real application, you would actually open the file in the try block, and you'd actually close the file in the finally block. The details of file manipulation have been eliminated to keep the example simple.

Exception Class Methods and Properties

So far you've been using the exception as a sentinel—that is, the presence of the exception signals the errors—but you haven't touched or examined the Exception object itself. The System.Exception class provides a number of useful methods and properties.

The Message property provides information about the exception, such as why it was thrown. The Message property is read-only; the code throwing the exception can pass in the message as an argument to the exception constructor, but the Message property cannot be modified by any method once set in the constructor.

The HelpLink property provides a link to a help file associated with the exception. This property is read/write. In Example 16-6, the Exception.HelpLink property is set and retrieved to provide information to the user about the DivideByZeroException. It is generally a good idea to provide a help file link for any exceptions you create, so that the user can learn how to correct the exceptional circumstance.

The read-only StackTrace property is set by the CLR. This property is used to provide a *stack trace* for the error statement. A stack trace is used to display the call stack: the series of method calls that lead to the method in which the exception was thrown.

Example 16-6. Inside the Exception class

```
using System;

namespace InsideTheExceptionClass
{
   class Tester
   {
      public void Run( )
      {
         try
         {
            Console.WriteLine( "Open file here" );
            double a = 12;
            double b = 0;
            Console.WriteLine( "{0} / {1} = {2}",
            a, b, DoDivide( a, b ) );
            Console.WriteLine(
            "This line may or may not print" );
         }

         // most derived exception type first
         catch (DivideByZeroException e )
         {
            Console.WriteLine(
            "\nDivideByZeroException! Msg: {0}",
            e.Message );
            Console.WriteLine(
            "\nHelpLink: {0}", e.HelpLink );
            Console.WriteLine(
            "\nHere's a stack trace: {0}\n",
            e.StackTrace );
         }
         catch
         {
            Console.WriteLine(
            "Unknown exception caught" );
         }
         finally
         {
            Console.WriteLine(
```

Example 16-6. Inside the Exception class (continued)

```
                  "Close file here." );
            }

      }

      // do the division if legal
      public double DoDivide( double a, double b )
      {
         if ( b == 0 )
         {
            DivideByZeroException e =
            new DivideByZeroException( );
            e.HelpLink =
            "http://www.libertyassociates.com";
            throw e;
         }
         if ( a == 0 )
            throw new ArithmeticException( );
         return a / b;
      }

      static void Main( )
      {
         Console.WriteLine( "Enter Main..." );
         Tester t = new Tester( );
         t.Run( );
         Console.WriteLine( "Exit Main..." );
      }
   }
}
```

The output looks like this:

```
Enter Main...
Open file here

DivideByZeroException! Msg: Attempted to divide by zero.

HelpLink: http://www.libertyassociates.com

Here's a stack trace:
  at ExceptionHandling.Tester.DoDivide(Double a, Double b) in class1.cs:line 54
  at ExceptionHandling.Tester.Run( ) in class1.cs:line 14

Close file here.
Exit Main...
```

In the output of Example 16-6, the stack trace lists the methods in the reverse order in which they were called; by reviewing this order, you can infer that the error occurred in DoDivide( ), which was called by Run( ). When methods are deeply nested, the stack trace can help you understand the order of method calls and thus track down the point at which the exception occurred.

In this example, rather than simply throwing a DivideByZeroException, you create a new instance of the exception:

```
DivideByZeroException e = new DivideByZeroException( );
```

You do not pass in a custom message, and so the default message is printed:

DivideByZeroException! Msg: **Attempted to divide by zero.**

 The designer of each Exception class has the option to provide a default message for that exception type. All the standard exceptions provide a default message, and it is a good idea to add a default message to your custom exceptions as well (see the section "Custom Exceptions," later in this chapter).

If you want, you can modify this line of code to pass in a custom message:

```
new DivideByZeroException(
  "You tried to divide by zero which is not meaningful");
```

In this case, the output message reflects the custom message:

```
DivideByZeroException! Msg:
You tried to divide by zero which is not meaningful
```

Before throwing the exception, set the HelpLink property:

```
e.HelpLink = "http://www.libertyassociates.com";
```

When this exception is caught, Console.WriteLine prints both the Message and the HelpLink:

```
catch (DivideByZeroException e)
{
 Console.WriteLine("\nDivideByZeroException! Msg: {0}",
 e.Message);
 Console.WriteLine("\nHelpLink: {0}", e.HelpLink);
```

The Message and HelpLink properties allow you to provide useful information to the user. The exception handler also prints the StackTrace by getting the StackTrace property of the Exception object:

```
Console.WriteLine("\nHere's a stack trace: {0}\n",
 e.StackTrace);
```

The output of this call reflects a full StackTrace leading to the moment the exception was thrown. In this case, only two methods were executed before the exception, DoDivide( ) and Run( ):

```
Here's a stack trace:
 at ExceptionHandling.Tester.DoDivide(Double a, Double b) in class1.cs:line 54
 at ExceptionHandling.Tester.Run( ) in class1.cs:line 14
```

Note that I've shortened the pathnames, so your printout might look a little different.

Custom Exceptions

The intrinsic exception types the CLR provides, coupled with the custom messages shown in the previous example, will often be all you need to provide extensive information to a catch block when an exception is thrown.

There will be times, however, when you want to provide more extensive information or need special capabilities in your exception. It is a trivial matter to create your own *custom exception* class. Example 16-7 illustrates the creation of a custom exception.

Example 16-7. A custom exception

```
using System;

namespace ACustomException
{
    // custom exception class
    public class MyCustomException :
    System.Exception
    {
        public MyCustomException( string message ):
        base( message ) // pass the message up to the base class
        {

        }
    }

    class Tester
    {
        public void Run()
        {
            try
            {
                Console.WriteLine( "Open file here" );
                double a = 0;
                double b = 5;
                Console.WriteLine( "{0} / {1} = {2}",
                a, b, DoDivide( a, b ) );
                Console.WriteLine(
                "This line may or may not print" );
            }

            // most derived exception type first
            catch ( System.DivideByZeroException e )
            {
                Console.WriteLine(
                "\nDivideByZeroException! Msg: {0}",
                e.Message );
                Console.WriteLine(
                "\nHelpLink: {0}\n", e.HelpLink );
            }
```

Example 16-7. A custom exception (continued)

```csharp
        // catch custom exception
        catch ( MyCustomException e )
        {
            Console.WriteLine(
            "\nMyCustomException! Msg: {0}",
            e.Message );
            Console.WriteLine(
            "\nHelpLink: {0}\n", e.HelpLink );
        }
        catch // catch any uncaught exceptions
        {
            Console.WriteLine(
            "Unknown exception caught" );
        }
        finally
        {
            Console.WriteLine( "Close file here." );
        }
    }

    // do the division if legal
    public double DoDivide( double a, double b )
    {
        if ( b == 0 )
        {
            DivideByZeroException e =
            new DivideByZeroException( );
            e.HelpLink =
            "http://www.libertyassociates.com";
            throw e;
        }
        if ( a == 0 )
        {
            // create a custom exception instance
            MyCustomException e =
            new MyCustomException(
            "Can't have zero divisor" );
            e.HelpLink =
            "http://www.libertyassociates.com/NoZeroDivisor.htm";
            throw e;
        }
        return a / b;
    }

    static void Main( )
    {
        Console.WriteLine( "Enter Main..." );
        Tester t = new Tester( );
        t.Run( );
        Console.WriteLine( "Exit Main..." );
    }
  }
}
```

The output looks like this:

```
Enter Main...
Open file here

MyCustomException! Msg: Can't have zero divisor

HelpLink: http://www.libertyassociates.com/NoZeroDivisor.htm

Close file here.
Exit Main...
```

MyCustomException is derived from System.Exception and consists of nothing more than a constructor that takes a string message that it passes to its base class.

The advantage of creating this custom exception class is that it better reflects the particular design of the Test class, in which it is not legal to have a zero divisor. Using the ArithmeticException rather than a custom exception would work as well, but it might confuse other programmers because a zero divisor wouldn't normally be considered an arithmetic error.

You are free, of course, to add methods and properties to your custom exception classes as needed.

Summary

- Throwing (or raising) an exception halts execution of your program in place, and execution proceeds in the most immediately available catch block (exception handler). If the exception was not raised within a try block, or there is no catch block, the stack is unwound until a catch block is found. If no catch block is ever found, the built-in exception handler is invoked, which terminates your program with an error message.

- An exception object can contain information about the circumstances that cause the exception to be raised. Typically, exception objects contain at least a text message explaining the exception.

- Exceptions can be derived from and can contain other exceptions within them to allow for very flexible error handling.

- A bug is a programming mistake that should be fixed before the program is released. An exception, however, is the result of a predictable but unpreventable problem that arises during run-time (for example, running out of disk space).

- All exceptions used in C# derive from System.Exception, and all exceptions in your program should derive from System.Exception.

- When a program encounters a problem that it cannot solve or work around, it may throw an exception to halt execution and allow the exception handler to fix the problem.

- You throw an exception yourself using the throw keyword.
- It is good programming practice to enclose code that has a high risk of throwing an exception within a try block and to provide an exception handler (a catch block) and perhaps a finally block.
- The catch block follows the try block and contains the code used to handle the exception.
- You can create dedicated catch statements to catch specific types of exceptions taking advantage of the inheritance hierarchy of exceptions.
- Any action that must be taken whether or not an exception is raised (such as closing a file) should be enclosed in a finally block.

Quiz

Question 16-1. What is an exception?

Question 16-2. What does the framework do if no exception handler is found in the method that throws an event?

Question 16-3. How do you create a handler?

Question 16-4. What is the syntax for throwing a new ArgumentNull exception?

Question 16-5. How do you write code to handle various exceptions differently?

Question 16-6. What is the finally statement?

Exercises

Exercise 16-1. Create a Cat class with one int property: Age. Write a program that creates a List of Cat objects in a try block. Create multiple catch statements to handle an ArgumentOutOfRangeException, and an unknown exception, and a finally block to simulate deallocating the Cat objects. Write test code to throw an exception that you will catch and handle.

Exercise 16-2. Modify Exercise 16-1 so that it does not throw an error. Create a custom error type CustomCatError that derives from System.Exception, and create a handler for it. Add a method to CatManager that checks the cat's age, and throws an error of type CustomCatError if the age is less than or equal to 0, with an appropriate message.

Delegates and Events

When a head of state dies, the President of the United States typically does not have time to attend the funeral personally. Instead, he dispatches a delegate. Often this delegate is the Vice President, but sometimes the VP is unavailable and the President must send someone else, such as the Secretary of State or even the First Lady. He does not want to "hardwire" his delegated authority to a single person; he might delegate this responsibility to anyone who is able to execute the correct international protocol.

The President defines in advance what responsibility will be delegated (attend the funeral), what parameters will be passed (condolences, kind words), and what value he hopes to get back (good will). He then assigns a particular person to that delegated responsibility at "runtime" as the course of his presidency progresses.

In programming, you are often faced with situations where you need to execute a particular action, but you don't know in advance which method, or even which object, you'll want to call upon to execute it. For example, a button might know that it must notify some object when it is pushed, but it might not know which object or objects need to be notified. Rather than wiring the button to a particular object, you will connect the button to a *delegate* and then resolve that delegate to a particular method when the program executes.

In the early, dark, and primitive days of computing, a program would begin execution and then proceed through its steps until it completed. If the user was involved, the interaction was strictly controlled and limited to filling in fields.

Today's Graphical User Interface (GUI) programming model requires a different approach, known as *event-driven programming*. A modern program presents the user interface and waits for the user to take an action. The user might take many different actions, such as choosing among menu selections, pushing buttons, updating text fields, clicking icons, and so forth. Each action causes an event to be raised. Other events can be raised without direct user action, such as events that correspond to timer ticks of the internal clock, email being received, file-copy operations completing, and so forth.

An *event* is the encapsulation of the idea that "something happened" to which the program must respond. Events and delegates are tightly coupled concepts because flexible event handling requires that the response to the event be dispatched to the appropriate event handler. An event handler is typically implemented in C# via a delegate.

Delegates are also used as callbacks so that one class can say to another "do this work and when you're done, let me know."

Delegates

In C#, delegates are first-class objects, fully supported by the language. Technically, a delegate is a reference type used to encapsulate a method with a specific signature and return type. You can encapsulate any matching method in that delegate.

A delegate is created with the delegate keyword, followed by a return type and the signature of the methods that can be delegated to it, as in the following:

```
public delegate int WhichIsFirst(object obj1, object obj2);
```

This declaration defines a delegate named WhichIsFirst, which will encapsulate any method that takes two objects as parameters and that returns an int.

Once the delegate is defined, you can encapsulate a member method with that delegate by instantiating the delegate, passing in a method that matches the return type and signature. As an alternative, you can use anonymous methods as described below. In either case, the delegate can then be used to invoke that encapsulated method.

Using Delegates to Specify Methods at Runtime

Delegates *decouple* the class that declares the delegate from the class that uses the delegate. For example, suppose that you want to create a simple generic container class called a Pair that can hold and sort any two objects passed to it. You can't know in advance what kind of objects a Pair will hold, but by creating methods within those objects to which the sorting task can be delegated, you can delegate responsibility for determining their order to the objects themselves.

Different objects will sort differently (for example, a Pair of Counter objects might sort in numeric order, while a Pair of Buttons might sort alphabetically by their name). As the author of the Pair class, you want the objects in the pair to have the responsibility of knowing which should be first and which should be second. To accomplish this, you will insist that the objects to be stored in the Pair must provide a method that tells you how to sort the objects.

You can define this requirement with interfaces, as well. Delegates are smaller and of finer granularity than interfaces. The Pair class does not need to implement an entire interface; it just needs to define the signature and return type of the method it wants to invoke. That is what delegates are for: they define the return type and signature of methods that can be invoked through the interface.

In this case, the Pair class will declare a delegate named WhichIsFirst. When the Pair needs to know how to order its objects, it will invoke the delegate passing in its two member objects as parameters. The responsibility for deciding which of the two objects comes first is delegated to the method encapsulated by the delegate:

```
public delegate Comparison WhichIsFirst( T obj1, T obj2 );
```

In this definition, WhichIsFirst is defined to encapsulate a method that takes two objects as parameters, and that returns an object of type Comparison. Comparison turns out to be an enumeration you will define:

```
public enum Comparison
{
    TheFirstComesFirst = 1,
    TheSecondComesFirst = 2
}
```

To test the delegate, you will create two classes: a Dog class and a Student class. Dogs and Students have little in common, except that they both implement methods that can be encapsulated by WhichComesFirst, and thus both Dog objects and Student objects are eligible to be held within Pair objects.

In the test program, you will create a couple of Students and a couple of Dogs, and store them each in a Pair. You will then create instances of WhichIsFirst to encapsulate their respective methods that will determine which Student or which Dog object should be first, and which second. Let's take this step by step.

You begin by creating a Pair constructor that takes two objects and stashes them away in a private array:

```
public Pair( T firstObject, T secondObject )
{
    thePair[0] = firstObject;
    thePair[1] = secondObject;
}
```

Note that the Pair<T> class uses generics, as discussed in Chapter 14. Therefore, firstObject and secondObject in the constructor above are of the generic type T, and the actual types will be assigned at runtime.

Next, you override ToString( ) to obtain the string value of the two objects:

```
public override string ToString()
{
    return thePair[0].ToString() + ", " +
        thePair[1].ToString();
}
```

You now have two objects in your `Pair` and you can print out their values. You're ready to sort them and print the results of the sort. You can't know in advance what kind of objects you will have, so you delegate the responsibility of deciding which object comes first in the sorted `Pair` to the objects themselves.

Both the `Dog` class and the `Student` class implement methods that can be encapsulated by `WhichIsFirst`. Any method that takes two objects and returns a `Comparison` can be encapsulated by this delegate at runtime.

You can now define the `Sort()` method for the `Pair` class:

```
public void Sort(WhichIsFirst theDelegatedFunc)
{
    if (theDelegatedFunc(thePair[0],thePair[1]) ==
        Comparison.theSecondComesFirst)
    {
        T temp = thePair[0];
        thePair[0] = thePair[1];
        thePair[1] = temp;
    }
}
```

This method takes a parameter: a delegate of type `WhichIsFirst` named `theDelegatedFunc`. The `Sort()` method delegates responsibility for deciding which of the two objects in the `Pair` comes first to the method encapsulated by that delegate. In the body of the `Sort()` method, it invokes the delegated method and examines the return value, which will be one of the two enumerated values of `Comparison`.

If the value returned is `theSecondComesFirst`, the objects within the pair are swapped; otherwise, no action is taken.

This is analogous to how the other parameters work. If you had a method that took an int as a parameter:

```
int SomeMethod (int myParam){//...}
```

The parameter name is `myParam`, but you can pass in any int value or variable. Similarly, the parameter name in the delegate example is `theDelegatedFunc`, but you can pass in any method that meets the return value and signature defined by the delegate `WhichIsFirst`.

Imagine you are sorting `Students` by name. You write a method that returns `theFirstComesFirst` if the first student's name comes first, and `theSecondComesFirst` if the second student's name does. If you pass in "Amy, Beth," the method will return `theFirstComesFirst`, and if you pass in "Beth, Amy," it will return `theSecondComesFirst`. If you get back `theSecondComesFirst`, the `Sort()` method reverses the items in its array, setting Amy to the first position and Beth to the second.

Now add one more method, ReverseSort( ), which will force the items in the array into the reverse of their normal order:

```
public void ReverseSort(WhichIsFirst theDelegatedFunc)
{
    if (theDelegatedFunc(thePair[0], thePair[1]) ==
            Comparison.theFirstComesFirst)
    {
        T temp = thePair[0];
        thePair[0] = thePair[1];
        thePair[1] = temp;
    }
}
```

The logic here is identical to Sort( ), except that this method performs the swap if the delegated method says that the first item comes first. Because the delegated function thinks the first item comes first, and this is a reverse sort, the result you want is for the second item to come first. This time, if you pass in "Amy, Beth," the delegated function returns theFirstComesFirst (Amy should come first), but because this is a *reverse* sort, it swaps the values, setting Beth first. This allows you to use the same delegated function as you used with Sort( ), without forcing the object to support a function that returns the reverse sorted value.

Now all you need are some objects to sort. You'll create two absurdly simple classes: Student and Dog. Assign Student objects a name at creation:

```
public class Student
{
    public Student(string name)
    {
        this.name = name;
    }
}
```

The Student class requires two methods: one to override ToString( ) and the other to be encapsulated as the delegated method.

Student must override ToString( ) so that the ToString( ) method in Pair, which invokes ToString( ) on the contained objects, will work properly; the implementation does nothing more than return the student's name (which is already a string object):

```
public override string ToString()
{
    return name;
}
```

It must also implement a method to which Pair.Sort( ) can delegate the responsibility of determining which of two objects comes first, called WhichStudentComesFirst( ) in this case:

```
public static Comparison WhichStudentComesFirst( Student s1, Student s2 )
{
    return (String.Compare(s1.name, s2.name) < 0 ?
```

```
        Comparison.theFirstComesFirst :
        Comparison.theSecondComesFirst);
    }
```

String.Compare() is a .NET Framework method on the String class that compares two strings and returns less than zero if the first is smaller, greater than zero if the second is smaller, and zero if they are the same. This method is discussed in some detail in Chapter 15. Notice that the logic here returns theFirstComesFirst only if the first string is smaller; if they are the same or the second is larger, this method returns theSecondComesFirst.

Notice that the WhichStudentComesFirst() method takes two objects as parameters and returns a Comparison. This qualifies it to be a Pair.WhichIsFirst delegated method, whose signature and return value it matches.

The second class is Dog. For our purposes, Dog objects will be sorted by weight, lighter dogs before heavier. Here's the complete declaration of Dog:

```
    public class Dog
    {
        public Dog(int weight)
        {
            this.weight=weight;
        }

        // dogs are ordered by weight
        public static Comparison WhichDogComesFirst(
            Object o1, Object o2)
        {
            Dog d1 = (Dog) o1;
            Dog d2 = (Dog) o2;
            return d1.weight > d2.weight ?
              Comparison.theSecondComesFirst :
                Comparison.theFirstComesFirst;
        }
        public override string ToString()
        {
            return weight.ToString();
        }
        private int weight;
    }
```

The Dog class also overrides ToString and implements a static method called Which-DogComesFirst() with the correct signature for the delegate. Notice also that the Dog and Student delegate methods do not have the same name. They do not need to have the same name, as they will be assigned to the delegate dynamically at runtime.

 You can call your delegated method names anything you like, but creating parallel names (such as WhichDogComesFirst and WhichStudent-ComesFirst) makes the code easier to read, understand, and maintain.

Example 17-1 is the complete program, which illustrates how the delegate methods are invoked.

Example 17-1. Working with delegates

```
using System;
using System.Collections.Generic;
using System.Text;

namespace WorkingWithDelegates
{
    public enum Comparison
    {
        TheFirstComesFirst = 1,
        TheSecondComesFirst = 2
    }

    // a simple collection to hold 2 items
    public class Pair<T>
    {

        // private array to hold the two objects
        private T[] thePair = new T[2];

        // the delegate declaration
        public delegate Comparison
            WhichIsFirst( T obj1, T obj2 );

        // passed in constructor take two objects,
        // added in order received
        public Pair(
            T firstObject,
            T secondObject )
        {
            thePair[0] = firstObject;
            thePair[1] = secondObject;
        }

        // public method which orders the two objects
        // by whatever criteria the object likes!
        public void Sort(
            WhichIsFirst theDelegatedFunc )
        {
            if ( theDelegatedFunc( thePair[0], thePair[1] )
                == Comparison.TheSecondComesFirst )
            {
                T temp = thePair[0];
                thePair[0] = thePair[1];
                thePair[1] = temp;
            }
        }
```

Example 17-1. Working with delegates (continued)

```
      // public method which orders the two objects
      // by the reverse of whatever criteria the object likes!
      public void ReverseSort(
          WhichIsFirst theDelegatedFunc )
      {
         if ( theDelegatedFunc( thePair[0], thePair[1] ) ==
              Comparison.TheFirstComesFirst )
         {
            T temp = thePair[0];
            thePair[0] = thePair[1];
            thePair[1] = temp;
         }
      }

      // ask the two objects to give their string value
      public override string ToString( )
      {
         return thePair[0].ToString( ) + ", "
             + thePair[1].ToString( );
      }
   }           // end class Pair

   public class Dog
   {
      private int weight;

      public Dog( int weight )
      {
         this.weight = weight;
      }

      // dogs are ordered by weight
      public static Comparison WhichDogComesFirst(
          Dog d1, Dog d2 )
      {
         return d1.weight > d2.weight ?
             Comparison.TheFirstComesFirst :
             Comparison.TheSecondComesFirst );
      }
      public override string ToString( )
      {
         return weight.ToString( );
      }
   }           // end class Dog

   public class Student
   {
      private string name;

      public Student( string name )
      {
         this.name = name;
      }
```

Example 17-1. Working with delegates (continued)

```
      // students are ordered alphabetically
      public static Comparison
          WhichStudentComesFirst( Student s1, Student s2 )
      {
         return ( String.Compare( s1.name, s2.name ) < 0 ?
             Comparison.theFirstComesFirst :
             Comparison.theSecondComesFirst );
      }

      public override string ToString()
      {
         return name;
      }
   }        // end class Student

   public class Test
   {
      public static void Main()
      {
         // create two students and two dogs
         // and add them to Pair objects
         Student Jesse = new Student( "Jesse" );
         Student Stacey = new Student( "Stacey" );
         Dog Milo = new Dog( 65 );
         Dog Fred = new Dog( 12 );

         Pair<Student> studentPair = new Pair<Student>( Jesse, Stacey );
         Pair<Dog> dogPair = new Pair<Dog>( Milo, Fred );
         Console.WriteLine( "studentPair\t\t\t: {0}",
             studentPair.ToString() );
         Console.WriteLine( "dogPair\t\t\t\t: {0}",
             dogPair.ToString() );

         // Instantiate  the delegates
         Pair<Student>.WhichIsFirst theStudentDelegate =
             new Pair<Student>.WhichIsFirst(
             Student.WhichStudentComesFirst );

         Pair<Dog>.WhichIsFirst theDogDelegate =
             new Pair<Dog>.WhichIsFirst(
             Dog.WhichDogComesFirst );

         // sort using the delegates
         studentPair.Sort( theStudentDelegate );
         Console.WriteLine( "After Sort studentPair\t\t: {0}",
             studentPair.ToString() );
         studentPair.ReverseSort( theStudentDelegate );
         Console.WriteLine( "After ReverseSort studentPair\t: {0}",
             studentPair.ToString() );

         dogPair.Sort( theDogDelegate );
         Console.WriteLine( "After Sort dogPair\t\t: {0}",
```

Example 17-1. Working with delegates (continued)

```
            dogPair.ToString( ) );
        dogPair.ReverseSort( theDogDelegate );
        Console.WriteLine( "After ReverseSort dogPair\t: {0}",
            dogPair.ToString( ) );
    }
  }
}
```

The output looks like this:

```
studentPair                 : Jesse, Stacey
dogPair                     : 65, 12
After Sort studentPair      : Jesse, Stacey
After ReverseSort studentPair : Stacey, Jesse
After Sort dogPair          : 12, 65
After ReverseSort dogPair   : 65, 12
```

The Test program creates two Student objects and two Dog objects and then adds them to Pair containers. The student constructor takes a string for the student's name and the dog constructor takes an int for the dog's weight.

```
Student Jesse = new Student( "Jesse" );
Student Stacey = new Student( "Stacey" );
Dog Milo = new Dog( 65 );
Dog Fred = new Dog( 12 );

Pair<Student> studentPair = new Pair<Student>( Jesse, Stacey );
Pair<Dog> dogPair = new Pair<Dog>( Milo, Fred );
Console.WriteLine( "studentPair\t\t\t: {0}",
    studentPair.ToString( ) );
Console.WriteLine( "dogPair\t\t\t\t: {0}",
    dogPair.ToString( ) );
```

It then prints the contents of the two Pair containers to see the order of the objects. The output looks like this:

```
studentPair         : Jesse, Stacey
dogPair             : 65, 12
```

As expected, the objects are in the order in which they were added to the Pair containers. You next instantiate two delegate objects:

```
Pair<Student>.WhichIsFirst theStudentDelegate =
    new Pair<Student>.WhichIsFirst(
    Student.WhichStudentComesFirst );

Pair<Dog>.WhichIsFirst theDogDelegate =
    new Pair<Dog>.WhichIsFirst(
    Dog.WhichDogComesFirst );
```

The first delegate, theStudentDelegate, is created by passing in the appropriate static method from the Student class. The second delegate, theDogDelegate, is passed a static method from the Dog class.

The delegates are now objects that can be passed to methods. You pass the delegates first to the Sort( ) method of the Pair object, and then to the ReverseSort( ) method. The results are printed to the console:

```
After Sort studentPair         : Jesse, Stacey
After ReverseSort studentPair  : Stacey, Jesse
After Sort dogPair             : 12, 65
After ReverseSort dogPair      : 65, 12
```

Multicasting

At times, it is desirable to call two (or more) implementing methods through a single delegate. This becomes particularly important when handling events (discussed later in this chapter).

The goal is to have a single delegate that invokes more than one method. For example, when a button is pressed, you might want to take more than one action. This process of calling more than one method with a single delegate is called *multicasting*.

Two delegates can be combined with the addition operator (+). The result is a new multicast delegate that invokes both of the original implementing methods. For example, assuming Writer and Logger are delegates, the following line will combine them and produce a new multicast delegate named myMulticastDelegate:

```
myMulticastDelegate = Writer + Logger;
```

You can add delegates to a multicast delegate using the plus-equals (+=) operator. This operator adds the delegate on the right side of the operator to the multicast delegate on the left. For example, assuming Transmitter and myMulticastDelegate are delegates, the following line adds Transmitter to myMulticastDelegate:

```
myMulticastDelegate += Transmitter;
```

The power of multicast delegates is best understood in terms of events, discussed in the next section. When an event such as a button press occurs, an associated multicast delegate can invoke a series of event handler methods that will respond to the event.

Events

GUIs, such as Microsoft Windows and web browsers, require that programs respond to *events*. An event might be a button push, a menu selection, the completion of a file transfer, and so forth. In short, something happens and you must respond to it. You cannot predict the order in which events will arise. The system is quiescent until the event, and then springs into action to handle it.

In a GUI environment, any number of controls can *raise* an event. For example, when you click a button, it might raise the `Click` event. When you add to a drop-down list, it might raise a `ListChanged` event.

Other classes will be interested in responding to these events. How they respond is not of interest to the class raising the event. The button says, "I was clicked," and the responding classes react appropriately.

Publishing and Subscribing

In C#, any object can *publish* a set of events to which other classes can *subscribe*. When the publishing class raises an event, all the subscribed classes are notified. With this mechanism, your object can say "Here are things I can notify you about," and other classes might sign up, saying "Yes, let me know when that happens." For example, a button might notify any number of interested observers when it is clicked. The button is called the *publisher* because the button publishes the `Click` event and the other classes are the *subscribers* because they subscribe to the `Click` event.

This design implements the Publish/Subscribe (Observer) Pattern described in the seminal work *Design Patterns* by Gamma, et al. (Addison Wesley, 1995).

Note that the publishing class does not know or care who (if anyone) subscribes; it just raises the event. Who responds to that event, and how they respond, is not the concern of the publishing class.

As a second example, a `Clock` might notify interested classes whenever the time changes by one second. The `Clock` class could itself be responsible for the User Interface representation of the time, rather than raising an event, so why bother with the indirection of using delegates? The advantage of the publish/subscribe idiom is that the `Clock` class need not know how its information will be used; the monitoring of the time is thus decoupled from the representation of that information. In addition, any number of classes can be notified when an event is raised. The subscribing classes do not need to know how the `Clock` works, and the `Clock` does not need to know what they are going to do in response to the event.

The publisher and the subscribers are decoupled by the delegate. This is highly desirable; it makes for more flexible and robust code. The `Clock` can change how it detects time without breaking any of the subscribing classes. The subscribing classes can change how they respond to time changes without breaking the `Clock`. The two classes spin independently of one another, and that makes for code that is easier to maintain.

Events and Delegates

Events in C# are implemented with delegates. The publishing class defines a delegate. The subscribing class does two things: first, it creates a method that matches the signature of the delegate, and then it creates an instance of that delegate type encapsulating that method. When the event is raised, the subscribing class's methods are invoked through the delegate.

A method that handles an event is called an *event handler*. You can declare your event handlers as you would any other delegate.

By convention, event handlers in the .NET Framework return void and take two parameters. The first parameter is the "source" of the event (that is, the publishing object). The second parameter is an object derived from EventArgs. It is recommended that your event handlers follow this design pattern.

EventArgs is the base class for all event data. Other than its constructor, the EventArgs class inherits all its methods from Object, though it does add a public static field named Empty, which represents an event with no state (to allow for the efficient use of events with no state). The EventArgs-derived class contains information about the event.

Suppose you want to create a Clock class that uses delegates to notify potential subscribers whenever the local time changes value by one second. Call this delegate SecondChangeEventHandler:

The declaration for the SecondChangeEventHandler delegate is:

```
public delegate void SecondChangeEventHandler (
    object clock,
    TimeInfoEventArgs timeInformation
    );
```

This delegate will encapsulate any method that returns void and that takes two parameters. The first parameter is an object that represents the clock (the object raising the event), and the second parameter is an object of type, TimeInfoEventArgs, that will contain useful information for anyone interested in this event. TimeInfoEventArgs is defined as follows:

```
public class TimeInfoEventArgs : EventArgs
{
    public TimeInfoEventArgs(int hour, int minute, int second)
    {
        this.hour = hour;
        this.minute = minute;
        this.second = second;
    }
    public readonly int Hour;
    public readonly int Minute;
    public readonly int Second;

}
```

The TimeInfoEventArgs object will have information about the current hour, minute, and second. It defines a constructor and three public, read-only integer variables.

In addition to its delegate, a Clock has three member variables—hour, minute, and second—as well as a single method, Run():

```
public void Run()
{
    for(;;)
    {
        // sleep 10 milliseconds
        Thread.Sleep(10);

        // get the current time
        System.DateTime dt = System.DateTime.Now;

        // if the second has changed
        // notify the subscribers
        if (dt.Second != second)
        {
            // create the TimeInfoEventArgs object
            // to pass to the subscriber
            TimeInfoEventArgs timeInformation =
              new TimeInfoEventArgs(
              dt.Hour,dt.Minute,dt.Second);

            // if anyone has subscribed, notify them
            if (SecondChanged != null)
            {
                SecondChanged(this,timeInformation);
            }
        }
        // update the state
        this.second = dt.Second;
        this.minute = dt.Minute;
        this.hour = dt.Hour;
    }
}
```

Run() creates an infinite for loop that periodically checks the system time. If the time has changed from the Clock object's current time, it notifies all its subscribers and then updates its own state.

The first step is to sleep for 10 milliseconds:

```
Thread.Sleep(10);
```

This makes use of a static method of the Thread class from the System.Threading namespace. The call to Sleep() prevents the loop from running so tightly that little else on the computer gets done.

After sleeping for 10 milliseconds, the method checks the current time:

```
System.DateTime dt = System.DateTime.Now;
```

About every 100 times it checks, the second will have incremented. The method notices that change and notifies its subscribers. To do so, it first creates a new TimeInfoEventArgs object:

```
if (dt.Second != second)
{
    // create the TimeInfoEventArgs object
    // to pass to the subscriber
    TimeInfoEventArgs timeInformation =
        new TimeInfoEventArgs(dt.Hour,dt.Minute,dt.Second);
```

It then notifies the subscribers by firing the SecondChanged event:

```
    // if anyone has subscribed, notify them
    if (SecondChanged != null)
    {
        SecondChanged(this,timeInformation);
    }
}
```

If an event has no subscribers registered, it will evaluate to null. The preceding test checks that the value is not null, ensuring that there are subscribers before calling SecondChanged.

You will remember that SecondChanged takes two arguments: the source of the event and the object derived from EventArgs. In the snippet, you see that the clock's this reference is passed because the clock is the source of the event. The second parameter is the TimeInfoEventArgs object, timeInformation, created in the preceding snippet.

Raising the event will invoke whatever methods have been registered with the Clock class through the delegate. We'll examine this in a moment.

Once the event is raised, you update the state of the Clock class:

```
this.second = dt.Second;
this.minute = dt.Minute;
this.hour = dt.Hour;
```

All that is left is to create classes that can subscribe to this event. You'll create two. First will be the DisplayClock class. The job of DisplayClock is not to keep track of time, but rather to display the current time to the console.

The example simplifies this class down to two methods. The first is a helper method named Subscribe( ) that is used to subscribe to the clock's SecondChanged delegate. The second method is the event handler TimeHasChanged( ):

```
public class DisplayClock
{
    public void Subscribe(Clock theClock)
    {
        theClock.SecondChanged +=
            new Clock.SecondChangeEventHandler(TimeHasChanged);
    }
```

```
    public void TimeHasChanged(
        object theClock, TimeInfoEventArgs ti)
    {
        Console.WriteLine("Current Time: {0}:{1}:{2}",
            ti.hour.ToString(),
            ti.minute.ToString(),
            ti.second.ToString());
    }
}
```

When the first method, Subscribe( ), is invoked, it creates a new SecondChangeHandler delegate, passing in its event handler method, TimeHasChanged( ). It then registers that delegate with the SecondChanged event of Clock.

You will create a second class that will also respond to this event, LogCurrentTime. This class would normally log the event to a file, but for our demonstration purposes, it will log to the standard console:

```
public class LogCurrentTime
{
    public void Subscribe(Clock theClock)
    {
        theClock.SecondChanged +=
            new Clock.SecondChangeHandler(WriteLogEntry);
    }

    // this method should write to a file
    // we write to the console to see the effect
    // this object keeps no state
    public void WriteLogEntry(
        object theClock, TimeInfoEventArgs ti)
    {
        Console.WriteLine("Logging to file: {0}:{1}:{2}",
            ti.hour.ToString(),
            ti.minute.ToString(),
            ti.second.ToString());
    }
}
```

Although in this example, these two classes are very similar, in a production program, any number of disparate classes might subscribe to an event.

All that remains is to create a Clock class, create the DisplayClock class, and tell it to subscribe to the event. You then will create a LogCurrentTime class and tell it to subscribe as well. Finally, you'll tell the Clock to run. All this is shown in Example 17-2 (you'll need to press Ctrl-C to terminate this application).

Example 17-2. Implementing events with delegates

```
using System;
using System.Collections.Generic;
using System.Text;
using System.Threading;
```

Example 17-2. Implementing events with delegates (continued)

```
namespace ImplementingEventsWithDelegates
{
    // a class to hold the information about the event
    // in this case it will hold only information
    // available in the clock class, but could hold
    // additional state information
    public class TimeInfoEventArgs : EventArgs
    {
        public TimeInfoEventArgs( int hour, int minute, int second )
        {
            this.hour = hour;
            this.minute = minute;
            this.second = second;
        }
        public readonly int hour;
        public readonly int minute;
        public readonly int second;
    }

    // our subject -- it is this class that other classes
    // will observe. This class publishes one delegate:
    // SecondChanged.
    public class Clock
    {
        private int hour;
        private int minute;
        private int second;

        // the delegate the subscribers must implement
        public delegate void SecondChangeHandler
          (
            object clock,
            TimeInfoEventArgs timeInformation
          );

        // an instance of the delegate
        public SecondChangeHandler SecondChanged;

        // set the clock running
        // it will raise an event for each new second
        public void Run( )
        {

            for ( ; ; )
            {
                // sleep 10 milliseconds
                Thread.Sleep( 10 );

                // get the current time
                System.DateTime dt = System.DateTime.Now;
```

Example 17-2. Implementing events with delegates (continued)

```
        // if the second has changed
        // notify the subscribers
        if ( dt.Second != second )
        {
            // create the TimeInfoEventArgs object
            // to pass to the subscriber
            TimeInfoEventArgs timeInformation =
                new TimeInfoEventArgs(
                dt.Hour, dt.Minute, dt.Second );

            // if anyone has subscribed, notify them
            if ( SecondChanged != null )
            {
                SecondChanged(
                    this, timeInformation );
            }
        }

        // update the state
        this.second = dt.Second;
        this.minute = dt.Minute;
        this.hour = dt.Hour;

    }
  }
}

// an observer. DisplayClock subscribes to the
// clock's events. The job of DisplayClock is
// to display the current time
public class DisplayClock
{
    // given a clock, subscribe to
    // its SecondChangeHandler event
    public void Subscribe( Clock theClock )
    {
        theClock.SecondChanged +=
            new Clock.SecondChangeHandler( TimeHasChanged );
    }

    // the method that implements the
    // delegated functionality
    public void TimeHasChanged(
        object theClock, TimeInfoEventArgs ti )
    {
        Console.WriteLine( "Current Time: {0}:{1}:{2}",
            ti.hour.ToString( ),
            ti.minute.ToString( ),
            ti.second.ToString( ) );
    }
}
```

Example 17-2. Implementing events with delegates (continued)

```csharp
    // a second subscriber whose job is to write to a file
    public class LogCurrentTime
    {
        public void Subscribe( Clock theClock )
        {
            theClock.SecondChanged +=
                new Clock.SecondChangeHandler( WriteLogEntry );
        }

        // this method should write to a file
        // we write to the console to see the effect
        // this object keeps no state
        public void WriteLogEntry(
            object theClock, TimeInfoEventArgs ti )
        {
            Console.WriteLine( "Logging to file: {0}:{1}:{2}",
                ti.hour.ToString( ),
                ti.minute.ToString( ),
                ti.second.ToString( ) );
        }
    }

    public class Test
    {
        public static void Main( )
        {
            // create a new clock
            Clock theClock = new Clock( );

            // create the display and tell it to
            // subscribe to the clock just created
            DisplayClock dc = new DisplayClock( );
            dc.Subscribe( theClock );

            // create a Log object and tell it
            // to subscribe to the clock
            LogCurrentTime lct = new LogCurrentTime( );
            lct.Subscribe( theClock );

            // Get the clock started
            theClock.Run( );
        }
    }
}
```

The output on my machine looks like this:

```
Current Time: 14:53:56
Logging to file: 14:53:56
Current Time: 14:53:57
Logging to file: 14:53:57
Current Time: 14:53:58
Logging to file: 14:53:58
```

```
Current Time: 14:53:59
Logging to file: 14:53:59
Current Time: 14:54:0
Logging to file: 14:54:0
```

The net effect of this code is to create two classes, DisplayClock and LogCurrentTime, both of which subscribe to a third class' event (Clock.SecondChanged).

SecondChanged is a multicast delegate field, initially referring to nothing. In time, it refers to a single delegate, and then later to multiple delegates. When the observer classes wish to be notified, they create an instance of the delegate and then add these delegates to SecondChanged. For example, in DisplayClock's Subscribe() method, you see this line of code:

```
theClock.SecondChanged +=
    new Clock.SecondChangeHandler(TimeHasChanged);
```

It turns out that the LogCurrentTime class also wants to be notified. In its Subscribe() method is very similar code:

```
public void Subscribe(Clock theClock)
{
  theClock.SecondChanged +=
    new Clock.SecondChangeHandler(WriteLogEntry);
}
```

Solving Delegate Problems with Events

There is a problem with Example 17-2, however. What if the LogCurrentTime class was not so considerate, and it used the assignment operator (=) rather than the subscribe operator (+=), as in the following:

```
public void Subscribe(Clock theClock)
{
  theClock.SecondChanged =
    new Clock.SecondChangeHandler(WriteLogEntry);
}
```

If you make that one tiny change to the example, you'll find that the Logger() method is called, but the DisplayClock method is *not* called. The assignment operator *replaced* the delegate held in the SecondChanged multicast delegate. This is not good.

A second problem is that other methods can call SecondChangeHandler directly. For example, you might add the following code to the Main() method of your Test class:

```
Console.WriteLine("Calling the method directly!");
System.DateTime dt = System.DateTime.Now.AddHours(2);

TimeInfoEventArgs timeInformation =
  new TimeInfoEventArgs(
  dt.Hour,dt.Minute,dt.Second);

theClock.SecondChanged(theClock, timeInformation);
```

Here, Main( ) has created its own TimeInfoEventArgs object and invoked SecondChanged directly. This runs fine, even though it is not what the designer of the Clock class intended. Here is the output:

```
Calling the method directly!
Current Time: 18:36:7
Logging to file: 18:36:7
Current Time: 16:36:7
Logging to file: 16:36:7
```

The problem is that the designer of the Clock class intended the methods encapsulated by the delegate to be invoked only when the event is fired. Here, Main( ) has gone around through the back door and invoked those methods itself. What is more, it has passed in bogus data (passing in a time construct set to two hours into the future!).

How can you, as the designer of the Clock class, ensure that no one calls the delegated method directly? You can make the delegate private, but then it won't be possible for clients to register with your delegate at all. What's needed is a way to say, "This delegate is designed for event handling: you may subscribe and unsubscribe, but you may not invoke it directly."

The event Keyword

The solution to this dilemma is to use the event keyword. The event keyword indicates to the compiler that the delegate can only be invoked by the defining class, and that other classes can only subscribe to and unsubscribe from the delegate using the appropriate += and -= operators, respectively.

To fix your program, change your definition of SecondChanged from:

```
public SecondChangeHandler SecondChanged;
```

to the following:

```
public event SecondChangeHandler SecondChanged;
```

Adding the event keyword fixes both problems. Classes can no longer attempt to subscribe to the event using the assignment operator (=), as they could previously, nor can they invoke the event directly, as was done in Main( ) in the preceding example. Either of these attempts will now generate a compile error:

```
The event 'Programming_CSharp.Clock.SecondChanged' can only appear on
the left-hand side of += or -= (except when used from within the type
'Programming_CSharp.Clock')
```

There are two ways of looking at SecondChanged now that you've modified it. In one sense, it is simply a delegate instance to which you've restricted access using the keyword event. In another, more important sense, SecondChanged *is* an event, implemented by a delegate of type SecondChangeHandler. These two statements mean the same thing, but the latter is a more object-oriented way of looking at it, and better reflects the intent of this keyword: to create an event that your object can raise, and to which other objects can respond.

The complete source, modified to use the event rather than the unrestricted delegate, is shown in Example 17-3.

Example 17-3. Using the event keyword

```
using System;
using System.Collections.Generic;
using System.Text;
using System.Threading;

namespace UsingTheEventKeyword
{
    // a class to hold the information about the event
    // in this case it will hold only information
    // available in the clock class, but could hold
    // additional state information
    public class TimeInfoEventArgs : EventArgs
    {
        public readonly int hour;
        public readonly int minute;
        public readonly int second;
        public TimeInfoEventArgs( int hour, int minute, int second )
        {
            this.hour = hour;
            this.minute = minute;
            this.second = second;
        }
    }

    // our subject -- it is this class that other classes
    // will observe. This class publishes one event:
    // SecondChanged. The observers subscribe to that event
    public class Clock
    {
        private int hour;
        private int minute;
        private int second;

        // the delegate the subscribers must implement
        public delegate void SecondChangeHandler
          (
          object clock,
          TimeInfoEventArgs timeInformation
          );

        // the keyword event controls access to the delegate
        public event SecondChangeHandler SecondChanged;

        // set the clock running
        // it will raise an event for each new second
```

Example 17-3. Using the event keyword (continued)

```csharp
    public void Run( )
    {

        for ( ; ; )
        {
            // sleep 10 milliseconds
            Thread.Sleep( 10 );

            // get the current time
            System.DateTime dt = System.DateTime.Now;

            // if the second has changed
            // notify the subscribers
            if ( dt.Second != second )
            {
                // create the TimeInfoEventArgs object
                // to pass to the subscriber
                TimeInfoEventArgs timeInformation =
                  new TimeInfoEventArgs(
                  dt.Hour, dt.Minute, dt.Second );

                // if anyone has subscribed, notify them
                if ( SecondChanged != null )
                {
                    SecondChanged(
                       this, timeInformation );
                }
            }

            // update the state
            this.second = dt.Second;
            this.minute = dt.Minute;
            this.hour = dt.Hour;

        }
    }
}

// an observer. DisplayClock subscribes to the
// clock's events. The job of DisplayClock is
// to display the current time
public class DisplayClock
{
    // given a clock, subscribe to
    // its SecondChangeHandler event
    public void Subscribe( Clock theClock )
    {
        theClock.SecondChanged +=
          new Clock.SecondChangeHandler( TimeHasChanged );
    }
```

Example 17-3. Using the event keyword (continued)

```
      // the method that implements the
      // delegated functionality
      public void TimeHasChanged(
        object theClock, TimeInfoEventArgs ti )
      {
        Console.WriteLine( "Current Time: {0}:{1}:{2}",
          ti.hour.ToString( ),
          ti.minute.ToString( ),
          ti.second.ToString( ) );
      }
    }

    // a second subscriber whose job is to write to a file
    public class LogCurrentTime
    {
      public void Subscribe( Clock theClock )
      {
        theClock.SecondChanged +=
          new Clock.SecondChangeHandler( WriteLogEntry );
      }

      // this method should write to a file
      // we write to the console to see the effect
      // this object keeps no state
      public void WriteLogEntry(
        object theClock, TimeInfoEventArgs ti )
      {
        Console.WriteLine( "Logging to file: {0}:{1}:{2}",
          ti.hour.ToString( ),
          ti.minute.ToString( ),
          ti.second.ToString( ) );
      }
    }

    public class Test
    {
      public static void Main( )
      {
        // create a new clock
        Clock theClock = new Clock( );

        // create the display and tell it to
        // subscribe to the clock just created
        DisplayClock dc = new DisplayClock( );
        dc.Subscribe( theClock );

        // create a Log object and tell it
        // to subscribe to the clock
        LogCurrentTime lct = new LogCurrentTime( );
        lct.Subscribe( theClock );
```

Example 17-3. Using the event keyword (continued)

```
        // Get the clock started
        theClock.Run( );
    }
  }
}
```

Using Anonymous Methods

In the previous example, you subscribed to the event by invoking a new instance of the delegate, passing in the name of a method that implements the event:

```
theClock.SecondChanged += new Clock.SecondChangeHandler(TimeHasChanged);
```

Later in the code, you must define TimeHasChanged as a method that matches the signature of the SecondChangeHandler delegate:

```
public void TimeHasChanged(
  object theClock, TimeInfoEventArgs ti)
{
  Console.WriteLine("Current Time: {0}:{1}:{2}",
    ti.hour.ToString( ),
    ti.minute.ToString( ),
    ti.second.ToString( ));
}
```

Anonymous methods allow you to pass a code block rather than the name of the method. This can make for more efficient and easier to maintain code, and the anonymous method has access to the variables in the scope in which they are defined.

```
clock.SecondChanged += delegate( object theClock, TimeInfoEventArgs ti )
{
  Console.WriteLine( "Current Time: {0}:{1}:{2}",
  ti.hour.ToString( ),
  ti.minute.ToString( ),
  ti.second.ToString( ) );
};
```

Notice that rather than registering an instance of a delegate, you use the keyword *delegate*, followed by the parameters that would be passed to your method, followed by the body of your method encased in braces and terminated by a semicolon.

This "method" has no name; hence, it is *anonymous*. You cannot invoke the method except through the delegate; but that is exactly what you want.

Summary

- Modern GUIs rely on events generated by the user (or by the system) to know what action to take.

- A delegate is a reference to a method of a particular signature and return type.

- The keyword event constrains a delegate's usage to the event handling semantics.
- Instead of implementing delegates as static fields, you can implement them as properties, so that you do not need to instantiate them if they are never used.
- You can combine delegates using the += operator.
- An object can publish a series of events to which other classes can subscribe. The publishing class defines a delegate and an event based on that delegate. The subscribing class creates a method that matches the signature of the delegate, and registers that method with an instance of the delegate.
- In .NET, all event handlers return void, and take two parameters. The first parameter is of type object and is the object that raises the event; the second argument is an object of type EventArgs or of a type derived from EventArgs, which may contain useful information about the event.
- Instead of passing a method name to a delegate, you can pass a block of code; this creates an anonymous method.

Quiz

Question 17-1. Define an event to signal that the phone has rung.

Question 17-2. Are delegates value types or reference types?

Question 17-3. What is the purpose of a delegate?

Question 17-4. How do you instantiate a delegate, such as the OnPhoneRings delegate described in the first question?

Question 17-5. Give an example of how you might call the delegated method through the delegate.

Question 17-6. What is multicasting?

Question 17-7. What does the event keyword do?

Question 17-8. If you want to pass information into the method that is called through the event, how do you do so?

Question 17-9. What properties or methods does System.EventArgs have?

Question 17-10. How can you create delegated methods anonymously?

Exercises

Exercise 17-1. Write a countdown alarm program that uses delegates to notify anyone who is interested that the designated amount of time has passed.

Exercise 17-2. Break the program you write in Exercise 17-1 by assigning a new handler to the delegate (deleting the old!).

Exercise 17-3. Fix the program you wrote in Exercise 17-1 by using the event keyword and test against changes you added in Exercise 17-2.

CHAPTER 18

Creating Windows Applications

All the previous chapters have used console applications to demonstrate the C# language. This allowed us to focus on the language itself, without being distracted by more complicated issues such as windows, mice, and controls.

That said, the only reason most people learn C# is to create Windows applications or web applications, or both. On the following pages, you will learn how to create Windows applications using the tools provided by Visual Studio (the next chapter shows you how to create web applications).

The application you will create in this chapter will bring together a number of C# techniques shown in earlier chapters and apply them to solving a real-world problem.

Creating a Simple Windows Form

The .NET Framework offers extensive support for Windows application development, the centerpiece of which is Windows Forms. The metaphor of a "form" was borrowed from Visual Basic, and is a hallmark of Rapid Application Development (RAD). Arguably, C# is the first development environment to marry the RAD tools of VB with the object-oriented and high-performance characteristics of a C++/Java-like language (though, of course, C# and Visual Basic 2005 are now virtually the same language with different syntactic coatings).

Using the Visual Studio Designer

While it is possible to build a Windows application using any text editor, and it is possible to compile from the command line, it is senseless to do so. Visual Studio 2005 increases your productivity, and integrates an editor, compiler, test environment, and debugger into a single work environment. Few serious .NET developers build commercial applications outside of Visual Studio.

To begin work on a new Windows application, first open Visual Studio and choose File → New → Project. In the New Project window, create a new C# Windows application and name it Learning CSharp Windows Forms, as shown in Figure 18-1.

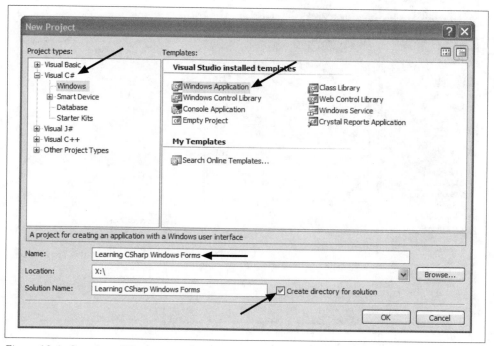

Figure 18-1. Creating a Windows Application project

Be sure to choose C# and Windows Application (see arrows). It is convenient to place each project in its own directory (see checkbox), and you may name the project anything you like (and the name may include spaces, as shown).

Visual Studio responds by creating a Windows Form application and, best of all, putting you into a design environment, as shown in Figure 18-2.

The Design window displays a blank Windows Form (Form1). A Toolbox window is also available, with a selection of Windows controls. If the Toolbox is not displayed, try selecting View → Toolbox on the Visual Studio menu. You can also use the keyboard shortcut Ctrl/Alt/X to display the Toolbox.*

Before proceeding, take a look around. The Toolbox is filled with controls that you can add to your Windows Form application. In the upper-right corner, you should see the Solution Explorer, a window that displays all the files in your projects (if not,

---

* Visual Studio allows a great deal of personalization; please verify all the keyboard shortcuts mentioned in this book to ensure that they work as expected in your environment.

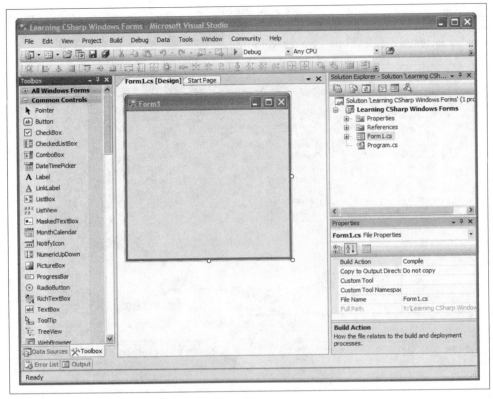

Figure 18-2. The design environment

click View → Solution Explorer). In the lower-right corner is the Properties window (View → Properties Window), which displays all the properties of the currently selected item.

Drag a label and a button from the Toolbox onto the form. Click on the label and take a look at its properties in the Properties window, as shown in Figure 18-3.

To add text to label1, you can type the words "Hello World" into the box to the right of its Text property.

If you want to change the font for the lettering in the HelloWorld label, click the + sign next to the Font property to expand it. Then click on the ellipsis next to the Name sub-property to open the Font editor, as shown in Figure 18-4.

Click on the button and change its text to Cancel. Run the application by clicking the Start Debugging button, or clicking F5, just as you would with a console application. You'll see your new form running in its own window. Click on the Cancel button. Oops, nothing happens. For the application to respond to the button click, you must provide an event handler. Click on the X to close your application and return to the Design view.

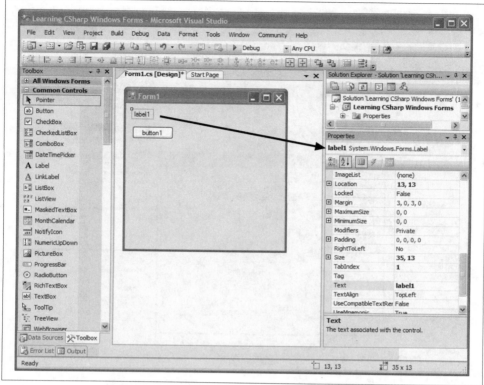

Figure 18-3. The properties for a control

Click on the button so that its properties are shown in the Properties window. Notice that at the top of the window are a series of buttons. As you hover the cursor over each, a tool tip tells you what it is for, as shown in Figure 18-5.

Click on the lightning bolt to change the Properties window to show all the events for the button. You'll want to create a handler for the Click event. You can type a name into the space next to Click or you can just double-click in the space and Visual Studio 2005 will create an event handler name for you. In either case, Visual Studio 2005 then places you in the editor for the event handler so you can add the logic. Add a line to the event so it looks like this:

```
private void button1_Click( object sender, EventArgs e )
{
    Application.Exit();
}
```

Visual Studio 2005 created the name by concatenating the control name (button1) with the event (Click), separated by an underscore. Your logic just says to exit the application when the button is clicked.

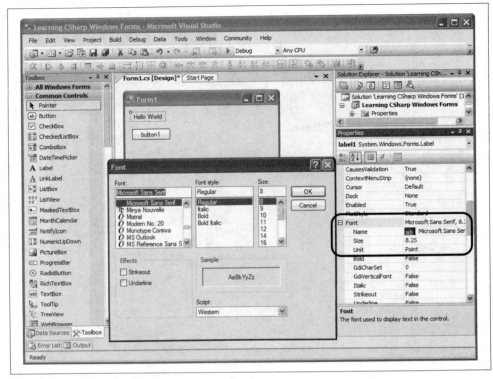

Figure 18-4. Editing the font

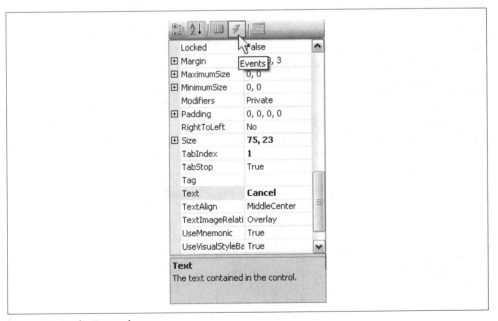

Figure 18-5. The Events button

Every control has a "default" event—the event most commonly handled by that control. In the button's case, the default event is click. You can save time by double-clicking on the control (in Design view) if you want Visual Studio 2005 to create and name an event handler for you. That is, rather than the steps above (click on the button, click on the lightning button, double-click on the space next to Click), you could have just double-clicked on the button; the effect would be the same because you are implementing the "default" event.

Notice that as you try to enter the method call Application.Exit( ), Visual Studio 2005's IntelliSense tries to help you. When you type A, the first possible object that begins with A is shown. Continue typing through Appl and then hit the period: the class Application is filled in for you, and the methods and properties of the Application object are available.

IntelliSense will remember your most recent choice of member for a given class, and that will be displayed first. Often this is a great convenience.

Type **Exi** and IntelliSense scrolls to the first method that begins with those letters, as shown in Figure 18-6.

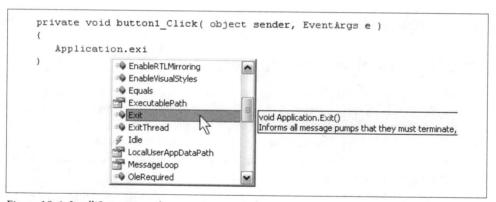

Figure 18-6. IntelliSense at work

Once you've found the method, just type the parentheses and semicolon.

In the IDE, the cursor flashes, making it easy to see where the code goes. For most readers, the cursor probably won't flash in this book.

The partial Keyword

Your code file (*Form1.cs*) has only the using directives and the constructor and event handler. If you have experience with previous versions of C#, you may be wondering where the code to initialize the controls is hiding. The class definition contains the keyword partial. This indicates that the rest of the class definition is contained in another file. If you click the Show All Files button at the top of the Solution Explorer (as shown in Figure 18-7), you will see that the designer has revealed another file, *Form1.Designer.cs*, that contains the boiler-plate code and the initialization for all the controls.

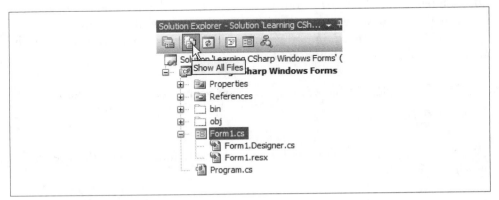

Figure 18-7. Show All Files button

Creating a Real-World Application

To see how Windows Forms can be used to create a more realistic Windows application, you'll build a utility named FileCopier that copies all files from a group of directories selected by the user to a single target directory or device, such as a floppy or backup hard drive on the company network. Although you won't implement every possible feature, this example will provide a good introduction to what it is like to build meaningful Windows applications.

For the purposes of this example and to keep the code simple, you'll focus on the user interface and the steps needed to *wire up* its various controls. The final application UI is shown in Figure 18-8.

The user interface for FileCopier consists of the following controls:

- Labels (Source Files, Target Files, and Status)
- Buttons (Clear, Copy, Delete, and Cancel)
- An "Overwrite if exists" checkbox
- A text box displaying the path of the selected target directory
- TreeView controls (source and target directories)

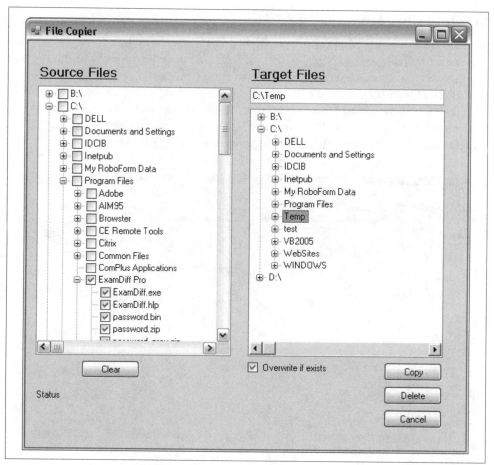

Figure 18-8. The FileCopier user interface

The goal is to allow the user to check files (or entire directories) in the left tree view (source). If the user clicks the Copy button, the files checked on the left side will be copied to the Target Directories specified on the right-side control. If the user clicks Delete, the checked files will be deleted.

 The example you're about to create is much more complex than anything you've done in this book so far. However, if you walk through the code slowly, you'll find that you've already learned everything you need in the previous chapters. The goal of creating Windows applications is to mix drag-and-drop design with rather straightforward C# blocks to handle the logic.

Creating the Basic UI Form

The first task is to open a new project named FileCopier. The IDE puts you into the designer, in which you can drag widgets onto the form. You can expand the form to the size you want. Drag, drop, and set the Name properties of labels (*lblSource*, *lblTarget*, *lblStatus*), buttons (*btnClear*, *btnCopy*, *btnDelete*, *btnCancel*), a checkbox (*chkOverwrite*), a text box (*txtTargetDir*), and tree view controls (*tvwSource*, *tvwTargetDir*) from the Toolbox onto your form. Then set the Text properties of the widgets until it looks more or less like the one shown in Figure 18-9.

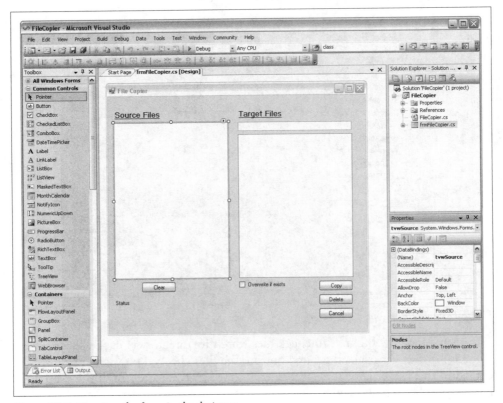

Figure 18-9. Creating the form in the designer

You want checkboxes next to the directories and files in the source selection window, but not in the target (where only one directory will be chosen). Set the CheckBoxes property on the left TreeView control, *tvwSource*, to true, and set the property on the right TreeView control, *tvwTargetDir*, to false. To do so, click each control in turn and adjust the values in the Properties window.

Once this is done, double-click the Cancel button to create its click event handler, like this:

```
protected void btnCancel_Click (object sender, System.EventArgs e)
{
    Application.Exit();
}
```

You can handle many different events for the various controls. An easy way to do so is by clicking the Events button in the Properties window. From there, you can create new handlers, just by filling in a new event handler method name or picking one of the existing event handlers. Visual Studio registers the event handler and opens the editor for the code, where it creates the header and puts the cursor in an empty method body.

So much for the easy part. Visual Studio generates code to set up the form and initializes all the controls, but it doesn't fill the TreeView controls. That you must do by hand.

Populating the TreeView Controls

The two TreeView controls work identically, except that the left control, tvwSource, lists the directories and files, whereas the right control, tvwTargetDir, lists only directories. The CheckBoxes property on tvwSource is set to true, and on tvwTargetDir, it is set to false. Also, although tvwSource will allow multiselect, which is the default for TreeView controls, you will enforce single selection for tvwTargetDir.

You'll factor the common code for both TreeView controls into a shared method FillDirectoryTree. You'll pass in the treeview control with a boolean (also called a *flag*) indicating whether to get the files that are currently present (you'll see how this works in a bit). You'll call this method from the Form's constructor, once for each of the two controls. Click on the Form1.cs tab at the top of the main window in Visual Studio to switch to the code for the form. Locate the constructor for the form (public Form1()), and add these two method calls:

```
FillDirectoryTree(tvwSource, true);
FillDirectoryTree(tvwTargetDir, false);
```

The FillDirectoryTree implementation names the TreeView parameter tvw. This will represent the source TreeView and the destination TreeView in turn. You'll need some classes from System.IO, so add a using System.IO statement at the top of *Form1.cs*.

Next, add the method declaration to *Form1.cs*:

```
private void FillDirectoryTree(TreeView tvw, bool isSource)
```

Right now, the code for *Form1.cs* should look like this:

```
using System;
using System.Collections.Generic;
using System.ComponentModel;
```

```
using System.Data;
using System.Drawing;
using System.Text;
using System.Windows.Forms;
using System.IO;

namespace FileCopier
{
    public partial class Form1 : Form
    {
        public Form1()
        {
            InitializeComponent();
            FillDirectoryTree(tvwSource, true);
            FillDirectoryTree(tvwTargerDir, false);
        }

        private void lblSource_Click(object sender, EventArgs e)
        {

        }

        private void btnCancel_Click(object sender, EventArgs e)
        {
            Application.Exit();
        }

        private void FillDirectoryTree(TreeView tvw, bool isSource)
        {

        }
    }
}
```

TreeNode objects

You're now going to fill in the code for the `FillDirectoryTree()` method you just created. The `TreeView` control has a property, `Nodes`, which gets a `TreeNodeCollection` object. The `TreeNodeCollection` is a collection of `TreeNode` objects, each of which represents a node in the tree. Start by emptying that collection.

```
tvw.Nodes.Clear();
```

The `TreeView`, the `TreeNodeCollection`, and the `TreeNode` class are all defined by the Framework Class Library, In fact, nearly all the classes used in this example are defined by the framework (as opposed to defined by you) and can be fully explored in the help files.

There is, unfortunately, no accepted convention to distinguish between individually user-defined classes (such as `frmFileCopier`) from framework-defined classes (such as `Environment`). On the other hand, if you haven't defined it explicitly, it is a safe bet that it is part of the framework, and you can confirm that with the help files documentation.

You are ready to fill the TreeView's Nodes collection by recursing through the directories of all the drives. First, you need to get all the logical drives on the local system. To do so, call a static method of the Environment object, GetLogicalDrives(). The Environment class provides information about and access to the current platform environment. You can use the Environment object to get the machine name, OS version, system directory, and so forth, from the computer on which you are running your program.

```
string[] strDrives = Environment.GetLogicalDrives();
```

GetLogicalDrives() returns an array of strings, each of which represents the root directory of one of the logical drives. You will iterate over that collection, adding nodes to the TreeView control as you go.

```
foreach (string rootDirectoryName in strDrives)
{
```

You process each drive within the foreach loop.

The very first thing you need to determine is whether the drive is available (that is, it is not a floppy drive with no floppy in it). My hack for that is to get the list of top-level directories from the drive by calling GetDirectories() on a DirectoryInfo object I created for the root directory:

```
DirectoryInfo dir = new DirectoryInfo(rootDirectoryName);
dir.GetDirectories();
```

The DirectoryInfo class exposes instance methods for creating, moving, and enumerating through directories, their files, and their subdirectories.

The GetDirectories() method returns a list of directories, but actually, this code throws the list away. You are calling it here only to generate an exception if the drive is not ready.

Wrap the call in a try block and take no action in the catch block. The effect is that if an exception is thrown, the drive is skipped.

Once you know that the drive is ready, create a TreeNode to hold the root directory of the drive and add that node to the TreeView control:

```
TreeNode ndRoot = new TreeNode(rootDirectoryName);
tvw.Nodes.Add(ndRoot);
```

To get the + signs right in the TreeView, you must find at least two levels of directories (so that the TreeView knows which directories have subdirectories and can write the + sign next to them). You don't want to recurse through all the subdirectories, however, because that would be too slow.

The job of the GetSubDirectoryNodes() method is to recurse two levels deep, passing in the root node, the name of the root directory, a flag indicating whether you want files, and the current level (you always start at level 1):

```
if ( isSource )
{
    GetSubDirectoryNodes(ndRoot, ndRoot.Text, true,1 );
}
else
{
    GetSubDirectoryNodes(ndRoot, ndRoot.Text, false,1 );
}
```

 You may be wondering why you need to pass in ndRoot.Text if you're already passing in ndRoot. You will see why this is needed when you recurse back into GetSubDirectoryNodes.

After the catch block, you throw in the following line:

```
Application.DoEvents();
```

This instructs the application to yield processing long enough to update the user interface. This keeps the user informed and happy, and avoids the problem of it looking like your program has hung while performing a long procedure.

You are now finished with FillDirectoryTree(). See Example 18-1 later in this chapter for a complete listing of this method.

Recursing through the subdirectories

Next, you need to create the method that gets the subdirectory nodes. Create that in a new method following the one you just finished. GetSubDirectoryNodes() begins by once again calling GetDirectories(), this time stashing away the resulting array of DirectoryInfo objects:

```
private void GetSubDireoctoryNodes(
  TreeNode parentNode, string fullName, bool getFileNames, int level)
{
    DirectoryInfo dir = new DirectoryInfo(fullName);
    DirectoryInfo[] dirSubs = dir.GetDirectories();
```

Notice that the node passed in is named parentNode. The current level of nodes will be considered children to the node passed in. This is how you map the directory structure to the hierarchy of the tree view.

Iterate over each subdirectory, skipping any that are marked Hidden:

```
foreach (DirectoryInfo dirSub in dirSubs)
{
    if ( (dirSub.Attributes & FileAttributes.Hidden) != 0 )
    {
        continue;
    }
```

`FileAttributes` is an enum; other possible values include `Archive`, `Compressed`, `Directory`, `Encrypted`, `Normal`, `ReadOnly`, and a few others, but they are rarely used.

The property `dirSub.Attributes` is the bit pattern of the current attributes of the directory. If you logically `AND` that value with the bit pattern `FileAttributes.Hidden`, a bit is set if the file has the `hidden` attribute; otherwise, all the bits are cleared. You can check for any hidden bit by testing whether the resulting `int` is something other than 0.

Next, create a `TreeNode` with the directory name and add it to the `Nodes` collection of the node passed in to the method (`parentNode`):

```
TreeNode subNode = new TreeNode(dirSub.Name);
parentNode.Nodes.Add(subNode);
```

Check the current level (passed in by the calling method) against a constant defined for the class.

By convention, member constants and variables are declared at the top of the class declaration:

```
partial class frmFileCopier : Form
{
    private const int MaxLevel = 2;
```

The constant makes sure you recurse only two levels deep. The following snippet is back in the foreach loop within `GetSubDirectoryNodes`:

```
if ( level < MaxLevel )
{
    GetSubDirectoryNodes(subNode, dirSub.FullName, getFileNames, level+1 );
}
```

 You pass in the node you just created as the new parent, the full path as the full name of the parent, and the flag you received, along with one greater than the current level (thus, if you started at level one, this next call will set the level to two).

The call to the `TreeNode` constructor uses the `Name` property of the `DirectoryInfo` object, while the call to `GetSubDirectoryNodes( )` uses the `FullName` property. If your directory is *C:\Windows\Media\Sounds*, the `FullName` property returns the full path, while the `Name` property returns just *Sounds*. Pass in only the name to the node because that is what you want displayed in the tree view. Pass in the full name with the path to the `GetSubDirectoryNodes( )` method so that the method can locate all the subdirectories on the disk. This answers the question asked earlier as to why you need to pass in the root node's name the first time you call this method. What is passed in isn't the name of the node; it is the full path to the directory represented by the node!

Getting the files in the directory

Once you've recursed through the subdirectories, it is time to get the files for the directory if the getFileNames flag is true. To do so, call the GetFiles( ) method on the DirectoryInfo object. An array of FileInfo objects is returned:

```
if (getFileNames)
{
 // Get any files for this node.
 FileInfo[] files = dir.GetFiles( );
```

The FileInfo class provides instance methods for manipulating files.

You can now iterate over this collection, accessing the Name property of the FileInfo object and passing that name to the constructor of a TreeNode, which you then add to the parent node's Nodes collection (thus creating a child node). There is no recursion this time because files don't have subdirectories:

```
foreach (FileInfo file in files)
{
    TreeNode fileNode = new TreeNode(file.Name);
    parentNode.Nodes.Add(fileNode);
}
```

That's all it takes to fill the two tree views. See Example 18-1 for a complete listing of this method.

If you found any of this confusing, I highly recommend building Example 18-1 and stepping through the code in the Visual Studio 2005 debugger. Pay particular attention to the recursion, watching as the TreeView build its nodes.

Handling TreeView Events

You must handle a number of events in this example. First, the user might click Cancel, Copy, Clear, or Delete. Second, the user might fire events in either TreeView. We'll consider the TreeView events first, as they are the more interesting, and potentially the more challenging.

Clicking the source TreeView

There are two TreeView objects, each with its own event handler. Consider the source TreeView object first. The user checks the files and directories he wants to copy from. Each time the user clicks the checkbox indicating a file or directory, a number of events are raised. The event you must handle is AfterCheck.

To do so, implement a custom event handler method you will create and name tvwSource_AfterCheck( ).The implementation of AfterCheck( ) delegates the work to a recursable method named SetCheck( ) that you'll also write. The SetCheck( ) method will recursively set the check mark for all the contained folders.

To add the AfterCheck( ) event, select the tvwSource control, click the Events icon in the Properties window, and then double-click AfterCheck. This will add the event, wire it up, and place you in the code editor where you can add the body of the method:

```
private void tvwSource_AfterCheck (
object sender, System.Windows.Forms.TreeViewEventArgs e)
{
    SetCheck(e.Node,e.Node.Checked);
}
```

The event handler passes in the sender object and an object of type TreeViewEventArgs. It turns out that you can get the node from this TreeViewEventArgs object (e). You then call SetCheck( ), passing in the node and the state of whether the node has been checked.

Each node has a Nodes property, which gets a TreeNodeCollection containing all the subnodes. SetCheck( ) recurses through the current node's Nodes collection, setting each subnode's check mark to match that of the node that was checked. In other words, when you check a directory, all its files and subdirectories are checked, recursively, all the way down.

For each TreeNode in the Nodes collection, check to see if it is a leaf. A node is a leaf if its own Nodes collection has a count of 0. If it is a leaf, set its check property to whatever was passed in as a parameter. If it is not a leaf, recurse:

```
private void SetCheck( TreeNode node, bool check )
{
    foreach ( TreeNode n in node.Nodes )
    {
        n.Checked = check;    // check the node

        if ( n.Nodes.Count != 0 )
        {
            SetCheck( n, check );
        }
    }
}
```

This propagates the check mark (or clears the check mark) down through the entire structure. In this way, the user can indicate that he wants to select all the files in all the subdirectories by clicking a single directory.

Expanding a directory

Each time you click a + sign next to a directory in the source (or in the target), you want to expand that directory. To do so, you'll need an event handler for the BeforeExpand event. Because the event handlers will be identical for both the source and the target tree views, you'll create a shared event handler (assigning the same event handler to both). Go back to the Design view, select the tvwSource control, double-click the BeforeExpand event, and add this code:

```
private void tvwExpand(object sender, TreeViewCancelEventArgs e)
{
    TreeView tvw = ( TreeView ) sender;
    bool getFiles = tvw == tvwSource;
    TreeNode currentNode = e.Node;
    string fullName = currentNode.FullPath;
    currentNode.Nodes.Clear( );
    GetSubDirectoryNodes( currentNode, fullName, getFiles, 1 );
}
```

Your second task is to determine whether you want to get the files in the directory you are opening, and you do only if the name of the TreeView that triggered the event is tvwSource.

You determine which node's + sign was checked by getting the Node property from the TreeViewCancelEventArgs that is passed in by the event:

```
TreeNode currentNode = e.Node;
```

Once you have the current node, you get its full pathname (which you will need as a parameter to GetSubDirectoryNodes) and then you must clear its collection of subnodes, because you are going to refill that collection by calling in to GetSubDirectoryNodes:

```
currentNode.Nodes.Clear( );
```

Why do you clear the subnodes and then refill them? Because this time you will go another level deep so that the subnodes know if *they* in turn have subnodes, and thus will know if they should draw a + sign next to their subdirectories.

Be sure to select the target TreeView and add the same code to its BeforeExpand event.

Clicking the target TreeView

The second event handler for the target TreeView (in addition to BeforeExpand) is somewhat trickier. The event itself is AfterSelect. (Remember that the target TreeView doesn't have checkboxes.) This time, you want to take the one directory chosen and put its full path into the text box at the upper-left corner of the form.

To do so, you must work your way up through the nodes, finding the name of each parent directory and building the full path:

```
private void tvwTargetDir_AfterSelect (
  object sender, System.Windows.Forms.TreeViewEventArgs e)
{
  string theFullPath = GetParentString(e.Node);
```

We'll look at GetParentString( ) in just a moment. Once you have the full path, you must lop off the backslash (if any) on the end, and then you can fill the text box:

```
if (theFullPath.EndsWith("\\"))
{
```

```
        theFullPath = theFullPath.Substring(0,theFullPath.Length - 1);
    }
    txtTargetDir.Text = theFullPath;
```

The `GetParentString( )` method takes a node and returns a string with the full path. To do so, it recurses upward through the path, adding the backslash after any node that is not a leaf:

```
private string GetParentString( TreeNode node )
{
    if ( node.Parent == null )
    {
        return node.Text;
    }
    else
    {
        return GetParentString( node.Parent ) + node.Text +
            ( node.Nodes.Count == 0 ? String.Empty : "\\" );
    }
}
```

You learned about the conditional operator (?) in Chapter 4. The logic is, "Test whether `node.Nodes.Count` is 0; if so, return the value before the colon (in this case, an empty string). Otherwise, return the value after the colon (in this case, a backslash)."

The recursion stops when there is no parent; that is, when you hit the root directory.

Handling the Clear button event

Given the `SetCheck( )` method developed earlier, handling the Clear button's `Click` event is trivial:

```
private void btnClear_Click( object sender, System.EventArgs e )
{
    foreach ( TreeNode node in tvwSource.Nodes )
    {
        SetCheck( node, false );
    }
}
```

Just call the `SetCheck( )` method on the root nodes and tell them to recursively uncheck all their contained nodes.

Implementing the Copy Button Event

Now that you can check the files and pick the target directory, you're ready to handle the Copy click event. The very first thing you need to do is to get a list of which files were selected. What you want is an array of `FileInfo` objects, but you have no idea how many objects will be in the list. This is a perfect job for a generic List. Delegate responsibility for filling the list to a method called GetFileList( ):

```
private void btnCopy_Click( object sender, System.EventArgs e )
{
    List<FileInfo> fileList = GetFileList();
```

Let's pick that method apart before returning to the event handler.

Start by instantiating a new List object to hold the strings representing the names of all the files selected:

```
private List<FileInfo> GetFileList( )
{
    List<string> fileNames = new List<string>( );
```

To get the selected filenames, you can walk through the source TreeView control:

```
foreach ( TreeNode theNode in tvwSource.Nodes )
{
    GetCheckedFiles( theNode, fileNames );
}
```

To see how this works, step into the GetCheckedFiles( ) method. This method is pretty simple: it examines the node it was handed. If that node has no children (node. Nodes.Count == 0), it is a leaf. If that leaf is checked, get the full path (by calling GetParentString( ) on the node) and add it to the ArrayList passed in as a parameter:

```
private void GetCheckedFiles( TreeNode node,List<string> fileNames )
{
    // if this is a leaf...
    if ( node.Nodes.Count == 0 )
    {

        // if the node was checked...
        if ( node.Checked )
        {
            // get the full path and add it to the arrayList
            string fullPath = GetParentString( node );
            fileNames.Add( fullPath );
        }
    }
```

If the node is *not* a leaf, recurse down the tree, finding the child nodes:

```
    else
    {
        foreach (TreeNode n in node.Nodes)
        {
            GetCheckedFiles(n,fileNames);
        }
    }
}
```

This returns the List filled with all the filenames. Back in GetFileList( ), you use this List of filenames to create a second List, this time to hold the actual FileInfo objects:

```
List<FileInfo> fileList = new List<FileInfo>( );
```

Notice the use of typesafe List objects to ensure that the compiler flags any objects added to the collection that aren't of type FileInfo.

Back in GetFileList( ), you can now iterate through the filenames in fileList, picking out each name and instantiating a FileInfo object with it. You can detect if it is a file or a directory by calling the Exists property, which will return false if the File object you created is actually a directory. If it is a File, you can add it to the new ArrayList:

```
foreach ( string fileName in fileNames )
{
    FileInfo file = new FileInfo( fileName );

    if ( file.Exists )
    {
        // both the key and the value are the file
        // would it be easier to have an empty value?
        fileList.Add( file );
    }
}
```

Sorting the list of selected files

You want to work your way through the list of selected files in large to small order so that you can pack the target disk as tightly as possible. You must therefore sort the List. You can call its Sort( ) method, but how will it know how to sort FileInfo objects?

To solve this, you must pass in an IComparer<T> interface. We'll create a class called FileComparer that will implement this generic interface for FileInfo objects:

```
public class FileComparer : IComparer<FileInfo>
{
```

This class has only one method, Compare( ), which takes two FileInfo objects as arguments:

```
public int Compare(FileInfo file1, FileInfo file2);
```

The normal approach is to return 1 if the first object (file1) is larger than the second (file2), to return -1 if the opposite is true, and to return 0 if they are equal. In this case, however, you want the list sorted from big to small, so you should reverse the return values.

Because this is the only use of the Compare method, it is reasonable to put this special knowledge (that the sort is from big to small) right into the Compare method itself. The alternative is to sort small to big, and have the *calling* method reverse the results.

To test the length of the FileInfo object, you must cast the Object parameters to FileInfo objects (which is safe because you know this method will never receive anything else):

```
public int Compare(FileInfo file1, FileInfo file2)
{

    if ( file1.Length > file2.Length )
    {
      return -1;
    }
    if ( file1.Length < file2.Length )
    {
      return 1;
    }
    return 0;
}
```

Returning to GetFileList( ), you were about to instantiate the IComparer reference and pass it to the Sort( ) method of fileList:

```
IComparer<FileInfo> comparer = ( IComparer<FileInfo> ) new FileComparer( );
        fileList.Sort( comparer );
```

That done, you can return fileList to the calling method:

```
return fileList;
```

The calling method was btnCopy_Click. Remember, you went off to GetFileList( ) in the first line of the event handler!

```
private void btnCopy_Click (object sender, System.EventArgs e)
{
    List<FileInfo> fileList = GetFileList( );
```

At this point, you've returned with a sorted list of File objects, each representing a file selected in the source TreeView.

You can now iterate through the list, copying the files and updating the UI:

```
foreach ( FileInfo file in fileList )
{
    try
    {
      lblStatus.Text = "Copying " + txtTargetDir.Text +
          "\\" + file.Name + "...";
      Application.DoEvents( );
```

```
        // copy the file to its destination location
        file.CopyTo( txtTargetDir.Text + "\\" +
            file.Name, chkOverwrite.Checked );
    }

    catch ( Exception ex )
    {
        MessageBox.Show( ex.Message );
    }
}
lblStatus.Text = "Done.";
```

As you go, write the progress to the `lblStatus` label and call `Application.DoEvents( )` to give the UI an opportunity to redraw. Then call `CopyTo( )` on the file, passing in the target directory obtained from the text field, and a Boolean flag indicating whether the file should be overwritten if it already exists.

The copy is wrapped in a try block because you can anticipate any number of things going wrong when copying files. For now, handle all exceptions by popping up a dialog box with the error; you might want to take corrective action in a commercial application.

That's it; you've implemented file copying!

Handling the Delete Button Event

The code to handle the `Delete` event is even more simple. The very first thing you do is ask the user if she is sure she wants to delete the files:

```
private void btnDelete_Click( object sender, System.EventArgs e )
{
    // ask them if they are sure
    System.Windows.Forms.DialogResult result =
        MessageBox.Show(
        "Are you quite sure?",                  // msg
        "Delete Files",                         // caption
        MessageBoxButtons.OKCancel,             // buttons
        MessageBoxIcon.Exclamation,             // icons
        MessageBoxDefaultButton.Button2 );      // default button
```

You can use the `MessageBox` static `Show( )` method, passing in the message you want to display, the title "Delete Files" as a string, and flags, as follows: `MessageBox.OKCancel` asks for two buttons: `OK` and `Cancel`. `MessageBox.IconExclamation` indicates that you want to display an exclamation mark icon. `MessageBox.DefaultButton.Button2` sets the second button (`Cancel`) as the default choice.

When the user chooses OK or Cancel, the result is passed back as a `System.Windows.Forms.DialogResult` enumerated value. You can test this value to see if the user selected OK:

```
if ( result == System.Windows.Forms.DialogResult.OK )
{
```

If so, you can get the list of fileNames and iterate through it, deleting each as you go:

```
List<FileInfo> fileNames = GetFileList();

foreach ( FileInfo file in fileNames )
  {
    try
    {
        // update the label to show progress
        lblStatus.Text = "Deleting " +
            txtTargetDir.Text + "\\" +
            file.Name + "...";
        Application.DoEvents();

        // Danger Will Robinson!
        file.Delete();
    }

    catch ( Exception ex )
    {
        // you may want to do more than
        // just show the message
        MessageBox.Show( ex.Message );
    }
  }
  lblStatus.Text = "Done.";
  Application.DoEvents();
```

This code is identical to the copy code, except that the method that is called on the file is Delete( ).

Example 18-1 provides the commented source code for this example.

Example 18-1. FileCopier source code

```
using System;
using System.Collections;
using System.Collections.Generic;  // for List<T>
using System.ComponentModel;
using System.Data;
using System.Drawing;
using System.IO;
using System.Windows.Forms;

/// <remarks>
///     File Copier - Windows Forms demonstration program
///     (c) Copyright 2006 Liberty Associates, Inc.
/// </remarks>
namespace FileCopier
{
    /// <summary>
    /// Form demonstrating Windows Forms implementation
    /// </summary>
    partial class frmFileCopier : Form
```

Example 18-1. FileCopier source code (continued)

```
{
    private const int MaxLevel = 2;
    public frmFileCopier( )
    {
        InitializeComponent( );
        FillDirectoryTree( tvwSource, true );
        FillDirectoryTree( tvwTarget, false );
    }

    /// <summary>
    ///     nested class which knows how to compare
    ///     two files we want to sort large to small,
    ///     so reverse the normal return values.
    /// </summary>
    public class FileComparer : IComparer<FileInfo>
    {
        public int Compare( FileInfo file1, FileInfo file2 )
        {
            if ( file1.Length > file2.Length )
            {
                return -1;
            }
            if ( file1.Length < file2.Length )
            {
                return 1;
            }
            return 0;
        }

        public bool Equals( FileInfo x, FileInfo y )
        {
            throw new NotImplementedException( );
        }

        public int GetHashCode( FileInfo x )
        {
            throw new NotImplementedException( );
        }

    }

    /// <summary>
    /// Factored out method for both directory trees
    /// </summary>
    /// <param name="tvw">which treeview called this handler</param>
    /// <param name="isSource">get the files if true</param>
    private void FillDirectoryTree( TreeView tvw, bool isSource )
    {
        // Populate tvwSource, the Source TreeView,
        // with the contents of
        // the local hard drive.
        // First clear all the nodes.
        tvw.Nodes.Clear( );
```

Example 18-1. FileCopier source code (continued)

```
        // Get the logical drives and put them into the
        // root nodes. Fill an array with all the
        // logical drives on the machine.
        string[] strDrives = Environment.GetLogicalDrives( );

        // Iterate through the drives, adding them to the tree.
        // Use a try/catch block, so if a drive is not ready,
        // e.g. an empty floppy or CD,
        //    it will not be added to the tree.
        foreach ( string rootDirectoryName in strDrives )
        {
          try
          {
            // Fill an array with all the first level
            // subdirectories. If the drive is
            // not ready, this will throw an exception.
            DirectoryInfo dir =
                new DirectoryInfo( rootDirectoryName );

            dir.GetDirectories( );       // force exception if drive not ready

            TreeNode ndRoot = new TreeNode( rootDirectoryName );

            // Add a node for each root directory.
            tvw.Nodes.Add( ndRoot );

            // Add subdirectory nodes.
            // If Treeview is the source,
            // then also get the filenames.
            if ( isSource )
            {
              GetSubDirectoryNodes(
                  ndRoot, ndRoot.Text, true, 1 );
            }
            else
            {
              GetSubDirectoryNodes(
                  ndRoot, ndRoot.Text, false, 1 );
            }
          }
          // Catch any errors such as
          // Drive not ready.
          catch
          {
          }
          Application.DoEvents( );
        }    // end foreach rootdirectory name
     }       // end FillSourceDirectoryTree

     /// <summary>
     /// Gets all the subdirectories below the
     /// passed in directory node.
```

Example 18-1. FileCopier source code (continued)

```
/// Adds to the directory tree.
/// The parameters passed in are the parent node
/// for this subdirectory,
/// the full path name of this subdirectory,
/// and a Boolean to indicate
/// whether or not to get the files in the subdirectory.
/// </summary>
private void GetSubDirectoryNodes(
    TreeNode parentNode, string fullName, bool getFileNames, int level )
{
    DirectoryInfo dir = new DirectoryInfo( fullName );
    DirectoryInfo[] dirSubs = dir.GetDirectories();

    //  Add a child node for each subdirectory.
    foreach ( DirectoryInfo dirSub in dirSubs )
    {
        // do not show hidden folders
        if ( ( dirSub.Attributes & FileAttributes.Hidden )
           != 0 )
        {
            continue;
        }

        /// <summary>
        ///     Each directory contains the full path.
        ///     We need to split it on the backslashes,
        ///     and only use
        ///     the last node in the tree.
        ///     Need to double the backslash since it
        ///     is normally
        ///     an escape character
        /// </summary>
        TreeNode subNode = new TreeNode( dirSub.Name );
        parentNode.Nodes.Add( subNode );

        //  Call GetSubDirectoryNodes recursively.
        if ( level < MaxLevel )
        {
            GetSubDirectoryNodes(
                subNode, dirSub.FullName, getFileNames, level + 1 );
        }
    }          // end foreach DirectoryInfo in dirSubs

    if ( getFileNames )
    {
        //  Get any files for this node.
        FileInfo[] files = dir.GetFiles();

        // After placing the nodes,
        // now place the files in that subdirectory.
        foreach ( FileInfo file in files )
        {
```

Example 18-1. FileCopier source code (continued)

```
            TreeNode fileNode = new TreeNode( file.Name );
            parentNode.Nodes.Add( fileNode );
      }      // end foreach FileInfo in files
   }         // end if get FileNames
}            // end GetSubDirectoryNodes method

/// <summary>
///    Create an ordered list of all
///    the selected files, copy to the
///    target directory
/// </summary>
private void btnCopy_Click( object sender,
    System.EventArgs e )
{
   // get the list
   List<FileInfo> fileList = GetFileList( );

   // copy the files
   foreach ( FileInfo file in fileList )
   {
      try
      {
         // update the label to show progress
         lblStatus.Text = "Copying " + txtTargetDir.Text +
             "\\" + file.Name + "...";
         Application.DoEvents( );

         // copy the file to its destination location
         file.CopyTo( txtTargetDir.Text + "\\" +
             file.Name, chkOverwrite.Checked );
      }

      catch ( Exception ex )
      {
         // you may want to do more than
         // just show the message
         MessageBox.Show( ex.Message );
      }
   }         // end foreach FileInfo in fileList
   lblStatus.Text = "Done.";
}

/// <summary>
///    Tell the root of each tree to uncheck
///    all the nodes below
/// </summary>
private void btnClear_Click( object sender, System.EventArgs e )
{
   // get the top most node for each drive
   // and tell it to clear recursively
   foreach ( TreeNode node in tvwSource.Nodes )
   {
```

Example 18-1. FileCopier source code (continued)

```
            SetCheck( node, false );
        }
    }

    /// <summary>
    ///     on cancel,  exit
    /// </summary>
    private void btnCancel_Click( object sender, EventArgs e )
    {
        Application.Exit( );
    }

    /// <summary>
    ///     Given a node and an array list
    ///     fill the list with the names of
    ///     all the checked files
    /// </summary>
    // Fill the List with the full paths of
    // all the files checked
    private void GetCheckedFiles( TreeNode node,
        List<string> fileNames )
    {
        // if this is a leaf...
        if ( node.Nodes.Count == 0 )
        {
            // if the node was checked...
            if ( node.Checked )
            {
                // get the full path and add it to the List
                string fullPath = GetParentString( node );
                fileNames.Add( fullPath );
            }
        }
        else  // if this node is not a leaf
        {
            // if this node is not a leaf
            foreach ( TreeNode n in node.Nodes )
            {
                GetCheckedFiles( n, fileNames );
            }
        }
    }

    /// <summary>
    ///     Given a node, return the
    ///     full path name
    /// </summary>
    private string GetParentString( TreeNode node )
    {
        // if this is the root node (c:\) return the text
        if ( node.Parent == null )
        {
```

Example 18-1. FileCopier source code (continued)

```
                    return node.Text;
            }
            else
            {
                // recurse up and get the path then
                // add this node and a slash
                // if this node is the leaf, don't add the slash
                return GetParentString( node.Parent ) + node.Text +
                    ( node.Nodes.Count == 0 ? "" : "\\" );
            } // end else
    }       // end GetParentString method


    /// <summary>
    ///     shared by delete and copy
    ///     creates an ordered list of all
    ///     the selected files
    /// </summary>
    private List<FileInfo> GetFileList()
    {
        // create an unsorted array list of the full file names
        List<string> fileNames = new List<string>();


        // fill the fileNames List with the
        // full path of each file to copy
        foreach ( TreeNode theNode in tvwSource.Nodes )
        {
            GetCheckedFiles( theNode, fileNames );
        }

        // Create a list to hold the FileInfo objects
        List<FileInfo> fileList = new List<FileInfo>();

        // for each of the file names we have in our unsorted list
        // if the name corresponds to a file (and not a directory)
        // add it to the file list
        foreach ( string fileName in fileNames )
        {
            // create a file with the name
            FileInfo file = new FileInfo( fileName );

            // see if it exists on the disk
            // this fails if it was a directory
            if ( file.Exists )
            {
                // both the key and the value are the file
                // would it be easier to have an empty value?
                fileList.Add( file );
            } // end if file exists
        }       // end foreach filename in filenames

        // Create an instance of the IComparer interface
        IComparer<FileInfo> comparer = (IComparer<FileInfo>)new FileComparer();
```

Example 18-1. FileCopier source code (continued)

```
            // pass the comparer to the sort method so that the list
            // is sorted by the compare method of comparer.
            fileList.Sort( comparer );
            return fileList;
        }

        /// <summary>
        ///     check that the user does want to delete
        ///     Make a list and delete each in turn
        /// </summary>
        private void btnDelete_Click( object sender, System.EventArgs e )
        {
            // ask them if they are sure
            System.Windows.Forms.DialogResult result =
                MessageBox.Show(
                "Are you quite sure?",              // msg
                "Delete Files",                     // caption
                MessageBoxButtons.OKCancel,         // buttons
                MessageBoxIcon.Exclamation,         // icons
                MessageBoxDefaultButton.Button2 );  // default button

            // if they are sure...
            if ( result == System.Windows.Forms.DialogResult.OK )
            {
                // iterate through the list and delete them.
                // get the list of selected files
                List<FileInfo> fileNames = GetFileList();

                foreach ( FileInfo file in fileNames )
                {
                    try
                    {
                        // update the label to show progress
                        lblStatus.Text = "Deleting " +
                            txtTargetDir.Text + "\\" +
                            file.Name + "...";
                        Application.DoEvents();

                        // Danger Will Robinson!
                        file.Delete();
                    }
                    catch ( Exception ex )
                    {
                        // you may want to do more than
                        // just show the message
                        MessageBox.Show( ex.Message );
                    } // end catch
                }     // end foreach FileInfo in filenames

                lblStatus.Text = "Done.";
                Application.DoEvents();
            }     // end if result = OK
        }         // end btnDelete_Click handler
```

Example 18-1. FileCopier source code (continued)

```
/// <summary>
///     Get the full path of the chosen directory
///     copy it to txtTargetDir
/// </summary>
private void tvwTargetDir_AfterSelect(
    object sender,
    System.Windows.Forms.TreeViewEventArgs e )
{
   // get the full path for the selected directory
   string theFullPath = GetParentString( e.Node );

   // if it is not a leaf, it will end with a back slash
   // remove the backslash
   if ( theFullPath.EndsWith( "\\" ) )
   {
      theFullPath =
          theFullPath.Substring( 0, theFullPath.Length - 1 );
   }
   // insert the path in the text box
   txtTargetDir.Text = theFullPath;
}

/// <summary>
///     Mark each node below the current
///     one with the current value of checked
/// </summary>
private void tvwSource_AfterCheck( object sender,
    System.Windows.Forms.TreeViewEventArgs e )
{
   // Call a recursible method.
   // e.node is the node which was checked by the user.
   // The state of the check mark is already
   // changed by the time you get here.
   // Therefore, we want to pass along
   // the state of e.node.Checked.
   SetCheck( e.Node, e.Node.Checked );
}

/// <summary>
///     recursively set or clear check marks
/// </summary>
private void SetCheck( TreeNode node, bool check )
{
   // find all the child nodes from this node
   foreach ( TreeNode n in node.Nodes )
   {
      n.Checked = check;    // check the node

      // if this is a node in the tree, recurse
      if ( n.Nodes.Count != 0 )
      {
         SetCheck( n, check );
```

Example 18-1. FileCopier source code (continued)

```
            }       // end if Nodes.Count not zero
        }           // end foreach TreeNode in Nodes
    }               // end SetCheck method

    /// <summary>
    /// Common event handler for beforeExpand event
    /// </summary>
    /// <param name="sender"></param>
    /// <param name="e"></param>
    private void tvwExpand( object sender, TreeViewCancelEventArgs e )
    {
        TreeView tvw = (TreeView)sender;
        bool getFiles = tvw == tvwSource;
        TreeNode currentNode = e.Node;
        string fullName = currentNode.FullPath;
        currentNode.Nodes.Clear( );
        GetSubDirectoryNodes( currentNode, fullName, getFiles, 1 );
    }       // end tvwExpand handler
}           // end frmFileCopier class
}           // end FileCopier namespace
```

XML Documentation Comments

C# supports a new *documentation comment* style, with three slash marks (///). You can see these comments sprinkled throughout Example 18-1. The Visual Studio editor recognizes these comments and helps format them properly.

> The C# compiler processes these comments into an XML file

You can generate the documentation in Visual Studio by clicking the FileCopier project icon in the Solution Explorer window, selecting View Property Pages on the Visual Studio menu, and then clicking Properties. Click the Build tab and then click the XML Documenation file and provide a path for where the XML should be placed, as shown in Figure 18-10.

Click the XML Documentation File checkbox and type in a name for the XML file you want to produce, such as Filecopier.XML. Rebuild the application.

 In at least some versions of Visual C# 2005 Express, you accomplish this by clicking the Properties button in the Solution Explorer window. Please check the documentation for the version of Visual Studio 2005 you are using.

An excerpt of the file that's produced for the FileCopier application of the previous section is shown in Example 18-2.

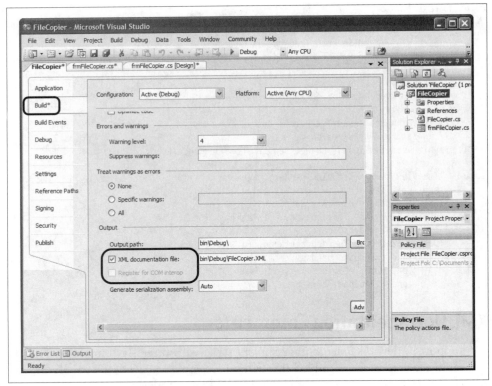

Figure 18-10. Setting the XML documentation path

Example 18-2. The XML output (excerpt) for file copy

```xml
<?xml version="1.0"?>
<doc>
    <assembly>
        <name>FileCopier</name>
    </assembly>
    <members>
        <member name="T:FileCopier.frmFileCopier">
            <summary>
            Form demonstrating Windows Forms implementation
            </summary>
        </member>
        <member name="M:FileCopier.frmFileCopier.FillDirectoryTree(System.Windows.Forms.
TreeView,System.Boolean)">
            <summary>
            Factored out method for both directory trees
            </summary>
            <param name="tvw">which treeview called this handler</param>
            <param name="isSource">get the files if true</param>
        </member>
```

The file is quite long, and although it can be read by humans, it isn't especially useful in that format. You could, however, write an XSLT file to translate the XML into HTML, or you could read the XML document into a database of documentation. You can also drag the file from File Explorer into Windows Explorer, which provides a nice interface for reading the XML, as shown in Figure 18-11.

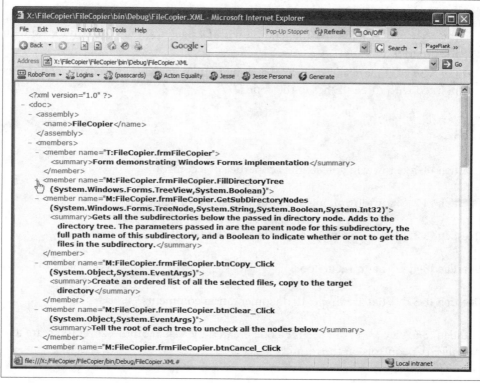

Figure 18-11. Reviewing the XML documentation in Internet Explorer

Internet Explorer provides a number of handy features for reading XML files, including the ability to expand and collapse nodes (see the + and – signs to the left of each node).

Summary

- C# and Visual Studio 2005 are designed to create Windows and web applications as well as web services.

- Visual Studio provides visual design tools that enable you to drag-and-drop controls onto a form.

- The Properties window allows you to change the properties of a control without having to edit the code by hand.
- The events window helps you to create event handlers for all the possible events for your control. Simply double-click the event, and Visual Studio 2005 will create a skeleton event handler, and then take you to the appropriate point in the code, so you can enter your logic.
- The partial keyword in the class definition indicates that the code to initialize the controls is in another file, ending with *Designer.cs*, that you can locate with the Solution Explorer.
- C# can automatically generate documentation in XML based on comments marked with three slashes in the code (*///*).

Quiz

Question 18-1. How can you set the properties of a control?

Question 18-2. How do you make a button respond to being clicked?

Question 18-3. Name two ways to create an event handler.

Question 18-4. What is recursion?

Question 18-5. What are the XML documentation comments?

Question 18-6. How do you see the code created by Visual Studio 2005 to create and initialize the controls on the form?

Exercises

Exercise 18-1. Create a Windows application that displays the word "Hello" in a label, and has a button that changes the display to "Goodbye."

Exercise 18-2. Create a Windows application that presents an order form that looks like Figure 18-12.

Figure 18-12. Exercise 2 order form

This figure represents an order form that that lets the user enter information through various controls such as buttons, checkboxes, radio buttons, DateTimePicker, and so forth. You don't need to write the back-end for the ordering system, but you can do the following:

- Simulate saving to the shopping cart with a message, and reset the form when the "Add to Shopping Cart" button is clicked.

- Set the minimum delivery date to be two days from now, and let the user select later dates.

Exercise 18-3. Modify the first exercise by dragging a timer (found in the Components section of the Toolbox) onto the form and having the timer change the message from "Hello" to "Goodbye" and back once per second. Change the button to turn this behavior on and off. Use the Microsoft Help files to figure out how to use the timer to accomplish this exercise.

CHAPTER 19

Programming ASP.NET Applications

In the previous chapter, you saw how to use C# to create Windows applications; in this chapter, you'll see how to use C# to create applications for the Web.

The .NET technology for building web applications (and dynamic web sites) is ASP. NET 2.0, which provides a rich collection of types for building web applications in its System.Web and System.Web.UI namespaces. There is a great deal to learn about ASP.NET, but much of it is language-independent. ASP.NET offers a rich suite of controls and related tools, including tools to validate data, display dates, present advertisements, interact with users, and so forth. Most of these require no coding whatsoever.

 For more on the details of ASP.NET, please see *Programming ASP. NET*, Third Edition, by Jesse Liberty and Dan Hurwitz (O'Reilly, 2005).

The role of the C# programmer in ASP.NET development is to write the event handlers that respond to user interaction. Many of the event handlers will either add data to a database or retrieve data and make it available to the controls.

With Web Forms, the application is deployed to a web server, and users interact with the application through a standard browser.

Understanding Web Forms

Web Forms bring Rapid Application Development (RAD) techniques (such as those used in Windows Forms) to the development of web applications. As with Windows Forms, you drag-and-drop controls onto a form and write the supporting code either inline or in *code-behind* pages.

ASP.NET 2.0 Web Forms are the successor to the enormously success-ful ASP.NET 1.x Web Forms, which in turn were the successor to ASP pages.

The goal of ASP.NET 2.0 was to reduce the amount of coding by 70 percent compared to ASP 1.x. This means that web programming is increasingly *declarative* rather than *programmatic*—that is, you declare controls on your Web Form rather than writing (and rewriting) boiler-plate code.

You still have the option of writing code (you can always write code), but for the vast majority of web programming, you'll write a lot less code with ASP.NET 2.0 than you did with 1.x.

Web Forms implement a programming model in which web pages are dynamically generated on a web server for delivery to a browser over the Internet. With Web Forms, you create an ASPX page with more or less static content consisting of HTML and Web Controls, and you write C# code to add additional dynamic content. The C# code *runs on the server*, and the data produced is integrated with the declared objects on your page to create an HTML page that is sent to the browser.

There are three critical points to pick up from the previous paragraph, and which you should keep in mind for this entire chapter:

- Web pages can have both HTML and Web Controls (described later).
- All processing is done on the server (you can have client-side processing with scripting languages, but that isn't part of ASP.NET).
- If you use ASP.NET Web Controls, what the browser sees is just HTML (there is an exception to this; with those browsers that Microsoft defines as "uplevel," some script may be sent as well).

In short, Web Forms are designed to be viewed through any browser, with the server generating the correct browser-compliant HTML. Just as with Windows Forms, you can create Web Forms in Notepad (or another editor of your choice) rather than in Visual Studio, but it makes no sense to do so and we will continue to use Visual Studio 2005 to enhance productivity and reduce errors.

Web Forms divide the user interface into two parts: the visual part or user interface (UI), and the logic that lies behind it. This is very similar to developing Windows Forms, as shown in Chapter 18. This is called *code separation*; all examples in this book use code separation, though it is possible to write the C# code in the same file with the user interface.

In Version 2.0 of ASP.NET, Visual Studio takes advantage of partial classes, allowing the code-separation page to be far simpler than it was in 1.x. Because the code-separation and declarative pages are part of the same class, there is no longer a need to have protected variables to reference the controls of the page, and the designer can hide its initialization code in a separate file.

The UI page is stored in a file with the extension *.aspx*. When you run the form, the server generates HTML sent to the client browser. This code uses the rich Web Forms types found in the System.Web and System.Web.UI namespaces of the .NET Framework Class Library (FCL).

With Visual Studio, Web Forms programming couldn't be simpler: open a form, drag some controls onto it, and write the code to handle events. Presto! You've written a web application.

On the other hand, even with Visual Studio, writing a robust and complete web application can be a daunting task; Web Forms offer a very rich UI and the number and complexity of Web Controls have greatly multiplied in recent years. User expectations about the look and feel of web applications have risen accordingly.

In addition, web applications are inherently distributed. Typically, the client will not be in the same building as the server. For most web applications, you must take network latency, bandwidth, and network server performance into account when creating the UI; a round trip from client to host might take a few seconds.

Web Form Events

Web Forms are event-driven. An *event* represents the idea that "something happened." An event is generated (or *raised*) when the user clicks a button, or selects from a ListBox, or otherwise interacts with the UI. Events can also be generated by the system starting or finishing work. For example, open a file for reading, and the system raises an event when the file has been read into memory.

The method that responds to the event is called the *event handler*. Event handlers are written in C# and are associated with controls in the HTML page through control attributes.

By convention, ASP.NET event handlers return void and take two parameters. The first parameter represents the object raising the event. The second, called the *event argument*, contains information specific to the event, if any. For most events, the event argument is of type EventArgs, which has no members and serves as a placeholder and as the base class for more specialized objects that provide properties needed by the event handler.

In web applications, most events are handled on the server and, therefore, require a round trip. ASP.NET supports only a limited set of events, such as button clicks and text changes. These are events that the user might expect to cause a significant change, as opposed to Windows events (such as mouse-over) that might happen many times during a single user-driven task.

Postback Versus Non-Postback Events

Postback events are those that cause the form to be sent (or posted) to the server and then to be returned to the browser (typically with updated data) The user's experience is that the page is updated after a brief delay.

A button click, for example, causes the page to be sent to the browser, the event handlers are run, and then the *same page* is sent back to the browser.

To avoid this round trip to the server happening too frequently, many events such as changing the text in a textbox or clicking a checkbox are *non-postback* events. When these events fire, the form is not posted back, but the event is saved by the control, and handled the next time the page is posted back.

> You can force non-postback controls to act as if they are postback controls by setting their AutoPostBack property to true.

State

The web does not maintain state. By design, it is a stateless environment. That means that the server would normally have no idea that a second post from a given user has any association with previous posts by that same user. That is fine if all you have are one or two pages that are information only, with no interaction, but it is obviously limiting if you want to create an interactive application.

ASP.NET solves this problem by maintaining three types of state: view state, session state, and application state:

View state

> Maintains the value of controls (what you've filled into text boxes, which choices you've made in lists) when you post a page to the server. There was a time you had to write code to do this, but it is now done for you in an efficient and reliable manner.

Session state

> Creates an artificial "connection" with the application, simulating the idea of an ongoing session for an individual user within a single application. This is so natural, you hardly notice it. You go to a site, and as you interact with it, remembers your input and responds accordingly, just like working with a desktop

application. Sessions typically end by "timing out" after about 20 minutes of inactivity; but in most cases, this is invisible to the user.

Application state

Preserves values across users within a given web application. Application state is beyond the scope of this chapter.

Creating a Web Form

To create the simple Web Form that will be used in the next example, start up Visual Studio .NET and select File → New Web Site. In the New Web Site menu, choose C# as your language, and choose ASP.NET Web Site as the template to use. Finally, locate your web site somewhere on your disk (at the bottom of the dialog), as shown in Figure 19-1.

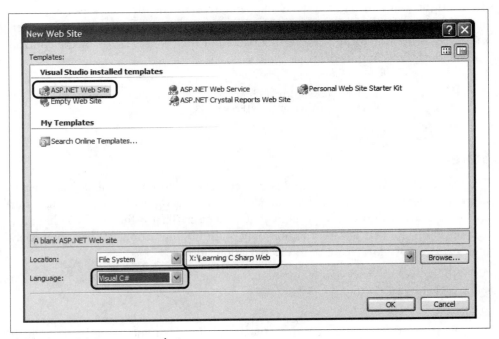

Figure 19-1. Creating a new web site

Visual Studio creates a folder named Learning C Sharp Web in the directory you've indicated, and within that directory, it creates your *Default.aspx* page (for the User interface), *Default.aspx.cs* (for your code), and a Data directory (currently empty, but often used to hold data files).

Code-Behind Files

Code-behind is the default coding model used by Visual Studio 2005. When a new web site is created, Visual Studio automatically creates two files: the content file, with a default name, such as *Default.aspx*, and a code-behind file with a matching name, such as *Default.aspx.cs* (assuming you are using C# as your programming language). If you change the name of the content file (highly recommended), the code-behind file will automatically assume the new name.

> *ASP.NET 1.1 programmers take note*: the code-behind model for ASP. NET has changed. In Versions 1.x, the code-behind file defined a class that derived from Page. This code-behind class contained instance variables for all the controls on the page, with explicit event binding using delegates and the *.aspx* page derived from the code-behind class.
>
> In Version 2.0, ASP.NET generates a single class from the combined *.aspx* page and partial class definitions in the code-behind file.
>
> ASP.NET can infer the control instances and derive event bindings from the markup during compilation; thus, the new code-behind file includes only the application code you need, such as event handlers, and doesn't need to include instance variables or explicit event binding. The new code-behind files are simpler, easier to maintain, and always in sync with the *.aspx* page.

Let's take a closer look at the *.aspx* and code-behind files that Visual Studio creates. Start by renaming *Default.aspx* to *HelloWeb.aspx*. To do this, close *Default.aspx*, and then right-click its name in the Solution Explorer. Choose Rename and enter the name HelloWeb.aspx. That renames the file, but not the class. To rename the class, right-click the *.aspx* page and choose View Code in the code page, then rename the class from _Default to HelloWeb. You'll see a small line next to the name, as shown in Figure 19-2.

```
public partial class HelloWeb : System.Web.UI.Page
{
    protected void Page_Load(object sender, EventArgs e)
    {

    }
}
```

Figure 19-2. Changing the class name

Click it and you'll open the smart tag that allows you to rename the class. Click Rename "_default" to "HelloWeb," and Visual Studio ensures that every occurrence of _Default is replaced with its new name, as shown in Figure 19-3.

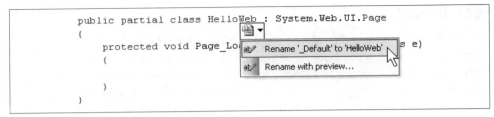

```
public partial class HelloWeb : System.Web.UI.Page
{
    protected void Page_Lo                              s e)
    {

    }
}
```

Rename '_Default' to 'HelloWeb'

Rename with preview...

Figure 19-3. Using Visual Studio to rename the class

You will be warned that references in "markup" will not be changed. This means that you must manually update the name of the class in the *.aspx* file:

```
<%@ Page Language="C#" AutoEventWireup="true"
CodeFile="HelloWeb.aspx.cs" Inherits="HelloWeb" %>
```

Within the HTML view of *HelloWeb.aspx*, you see an HTML form tag within the body of the page, like this:

```
<form id="Form1" runat="server">
```

This tag specifies the form to use for your page. Web Forms assumes that you need at least one form to manage the user interaction, and creates one when you open a project. The attribute runat="server" within the form tag is the key to the server-side magic. Any tag that includes this attribute is considered a *server-side control* to be executed by the ASP.NET framework on the server. Visual Studio has placed div tags in the form to facilitate placing your controls and text.

Look for the title tag and change it to "Hello Web"—it makes the browser window look nicer, as you'll see in just a moment.

Having created an empty Web Form, the first thing you might want to do is add some text to the page. By switching to HTML view, you can add script and HTML directly to the file just as you could with classic ASP. Adding the following line to the body segment of the HTML page (between the opening and closing div tags) will cause it to display a greeting and the current local time:

```
Hello World! It is now <% = DateTime.Now.ToString() %>
```

The <% and %> marks surround snippets of C# code. The = sign immediately following the opening tag causes ASP.NET to display the value, just like a call to Response. Write( )—that is, it writes directly to the HTML page. You could just as easily write the line as:

```
Hello World! It is now
<% Response.Write(DateTime.Now.ToString()); %>
```

Run the page by pressing F5 (or save it and navigate to it in your browser). You should see the string printed to the browser, as in Figure 19-4.

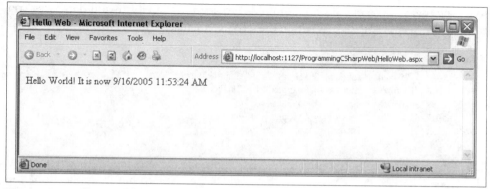

Figure 19-4. Hello World from ASP.NET 2.0

Enabling Debugging

When you press F5, you begin the debugger. It's likely that Visual Studio will notice that you don't have a *Web.config* file for this application (which is required for debugging), and the Debugging Not Enabled dialog box will appear, as shown in Figure 19-5.

The default in this dialog box is to modify (and if needed, create) the *Web.config* file. Go ahead, and press OK to enable debugging for your application.

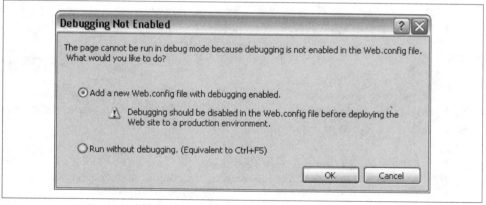

Figure 19-5. You'll see this if you start debugging before you have a Web.config file

Adding Controls

You can add Server Controls to a Web Form in three ways: by writing HTML into the HTML page, by dragging controls from the toolbox to the Design page, or by programmatically adding them at runtime. For example, suppose you want to use buttons to let the user choose one of three shippers provided in the Northwind database. You can write the following HTML within the <div> elements, in the HTML window:

```
<div>
  <asp:RadioButton GroupName="Shipper" id="Speedy"
    text = "Speedy Express" Checked="True" runat="server" />
  <asp:RadioButton GroupName="Shipper" id="United"
    text = "United Package" runat="server"/>
  <asp:RadioButton GroupName="Shipper" id="Federal"
    text = "Federal Shipping" runat="server" />
</div>
```

The asp tags declare server-side ASP.NET controls that are replaced with normal HTML when the server processes the page. When you run the application, the browser displays three radio buttons in a button group; pressing one deselects the others.

You can create the same effect more easily by dragging three buttons from the Visual Studio toolbox onto the Form, or, to make life even easier, follow these steps:

1. Switch to Design view.
2. Drag a RadioButtonList control from the toolbox onto the form.
3. Click on the control's the smart tag to open it.
4. Choose Edit Items to open theListItem Collection Editor dialog box.
5. Click Add three times to add three radio buttons.

 You could instead click on Choose a Data Source and bind to a collection, perhaps one you've obtained from a database.

Each radio button is given the default name ListItem, but you may edit its text and value in the ListItem properties, where you can also decide which of the radio buttons is selected, as shown in Figure 19-6.

 You can add controls to a page in one of two modes. The default mode is FlowLayout. With FlowLayout, the controls are added to the form from top to bottom, as in a Microsoft Word document. The alternative is GridLayout, in which the controls are arranged in the browser using absolute positioning (x- and y-coordinates).

To change from Grid to Layout or back, change the pageLayout property of the document in Visual Studio .NET. You can improve the look of your radio button list by changing properties in the Properties window, including the font, colors, number of columns, repeat direction (vertical is the default), and so forth.

Click OK to close the editor and then switch back and forth between the Design and Source tabs to see the effect of your changes, as shown in Figure 19-7.

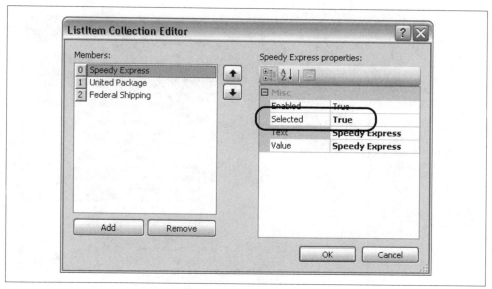

Figure 19-6. Editing a collection of list items

I've numbered a few areas of interest in Figure 19-7. Number 1 shows the RadioButtonList control in the toolbox. Number 2 shows the smart tag on the RadioButtonList control on the form. Number 3 shows that you are looking at the properties of the RadioButtonList control, which has been named RadioButtonList1 for you by Visual Studio 2005 (but of course, you are free to change that in the Properties window), and Number 4 shows that the current RepeatDirection property is set to Vertical (setting it to horizontal will lay out the radio buttons horizontally).

Server Controls

Web Forms offer two types of Server Controls. The first is server-side HTML controls. These are HTML controls that you tag with the attribute runat=Server. Although these work, we won't spend time on them in this chapter.

Instead, we will focus on ASP.NET Server Controls* that Microsoft designed to augment and replace the standard HTML controls. Server Controls provide a more consistent object model and more consistently named attributes. For example, with traditional and server-side HTML controls, input is not handled consistently:

```
<input type="radio">
<input type="checkbox">
<input type="button">
<input type="text">
<textarea>
```

---

* Some programmers also call these "ASP Controls" or "Web Controls."

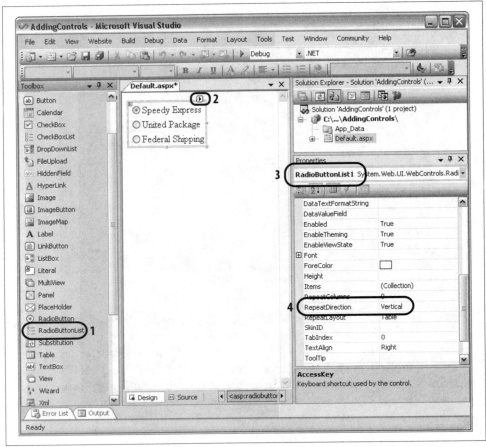

Figure 19-7. Switching between design and source tabs after adding a radio group

Each input type behaves differently and takes different attributes, and text is handled with different types of controls depending on whether you want a single line or multi-line input. The Server Controls try to use attributes consistently. The Server Controls that correspond to the preceding HTML Server Controls are as follows:

```
<asp:RadioButton>
<asp:CheckBox>
<asp:Button>
<asp:TextBox rows="1">
<asp:TextBox rows="5">
```

When you use the Server Controls, ASP.NET translates them into ordinary HTML before sending the page back to the browser. What is seen on the browser is always industry-standard HTML and will run on virtually any browser by any manufacturer.

Data Binding

Various technologies have offered programmers the opportunity to bind controls to data so that as the data was modified, the controls responded automatically. Generally speaking, they made for great demos, but were of limited use to real programmers writing commercial applications. They tended to constrain the developer with severe limitations in how the control looked and performed. It came down to this: "If you want to do what we expect, it is wicked easy, but if you want to do anything else, may the Gods be kind."

The ASP.NET designers set out to provide a suite of robust data-bound controls, which simplify display and modification of data, sacrificing neither performance nor control over the UI. In Version 2.0, they have expanded the list of bindable controls and provided even more out-of-the-box functionality.

In the previous section, you hard-coded radio buttons onto a form, one for each of three shippers in the Northwind database. That can't be the best way to do it; if you change the shippers in the database, you have to go back and rewire the controls. This section shows you how to create these controls dynamically, binding them to data from the database.

Create a new web site called DisplayShippers and drag a RadioButtonList onto the form. Click on the smart tag, and then click on Choose Data Source.... The Choose Data Source dialog opens, as shown in Figure 19-8.

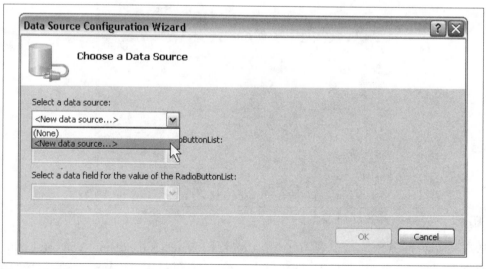

Figure 19-8. Data Source Configuration Wizard

Drop down the Select a data source menu and choose <New Data Source>. You are prompted to choose a data source from the datatypes on your machine. Select

Database, (you can specify a name, or use the default name of SqlDataSource1). Click OK and the Configure Data Source dialog box opens.

Choose New Connection to configure a new data source, and the Add Connection dialog box opens, offering you an opportunity to pick a server and to use either Windows or database authorization. Fill in the required information, and choose Northwind as your database name. Be sure to test the connection, as shown in Figure 19-9.

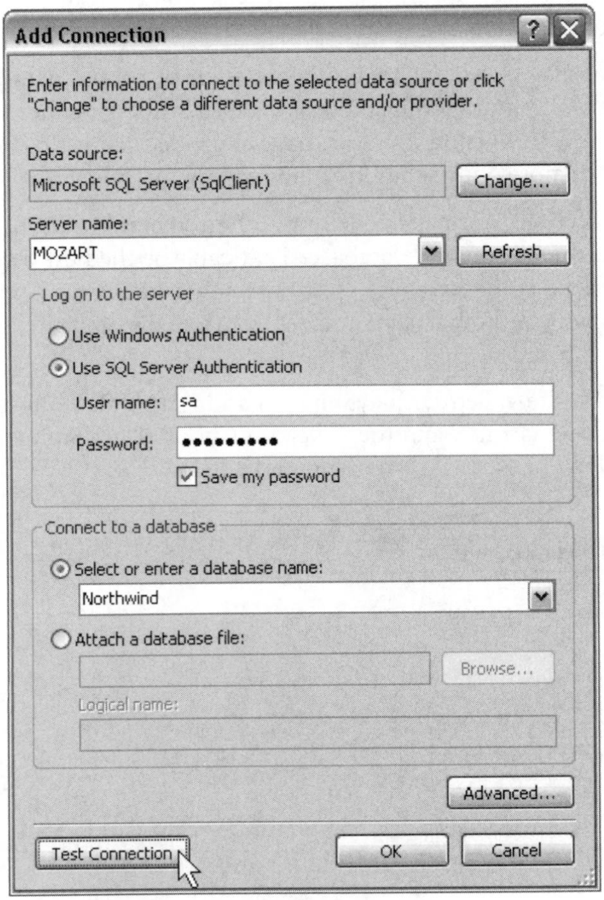

Figure 19-9. Adding a connection

When you click OK, you'll return to the Configure Data Source dialog. You can examine the connection string if you'd like or just press Next to go on to the next step, where you are asked if you'd like to save this connection in the application configuration file. Click Yes and give it a name without spaces, such as NorthwindConnectionString.

The next step is to specify either a stored procedure or SQL statement to use for your query, or to build your query by picking the table or view and then the columns you want, as shown in Figure 19-10.

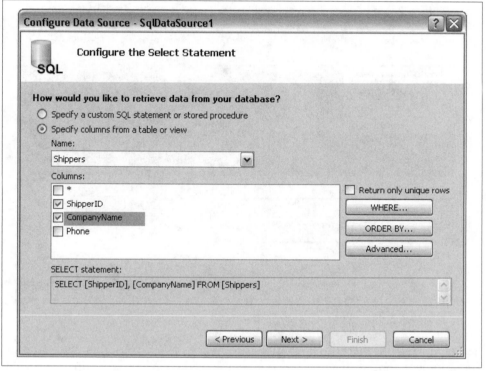

Figure 19-10. Selecting fields in the shippers table

When you click Next, you are brought to a dialog in which you can test the results of your query, which you can examine as shown circled in Figure 19-11.

When you click Finish, the data source is created. You are returned to the Data Source Configuration Wizard, where you will make three choices:

1. The data source to use (in this case, you have only one)
2. The data field to display in the radio button list
3. The data field to use for the value

These choices are shown in Figure 19-12.

The distinction between the display field and the data field allows you to display the company name in the radio button list, but retrieve the actual shipper ID when processing the user's request. Run the application (accept the offered Web.config file as previously) and note that the radio button list is dynamically populated with the three values from the database table.

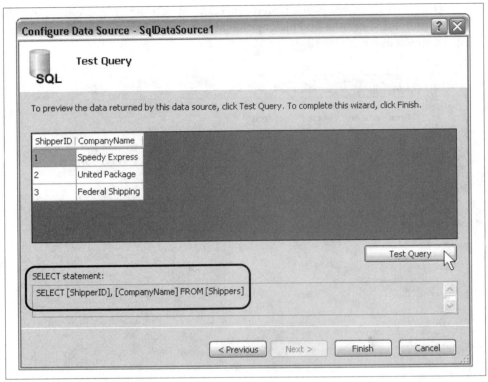

Figure 19-11. Testing the query

Before moving on, there are a few things to notice. When you press F5 to run this application, it appears in a web browser, and the radio buttons come up as expected. Choose View → Source and you'll see that what is being sent to the browser is simple HTML, as shown in Figure 19-13.

Notice that the HTML has no RadioButtonList; it has a table, with cells, within which are standard HTML *input* objects and labels. ASP.NET has translated the developer controls to HTML understandable by any browser.

Adding Controls and Events

By adding just a few more controls, you can create a complete form with which users can interact. You will do this by adding a more appropriate greeting ("Welcome to Northwind"), a text box to accept the name of the user, two new buttons (Order and Cancel), and text that provides feedback to the user. Figure 19-14 shows the form.

This form won't win any awards for design, but its use will illustrate a number of key points about Web Forms. Example 19-1 is the complete HTML for the *.aspx* file.

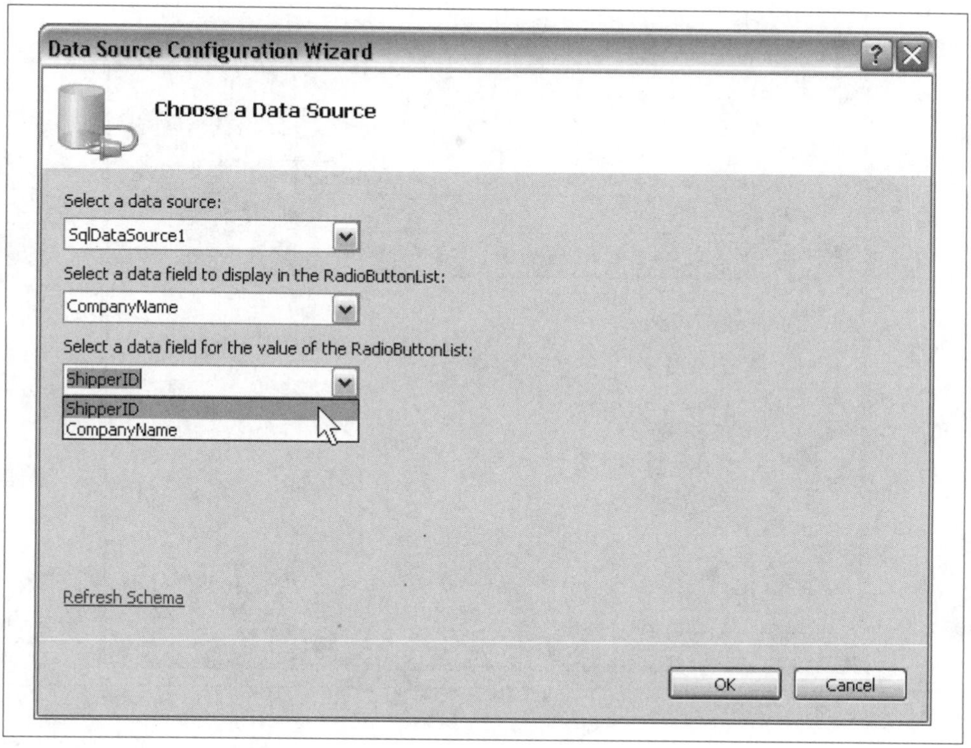

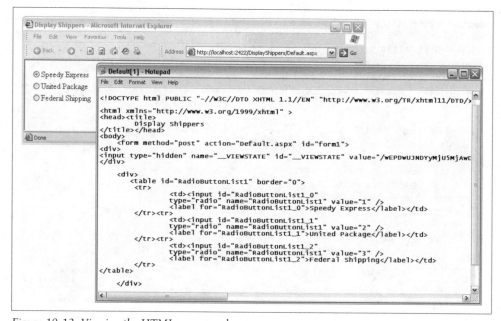

Figure 19-12. Choosing the data fields

Figure 19-13. Viewing the HTML source code

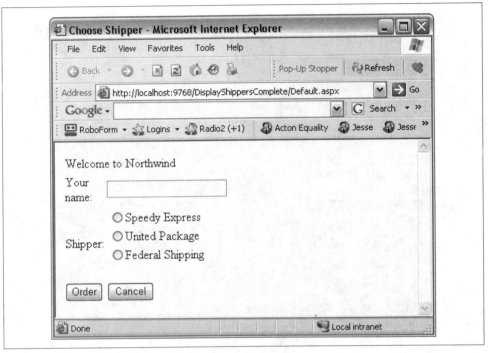

Figure 19-14. The shipper form

Example 19-1. Completed shipper form Default.aspx

```
<%@ Page AutoEventWireup="true" CodeFile="Default.aspx.cs"
Inherits="_Default" Language="C#" %>

<!DOCTYPE html PUBLIC "-//W3C//DTD XHTML 1.1//EN"
"http://www.w3.org/TR/xhtml11/DTD/xhtml11.dtd">
<html xmlns="http://www.w3.org/1999/xhtml">
<head id="Head1" runat="server">  <title>Choose Shipper</title>
</head>
<body>
  <form id="form1" runat="server">
    <table style="width: 166px; height: 33px">
      <tr>
        <td colspan="2" style="height: 20px">
          Welcome to Northwind
        </td>
      </tr>
      <tr>
        <td>Your name:</td>
        <td><asp:TextBox ID="txtName" runat="server" /></td>
      </tr>
      <tr>
        <td>Shipper:</td>
        <td>
          <asp:RadioButtonList ID="RadioButtonList1" runat="server"
```

Example 19-1. Completed shipper form Default.aspx (continued)

```
            DataSourceID="SqlDataSource1"
            DataTextField="CompanyName" DataValueField="ShipperID">
        </asp:RadioButtonList>

        <asp:SqlDataSource ID="SqlDataSource1" runat="server"
        ConnectionString="<%$ ConnectionStrings:NorthwindConnectionString %>"
        SelectCommand="SELECT [ShipperID], [CompanyName]FROM [Shippers]" />
        <br />
      </td>
    </tr>
    <tr>
      <td><asp:Button ID="btnOrder" runat="server" Text="Order" /></td>
      <td><asp:Button ID="btnCancel" runat="server" Text="Cancel" /></td>
    </tr>
    <tr>
      <td colspan="2"><asp:Label ID="lblMsg" runat="server" /></td>
    </tr>
  </table>
 </form>
</body>
</html>
```

When the user clicks the Order button, you'll check that the user has filled in his name, and you'll also provide feedback on which shipper was chosen. Remember, at design time, you can't know the name of the shipper (this is obtained from the database), so you'll have to ask the ListBox for the chosen name (and ID).

To accomplish all of this, switch to Design mode and double-click the Order button. Visual Studio will put you in the code-behind page, and will create an event handler for the button's Click event.

You add the event-handling code, setting the text of the label to pick up the text from the text box and the text and value from the RadioButtonList:

```
protected void btnOrder_Click( object sender, EventArgs e )
{
    lblMsg.Text = "Thank you " +
        txtName.Text.Trim( ) +
        ". You chose " +
        rblShippers.SelectedItem.Text.ToString( ) +
        " whose ID is " +
        rblShippers.SelectedValue.ToString( );
}
```

When you run this program, you'll notice that none of the radio buttons are selected. Binding the list did not specify which one is the default. There are a number of ways around this, but the simplest is to override the OnLoad event and set the first radio button to be selected.

Return to the *Shipper.aspx.cs* and type **protected override**. You will see a scrolling list of all the overrideable methods, properties, etc. Start typing the first letters of OnLoad, as shown in Figure 19-15.

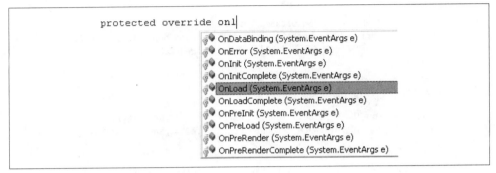

Figure 19-15. Using IntelliSense to override OnLoad

When OnLoad is highlighted, press Tab to accept the method. The stub for the over-ridden method is created, but its default body throws the NotImplementedException.

Delete the exception and replace it with this code:

```
rblShippers.SelectedIndex = 0;
```

This selects the first radio button in the RadioButtonList. The problem with this solution is subtle. If you run the application, you'll see that the first button is selected, but if you choose the second (or third) button and click OK, you'll find that the first button is reset. You can't seem to choose any but the first selection. This is because each time the page is loaded, the OnLoad event is run, and in that event handler, you are (re-)setting the selected index.

The fact is that you only want to set this button the first time the page is selected, not when it is posted back to the browser as a result of the OK button being clicked.

To solve this, wrap the setting in an if statement that tests if the page has been posted back:

```
protected override void OnLoad( EventArgs e )
{
   if ( !IsPostBack )
   {
      rblShippers.SelectedIndex = 0;
   }
}
```

When you run the page, the IsPostBack property is checked. The first time the page is posted, this value is false and the radio button is set. If you click a radio button and then click OK, the page is sent to the server for processing (where the btnOrder_Click handler is run), and then the page is posted back to the user. This time, the

IsPostBack property is true, and thus the code within the if statement isn't run, and the user's choice is preserved, as shown in Figure 19-16.

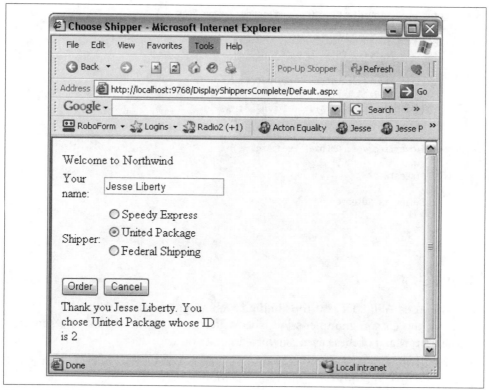

Figure 19-16. The completed shipper form

The complete code-behind form is shown in Example 19-2.

Example 19-2. Code-behind form for Shipper.aspx.cs

```
using System;
using System.Data;
using System.Configuration;
using System.Web;
using System.Web.Security;
using System.Web.UI;
using System.Web.UI.WebControls;
using System.Web.UI.WebControls.WebParts;
using System.Web.UI.HtmlControls;

public partial class _Default : System.Web.UI.Page
{

    protected void Page_Load(object sender, EventArgs e)
    {
```

Example 19-2. Code-behind form for Shipper.aspx.cs (continued)

```
    }

    protected void btnOrder_Click( object sender, EventArgs e )
    {
        lblMsg.Text = "Thank you " +
            txtName.Text.Trim( ) +
            ". You chose " +
            rblShippers.SelectedItem.Text.ToString( ) +
            " whose ID is " +
            rblShippers.SelectedValue.ToString( );
    }

    protected override void OnLoad( EventArgs e )
    {
        if ( !IsPostBack )
        {
            rblShippers.SelectedIndex = 0;
        }
    }
}
```

Summary

- .NET uses ASP.NET 2.0 for building web applications. In ASP.NET development, the C# programmer's job is to write the event handlers that respond to the user. Many of these events involve interaction with data.

- As with Windows Forms, Visual Studio 2005 provides a visual design area where you can drag and drop controls onto the form surface.

- The C# code for ASP.NET Web Forms runs on the server, not on the client. The server typically delivers only HTML to the browser.

- Web Forms separate the visual part of the program from the logic. The interface is stored in a file with an *.aspx* extension. The logic, also called the code-behind file, is stored in a *.cs* file.

- Like Windows Forms, Web Forms are event-driven and use the same system of delegates and events as Windows Forms do.

- A postback event is one that causes the form to be sent to the server where event-handling code is run, and then the page is recreated and returned to the browser.

- A non-postback event is one that does not force a postback. Non-postback events are handled when the next postback event is fired.

- View state encodes the value of each control during the round trip to the server, so that the page delivered back to the browser retains these values.

- Session state is used to maintain values across pages during a user's session.
- ASP.NET provides a set of data-bound controls that enable the controls to respond automatically as the data is changed.

Quiz

Question 19-1. What are the two most significant and commonly used namespaces for ASP.NET?

Question 19-2. Where does ASP.NET code run?

Question 19-3. How do you ensure that a radio button selection or checkbox selection will be immediately posted to the server?

Question 19-4. What is view state?

Question 19-5. If you rename your class, all references to the class name will be updated, except that you will be warned that the reference in "markup" will not be changed. What does this mean?

Question 19-6. If you click F5 to run your program, you may see a dialog box saying that debugging is not enabled. What should you do?

Question 19-7. What are the three ways to add Server Controls to your form?

Question 19-8. What property must every Server Control have?

Question 19-9. Which control is used to enable data binding from a database to controls on a Web Form?

Question 19-10. When you create an <ASP:RadioButtonList> with <ASP:RadioButton> controls in it, what is sent to the browser?

Question 19-11. How do you ensure that an action you want to take happens only the first time the page is shown, and does not happen if the user clicks a button or takes another action to post the page back to the server for processing?

Exercises

Exercise 19-1. Create a web application that displays the words "Hello" and has a button that changes the display to "Goodbye."

Exercise 19-2. Create a web application that presents an order form that lets the user enter information through various controls such as buttons, checkboxes, radio buttons, and lets the user pick a date, as shown in Figure 19-17.

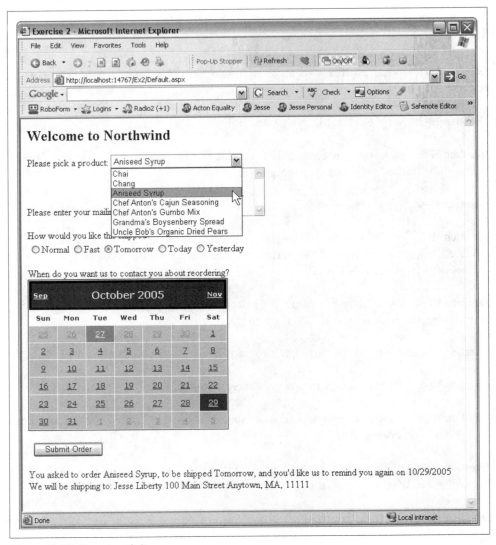

Figure 19-17. Exercise 19-2

Exercise 19-3. Modify the second exercise to populate the radio buttons and the contents of drop downs from tables in the Northwind database, as shown in Figure 19-18.

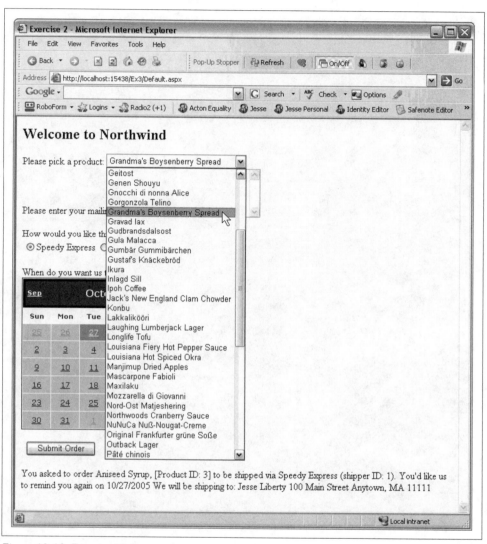

Figure 19-18. Exercise 19-3

Answers to Quizzes and Exercises

Chapter 1: C# and .NET Programming

Quiz

Solution to Question 1-1. The Common Language Runtime is the platform for .NET applications that allow you to develop your application in any .NET languages (C#, Visual Basic 2005, etc.) and have them all run seamlessly on a single platform.

Solution to Question 1-2. Console, Windows, Web, and Web Services.

Solution to Question 1-3. The Framework specifies how .NET constructs intrinsic types, classes, interfaces, etc.

Solution to Question 1-4. The Framework Class Library provides a very large suite of predefined classes that you can use in building your application.

Solution to Question 1-5. This refers to "type safety"—the ability of the compiler to ensure that the objects you create are of the expected type.

Solution to Question 1-6. Keywords are reserved for use by the language and cannot be used to identify objects or methods you create.

Solution to Question 1-7. Namespaces are used to ensure that identifiers are unique across libraries of classes.

Solution to Question 1-8. The job of the compiler is to turn your source code into MSIL.

Solution to Question 1-9. The Microsoft Intermediate Language is the native language for .NET and is compiled into an executable application by the JIT.

Solution to Question 1-10. The Just In Time compiler turns your MSIL code into an application in memory.

Exercise

Solution to Exercise 1-1. The instructions for creating this program are found in Chapter 1.

Chapter 2: Visual Studio 2005

Quiz

Solution to Question 2-1. A project results in the production of an executable or a library. Most solutions consist of a single project, but many consist of two or more.

Solution to Question 2-2. Click and drag on the title bar; use the indicators for placement.

Solution to Question 2-3. Toggles between lock in place, and hide as a tab.

Solution to Question 2-4. F5 indicates run with debugging; Ctrl-F5 indicates run without debugging.

Solution to Question 2-5. Allows you to store more than one item on the clipboard.

Solution to Question 2-6. Ctrl-Shift-V cycles through all the selections.

Solution to Question 2-7. Allows you to search for symbols (namespaces, classes, and interfaces) and their members (properties, methods, events, and variables).

Solution to Question 2-8. A tool for returning to a specific place in your code.

Solution to Question 2-9. An editing tool to help you find the right method and/or the correct parameters and much more.

Solution to Question 2-10. A complete outline of a commonly used programming structure with replaceable items to speed development.

Exercises

Solution to Exercise 2-1. Insert a bookmark before the `Console.Writeline()` statement in Hello World. Navigate away from it and then use the Bookmarks menu item to return to it.

Your Visual Studio window should look something like Figure A-1.

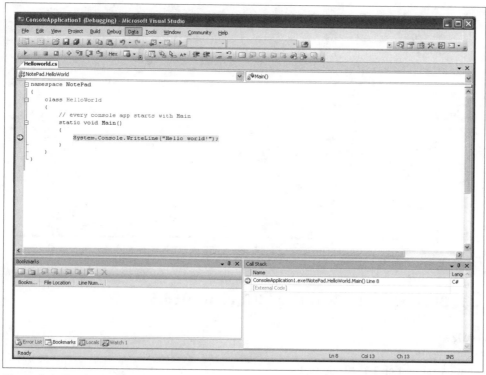

Figure A-1. Exercise 2-1

Solution to Exercise 2-2. Undock the Solution Explorer window from the right side of the IDE and move it to the left. Leave it there if you like or move it back.

Your Visual Studio window should look something like Figure A-2.

Solution to Exercise 2-3. Insert a code snippet for a `for` loop from the Edit → Intellisense menu into your Hello World program. (It won't do anything for now; you'll learn about for loops in Chapter 4.)

Your Visual Studio window should look something like Figure A-3.

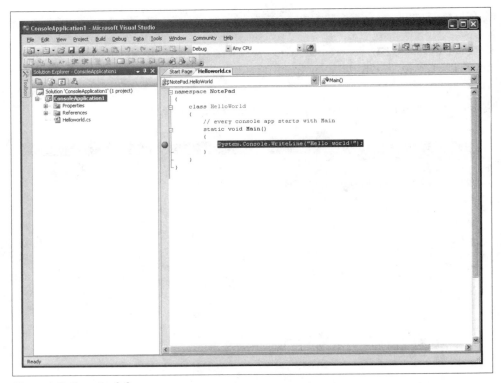

Figure A-2. Exercise 2-2

Chapter 3: C# Language Fundamentals

Quiz

Solution to Question 3-1. True or False.

Solution to Question 3-2. int is the C# alias for the .NET Int32 type. They can be used interchangeably.

Solution to Question 3-3. All except the last, which requires an explicit cast:

```
int newInt = (int) myLong;
```

Solution to Question 3-4. A uint is an unsigned int and can hold only positive numbers, but it can hold a positive value twice as big as an int (4 million+ rather than 2 million+).

Solution to Question 3-5. A float takes four bytes and a double takes eight bytes, and thus a double can represent much larger values with greater precision.

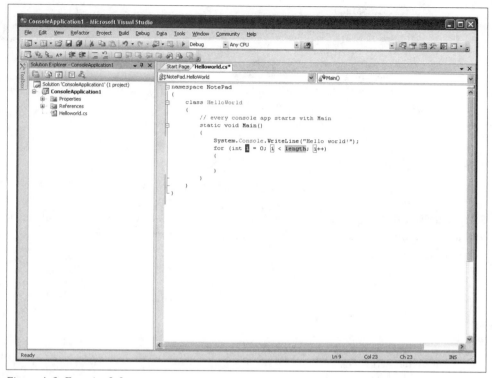

Figure A-3. Exercise 2-3

Solution to Question 3-6. In C, if you wish to use a variable of any type (pass it as a parameter to a method), you must assign it a value.

Solution to Question 3-7. You refer to the constant like this:

```
Temperatures.LightJacketWeather
```

Its value is 33.

Solution to Question 3-8. Any statement that evaluates to a value.

Exercises

Solution to Exercise 3-1. Write a short program creating and initializing each of the following types of variables: int, float, double, char, and then outputting the values to the console.

```
namespace fundamentals
{
    class exercise
    {
```

```
static void Main()
{
    int myInt = 3;
    float myFloat = 4.25f;
    double myDouble = 123456789.9867;
    char myChar = 'A';
    System.Console.WriteLine("myInt: {0}, myFloat: {1}, myDouble: {2},
        myChar: {3}.", myInt, myFloat, myDouble, myChar);
}
    }
}
```

The output should look like this:

```
myInt: 3, myFloat: 4.25, myDouble: 123456789.9876, myChar: A.
```

Solution to Exercise 3-2. Modify the program in Exercise 3-1 to change the values of variables and output the values to the console a second time:

```
namespace fundamentals
{
    class exercise
    {
        static void Main()
        {
            // round one

            int myInt = 3;
            float myFloat = 4.25f;
            double myDouble = 123456789.9867;
            char myChar = 'A';
            System.Console.WriteLine("Round 1: myInt: {0}, myFloat: {1},
                myDouble: {2}, myChar: {3}.", myInt, myFloat, myDouble,
                myChar);

            // round two

            myInt = 5;
            float myFloat = 25.267f;
            myDouble = 987654321.1234;
            myChar = 'Z';
            System.Console.WriteLine("Round 2: myInt: {0}, myFloat: {1},
                myDouble: {2}, myChar: {3}.", myInt, myFloat, myDouble,
                myChar);
        }
    }
}
```

The output should look like this:

```
Round 1: myInt: 3, myFloat: 4.25, myDouble: 123456789.9876, myChar: A.
Round 2: myInt: 5, myFloat: 25.267, myDouble: 987654321.1234, myChar: Z.
```

Solution to Exercise 3-3. Modify the program in Exercise 3-2 to declare a constant float Pi equal to 3.14159. Then assign a new value to pi (3.1) and output its value with the other variables statement. What happens when you try to compile this program?

```
namespace fundamentals
{
    class exercise
    {
        static void Main()
        {
            const float pi = 3.14159f;

            int myInt = 3;
            float myFloat = 4.25f;
            double myDouble = 123456789.9867;
            char myChar = 'A';
            pi = 3.1f;
            System.Console.WriteLine("Round 1: myInt: {0}, myFloat: {1},
                myDouble: {2}, myChar: {3}.  Pi: {4}", myInt, myFloat,
                myDouble, myChar, pi);

        }
    }
}
```

This program won't compile, because you're trying to assign a value to a constant. Instead, you receive a compiler error that reads, "The left-hand side of an assignment must be a variable, property or indexer."

Chapter 4: Operators

Quiz

Solution to Question 4-1. The output of the operations is:

```
32
6
4
```

Solution to Question 4-2. The expressions evaluate to:

```
True
True
False
5
True
```

The fourth expression evaluates to 5, not to true. Thus, if you write:

```
z = x = y;
```

and y has the value 5, then the order of operations is that the value in y (5) is assigned to x, and the value of the expression x=y, which is 5, is assigned to z.

Solution to Question 4-3. The prefix operator increments the original value, and then assigns the new value to the result. The postfix operator assigns the original value to the result, and then increments the original value.

Solution to Question 4-4. The correct order of operations is:

```
++
%
!=
&&
?:
```

Exercises

Solution to Exercise 4-1. Write a program that assigns the value 25 to variable x, and 5 to variable y. Output the sum, difference, product, quotient, and modulus of x and y.

```
namespace operators
{
   class exercise
   {
      static void Main()
      {
         int x = 25;
         int y = 5;
         System.Console.WriteLine("sum: {0}, difference: {1},
            product: {2}, quotient: {3}, modulus: {4}.", x + y, x - y,
            x * y, x / y, x % y);
      }
   }
}
```

The output looks like this:

```
sum: 30, difference: 20, product: 125, quotient: 5, modulus: 0.
```

Solution to Exercise 4-2. What will be the output of the following method?

```
static void Main()
{
   int varA = 5;
   int varB = ++varA;
   int varC = varB++;
   Console.WriteLine( "A: {0}, B: {1}, C: {2}", varA, varB, varC );
}
```

The output looks like this:

```
A: 6, B: 7, C: 6
```

Solution to Exercise 4-3. Write a program that demonstrates the difference between the prefix and postfix operators.

```
namespace operators
{
   class exercise
   {
      static void Main( )
      {
         int myInt = 5;
         int myOtherInt = myInt;
         System.Console.WriteLine("initial values: myInt: {0},
            myOtherInt: {1}\n", myInt, myOtherInt);

         // prefix evaluation
         myOtherInt = ++myInt;
         System.Console.WriteLine("prefix evaluation myInt: {0},
            myOtherInt: {1}\n", myInt, myOtherInt);

         // postfix evaluation
         myInt = 5;
         myOtherInt = 5;
         myOtherInt = myInt++;
         System.Console.WriteLine("postfix evaluation myInt: {0},
            myOtherInt: {1}\n", myInt, myOtherInt);
      }
   }
}
```

The output looks like this:

```
initial values: myInt: 5, myOtherInt: 5
prefix evaluation myInt: 6, myOtherInt: 6
postfix evaluation myInt: 6, myOtherInt: 5
```

Chapter 5: Branching

Quiz

Solution to Question 5-1. `if`, `else`, `switch`.

Solution to Question 5-2. False. In C#, an `if` statement's condition must evaluate to a *Boolean* expression.

Solution to Question 5-3. The braces make maintenance easier. If you add a second statement later, you are less likely to create a logic error because it is obvious what "block" of statements the `if` refers to.

Solution to Question 5-4. Either a numeric value or a string.

Solution to Question 5-5. False. If the statement has no body, then you can fall through. For example:

```
case morning:
case afternoon:
    someAction( );
    break;
```

Solution to Question 5-6. Two uses of goto are:

- To go to a label in your code
- To go to a different case statement in a switch statement

Solution to Question 5-7. do...while evaluates its condition is at the end of the statement rather than at the beginning, and thus is guaranteed to run at least once.

Solution to Question 5-8. In a loop, it causes the remainder of the body of the loop to be skipped and the next iteration of the loop to begin immediately.

Solution to Question 5-9. Two ways of creating an infinite loop are:

```
for (;;)
while(true)
```

Exercises

Solution to Exercise 5-1. Create a method that counts from 1–10 using each of the while, do...while, and for statements.

```
using System;
class Exercises
{
    static void Main( )
    {
        Console.WriteLine( "while" );
        int counter = 1;
        while ( counter <= 10 )
        {
            Console.Write( counter );
            if ( counter < 10 )
            {
                Console.Write( ", " );
            }
            ++counter;
        }

        Console.WriteLine( "\nDo..while" );
        counter = 1;
        do
        {
```

```
            Console.Write( counter );
            if ( counter < 10 )
            {
                Console.Write( ", " );
            }
            ++counter;
        } while ( counter <= 10 );

        Console.WriteLine( "\nfor" );
        for ( int ctr = 1; ctr <= 10; ctr++ )
        {
            Console.Write( counter );
            if ( counter < 10 )
            {
                Console.Write( ", " );
            }
        }
        Console.WriteLine( "\nDone" );
    }
}
```

Solution to Exercise 5-2. Create a program that evaluates whether a given input is odd or even, a multiple of 10, or too large (over 100) by using four levels of if statement. Then expand the program to do the same work with a switch statement.

```
using System;
class Exercises
{
    enum numericCondition
    {
        even,
        multiple,
        odd,
        tooBig,
        unknown,
        zero,
    };

    static void Main()
    {
        // possible input conditions


        while ( true )
        {
            // entering any symbol except a number will throw an exception
            // -- no error handling in this simple example
            Console.Write( "Enter a number please: " );
            string theEntry = Console.ReadLine();
            int theNumber = Convert.ToInt32(theEntry) ;
            Console.Write( "NestedIf {0}: ", theNumber );
```

```
        // Logic: if the number is greater than 100, say it is too big
        // if it is even but not a multiple of 10 say it is even
        // if it is a multiple of ten, say so
        // if it is not even, say it is odd
        if ( theNumber <= 100 )
        {
          if ( theNumber % 2 == 0 )
          {
            if ( theNumber == 0 )
            {
              Console.WriteLine( "zero is not even or odd nor a multiple of 10" );
            }
            else
            {
              if ( theNumber % 10 == 0 )
              {
                Console.WriteLine( "You have picked a multiple of 10" );
              }
              else
              {
                Console.WriteLine( "Your number is even" );
              } // end else not a multiple of 10
            } // end else not zero
          } // end if even
          else
          {
            Console.WriteLine( "What an odd number to enter" );
          }
        } // end if not too big
        else
        {
          Console.WriteLine( "Your number is too big for me." );
        }


        Console.Write( "SwitchMethod {0}: ", theNumber  );


    // same logic, different implementation
        // set the enumerated condition
        numericCondition condition = numericCondition.unknown;  // initialize
        condition = ( theNumber  % 2 == 0 ) ?
             numericCondition.even : numericCondition.odd;
        if ( theNumber % 10 == 0 ) condition = numericCondition.multiple;
        if ( theNumber == 0 ) condition = numericCondition.zero;
        if ( theNumber > 100 ) condition = numericCondition.tooBig;

        // switch on the condition and display the correct message
        switch ( condition )
        {
          case numericCondition.even:
            Console.WriteLine( "Your number is even" );
            break;
          case numericCondition.multiple:
```

```
          Console.WriteLine( "You have picked a multiple of 10" );
          break;
      case numericCondition.odd:
          Console.WriteLine( "What an odd number to enter" );
          break;
      case numericCondition.tooBig:
          Console.WriteLine( "Your number is too big for me." );
          break;
      case numericCondition.zero:
          Console.WriteLine( "zero is not even or odd nor a multiple of 10" );
          break;
      default:
          Console.WriteLine( "I'm sorry, I didn't understand that." );
          break;
      }
    }
  }
}
```

Solution to Exercise 5-3. Create a program that initializes a variable i at 0 and counts up, and initializes a second variable j at 25 and counts down. Use a for loop to increment i and decrement j simultaneously. When i is greater than j, end the loop and print out the message "Crossed over!".

```
using System;
class Exercises
{
    static void Main( )
    {
        int i = -1;
        int j = -1;
        for (i = 0, j = 25; i < j; ++i, --j )
        {
            Console.WriteLine("i: {0}; j: {1}", i, j);
        }
        Console.WriteLine( "Crossed over! i: {0}; j: {1}", i, j );

    }
}
```

The output looks like this:

```
i: 0; j: 25
i: 1; j: 24
i: 2; j: 23
i: 3; j: 22
i: 4; j: 21
i: 5; j: 20
i: 6; j: 19
i: 7; j: 18
i: 8; j: 17
i: 9; j: 16
i: 10; j: 15
i: 11; j: 14
```

```
i: 12; j: 13
Crossed over! i: 13; j: 12
```

Chapter 6: Object-Oriented Programming

Quiz

Solution to Question 6-1. New (user-defined) types are most often created in C# with the keyword class.

Solution to Question 6-2. A class defines a new type; an object is an instance of that type.

Solution to Question 6-3. Making your member fields private allows you to change how you store that data (as a member variable, in a database) without breaking your client's code.

Solution to Question 6-4. Encapsulation is the principle of keeping each class discreet and self-contained, so you can change the implementation of one class without affecting any other class.

Solution to Question 6-5. Specialization allows a new class to "inherit" many of the characteristics of an existing class, and to be used polymorphically with that class. Specialization is implemented in C# through inheritance.

Solution to Question 6-6. Polymorphism is the ability to treat derived classes as if they were all instances of their base class, yet have each derived class specialize its own implementation of the base class's methods.

Solution to Question 6-7. The is-a relationship is established through inheritance. The has-a relationship is implemented through aggregation (making one type a member variable of another type).

Solution to Question 6-8. Access modifiers indicate which class' methods have access to a given field, property or method of a class. Public members are available to methods of any class; private members are available only to methods of instances of the same class.

Solution to Question 6-9. State is the current conditions and values of an object, and is implemented with properties and member variables. Capabilities are what the object can do, exposed through public methods. Responsibilities are the promises a well-designed class makes to the clients of that class.

Solution to Question 6-10. A use-case scenario is a tool for the analysis of a problem. In a use-case scenario, you walk through the details of how your product will be used by one user to accomplish one task, noting which classes interact and what their responsibilities are.

Exercises

Solution to Exercise 6-1. Draw a class diagram for a class named "vehicle" and show how the classes "car," "truck," and "motorcycle" derive from it. (See Figure A-4.)

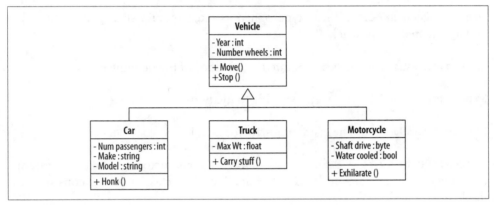

Figure A-4. Exercise 6-1

Solution to Exercise 6-2. Define a class Book, in which a book has a title, author, and ISBN, and the book can be read or shelved:

```
class Book
{
  private String title;
  private String author;
  private String ISBN;

  public Book (string title, string author, string ISBN)
  {
     this.title = title;
     this.author = author;
     this.ISBN = ISBN;
  }
  public void Read()     // member method
  {
    // code here to read book
  }
  public void Shelve()   // member method
  {
    // code here to shelve book
};
```

Chapter 7: Classes and Objects

Quiz

Solution to Question 7-1. A class defines a new type; an object is a single instance of that type.

Solution to Question 7-2. Instances of classes are reference types and are created on the heap.

Solution to Question 7-3. Intrinsic types (such as integers) and structs are value types and are created on the stack.

Solution to Question 7-4. Access is limited to methods of the defining class.

Solution to Question 7-5. Access is available to methods in any class.

Solution to Question 7-6. The class's constructor is called.

Solution to Question 7-7. A default constructor is a constructor that takes no parameters. If you do not create any constructor at all for your class, a default constructor is implicitly created.

Solution to Question 7-8. None. A constructor is not defined to return a type, and is not marked void.

Solution to Question 7-9. Either in the constructor, using assignment, or when the member variable is created:

```
private int myVariable = 88;
```

Technically, only the latter is truly initialization; assigning it in the constructor is not as efficient.

Solution to Question 7-10. this refers to the object itself—the current instance of the class.

Solution to Question 7-11. A static method has no this reference. It does not belong to an instance; it belongs to the class and can only call other static methods.

You access a static method through the name of the class:

```
Dog myDog = new Dog( );
myDog.InstanceMethod( );
Dog.StaticMethod( );
```

Of course, from within any method (including static methods), you can instantiate a class, and then call methods on that instance.

You can even instantiate an instance of your own class, and then call *any* non-static method of that object, as we did with [static] Main( ) calling [non-static] Test( ).

Solution to Question 7-12. The using statement automatically calls the dispose method on the object once the statement completes.

Exercises

Solution to Exercise 7-1. Write a program with a Math class that has four methods: Add, Subtract, Multiply, and Divide, each of which takes two parameters. Call each method from Main( ).

```
using System;
using System.Collections.Generic;
using System.Text;

namespace ConsoleApplication2
{
    class Math
    {
        public int Add( int left, int right )
        {
            return left + right;
        }

        public int Subtract( int left, int right )
        {
            return left - right;
        }

        public int Multiply( int left, int right )
        {
            return left * right;
        }

        public float Divide( float left, float right )
        {
            return left / right;
        }
    }   // end class Math


    class Program
    {
        static void Main( string[] args )
        {
            Math m = new Math( );
            int sum =        m.Add(3,5);
```

```
            int difference =  m.Subtract(3,5);
            int product =      m.Multiply(3,5);
            float quotient =   m.Divide(3.0f, 5.0f);

            Console.WriteLine(
               "sum: {0}, difference: {1}, product: {2}, quotient: {3}",
               sum, difference, product, quotient);

      }
   }
}
```

Solution to Exercise 7-2. Modify the program from Exercise 7-1 so that you do not have to create an instance of Math to call the four methods:

```
using System;
using System.Collections.Generic;
using System.Text;

namespace ConsoleApplication2
{
   class Math
   {
      static public int Add( int left, int right )
      {
         return left + right;
      }

      static public int Subtract( int left, int right )
      {
         return left - right;
      }

      static public int Multiply( int left, int right )
      {
         return left * right;
      }

      static public float Divide( float left, float right )
      {
         return left / right;
      }
   }     // end class Math


   class Program
   {
      static void Main( string[] args )
      {

         int sum =         Math.Add( 3, 5 );
         int difference =  Math.Subtract(3,5);
```

```
        int product =      Math.Multiply(3,5);
        float quotient =  Math.Divide(3.0f, 5.0f);

        Console.WriteLine(
            "sum: {0}, difference: {1}, product: {2}, quotient: {3}",
            sum, difference, product, quotient);

      }
    }
  }
```

Chapter 8: Inside Methods

Quiz

Solution to Question 8-1. Method overloading allows the author of the class to create a method with varying (number and/or type of) parameters, rather than having to have many methods with similar but different names.

Solution to Question 8-2. The signature of a method is its name and its parameter list.

Solution to Question 8-3. Properties are public accessors to your encapsulated data. Properties appear to the class creator as methods, but to the class's clients as fields.

Solution to Question 8-4. Do not implement the set part of the property. No special notation is required.

Solution to Question 8-5. By passing in parameters by reference and getting the results back in those parameters.

Solution to Question 8-6. If you want to pass a value object (variable) by reference, you can use the keyword ref in the call to the method and in the declaration of the method.

Solution to Question 8-7. If you want to pass a value object by reference, but do not want to initialize it, you must use the keyword out in the call to the method and in the declaration of the method.

Exercises

Solution to Exercise 8-1. Write a program with an overloaded method for doubling the value of the argument. One version of the method should double an int value, and the other version should double a float value. Call both methods to demonstrate that they work.

```
using System;

namespace InsideMethods
{
   class Tester
   {
      public void Run()
      {
         int x = 5;
         float y = 5.2f;
         Console.WriteLine( "Double {0} = {1}", x, Doubler( x ) );
         Console.WriteLine( "Double {0} = {1}", y, Doubler( y ) );
      }

      static int Doubler( int theVal )
      {
         return theVal * 2;
      }

      static float Doubler( float theVal )
      {
         return theVal * 2.0f;
      }

      static void Main()
      {
         Tester t = new Tester();
         t.Run();
      }

   }
}
```

Solution to Exercise 8-2. Write a program with one method that takes an int value, and returns both double and triple that value. You'll need to use reference parameters.

```
using System;

namespace InsideMethods
{
   class Tester
   {
      public void Run()
      {
         int x = 5;
         int doubleX = 0;
         int tripleX =0;
         DoublerAndTripler( x, ref doubleX, ref tripleX );
         Console.WriteLine( "Double {0} = {1}; triple {2} = {3}",
            x, doubleX, x, tripleX );

      }
```

```
static void DoublerAndTripler(
   int theVal, ref int doubleValue, ref int tripleValue )
{
   doubleValue = theVal * 2;
   tripleValue = theVal * 3;
}

static void Main( )
{
   Tester t = new Tester( );
   t.Run( );
}

   }
}
```

Solution to Exercise 8-3. Modify the program from Exercise 8-2 so that you don't need
to initialize the variables that will hold the doubled and tripled values before calling
the method:

```
using System;

namespace InsideMethods
{
   class Tester
   {
      public void Run( )
      {
         int x = 5;
         int doubleX;      // uninitialized
         int tripleX;      // uninitialized
         DoublerAndTripler( x, out doubleX, out tripleX );
         Console.WriteLine( "Double {0} = {1}; triple {2} = {3}",
            x, doubleX, x, tripleX );

      }

      static void DoublerAndTripler(
         int theVal, out int doubleValue, out int tripleValue )
      {
         doubleValue = theVal * 2;
         tripleValue = theVal * 3;
      }

      static void Main( )
      {
         Tester t = new Tester( );
         t.Run( );
      }

   }
}
```

Chapter 9: Basic Debugging

Quiz

Solution to Question 9-1. Go to the line where you want execution to stop, and click in the margin. A red dot will appear on the line.

Solution to Question 9-2. Pressing F10 steps over a method; F11 steps into the method.

Solution to Question 9-3. Right-click on the line and choose breakpoints and then disable breakpoint, or right-click on the breakpoint and choose disable.

Solution to Question 9-4. The Locals window shows all the variables that are in scope. The Autos window shows variables used in the current and previous statement.

Solution to Question 9-5. Either right-click on the variable and choose "Add to Watch window" or just click and drag the variable directly onto the Watch window.

Solution to Question 9-6. Right-click on the variable and choose "QuickWatch," or select Debug → QuickWatch.

Solution to Question 9-7. The call stack shows which method called the current method, and which method called that method, etc. This allows you to determine the exact path your code followed to bring you to the current method.

Exercises

Solution to Exercise 9-1. You'll use the following program for this exercise. Either type it into Visual Studio, or copy it from this book's web site. Note that this is spaghetti code—you'd never write method calls like this, but that's why this is the debugging chapter.

```
using System;

namespace Debugging
{
    class Tester
    {
        public void Run()
        {
            int myInt = 42;
            float myFloat = 9.685f;
```

```
        System.Console.WriteLine("Before staring: \n value of myInt: {0} \n
        value of myFloat: {1}", myInt, myFloat);

        // pass the variables by reference
        Multiply( ref myInt, ref myFloat );

        System.Console.WriteLine("After finishing: \n value of myInt: {0} \n
        value of myFloat: {1}", myInt, myFloat);

    }

    private static void Multiply (ref int theInt, ref float theFloat)
    {
        theInt = theInt * 2;
        theFloat = theFloat *2;

        Divide( ref theInt, ref theFloat);
    }

    private static void Divide (ref int theInt, ref float theFloat)
    {
        theInt = theInt / 3;
        theFloat = theFloat / 3;

        Add(ref theInt, ref theFloat);
    }

    public static void Add(ref int theInt, ref float theFloat)
    {
        theInt = theInt + theInt;
        theFloat = theFloat + theFloat;
    }

    static void Main( )
    {
        Tester t = new Tester( );
        t.Run( );
    }
  }
}
```

1. Place a breakpoint in Run( ) on the following line:

```
        System.Console.WriteLine("Before staring: \n value of myInt: {0} \n
                value of myFloat: {1}", myInt, myFloat);
```

2. Step into the Multiply( ) method, up to the call to Divide( ). What are the values of theInt and theFloat at this point?

3. Run the program again, and when it reaches the breakpoint in Run( ), set a watch on myInt. Step through the methods. When does the value of myInt change?

4. Set another breakpoint in Add( ) at this line:

```
        theInt = theInt + theInt;
```

Run the program. How many calls are in the call stack when the program reaches this breakpoint?

Answers:

1. As shown in the Locals window, myInt is 42 and myFloat is 9.685, because both have just been set.

2. Use theInt is 84 and theFloat is 19.37.

3. The value of myInt doesn't change until control returns to Run( ), after the Multiply( ) method has finished.

4. There are five calls in the call stack at this point: Main( ), Run( ), Multiply( ), Divide( ), and Add( ).

Solution to Exercise 9-2. The program in this exercise is similar to the first, but it has a logic error. Type this program into Visual Studio or download it from this book's web site.

```
using System;

namespace Debugging
{

    class Tester
    {
        public void Run( )
        {

            int myInt = 42;
            float myFloat = 9.685f;

            System.Console.WriteLine("Before staring: \n value of myInt: {0} \n
            value of myFloat: {1}", myInt, myFloat);

            // pass the variables by reference
            Multiply( ref myInt, ref myFloat );

            System.Console.WriteLine("After finishing: \n value of myInt: {0} \n
            value of myFloat: {1}", myInt, myFloat);

        }

        private static void Multiply (ref int theInt, ref float theFloat)
        {
            theInt = theInt * 2;
            theFloat = theFloat *2;
            Divide( ref theInt, ref theFloat);
        }

        private static void Divide (ref int theInt, ref float theFloat)
        {
            theInt = theInt * 3;
            theFloat = theFloat * 3;
            Add(ref theInt, ref theFloat);
        }
```

```
        public static void Add(ref int theInt, ref float theFloat)
        {
            theInt = theInt - theInt;
            theFloat = theFloat - theFloat;
        }

        static void Main()
        {
            Tester t = new Tester();
            t.Run();
        }
    }
}
```

If you run this program, you will not get the same results as you did in the previous example. Use the debugging tools you just learned about to find the error. Correct the error, and then run the program again to see if the results are correct.

You could find this error by setting a breakpoint on the call to Run( ), and stepping through the code from there, watching the values of theInt and theFloat. You could also find it by setting breakpoints on each of the method calls and examining the values of theInt and theFloat each time.

The first errors you'll probably find are these in Divide( ):

```
theInt = theInt * 3;
theFloat = theFloat * 3;
```

theInt and theFloat are multiplied by 3, not divided. However, if you fix these errors and run the program, the result is still 0 for both variables. That's because there are two more errors in Add( ):

```
theInt = theInt - theInt;
theFloat = theFloat - theFloat;
```

As you can see, the programmer isn't a very good typist—the variables are subtracted instead of added. If you fix these errors, the program will run as expected.

Chapter 10: Arrays

Quiz

Solution to Question 10-1. 6. Arrays always begin with index (or offset) zero.

Solution to Question 10-2. Yes. Every array declares the type of objects it will hold. You can undermine the type-safety by creating an array of objects (which will hold anything, because everything derives from objects), but that is not advised.

Solution to Question 10-3. Arrays are reference types and created on the heap.

Solution to Question 10-4. If the elements of the array are of value types, they are created in the allocated memory for the array; otherwise, they are created elsewhere on the heap and a reference is stored in the array.

Solution to Question 10-5. You can explicitly call new or just imply the size of the array. For example, if you have three employee objects named moe, larry, and curley:

```
Employee[] myEmpArray = new Employee[3] = { moe, larry, curley };
```

or:

```
Employee[] myEmpArray = { moe, larry, curley };
```

Solution to Question 10-6. Allows you to pass in an indefinite number of parameters, all of the same type, which will be treated as an array. You can, if you wish, also pass in an array.

Solution to Question 10-7. A rectangular array is a multidimensional array; a jagged array is an array of arrays.

Exercises

Solution to Exercise 10-1. Declare a Dog class with two private members: weight (an int), and name (a string). Be sure to add properties to access the members. Then create an array that holds three Dog objects (Milo, 26 pounds; Frisky, 10 pounds; and Laika, 50 pounds). Output each dog's name and weight.

```
using System;
namespace Exercises
{
    public class Dog
    {

        public Dog(int theWeight, string theName)
        {
            this.weight = theWeight;
            this.name = theName;
        }

        public int Weight
        {
            get
            {
                return weight;
            }
            set
            {
                weight = value;
            }
        }
```

```
        public string Name
        {
            get
            {
                return name;
            }
            set
            {
                name = value;
            }
        }


        private int weight;
        private string name;
    }
    public class Tester
    {
        public void Run()
        {
            Dog milo = new Dog(26, "Milo");
            Dog frisky = new Dog(10, "Frisky");
            Dog laika = new Dog(50, "Laika");

            Dog[] dogArray = {milo, frisky, laika};


            // output array values

            foreach (Dog d in dogArray)
            {
                Console.WriteLine("Dog {0} weighs {1} pounds.", d.Name, d.Weight);
            }

        }
        static void Main()
        {
            Tester t = new Tester();
            t.Run();
        }
    }
}
```

Solution to Exercise 10-2. Create an array of 10 integers. Populate the array by having the user enter integers at the console (use Console.Readline). Don't worry about error checking for this exercise. Output the integers sorted from greatest to least.

```
using System;
namespace Exercises
{

    public class Tester
    {
```

```
    public void Run( )
    {
        int[] intArray = new int[10];

        Console.WriteLine("You'll be asked to enter 10 integers");

        // enter data into the array
        for (int i = 0; i < intArray.Length; i++ )
        {
            Console.Write("Enter an integer: ");
            string theEntry = Console.ReadLine( );
            intArray[i] = Convert.ToInt32(theEntry);
        }

        // sort and reverse the array
        Array.Sort(intArray);
        Array.Reverse(intArray);

        Console.WriteLine("\nValues:");
        foreach (int j in intArray)
        {
            Console.WriteLine("{0}", j);
        }

    }
    static void Main( )
    {
        Tester t = new Tester( );
        t.Run( );
    }
}
}
```

Solution to Exercise 10-3. Extend Exercise 10-1 by creating a two-dimensional array that represents a collection of strings that indicate the awards each dog has won at dog shows. Each dog may have a different number of awards won. Output the contents of the array to check its validity.

```
using System;
namespace exercise
{
    public class Dog
    {

        public Dog(int theWeight, string theName)
        {
            this.weight = theWeight;
            this.name = theName;
        }

        public int Weight
        {
            get
```

```
            {
                return weight;
            }
            set
            {
                weight = value;
            }
        }

        public string Name
        {
            get
            {
                return name;
            }
            set
            {
                name = value;
            }
        }


        private int weight;
        private string name;
    }
    public class Tester
    {
        public void Run( )
        {
            const int rows = 3;

            // declare and populate the dogs array
            Dog milo = new Dog(26, "Milo");
            Dog frisky = new Dog(10, "Frisky");
            Dog laika = new Dog(50, "Laika");

            Dog[] dogArray = {milo, frisky, laika};


            // declare the dogAwards array as 3 rows high
            string[][] dogAwardsArray = new string[rows][];

            // declare the rows
            dogAwardsArray[0] = new string[3];
            dogAwardsArray[1] = new string[1];
            dogAwardsArray[2] = new string[2];

            // Populate the rows
            dogAwardsArray[0][0] = "Best in Show";
            dogAwardsArray[0][1] = "Best of Breed";
            dogAwardsArray[0][2] = "Judge's Cup";
            dogAwardsArray[1][0] = "Best Toy Tog";
            dogAwardsArray[2][0] = "Best Working Dog";
            dogAwardsArray[2][1] = "Best Large Dog";
```

```
        // Output the contents
        for (int i = 0; i < dogAwardsArray.Length; i++)
        {
            Console.WriteLine("{0}'s awards: ", dogArray[i].Name);
            for (int j = 0; j < dogAwardsArray[i].Length; j++)
            {
                Console.WriteLine("\t{0}", dogAwardsArray[i][j]);
            }
        }
    }
    static void Main()
    {
        Tester t = new Tester();
        t.Run();
    }
}
}
```

Solution to Exercise 10-4. Create a two-dimensional array that represents a chessboard (an 8×8 array). Each element in the array should contain either the string "black" or "white," depending on where it is on the board. Create a method that initializes the array with the strings. Then create a method that asks the reader to enter two integers for the coordinates of a square, and returns whether that square is black or white.

```
using System;

namespace exercises
{
    public class Tester
    {
        public void Run()
        {
            const int rows = 8;
            const int columns = 8;

            // create an 8x8 array
            string[,] chessboardArray = new string[rows, columns];

            // populate the chessboard array

            for (int i = 0; i < rows; i++)
            {
                // if row starts with a black square
                if ((i % 2) == 0)
                {
                    for (int j = 0; j < columns; j++)
                    {
                        if ((j % 2) == 0)
                        {
                            chessboardArray[i,j] = "black";
```

```
            }
            else
            {
                chessboardArray[i,j] = "white";
            }
        }
    }
    // else row starts with a white square
    else
    {
        for (int j = 0; j < columns; j++)
        {
            if ((j % 2) == 0)
            {
                chessboardArray[i,j] = "white";
            }
            else
            {
                chessboardArray[i,j] = "black";
            }
        }
    }
}

    // ask the user for coordinates to test
    Console.Write("Enter the row to test (1 through 8): ");
    string rowEntry = Console.ReadLine();
    int testRow = Convert.ToInt32(rowEntry);
    Console.Write("Enter the column to test (1 through 8): ");
    string colEntry = Console.ReadLine();
    int testCol = Convert.ToInt32(colEntry);

    // output the value at those coordinates
    Console.WriteLine("The square at {0}, {1} is {2}.", testRow,
    testCol, chessboardArray[(testRow - 1), (testCol - 1)]);
}

static void Main()
{
    Tester t = new Tester();
    t.Run();
}
    }
}
```

Chapter 11: Inheritance and Polymorphism

Quiz

Solution to Question 11-1. This relationship is reciprocal: if you have three types with similar functionality, you can refactor that similarity out of the three types into a generalized type. At the same time, each of the three types are now specialized forms of the more generalized type.

Inheritance is also implicitly hierarchical: you can imagine a tree with the most generalized type at the top and each level of specialization descending from levels above. A generalized type may have many specializations, but each specialized type may have only one generalization.

Solution to Question 11-2. Through inheritance.

Solution to Question 11-3. `class <identifier> : <base class>`

Solution to Question 11-4. Create a virtual method in the base class, and then override it in the derived class.

Solution to Question 11-5. The more usual meaning is to allocate memory on the heap. The special meaning in inheritance is that you are not overriding a base method; you are creating a new method that intentionally hides and replaces the base class method.

Solution to Question 11-6. After the parameter list, but before the opening brace, put a colon followed by the keyword base and two parentheses. Pass the parameters for the base class constructor within the parentheses.

Solution to Question 11-7. A member of class A is visible to class B if it is marked `public`, or if it is marked `protected` *and* class B derives directly or indirectly from A. If the member is marked private in A, it is always invisible to class B.

Solution to Question 11-8. An abstract method has no implementation in the base class, but must be overridden and implemented in any derived class that does not itself want to be abstract. Any class with an abstract method (even if inherited) is itself abstract and may not be instantiated.

Solution to Question 11-9. A sealed class is one that the compiler will not let you derive from. Classes are marked sealed when the designer of the class does not want anyone to create a derived version.

Solution to Question 11-10. Object (which is the ultimate base class (root) of all types in C#).

Solution to Question 11-11. Object.

Solution to Question 11-12. If you use a value type where an Object is expected, the value type will be automatically and invisibly wrapped in an Object and will take on reference characteristics.

Solution to Question 11-13. When you return a boxed type back to its original type, you must unbox it and explicitly cast it.

Exercises

Solution to Exercise 11-1. Create a base class, Telephone, and derive a class Electronic-Phone from it. In Telephone, create a protected string member phonetype, and a public method Ring( ) that outputs a text message such as: "Ringing the <phonetype>." In ElectronicPhone, the constructor should set the phonetype to "Digital." In the Run( ) method, call Ring( ) on the ElectronicPhone to test the inheritance.

```
using System;
public class Tester
{

    public class Telephone
    {
        protected string phonetype;
        public void Ring( )
        {
            Console.WriteLine( "Ringing the {0} phone...", phonetype );
        }
    }

    public class ElectronicPhone : Telephone
    {
        public ElectronicPhone( )
        {
            this.phonetype = "Digital";   // access protected member
        }
    }

    public void Run( )
    {
        ElectronicPhone phone = new ElectronicPhone( );
        phone.Ring( ); // accessing the base method
    }

    static void Main( )
    {
        Tester t = new Tester( );
        t.Run( );
    }
}
```

Solution to Exercise 11-2. Extend Exercise 11-1 to illustrate a polymorphic method. Have the derived class override the Ring( ) method to display a different message.

```
using System;
public class Tester
{

    public class Telephone
    {
        protected string phonetype;
        public virtual void Ring()  // now virtual
        {
            Console.WriteLine( "Ringing the {0} phone. Ring Ring.", phonetype );
        }
    }

    public class ElectronicPhone : Telephone
    {
        public ElectronicPhone()
        {
            this.phonetype = "Digital";   // access protected member
        }
        public override void Ring()      // override
        {
            Console.WriteLine( "Ringing the {0} phone. Beep Beep.", phonetype );
        }
    }

    public void Run()
    {
        // assign derived instance to base reference
        Telephone phone = new ElectronicPhone();
        phone.Ring(); // accessing the polymorphic method
    }

    static void Main()
    {
        Tester t = new Tester();
        t.Run();
    }
}
```

Solution to Exercise 11-3. Change the Telephone class to abstract, and make Ring( ) an abstract method. Derive two new classes from Telephone: DigitalPhone and Talking-Phone. Each derived class should set the phonetype, and override the Ring( ) method.

```
using System;
public class Tester
{
```

```
public abstract class Telephone
{
   protected string phonetype;
   public abstract void Ring( ); // now abstract
}

public class DigitalPhone : Telephone
{
   public DigitalPhone( )
   {
      this.phonetype = "Digital";   // access protected member
   }
   public override void Ring( )      // implement
   {
      Console.WriteLine( "Ringing the {0} phone. Beep Beep.", phonetype );
   }
}

public class TalkingPhone : Telephone
{
   public TalkingPhone( )
   {
      this.phonetype = "Talking";   // access protected member
   }
   public override void Ring( )      // implement
   {
      Console.WriteLine( "Ringing the {0} phone. You have a call.",
                         phonetype );
   }
}


public void Run( )
{
   // assign derived instance to base reference
   Telephone phone1 = new DigitalPhone( );
   Telephone phone2 = new TalkingPhone( );
   phone1.Ring( ); // accessing the polymorphic method
   phone2.Ring( ); // accessing the polymorphic method

}

static void Main( )
{
   Tester t = new Tester( );
   t.Run( );
}
}
```

Chapter 12: Operator Overloading

Quiz

Solution to Question 12-1. The process of writing methods for your class that allow clients of your class to interact with your class using standard operators (+, ==).

Solution to Question 12-2. Static methods.

Solution to Question 12-3. Call to:

```
public static Fraction operator+(f2, f1)
```

Solution to Question 12-4. Overload the Equals( ) method.

Solution to Question 12-5. Use implicit conversion when you know the conversion will succeed without the risk of losing information. Use explicit conversion if information might be lost.

Exercises

Solution to Exercise 12-1. Create a class Invoice, that has a string property vendor and a double property amount. Overload the addition operator so that if the vendor properties match, the amount properties of the two invoices are added together in a new invoice. If the vendor properties do not match, the new invoice is blank.

```
using System;

public class Invoice
{
    private string vendor;
    private double amount;

    public string Vendor
    {
        get
        {
            return vendor;
        }
        set
        {
            vendor = value;
        }
    }

    public double Amount
    {
        get
```

```
        {
            return amount;
        }
        set
        {
            amount = value;
        }
    }

    // constructor
    public Invoice(string vendor, double amount)
    {
        this.vendor = vendor;
        this.amount = amount;
    }

    // Overloaded operator + takes two invoices.
    // If the vendors are the same, the two amounts are added.
    // If not, the operation fails, and a blank invoice is returned.

    public static Invoice operator +(Invoice lhs, Invoice rhs)
    {
        if (lhs.vendor == rhs.vendor)
        {
            return new Invoice(lhs.vendor, lhs.amount + rhs.amount);
        }
        else
        {
            Console.WriteLine("Vendors don't match; operation failed.");
            return new Invoice("", 0);
        }
    }

    public void PrintInvoice()
    {
        Console.WriteLine("Invoice from {0} for ${1}.", this.vendor,
                          this.amount);
    }
}


public class Tester
{
    public void Run()
    {
        Invoice firstInvoice = new Invoice("TinyCorp", 345);
        Invoice secondInvoice = new Invoice("SuperMegaCo", 56389.53);
        Invoice thirdInvoice = new Invoice("SuperMegaCo", 399.65);

        Console.WriteLine("Adding first and second invoices.");
        Invoice addedInvoice = firstInvoice + secondInvoice;
        addedInvoice.PrintInvoice();
```

```
            Console.WriteLine("Adding second and third invoices.");
            Invoice otherAddedInvoice = secondInvoice + thirdInvoice;
            otherAddedInvoice.PrintInvoice();


        }
        static void Main()
        {
            Tester t = new Tester();
            t.Run();
        }
    }
```

Solution to Exercise 12-2. Modify the Invoice class so that two invoices are considered equal if the vendor and amount properties match. Test your methods.

```
using System;

public class Invoice
{
    private string vendor;
    private double amount;

    public string Vendor
    {
        get
        {
            return vendor;
        }
        set
        {
            vendor = value;
        }
    }

    public double Amount
    {
        get
        {
            return amount;
        }
        set
        {
            amount = value;
        }
    }

    // constructor
    public Invoice(string vendor, double amount)
    {
        this.vendor = vendor;
        this.amount = amount;
    }
```

```
// Overloaded operator + takes two invoices.
// If the vendors are the same, the two amounts are added.
// If not, the operation fails, and a blank invoice is returned.

public static Invoice operator+ (Invoice lhs, Invoice rhs)
{
    if (lhs.vendor == rhs.vendor)
    {
        return new Invoice(lhs.vendor, lhs.amount + rhs.amount);
    }
    else
    {
        Console.WriteLine("Vendors don't match; operation failed.");
        return new Invoice("", 0);
    }
}


// overloaded equality operator
public static bool operator== (Invoice lhs, Invoice rhs)
{
    if ( lhs.vendor == rhs.vendor && lhs.amount == rhs.amount )
    {
        return true;
    }
    return false;
}

// overloaded inequality operator, delegates to ==
public static bool operator !=(Invoice lhs, Invoice rhs)
{
    return !(lhs == rhs);
}

// method for determining equality; tests for same type,
// then delegates to ==
public override bool Equals(object o)
{
    if (!(o is Invoice))
    {
        return false;
    }
    return this == (Invoice)o;
}

public void PrintInvoice()
{
    Console.WriteLine("Invoice from {0} for ${1}.", this.vendor,
                    this.amount);
}
}


public class Tester
{
```

```
    public void Run()
    {
        Invoice firstInvoice = new Invoice("TinyCorp", 399.65);
        Invoice secondInvoice = new Invoice("SuperMegaCo", 56389.53);
        Invoice thirdInvoice = new Invoice("SuperMegaCo", 399.65);

        Invoice testInvoice = new Invoice("SuperMegaCo", 399.65);

        if (testInvoice == firstInvoice)
        {
            Console.WriteLine("First invoice matches.");
        }
        else if (testInvoice == secondInvoice)
        {
            Console.WriteLine("Second invoice matches.");
        }
        else if (testInvoice == thirdInvoice)
        {
            Console.WriteLine("Third invoice matches.");
        }
        else
        {
            Console.WriteLine("No matching invoices.");
        }

    }
    static void Main()
    {
        Tester t = new Tester();
        t.Run();
    }
}
```

Chapter 13: Interfaces

Quiz

Solution to Question 13-1. The interface defines the methods, properties, etc. that the implementing class must provide. The implementing class provides these members and, optionally, additional members.

Solution to Question 13-2. Every class has exactly one base class, but may implement zero, one, or more interfaces. An abstract base class serves as the base to a derived class that must implement all its abstract methods or that derived class is also abstract.

Solution to Question 13-3. `class MyClass : MyBase, ISuppose, IDo {}`

Note that the base class must come first after the colon.

Solution to Question 13-4. The is and the as operator.

Solution to Question 13-5. is returns false if the interface is not implemented; as returns null. Using the as operator can be more efficient.

Solution to Question 13-6. Extending an interface is very much like deriving a class. The new interface inherits all the members of the parent interface, and can also include additional methods.

Solution to Question 13-7. *ExtendedInterface : OriginalInterface*

For example, read:

```
ILoggedCompressible : ICompressible
```

as "ILoggb[edCompressible extends ICompressible."

Solution to Question 13-8. The class implementing a method of the interface can mark that method virtual, and the implementation of the method can be overridden in derived classes.

Solution to Question 13-9. Explicit interface implementation identifies the member of the interface by naming the interface itself (e.g., IStorable.Write( )). This is done to differentiate implementation methods when there might otherwise be an ambiguity, such as when implementing more than one interface that have methods with the same signature.

Exercises

Solution to Exercise 13-1. Define an interface IConvertible that indicates that the class can convert a string to C# or VB2005. The interface should have two methods: ConvertToCSharp and ConvertToVB2005. Each method should take a string, and return a string.

```
using System;

namespace Exercises
{
    interface IConvertible
    {
        string ConvertToCSharp( string stringToConvert );
        string ConvertToVB2005( string stringToConvert );
    }
}
```

Solution to Exercise 13-2. Implement that interface and test it by creating a class ProgramHelper that implements IConvertible. You can use simple string messages to simulate the conversion.

```csharp
using System;

namespace Exercises
{
    interface IConvertible
    {
        string ConvertToCSharp( string stringToConvert );
        string ConvertToVB2005( string stringToConvert );
    }


    public class ProgramHelper : IConvertible
    {
        public ProgramHelper( )
        {
            Console.WriteLine( "Creating ProgramHelper" );
        }

        public virtual string ConvertToCSharp( string stringToConvert )
        {
            return "Converting the string you passed in to CSharp syntax";
        }

        public virtual string ConvertToVB2005( string stringToConvert )
        {
            return "Converting the string you passed in to VB 2005 syntax";
        }

    } // end class ProgramHelper

    class Tester
    {

        static void Main( )
        {
            Tester t = new Tester();
            t.Run();
        }

        public void Run( )
        {
            // Create a ProgramHelper object
            ProgramHelper theProgramHelper = new ProgramHelper();

            // convert a line of CSharp to vb
            string vbString = (
                "Public Sub Read() Implements IStorable.Read " +
                "Console.WriteLine(\"Implementing the Read Method for IStorable\")"
                + "End Sub 'Read\")" );
```

```
            Console.WriteLine( vbString );

            // convert the converted line back to CSharp
            string cSharpString = theProgramHelper.ConvertToCSharp( vbString );

            Console.WriteLine( cSharpString );

        } // end run
    } // end class Tester
} // end namespace
```

Solution to Exercise 13-3. Extend the interface by creating a new interface, IConvertible. The new interface should implement one new method, CodeCheckSyntax, which takes two strings: the string to check, and the language to use. The method should return a bool. Revise the ProgramHelper class from Exercise 13-2 to use the new interface.

```
using System;

namespace Exercises
{
    interface IConvertible
    {
        string ConvertToCSharp( string stringToConvert );
        string ConvertToVB2005( string stringToConvert );
    }

    interface ICodeChecker : IConvertible
    {
        bool CheckCodeSyntax( string stringToCheck, string whichLang );
    }


    public class ProgramHelper : ICodeChecker
    {
        public ProgramHelper( )
        {
            Console.WriteLine( "Creating ProgramHelper" );
        }

        public virtual string ConvertToCSharp( string stringToConvert )
        {
            return "Converting the string you passed in to CSharp syntax";
        }

        public virtual string ConvertToVB2005( string stringToConvert )
        {
            return "Converting the string you passed in to VB 2005 syntax";
        }

        public bool CheckCodeSyntax ( string stringToCheck, string whichLang)
        {
            switch ( whichLang )
            {
```

```
        case "CSharp":
            Console.WriteLine(
                "Checking the string \"{0}\" for C# Syntax", stringToCheck );
            return true;
        case "VB2005":
            Console.WriteLine(
                    "Checking the string \"{0}\" for VB 2005 Syntax",
                    stringToCheck );
            return true;
        default:
            return false;
    }

    }

}   // end class ProgramHelper

class Tester
{

    static void Main( )
    {
        Tester t = new Tester( );
        t.Run( );
    }

    public void Run( )
    {
        // Create a ProgramHelper object
        ProgramHelper theProgramHelper = new ProgramHelper( );

        // convert a line of CSharp to VB
        string cSharpString = theProgramHelper.ConvertToCSharp(
            "Public Sub Read( ) Implements IStorable.Read " +
            "Console.WriteLine(\"Implementing the Read Method for IStorable\")"
            + "End Sub 'Read\")" );

        Console.WriteLine( cSharpString );
        Console.WriteLine (
            "Checking \"{0}\" for syntax... Result {1}", cSharpString,
             theProgramHelper.CheckCodeSyntax(cSharpString, "CSharp"));

        // convert the converted line back to VB
        string vbString = theProgramHelper.ConvertToCSharp( cSharpString );

        Console.WriteLine( vbString );
        Console.WriteLine (
         "Checking \"{0}\" for syntax... Result {1}", vbString,
          theProgramHelper.CheckCodeSyntax(vbString,"VB2005"));

    } // end run
    }   // end class Tester
}       // end namespace
```

Solution to Exercise 13-4. Demonstrate the use of is and as. Create a new class, ProgramConverter, that implements IConvertible. ProgramConverter should implement the ConvertToCSharp( ) and ConvertToVB( ) methods. Revise ProgramHelper so that it derives from ProgramConverter, and implements ICodeChecker.

```csharp
using System;

namespace Exercises
{
    interface IConvertible
    {
        string ConvertToCSharp( string stringToConvert );
        string ConvertToVB2005( string stringToConvert );
    }

    interface ICodeChecker : IConvertible
    {
        bool CheckCodeSyntax( string stringToCheck, string whichLang );
    }

    public class ProgramConverter : IConvertible
    {
        public ProgramConverter( )
        {
            Console.WriteLine( "Creating ProgramConverter" );
        }
        public virtual string ConvertToCSharp( string stringToConvert )
        {
            return "Converting the string you passed in to CSharp syntax";
        }
        public virtual string ConvertToVB2005( string stringToConvert )
        {
            return "Converting the string you passed in to VB 2005 syntax";
        }

    }

    public class ProgramHelper : ProgramConverter, ICodeChecker
    {
        public ProgramHelper( )
        {
            Console.WriteLine( "Creating ProgramHelper" );
        }

        public bool CheckCodeSyntax( string stringToCheck, string whichLang )
        {
            switch ( whichLang )
            {
                case "CSharp":
                    Console.WriteLine(
                        "Checking the string {0} for C# Syntax", stringToCheck );
                    return true;
                case "VB2005":
```

```
                    Console.WriteLine(
                        "Checking the string {0} for VB 2005 Syntax", stringToCheck );
                    return true;
                default:
                    return false;
        }           // end switch
    }               // end method Check Code Syntax
}                   // end class ProgramHelper

class Tester
{

    static void Main( )
    {
        Tester t = new Tester( );
        t.Run( );
    }

    public void Run( )
    {
        ProgramConverter[] converters = new ProgramConverter[4];
        converters[0] = new ProgramConverter( );
        converters[1] = new ProgramHelper( );
        converters[2] = new ProgramHelper( );
        converters[3] = new ProgramConverter( );

        foreach ( ProgramConverter pc in converters )
        {
            string vbString =
                pc.ConvertToCSharp( "Public Sub Read() Implements IStorable.Read "
                + "Console.WriteLine(\"Implementing the Read Method for
                                    IStorable\")"
                + "End Sub 'Read\")" );

            Console.WriteLine( vbString );

            ProgramHelper ph = pc as ProgramHelper;
            if ( ph != null )
            {
                ph.CheckCodeSyntax( vbString, "VB2005" );
            }
            else
            {
                Console.WriteLine( "No vb syntax check - not a Program helper" );
            }

            string cSharpString = pc.ConvertToCSharp( vbString );
            Console.WriteLine( cSharpString );
            if ( ph != null )
            {
                ph.CheckCodeSyntax( vbString, "CSharp" );
            }
            else
            {
```

```
        Console.WriteLine(
            "No csharp syntax check - not a Program helper" );
        }
    } // end foreach in converters
  } // end run
 } // end class Tester
} // end namespace
```

Chapter 14: Generics and Collections

Quiz

Solution to Question 14-1. Indexers are unnamed. You use the this keyword to create an indexer:

```
public string this[int index]
```

Solution to Question 14-2. Any type can be used, although it's most common to use integers.

Solution to Question 14-3. The elements of the array must implement IComparable.

Solution to Question 14-4. Generics allow you to create type-safe collections without specifying the type the collection will hold when you create the collection.

Solution to Question 14-5. It allows your collection to support a foreach loop.

Solution to Question 14-6. The size of an array is fixed when you create it. A List<T> expands dynamically when you add more elements.

Solution to Question 14-7. A List is like an expandable array. A Stack is a "Last In, First Out" collection, a Queue is a "First In, First Out" collection, and a Dictionary is a collection of key/value pairs where you can retrieve the value given a key.

Exercises

Solution to Exercise 14-1. Create an abstract Animal class that has private members weight and name, and abstract methods Speak( ), Move( ), and ToString( ). Derive from Animal a Cat and Dog class that override the methods appropriately. Create an Animal array, populate it with Dogs and Cats, and then call each member's overridden virtual method.

```
using System;

abstract public class Animal
{
```

```
    protected int weight;
    protected string name;
    public Animal(int weight, string name)
    {
        this.weight = weight;
        this.name = name;
    }
    abstract public  void Speak();
    abstract public  void Move();
    public override string  ToString()
    {
        throw new Exception("The method or operation is not implemented.");
    }
}

public class Dog : Animal
{
    private string breed;

    public string Breed
    {
        get { return breed; }
        set { breed = value; }
    }
    public Dog (int weight, string name, string breed):
    base(weight,name)
    {
        this.breed = breed;
    }

    public override void Speak()
    { Console.WriteLine ("Woof"); }

    public override void Move ()
    { Console.WriteLine ("Run, run, run, drool.");  }

    public override string  ToString()
    {
        return "My name is " + this.name + " I weigh " + this.weight +
        " and I am a " + this.breed + "\n";
    }
}


public class Cat : Animal
{

    public Cat (int weight, string name):
    base(weight,name)
    {}

    public override void Speak()
    { Console.WriteLine ("Meow"); }
```

```
    public override void Move ()
    { Console.WriteLine ("Run, tumble, nap."); }

    public override string ToString()
    {
        return "My name is " + this.name + " I weigh " + this.weight +
        " and I know how to purr!\n";
    }

    public void Purr()
    {
        Console.WriteLine("Purrrrrrrrrrrrrrrrrrrrrrrrrrrrrrr\n");
    }

}

public class Tester
{
    static void Main()
    {
        Animal[] myAnimals = new Animal[5];
        myAnimals[0] = new Dog( 72, "Milo", "Golden" );
        myAnimals[1] = new Cat( 12, "Shakespeare");
        myAnimals[2] = new Cat( 10, "Allegra");
        myAnimals[3] = new Dog( 50, "Dingo", "mixed breed" );
        myAnimals[4] = new Dog( 20, "Brandy", "Beagle" );

        foreach ( Animal a in myAnimals )
        {
            a.Speak();
            a.Move();
            Console.WriteLine(a);

            Cat c = a as Cat;  // cast to cat
            if ( c != null )   // if it is a cat
            {
                c.Purr();       // only cats purr
            }
        }
    }
}
```

Solution to Exercise 14-2. Replace the array in Exercise 14-1 with a List. Sort the animals by size. You can simplify by just calling ToString( ) before and after the sort. Remember that you'll need to implement IComparable.

```
using System;
using System.Collections.Generic;

abstract public class Animal : IComparable
{
    protected int weight;
    protected string name;
```

```csharp
    public Animal(int weight, string name)
    {
        this.weight = weight;
        this.name = name;
    }
    abstract public  void Speak();
    abstract public  void Move();

    public override string  ToString()
    {
        throw new Exception("The method or operation is not implemented.");
    }

    public int CompareTo( Object rhs )
    {
        Animal otherAnimal = rhs as Animal;
        if ( otherAnimal != null )
        {
            return this.weight.CompareTo( otherAnimal.weight );
        }
        else
        {
            throw new ApplicationException("Expected to compare animals");
        }
    }
}

public class Dog : Animal
{
    private string breed;

    public string Breed
    {
        get { return breed; }
        set { breed = value; }
    }
    public Dog (int weight, string name, string breed):
    base(weight,name)
    {
        this.breed = breed;
    }

    public override void Speak()
    { Console.WriteLine ("Woof"); }

    public override void Move ()
    { Console.WriteLine ("Run, run, run, drool.");  }

    public override string  ToString()
    {
        return "My name is " + this.name + " I weigh " + this.weight +
        " and I am a " + this.breed ;
    }
}
```

```
public class Cat : Animal
{

    public Cat (int weight, string name):
    base(weight,name)
    {}

    public override void Speak()
    { Console.WriteLine ("Meow"); }

    public override void Move ()
    { Console.WriteLine ("Run, tumble, nap.");  }

    public override string ToString()
    {
        return "My name is " + this.name + " I weigh " + this.weight +
        " and I know how to purr!";
    }

    public void Purr()
    {
        Console.WriteLine("Purrrrrrrrrrrrrrrrrrrrrrrrrrrr\n");
    }
}

public class Tester
{
    static void Main()
    {
        List<Animal> myAnimals = new List<Animal>();
        myAnimals.Add(new Dog( 72, "Milo", "Golden" ));
        myAnimals.Add(new Cat( 12, "Shakespeare"));
        myAnimals.Add(new Cat( 10, "Allegra"));
        myAnimals.Add(new Dog( 50, "Dingo", "mixed breed" ));
        myAnimals.Add(new Dog( 20, "Brandy", "Beagle" ));

        foreach ( Animal a in myAnimals )
        {
            Console.WriteLine(a);
        }

        Console.WriteLine( "\nAfter sorting by size..." );
        myAnimals.Sort();
        foreach ( Animal a in myAnimals )
        {
            Console.WriteLine( a );
        }
    }
}
```

Solution to Exercise 14-3.   Replace the list from Exercise 14-2 with both a Stack and a Queue, and see the difference in the order in which the animals are returned.

The animal definitions are unchanged; the Tester class has the changes:

```
Using System.Collections.Generic;

public class Tester
{
    static void Main( )
    {
        Console.WriteLine(
          "Adding in the order: Milo, Shakespeare, Allegra, Dingo, Brandy" );

        Stack<Animal> myStackOfAnimals = new Stack<Animal>( );
        myStackOfAnimals.Push( new Dog( 72, "Milo", "Golden" ) );
        myStackOfAnimals.Push( new Cat( 12, "Shakespeare" ) );
        myStackOfAnimals.Push( new Cat( 10, "Allegra" ) );
        myStackOfAnimals.Push( new Dog( 50, "Dingo", "mixed breed" ) );
        myStackOfAnimals.Push( new Dog( 20, "Brandy", "Beagle" ) );

        Queue<Animal> myQueueOfAnimals = new Queue<Animal>( );
        myQueueOfAnimals.Enqueue( new Dog( 72, "Milo", "Golden" ) );
        myQueueOfAnimals.Enqueue( new Cat( 12, "Shakespeare" ) );
        myQueueOfAnimals.Enqueue( new Cat( 10, "Allegra" ) );
        myQueueOfAnimals.Enqueue( new Dog( 50, "Dingo", "mixed breed" ) );
        myQueueOfAnimals.Enqueue( new Dog( 20, "Brandy", "Beagle" ) );


        Console.WriteLine( "The stack..." );
        foreach ( Animal a in myStackOfAnimals )
        {
            Console.WriteLine(a);
        }

        Console.WriteLine( "The queue..." );
        foreach ( Animal a in myQueueOfAnimals )
        {
            Console.WriteLine( a );
        }
    }
}
```

Solution to Exercise 14-4.   Rewrite Exercise 14-2 to allow Animals to be sorted either by weight or alphabetically by name:

```
using System;
using System.Collections.Generic;

// simplified to show comparision
abstract public class Animal : IComparable<Animal>
{
    protected int weight;
    protected string name;

    public Animal( int weight, string name )
    {
```

```csharp
      this.weight = weight;
      this.name = name;
   }

   // ** new **
   public static AnimalComparer GetComparer()
   {
      return new Animal.AnimalComparer();
   }

   public int CompareTo( Animal rhs )
   {
      return this.weight.CompareTo( rhs.weight );
   }

   // ** new **
   public int CompareTo( Animal rhs,
      Animal.AnimalComparer.ComparisonType whichComparison )
   {
      switch ( whichComparison )
      {
         case AnimalComparer.ComparisonType.name:
            return this.name.CompareTo( rhs.name );
         case AnimalComparer.ComparisonType.size:
            return this.weight.CompareTo( rhs.weight );
      }
      return -1;  // gotta have all paths return a value

   }

   // nested class    ** new **
   public class AnimalComparer : IComparer<Animal>
   {
      // how do you want to compare?
      public enum ComparisonType
      {
         Size,
         Name
      };

      private Animal.AnimalComparer.ComparisonType whichComparison;
      public Animal.AnimalComparer.ComparisonType WhichComparison
      {
         get { return whichComparison; }
         set { whichComparison = value; }
      }

      // compare two Animals using the previously set
      // whichComparison value
      public int Compare( Animal lhs, Animal rhs )
      {
         return lhs.CompareTo( rhs, whichComparison );
      }
```

```
      // required to fulfill implementation
      public bool Equals( Animal lhs, Animal rhs )
      {
         return this.Compare( lhs, rhs ) == 0;
      }

      // required to fulfill implementation
      public int GetHashCode( Animal a )
      {
         return a.weight.GetHashCode();
      }
   }     // end nested class
}         // end class Animal


public class Dog : Animal
{
   public Dog( int weight, string name, string breed ) :
   base( weight, name )
   {}

   public override string ToString()
   {
      return "My name is " + this.name + " I weigh " + this.weight;
   }
}

public class Cat : Animal
{

   public Cat( int weight, string name ) :
   base( weight, name )
   { }

   public override string ToString()
   {
      return "My name is " + this.name + " I weigh " + this.weight;
   }
}

public class Tester
{
   static void Main()
   {

      List<Animal> myAnimals = new List<Animal>();
      myAnimals.Add( new Dog( 70, "Milo", "Golden" ) );
      myAnimals.Add( new Cat( 10, "Shakespeare" ) );
      myAnimals.Add( new Cat( 15, "Allegra" ) );
      myAnimals.Add( new Dog( 50, "Dingo", "mixed breed" ) );
      myAnimals.Add( new Dog( 20, "Brandy", "Beagle" ) );

      Console.WriteLine( "Before sorting..." );
      foreach ( Animal a in myAnimals )
```

```
        {
            Console.WriteLine( a );
        }

        Console.WriteLine( "\nAfter sorting by default (weight)..." );
        myAnimals.Sort();
        foreach ( Animal a in myAnimals )
        {
            Console.WriteLine( a );
        }

        Console.WriteLine( "\nAfter sorting by name..." );
        Animal.AnimalComparer animalComparer = Animal.GetComparer();
        animalComparer.WhichComparison = Animal.AnimalComparer.ComparisonType.name;
        myAnimals.Sort( animalComparer );
        foreach ( Animal a in myAnimals )
        {
            Console.WriteLine( a );
        }

        Console.WriteLine( "\nAfter sorting explicitly by size..." );
        animalComparer.WhichComparison = Animal.AnimalComparer.ComparisonType.size;
        myAnimals.Sort( animalComparer );
        foreach ( Animal a in myAnimals )
        {
            Console.WriteLine( a );
        }
    }       // end main
}           // end tester
```

Chapter 15: Strings

Quiz

Solution to Question 15-1.   string (lowercase) is the C# keyword that maps to the .NET Framework String class. They may be used interchangeably.

Solution to Question 15-2.

IComparable
  Guarantees that strings can be sorted

ICloneable
  Guarantees that you can call the Clone method on a string object and get back a new duplicate string

IConvertible
  Allows strings to be converted to other types (such as integers)

IEnumerable
  Guarantees that strings can be iterated over in foreach loops

Solution to Question 15-3. A quoted string, provided by the programmer, such as "Hello."

Solution to Question 15-4. An escape character embedded in a string indicates that the character or punctuation that follows is to be treated as an instruction rather than as part of the string. \n indicates a new line. \" indicates that the quote symbol is in the string, not terminating it.

Solution to Question 15-5. Verbatim strings are taken "as is" and thus do not require escape characters. Where \\ would indicate a single backslash in a normal string, in a verbatim string, it indicates two backslashes.

Solution to Question 15-6. Strings cannot be changed. When you appear to change a string, what actually happens is that a new string is created and the old string is destroyed by the garbage collector if it is no longer referenced.

Solution to Question 15-7. It is not possible to derive from the String class (or any other sealed class).

Solution to Question 15-8. You can call the Concat method of the String class, but it is more common to use the overloaded + operator.

Solution to Question 15-9. Given an array of delimiters, Split( ) returns the substrings of the original string.

Solution to Question 15-10. StringBuilder objects are mutable. When the StringBuilder has the complete set of characters you want, you call ToString( ) to get back a string object.

Solution to Question 15-11. Regular expressions constitute a language for identifying and manipulating strings using both literal and metacharacters.

Exercises

Solution to Exercise 15-1. Create the following six strings:

- String 1: "Hello"
- String 2: "World"
- String 3 (a verbatim string): "Come visit us at http://www.LibertyAssociates.com"
- String 4: a concatenation of strings 1 and 2
- String 5: "world"
- String 6: a copy of string 3

Once you have the strings created, do the following:

1. Output the length of each string.
2. Output the third character in each string.
3. Output whether the character "H" appears in each string.
4. Output which strings are the same as string 2.
5. Output which strings are the same as string 2, ignoring case.

```
using System;

namespace StringManipulation
{
    class Tester
    {
        public void Run( )
        {
            string s1 = "Hello ";
            string s2 = "World";
            string s3 = @"Come visit us at http://www.LibertyAssociates.com";
            string s4 = s1 + s2;
            string s5 = "world";
            string s6 = string.Copy( s3 );

            Console.WriteLine("Here's how long our strings are...");
            Console.WriteLine( "s1: {0} [{1}]", s1.Length, s1 );
            Console.WriteLine( "s2: {0} [{1}]", s2.Length, s2 );
            Console.WriteLine( "s3: {0} [{1}]", s3.Length, s3 );
            Console.WriteLine( "s4: {0} [{1}]", s4.Length, s4 );
            Console.WriteLine( "s5: {0} [{1}]", s5.Length, s5 );
            Console.WriteLine( "s6: {0} [{1}]", s6.Length, s6 );


            Console.WriteLine( "\nHere's the third character in each string..." );
            Console.WriteLine( "s1: {0} [{1}]", s1[2], s1 );
            Console.WriteLine( "s2: {0} [{1}]", s2[2], s2 );
            Console.WriteLine( "s3: {0} [{1}]", s3[2], s3 );
            Console.WriteLine( "s4: {0} [{1}]", s4[2], s4 );
            Console.WriteLine( "s5: {0} [{1}]", s5[2], s5 );
            Console.WriteLine( "s6: {0} [{1}]", s6[2], s6 );

            Console.WriteLine( "\nIs there an h in the string?" );
            Console.WriteLine( "s1: {0} [{1}]",
                s1.ToUpper( ).IndexOf( 'H' ) >= 0 ? "yes" : "nope", s1 );
            Console.WriteLine( "s2: {0} [{1}]",
                s2.ToUpper( ).IndexOf( 'H' ) >= 0 ? "yes" : "nope", s2 );
            Console.WriteLine( "s3: {0} [{1}]",
                s3.ToUpper( ).IndexOf( 'H' ) >= 0 ? "yes" : "nope", s3 );
            Console.WriteLine( "s4: {0} [{1}]",
                s4.ToUpper( ).IndexOf( 'H' ) >= 0 ? "yes" : "nope", s4 );
            Console.WriteLine( "s5: {0} [{1}]",
                s5.ToUpper( ).IndexOf( 'H' ) >= 0 ? "yes" : "nope", s5 );
            Console.WriteLine( "s6: {0} [{1}]",
                s6.ToUpper( ).IndexOf( 'H' ) >= 0 ? "yes" : "nope", s6 );
```

```
        Console.WriteLine( "\nWhich strings are the same as s2 [{0}]?", s2 );
        Console.WriteLine( "s1: {0} [{1}]",
            String.Compare( s1, s2 ) == 0 ? "Same!" : "Different", s1 );
        Console.WriteLine( "s2: {0} [{1}]",
            String.Compare( s2, s2 ) == 0 ? "Same!" : "Different", s2 );
        Console.WriteLine( "s3: {0} [{1}]",
            String.Compare( s3, s2 ) == 0 ? "Same!" : "Different", s3 );
        Console.WriteLine( "s4: {0} [{1}]",
            String.Compare( s4, s2 ) == 0 ? "Same!" : "Different", s4 );
        Console.WriteLine( "s5: {0} [{1}]",
            String.Compare( s5, s2 ) == 0 ? "Same!" : "Different", s5 );
        Console.WriteLine( "s6: {0} [{1}]",
            String.Compare( s6, s2 ) == 0 ? "Same!" : "Different", s6 );

        Console.WriteLine(
            "\nWhich strings are the same as s2 [{0}] ignoring case ?", s2 );
        Console.WriteLine( "s1: {0} [{1}]",
            String.Compare( s1, s2, true ) == 0 ? "Same!" : "Different", s1 );
        Console.WriteLine( "s2: {0} [{1}]",
            String.Compare( s2, s2, true ) == 0 ? "Same!" : "Different", s2 );
        Console.WriteLine( "s3: {0} [{1}]",
            String.Compare( s3, s2, true ) == 0 ? "Same!" : "Different", s3 );
        Console.WriteLine( "s4: {0} [{1}]",
            String.Compare( s4, s2, true ) == 0 ? "Same!" : "Different", s4 );
        Console.WriteLine( "s5: {0} [{1}]",
            String.Compare( s5, s2, true ) == 0 ? "Same!" : "Different", s5 );
        Console.WriteLine( "s6: {0} [{1}]",
            String.Compare( s6, s2, true ) == 0 ? "Same!" : "Different", s6 );
    }

    static void Main()
    {
        Tester t = new Tester();
        t.Run();
    }
  }
}
```

Solution to Exercise 15-2. Take the following string:

We hold these truths to be self-evident, that all men are created equal, that they are endowed by their Creator with certain unalienable Rights, that among these are Life, Liberty and the pursuit of Happiness.

Use a regular expression to split the string into words:

```
using System;
using System.Text;
using System.Text.RegularExpressions;

namespace RegularExpressions
{
    class Tester
    {
```

```
        public void Run()
        {
            string importantString =
            "We hold these truths to be self-evident, " +
            "that all men are created equal, " +
            "that they are endowed by their Creator with certain " +
            "unalienable Rights, that among " +
            "these are Life, Liberty and the pursuit of Happiness.";

            Regex theRegex = new Regex( " |, |," );
            StringBuilder sBuilder = new StringBuilder();
            int id = 1;

            foreach ( string subString in theRegex.Split( importantString ) )
            {
                sBuilder.AppendFormat(
                "{0}: {1}\n", id++, subString );
            }
            Console.WriteLine( "{0}", sBuilder );
        }

        static void Main()
        {
            Tester t = new Tester();
            t.Run();
        }
    }
}
```

Chapter 16: Throwing and Catching Exceptions

Quiz

Solution to Question 16-1. An exception is an object (derived from `System.Exception`) that contains information about a problematic event. The framework supports throwing exceptions to stop processing and catching events to handle the problem and resume processing.

Solution to Question 16-2. The stack is unwound until a handler is found, or else the exception is handled by the CLR, which terminates the program.

Solution to Question 16-3. You create a try/catch block; the catch part is the exception handler.

Solution to Question 16-4. The syntax is:

```
throw new Sytem.Arg'umentNullException()
```

Solution to Question 16-5. You can write multiple exception handlers to handle different exceptions; the first handler that catches the thrown exception will prevent further handling. Beware of inheritance complications in the ordering of your handlers.

Solution to Question 16-6. If you have code that must run whether or not an exception is thrown (to close a file, for example), place that code in the finally block. You must have a try for the finally, but a catch is optional.

Exercises

Solution to Exercise 16-1. Create a Cat class with one int property: Age. Write a program that creates a List of Cat objects in a try block. Create multiple catch statements to handle an ArgumentOutOfRangeException, and an unknown exception, and a finally block to simulate deallocating the Cat objects. Write test code to throw an exception that you will catch and handle.

```
using System;
using System.Collections.Generic;

namespace ConsoleApplication1
{

    class Cat
    {
        private int age;

        public int Age
        {
            get { return age; }
            set { age = value; }
        }
        public Cat( int age )
        {
            this.age = age;
        }

    }


    class Tester
    {

        private void CatManager(Cat kitty)
        {
            Console.WriteLine ("Managing a cat who is " + kitty.Age +
                                " years old");
        }

        public void Run( )
        {
```

```
        try
        {
            Console.WriteLine(
              "Allocate resource that must be deallocated here" );

            List<Cat> cats = new List<Cat>();
            cats.Add( new Cat( 5 ) );
            cats.Add( new Cat( 7 ) );

            CatManager( cats[1] ); // pass in the second cat
            CatManager( cats[2] ); // pass in the non-existent third cat

            Console.WriteLine(
            "This line may or may not print" );
        }

        catch ( System.ArgumentOutOfRangeException )
        {
            Console.WriteLine(
          "I've often seen a cat without a smile, \nbut this is " +
          "the first time I've seen a smile without a cat" );
        }

        catch (Exception e)
        {
            Console.WriteLine( "Unknown exception caught"  + e.Message);
        }

        finally
        {
            Console.WriteLine( "Deallocation of resource here." );
        }

    }


    static void Main()
    {
        Console.WriteLine( "Enter Main..." );
        Tester t = new Tester();
        t.Run();
        Console.WriteLine( "Exit Main..." );
    }
  }
}
```

The output from this example would look like this:

```
Enter Main...
Allocate resource that must be deallocated here
Managing a cat who is 7 years old
I've often seen a cat without a smile,
but this is the first time I've seen a smile without a cat
```

```
    Deallocation of resource here.
    Exit Main...
```

Your output may vary, depending on how you wrote your test code.

Solution to Exercise 16-2. Modify Exercise 16-1 so that it does not throw an error. Create a custom error type CustomCatError that derives from System.ApplicationException, and create a handler for it. Add a method to CatManager that checks the cat's age, and throws an error of type CustomCatError if the age is less than or equal to 0, with an appropriate message.

```
using System;
using System.Collections.Generic;

namespace ConsoleApplication1
{

    class Cat
    {
        private int age;

        public int Age
        {
            get { return age; }
            set { age = value; }
        }
        public Cat(int age)
        {
            this.age = age;
        }

    }

    // custom exception class
    public class CustomCatException :
    System.ApplicationException
    {
        public CustomCatException(string message)
            :
        base(message) // pass the message up to the base class
        {

        }
    }


    class Tester
    {

        private void CheckCat(Cat testCat)
        {
            if (testCat.Age <= 0)
            {
```

```
        // create a custom exception instance
        CustomCatException e =
        new CustomCatException("Your cat does not exist");
        e.HelpLink =
        "http://www.libertyassociates.com/NoZeroDivisor.htm";
        throw e;
    }
}


private void CatManager(Cat kitty)
{
    CheckCat(kitty);
    Console.WriteLine("Managing a cat who is " + kitty.Age +
                    " years old");
}

public void Run()
{
    try
    {
        Console.WriteLine("Allocate resource that must be deallocated
                        here");

        List<Cat> cats = new List<Cat>();
        cats.Add(new Cat(7));
        cats.Add(new Cat(-2));

        CatManager(cats[0]); // pass in the first cat
        CatManager(cats[1]); // pass in the second cat

        Console.WriteLine(
        "This line may or may not print");
    }

    // catch custom exception
    catch (CustomCatException e)
    {
        Console.WriteLine(
        "\nCustomCatException! Msg: {0}",
        e.Message);
        Console.WriteLine(
        "\nHelpLink: {0}\n", e.HelpLink);
    }

    catch (System.ArgumentOutOfRangeException)
    {
        Console.WriteLine(
        "I've often seen a cat without a smile, \nbut this is " +
        "the first time I've seen a smile without a cat");
    }

    catch (Exception e)
    {
```

```
            Console.WriteLine("Unknown exception caught" + e.Message);
        }

        finally
        {
            Console.WriteLine("Deallocation of resource here.");
        }

    }

    static void Main( )
    {
        Console.WriteLine("Enter Main...");
        Tester t = new Tester( );
        t.Run( );
        Console.WriteLine("Exit Main...");
    }
}
}
```

Chapter 17: Delegates and Events

Quiz

Solution to Question 17-1. The following is the standard way to define a delegate:

```
public delegate void PhoneRangHandler
( object sender, EventArgs e );

public event PhoneRangHandler PhoneRang;
```

Solution to Question 17-2. Reference types.

Solution to Question 17-3. To decouple the method(s) called from the calling code. It allows the designer of an object to define the delegate, and the user of the object to define which method will be called when the delegate is invoked.

Solution to Question 17-4. You instantiate a delegate like this:

```
OnPhoneRings myDelegate = new OnPhoneRings(myMethod);
```

Solution to Question 17-5. Here is how to call a delegated method:

```
OnPhoneRings(object this, new EventArgs( ));
```

Solution to Question 17-6. The ability for more than one method to be called through a single delegate.

Solution to Question 17-7. Limits the use of the delegate in the following ways:

- You can only add a method using +=.
- You can only remove a method using -=.
- The delegate can only be invoked by the class that defines it.

Solution to Question 17-8. Define the delegate to take, as its second parameter, an object of a type derived from EventArgs. Pass the information through properties of that object.

Solution to Question 17-9. None.

Solution to Question 17-10. Rather than creating a method that matches the delegate's signature and then assigning the name of that method to the delegate, you can directly assign an unnamed delegate method by providing the implementation in line with the assignment.

Exercises

Solution to Exercise 17-1. Write a countdown alarm program that uses delegates to notify anyone who is interested that the designated amount of time has passed:

```
using System;
using System.Collections.Generic;
using System.Text;
using System.Threading;

namespace Exercise1
{
    // a class to hold the message to display
    public class CountDownClockEventArgs : EventArgs
    {
        public readonly string message;
        public CountDownClockEventArgs( string message )
        {
            this.message = message;
        }
    }

    // The subject (publisher). The class to which other
    // classes will subscribe. Provides the delegate TimeExpired
    // that fires when the requested amount of time has passed
    public class CountDownClock
    {
        private DateTime startingTime;
        private DateTime targetTime;
        private string message;
```

```csharp
      // tell me the message to display, and how much time
      //(hours, minutes seconds) to wait
      public CountDownClock( string message, int hours, int mins, int seconds )
      {
         this.message = message;
         startingTime = DateTime.Now;
         TimeSpan duration = new TimeSpan( hours, mins, seconds );
         targetTime = startingTime + duration;
      }

      // the delegate
      public delegate void TimesUpEventHandler
      (
          object countDownClock,
          CountDownClockEventArgs alarmInformation
      );

      // an instance of the delegate
      public TimesUpEventHandler TimeExpired;

      // Check 10 times a second to see if the time has elapsed
      // if so, if anyone is listening, send then message
      public void Run( )
      {
         for ( ; ; )
         {
            // sleep 1/10 of a second
            Thread.Sleep( 100 );   // milliseconds

            // get the current time
            System.DateTime rightNow = System.DateTime.Now;

            if ( rightNow >= this.targetTime )
            {
               if ( TimeExpired != null )
               {
                  // Create the CountDownClockEventArgs to hold the message
                  CountDownClockEventArgs e =
                     new CountDownClockEventArgs( this.message );
                  // fire the event
                  TimeExpired( this, e );
                  // stop the timer
                  break;
               }   // end if registered delegates
            }   // end if time has passed
         }   // end forever loop
      }   // end run
   }   // end class

// an observer.
public class CountDownTimerDisplay
{
   CountDownClock.TimesUpEventHandler myHandler;
```

```csharp
    public CountDownTimerDisplay(CountDownClock cdc)
    {
        myHandler = new CountDownClock.TimesUpEventHandler( TimeExpired );

        // register the event handler and start the timer
        cdc.TimeExpired += myHandler;
    }

    // Alert the user that the time has expired
    public void TimeExpired( object theClock, CountDownClockEventArgs e )
    {
        Console.WriteLine( e.message );
    }
}

// an observer.
public class CountDownTimerLog
{
    CountDownClock.TimesUpEventHandler myHandler;

    public CountDownTimerLog( CountDownClock cdc )
    {
        myHandler = new CountDownClock.TimesUpEventHandler( TimeExpired );

        // register the event handler and start the timer
        cdc.TimeExpired += myHandler;
    }

    // Alert the user that the time has expired
    public void TimeExpired( object theClock, CountDownClockEventArgs e )
    {
        Console.WriteLine( "logging " + e.message );
    }
}

public class Test
{
    public static void Main( )
    {
        Console.Write( "Message: " );
        string message = Console.ReadLine( );

        // NB: You would of course create a more sophisticated interface to
        // let the user set the correct amount of time. For now, we'll just
        // ask for how many seconds to wait
        Console.Write( "How many seconds?: " );
        int seconds = Convert.ToInt32( Console.ReadLine( ) );

        CountDownClock cdc = new CountDownClock( message, 0, 0, seconds );
        CountDownTimerDisplay display = new CountDownTimerDisplay( cdc );
```

```
                  CountDownTimerLog logger = new CountDownTimerLog (cdc);
                  cdc.Run( );

          }
      }
}
```

Solution to Exercise 17-2. Break the program you write in Exercise 17-1 by assigning a new handler to the delegate (deleting the old!).

The only change is in the registration of the handler, using = rather than +=:

```
public class CountDownTimerLog
{
    CountDownClock.TimesUpEventHandler myHandler;

    public CountDownTimerLog( CountDownClock cdc )
    {
        myHandler = new CountDownClock.TimesUpEventHandler( TimeExpired );

        // register the event handler and start the timer
        cdc.TimeExpired = myHandler;
    }

    // Alert the user that the time has expired
    public void TimeExpired( object theClock, CountDownClockEventArgs e )
    {
        Console.WriteLine( "logging " + e.message );
    }
}
```

Solution to Exercise 17-3. Fix the program you wrote in Exercise 17-1 by using the event keyword and test against changes you added in Exercise 17-2.

The only change is in the declaration of the instance of the delegate, adding the keyword event, which will make Exercise 17-2 fail at compile time. Repairing it from = to += will let it run as an event.

```
// the delegate
public delegate void TimesUpEventHandler
(
    object countDownClock,
    CountDownClockEventArgs alarmInformation
);

// an instance of the delegate
public event TimesUpEventHandler TimeExpired;
```

Chapter 18: Creating Windows Applications

Quiz

Solution to Question 18-1. Click on the control on the form, then set the properties in the Properties window.

Solution to Question 18-2. Implement an event handler.

Solution to Question 18-3. The two ways to create an event handler are as follows:

- Go to the Properties window, click on the lightning button to open the events, then fill in a name or double-click next to the event to let Visual Studio 2005 create the name.
- Double-click on the control to create the default handler with a name provided by Visual Studio 2005.

Solution to Question 18-4. A method calling itself (such as calling MethodA( ) from within the body of MethodA( )).

Solution to Question 18-5. XML documentation comments are preceded with three slashes, and are used to generate XML documents that can be used to document the application.

Solution to Question 18-6. Click the ShowAllFiles button on the Solution Explorer and examine the <FormName>.Designer file.

Exercises

Solution to Exercise 18-1. Create a Windows application that displays the word "Hello" in a label, and has a button that changes the display to "Goodbye."

See the source code solution *Chapter18Exercise1* on the web site for this book. Figure A-5 is a picture of the form.

Here is the event handler for the button:

```
private void button1_Click( object sender, EventArgs e )
{
   label1.Text = "Goodbye";
}
```

Figure A-5. Exercise 18-1: the form

Solution to Exercise 18-2. Create a Windows application that presents an order form that looks like Figure A-6.

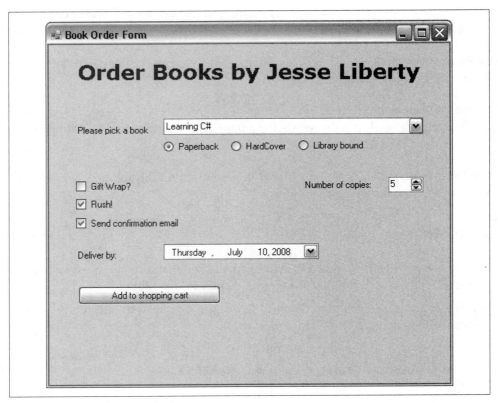

Figure A-6. Exercise 18-2: order form

This figure represents an order form that that lets the user enter information through various controls such as buttons, checkboxes, radio buttons, DateTimePicker, and so forth. You don't need to write the back-end for the ordering system, but you can do the following:

- Simulate saving to the shopping cart with a message, and reset the form when the "Add to Shopping Cart" button is clicked.

- Set the minimum delivery date to be two days from now, and let the user select later dates.

For one example solution, please see the source code solution *Chapter18Exercise2* available on the web site for this book.

To make this work the way I wanted, I added a bit of code to support the UI (though not to support actually recording the data). That code follows:

```
using System;
using System.Collections.Generic;
using System.ComponentModel;
using System.Data;
using System.Drawing;
using System.Text;
using System.Windows.Forms;

namespace Chapter18Exercise2
{
    public partial class OrderForm : Form
    {
        public OrderForm( )
        {
            InitializeComponent( );
            ResetValues( );
            ResetDeliveryDate( );
        }

        // When you click the Add button we reset for next choice
        // and we do the work of adding the current order to the cart
        private void btnAdd_Click( object sender, EventArgs e )
        {
            ResetValues( );
            SaveToShoppingCart( );
        }

        // set all the controls to their starting values
        private void ResetValues( )
        {
            this.ddlBooks.SelectedIndex = -1;
            this.ddlBooks.Text = "Please pick a book";
            this.numCopies.Value = 1;
            this.rbHardcover.Checked = false;
            this.rbLibrary.Checked = false;
            this.rbPaperback.Checked = true;
```

```
            this.cbConfirm.Checked = false;
            this.cbGiftWrap.Checked = false;
            this.cbRush.Checked = false;
        }

        // broken out in case we need to set this separately
        private void ResetDeliveryDate( )
        {
            // minimum delivery date is 2 days from now
            this.deliveryDate.MinDate = DateTime.Now + new TimeSpan( 2, 0, 0, 0 );
            // initialize the control to the MinDate
            this.deliveryDate.Value = this.deliveryDate.MinDate;
        }

        // handle work to save to shopping cart and update status
        private void SaveToShoppingCart( )
        {
            // work here to record choices
            this.lblStatus.Text = "Saved to Shopping Cart.";
        }

        // hack to allow touching any control other than button
        // to turn off the status (to avoid confusion)
        private void UniversalEventHandler( object sender, EventArgs e )
        {
            this.lblStatus.Text = string.Empty;
        }
    }      // end class
}          // end namespace
```

Solution to Exercise 18-3. Modify the first exercise by dragging a timer (found in the Components section of the Toolbox) onto the form and having the timer change the message from "Hello" to "Goodbye" and back once per second. Change the button to turn this behavior on and off. Use the Microsoft Help files to figure out how to use the timer to accomplish this exercise.

1. Create a new project named *Chapter18Exercise3*.

2. Set the form to the size of the form in Exercise 18-1 (196,128).

3. Optionally copy the two controls (label and button) from the first exercise (or drag on new ones).

4. Set the form's text to "Hello Goodbye."

5. Drag a timer onto the form; it will appear in the tray, as shown in Figure A-7.

6. Set the timer's Interval property to 1000 and Enabled to false.

7. Double-click on the timer to create the timer1_Tick event handler that will fire every 1,000 milliseconds (every 1 second). It will alternate the text in the label by checking (and changing) the Boolean value isHello.

8. Change the button event handler to test if the timer is running (if so, its IsEnabled property is true) to start the timer and set the button's text to stop, or to stop the timer and set the button's text to start.

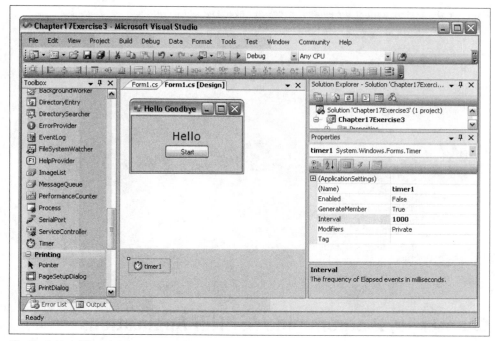

Figure A-7. Adding the timer

The source code for this example is presented in Example A-1.

Example A-1. Using a timer to switch the message every second

```csharp
using System;
using System.Collections.Generic;
using System.ComponentModel;
using System.Data;
using System.Drawing;
using System.Text;
using System.Windows.Forms;

namespace Chapter18Exercise3
{
   public partial class Form1 : Form
   {
      bool isHello = true;
      public Form1()
      {
         InitializeComponent();
      }

      private void button1_Click( object sender, EventArgs e )
      {
         if ( !timer1.Enabled )
         {
            timer1.Start();
```

Example A-1. Using a timer to switch the message every second (continued)

```
            this.button1.Text = "Stop";
        }
        else
        {
            timer1.Stop( );
            this.button1.Text = "Start";
        }

    }

    private void timer1_Tick( object sender, EventArgs e )
    {
        isHello = !isHello;
        if ( isHello )
            label1.Text = "Hello";
        else
            label1.Text = "Goodbye";
    }
}
}
```

Chapter 19: Programming ASP.NET Applications

Quiz

Solution to Question 19-1. System.Web and System.Web.UI.

Solution to Question 19-2. On the server (though occasionally some Web Controls will write script to run on the client).

Solution to Question 19-3. Making a non-postback event into a postback event is accomplished simply by setting the AutoPostBack property to true.

Solution to Question 19-4. View state is the ability of ASP.NET pages to store the state of their controls during a post-back; the net effect is that the programmer does not have to write code to maintain the state of controls when a page is posted back to the server.

Solution to Question 19-5. You must update the Page directive to ensure that the Inherits property is set to the new class name.

Solution to Question 19-6. Click "Add a new web.config file with debugging enabled," and Visual Studio 2005 will create a web.config file for you, or alternatively, you can create the file yourself (by hand) and then add it to the project.

Solution to Question 19-7. The three ways are as follows:

- Drag them from the toolbox.
- Write the code in the HTML markup window.
- Add them programmatically.

Solution to Question 19-8. Every Server Control must have this property:

```
runat="Server"
```

Solution to Question 19-9. The DataSource control.

Solution to Question 19-10. A series of <input> elements of type "radio" with associated <label> controls, all contained within a <table>.

Solution to Question 19-11. Test for the IsPostBack property of the page. If true, the page has been posted back.

Exercises

For the answers to these exercises, please download the ASP.NET project files that are available on this book's web site.

Index

Symbols

A

We'd like to hear your suggestions for improving our indexes. Send email to *index@oreilly.com*.

new keyword, 130
New Project dialog box, 21
New Web Site menu, 414
Next( ) method, 283
Nodes property, 389
nodes, TreeNode objects, 384
non-numeric types, 45
non-postback events, 413
Not operator (!), 66
Notepad, Hello World, 8
not-equals operator (!=), 227
numeric types, 44

O

Object Browser window, 36
Object class, 211
object-oriented programming, 3
  analysis, 111
  classes, 106
    defining, 107
    relationships, 108
  design, 111
  encapsulation, 109
  models, 106
  objects, 106
  polymorphism, 111
  specialization, 110
objects
  arrays
    accessing elements, 176–179
    applying, 174
    declaring, 175
    default values, 176
    foreach statements, 179
    initializing elements, 179
    methods, 188
    multidimensional, 181–188
    params keyword, 180
    sorting, 189–191
  casting, 54
  classes, 11
    constructors, 123–125
    defining, 116–121
    destroying, 133–135
    initializers, 125–127
    instance members, 128–133
    memory allocation, 135–142
    static members, 128–133
    this keyword, 127
  delegates, 348–357
  deriving, 196

  instantiating, 117
  IStorable, 238
  lists, sorting, 282
  metaphors for, 105
  object-oriented programming, 106
  runtime types, 205
  strings, 55
  tracking, 166
  TreeNode, 384
  TreeView, handling events, 388
offset properties, 298
omitting iterators, 99
OnLoad event, overriding, 427
operator keyword, 219–222
operators
  addition (+), 60, 357
  And (&&), 66
  as, 246–251
  assignment (=), 59, 308
  calculate, 62
  conditionals, 67
  conversion, 229–233
  decrement (- -), 62–65
  division (/), 60
  dot (.), 11, 120
  equality (==), 309
  equals (==), 223–229
  greater than (>), 65, 227
  greater than or equal to (>=), 65, 227
  increment (++), 62–65, 222
  index ([ ]), 176, 313
  is, 246–251
  less than (<), 227
  less than or equal to (<=), 227
  logical with conditionals, 66
  mathematical, 60–62
  modulus (%), 61
    controlling for loops, 94
  multiplication (*), 60
  Not (!), 66
  not-equals (!=), 227
  Or (||), 66
  overloading, creating useful, 222
  plus sign (+), 219
  plus-equals (+=), 357
  postfix, 63
  precedence, 67
  prefix, 63
  reassign, 62
  relational, 65–69
  subtraction (-), 60
  ternary, 67

U

UI forms, creating, 382
UML (Unified Modeling Language),
    specialization, 195
unboxing types, 213–215
Uncompress( ) method, 244
unconditional branching statements, 73
unhandled exceptions, 329
Unified Modeling Language (UML),
    specialization, 195
unsigned numeric types, 44
unwinding stacks, 329, 333
Use checkbox, 27
use-case scenarios, 111
utilities
    debuggers, setting breakpoints, 160–164
    FileCopier, 380
        source code, 396–405
    Find in Files, 27
    ILDasm, 238

V

value keyword, 151
values
    constants, 50–55
    debugging, viewing, 164–167
    default, arrays, 176
    dictionaries, 297–300
    expressions, 55
    indexers, assigning, 271
    initializers, 125–127
    integers, indexers, 272
    multiple, returning, 152–158
    primitive types, 124
    references, passing types by, 154
    types, 136
variables, 44, 47–49
    definite assignment, 49
    expanding, 165
    initializers, 125–127
    local, 135–142
    tracking, 166
verbatim strings, 304
versioning with new/override keywords, 205
vertical bar (|), 322
View menu, 32
viewing
    attributes, 238
    breakpoints, 163
    HTML source code, 425

programs, 10–14
    values, debugging, 164–167
views, HTML, 416
virtual methods, overriding, 202
Visual Studio 2005
    applications, building and running, 24
    classes, renaming, 415
    Designer, 374–379
    menus, 25–40
    navigating, 21–23
    projects and solutions, 18–21
    Start Page, 18
    toolbars, 25–40
    Web Forms, 412
    XML documentation comments, 405
void keyword, 12

W

warnings, removing, 207
Watch window, 166
web applications, creating, 20
Web Forms, 410–412
    controls
        adding, 417–419
        server, 419
    creating, 414–417
    events, 412–414
web sites, New Web Site menu, 414
while (true) construct, 100
while loops, 91
whitespace, 56
wildcards, 27
Wiltamuth, Scott, 3
Window menu, 39
Windows
    applications, 6
    controls, 116
    forms
        creating, 374–380
        creating real-world
            applications, 380–405
    .NET Framework, 2
windows
    Auto Hide, 23
    Autos, 164–167, 228
    Bookmark, 36
    Breakpoints, 163
    Call Stack, 169
    Code Definition, 33
    Command, 36
    Dockable, 23

About the Authors

Jesse Liberty, Microsoft MVP, is the best-selling author of *Programming ASP.NET*, *Programming C#* (both from O'Reilly), and a dozen other books on web and object-oriented programming. He is president of Liberty Associates, Inc., where he provides contract programming, consulting, and on-site training in ASP.NET, C#, and related topics. Jesse was a Distinguished Software Engineer at AT&T and vice president for technology development at Citibank.

Brian MacDonald is an editor of programming and networking books. He has edited books for several major publishers on topics ranging from securing Windows servers to PHP web programming to running an eBay business. His work for O'Reilly includes *Programming ASP.NET* and *Programming .NET Components*. He lives in southeastern Pennsylvania with his wife and son.

Colophon

The animal on the cover of *Learning C# 2005*, Second Edition is a goldfish. Goldfish are freshwater fish popular in aquariums and ponds. Though they are native to China, goldfish are one of the most common household pets all over the world. They were first domesticated centuries ago when it was discovered that carp, which are usually olive-colored, can have color mutations causing some of their scales to be red or gold. These mutated fish were bred to create many different varieties of goldfish, including the oranda, ryukin, lionhead, pearlscale, telescoped eye, and bubble eye types.

Most commercial goldfish are scaled and have metallic red, gold, white, silver, or black sheens. But the more rare "scaleless" fish have transparent scales, making them appear bright red, blue, purple, or calico-patterned. Though the wild carp from which goldfish are bred can measure up to 16 inches in length, most commercial goldfish are between 1 and 4 inches long.

The cover image is a 19th-century engraving from the Dover Pictorial Archive. The cover font is Adobe ITC Garamond. The text font is Linotype Birka; the heading font is Adobe Myriad Condensed; and the code font is LucasFont's TheSans Mono Condensed.

Better than e-books

Buy *Learning C# 2005*, 2nd Edition and access
the digital edition FREE on Safari for 45 days.

Go to www.oreilly.com/go/safarienabled
and type in coupon code ZRN1-6RSP-91PP-V8PN-QPKJ

Search
thousands of
top tech books

Download
whole chapters

Cut and Paste
code examples

Find
answers fast

Search Safari! The premier electronic reference
library for programmers and IT professionals.

Related Titles from O'Reilly

.NET

ADO.NET Cookbook

ASP.NET 2.0 Cookbook

ASP.NET 2.0: A Developer's Notebook

C# Cookbook, *2nd Edition*

C# in a Nutshell, *2nd Edition*

C# Language Pocket Guide

Learning C#, *2nd Edition*

.NET and XML

.NET Gotchas

Programming .NET Components, *2nd Edition*

Programming .NET Security

Programming .NET Web Services

Programming ASP.NET, *3rd Edition*

Programming C#, *4th Edition*

Programming MapPoint in .NET

Programming Visual Basic 2005

Programming Windows Presentation Foundation

Visual Basic 2005: A Developer's Notebook

Visual Basic 2005 in a Nutshell, *3rd Edition*

Visual Basic 2005 Jumpstart

Visual C# 2005: A Developer's Notebook

Visual Studio Hacks

Our books are available at most retail and online bookstores.

To order direct: 1-800-998-9938 • *order@oreilly.com* • *www.oreilly.com*

Online editions of most O'Reilly titles are available by subscription at *safari.oreilly.com*